Greek Prostitutes in the Ancient Mediterranean, 800 BCE–200 CE

Publication of this volume has been made possible, in part,
through the generous support and enduring vision of
WARREN G. MOON
and through support from
the IOWA STATE UNIVERSITY PUBLICATION SUBVENTION funds.

Greek Prostitutes in the Ancient Mediterranean, 800 BCE–200 CE

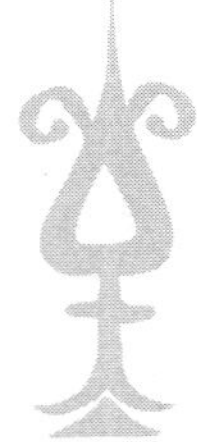

Edited by

ALLISON GLAZEBROOK

and

MADELEINE M. HENRY

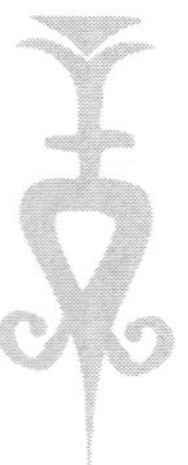

The University of Wisconsin Press

The University of Wisconsin Press
1930 Monroe Street, 3rd Floor
Madison, Wisconsin 53711-2059
uwpress.wisc.edu

3 Henrietta Street
London WC2E 8LU, England
eurospanbookstore.com

1 3 5 4 2

Printed in the United States of America

Library of Congress Cataloging-in-Publication Data
Greek prostitutes in the ancient Mediterranean, 800 BCE–200 CE /
edited by Allison Glazebrook and Madeleine M. Henry.
p. cm.—(Wisconsin studies in classics)
Includes bibliographical references and index.
ISBN 978-0-299-23564-2 (pbk.: alk. paper)
ISBN 978-0-299-23563-5 (e-book)
1. Prostitutes—Greece—History. 2. Prostitutes—Rome—History.
I. Glazebrook, Allison, 1966– II. Henry, Madeleine Mary, 1949–
III. Series: Wisconsin studies in classics.
HQ113.G74 2011
306.740938'09014—dc22
2010011575

Contents

Acknowledgments

This project began over breakfast at the 2005 APA/AIA meetings in Boston. The first step was a panel at the AIA in San Diego in 2007. We wish to thank Laura K. McClure for suggesting at the end of that session that we consider publishing the papers as a collection. The volume is not simply a publication of those papers, however, but a continuation and an expansion of the explorations on the brothel, the *pornē*, and the sociocultural history of prostitution begun there.

Many have helped this project become a book. We are grateful to our students for their assistance with various stages in the preparation of the manuscript: Matthew Caffrey, Carrie Carlson, Bethany Mathes, Helen Taylor, and especially Nicole Daniel. We are thankful to our institutions for their financial support: Iowa State University Publication Subvention Grants Program, Humanities Research Institute at Brock University, and the Brock University Advancement Fund. We also wish to thank the editorial staff at the University of Wisconsin Press for making the process a smooth one and the anonymous reviewers for their thoughtful comments. We especially wish to thank our contributors for their thoughts and enthusiasm for this topic and their cooperation throughout the editorial process. A special thanks to Claudia Mueller, secretary of the World Languages and Cultures Department at Iowa State University, and to Frances Meffe, administrative assistant of the Department of Classics at Brock University.

Finally, we are most thankful to the support and encouragement of our partners, Dave and Dean. Allison also wishes to thank her parents, George and Marion Glazebrook, for their continued enthusiasm for her work.

We hope these papers will encourage further research and generate more interest in the complex relationship between prostitution and women, slavery, gender, sexuality, economy, and culture.

Abbreviations and Transliterations

Abbreviations of ancient authors and works follow the *Oxford Classical Dictionary*. Abbreviations of standard reference works appear below. Full details for all other references can be found in the references. In transliterating Greek, we have used Latinized spellings for well-known Greek authors, such as Isaeus, following the spelling in the *Oxford Classical Dictionary*. We use a direct transliteration from Greek for all other Greek names and terms.

Add	T. Carpenter, T. Mannack, and M. Mendonca. *Beazley Addenda: Additional References to ABV, ARV*[2] *and Paralipomena*. 2nd ed. Oxford, 1989.
ARV	J. D. Beazley. *Attic Red-Figure Vase-Painters*. 1st ed. Oxford, 1942.
ARV[2]	J. D. Beazley. *Attic Red-Figure Vase-Painters*. 2nd ed. Oxford, 1963.
Brill's New Pauly	H. Cancik, H. Schneider, and M. Landfester, eds. *Brill's New Pauly: Encyclopedia of the Ancient World*. Leiden, 2002–.
Broughton *MRR*	T. R. S. Broughton. *The Magistrates of the Roman Republic*. New York, 1951–52.
Chantraine	P. Chantraine. *Dictionnaire étymologique de la langue grecque: Histoire des mots*. Paris, 1968.
Conomis	N. C. Conomis, ed. *Dinarchus: Orationes cum fragmentis*. Leipzig, 1975.
Cramer	J. A. Cramer. *Anecdota graeca*. Oxford, 1835–37.
CVA	*Corpus vasorum antiquorum*. 1922–.
Davies *APF*	J. K. Davies. *Athenian Propertied Families, 600–300 B.C.* Oxford, 1971.
Diels-Kranz	H. Diels and W. Kranz, eds. *Die Fragmente der Vorsokratiker*. Berlin, 1906–10.
Dindorf	G. Dindorf, ed. *Harpocrationis Lexicon in decem oratores atticos*. Oxford, 1853.

EM	T. Gaisford, ed. *Etymologicum magnum*. Oxford, 1848.
Etym. gen.	F. Lasserre and N. A. Livadarus, eds. *Etymologicum genuinum*. Rome, 1976–.
Etym. gud.	E. L. de Stefani, ed. *Etymologicum gudianum*. Leipzig, 1909–20.
FAC	J. M. Edmonds, ed. *The Fragments of Attic Comedy*. Leiden, 1957–61.
FGrH	F. Jacoby, ed. *Die Fragmente der griechischen Historiker*. Berlin, 1923–.
Fischer	E. Fischer, ed. *Die Ekloge des Phrynichos*. Berlin, 1974.
FLG	G. Hermann, ed. *Fragmentum lexici graeci*. In *De emendanda rationae graecae grammaticae*. Leipzig, 1801.
Frisk	H. Frisk. *Griechisches Etymologisches Wörterbuch*. Heidelberg, 1961.
Gentili	B. Gentili. *Anacreon*. Rome, 1958.
GD	P. Bruneau. *Guide de Délos*. Paris, 1983.
Helm	R. Helm, ed. *Die Chronik der Hieronymus*. Berlin, 1984.
Hercher	R. Hercher. *Epistolographi graeci*. Paris, 1873.
ID	A. Plassart, J. Coupy, F. Durrbach, P. Roussel, and M. Launy, eds. *Inscriptions de Délos*. 7 vols. Paris, 1926–72.
IG	*Inscriptiones graecae*. Vols. 1–3: *Attica*. Berlin, 1873–.
Kaibel	G. Kaibel, ed. *Comicorum graecorum fragmenta*. Berlin, 1890–.
Kenyon	F. G. Kenyon. *Hyperidis orationes et fragmenta*. Oxford, 1907.
Kühn	C. G. Kühn. *Claudii Galeni opera omnia*. Leipzig, 1821–33; repr., Hildesheim, 1964–65.
Lewis and Short	C. T. Lewis and C. Short. *A Latin Dictionary Founded upon Andrew's Edition of Freund's Latin Dictionary*. Oxford, 1879.
LGPN 2	M. J. Osborne and S. G. Byrne. *Lexicon of Greek Personal Names*. Vol. 2: *Attica*. Oxford, 1994.
Lobel-Page	E. Lobel and D. L. Page, eds. *Poetarum lesbiorum fragmenta*. Oxford, 1955.
LSJ	H. G. Liddell, R. Scott, H. S. Jones, and R. McKenzie. *A Greek-English Lexicon with a Revised Supplement*. Oxford, 1996.
Meineke	A. Meineke. *Corpus scriptorum historiae byzantinae*. Bonn, 1836.
Nauck	A. Nauck. *Aristophanis Byzantii grammatici alexandrini fragmenta*. Halle, 1848; repr., Hildesheim, 1963.

Nickau	K. Nickau, ed. *Ammonii qui dicitur liber de "Adfinium vocabularum differentia."* Leipzig, 1966.
OED	*Oxford English Dictionary*. Oxford, 2002.
OLD	P. G. W. Glare, ed. *Oxford Latin Dictionary*. Oxford, 1982.
Para	J. D. Beazley. *Paralipomena: Additions to Attic Black-Figure Vase-Painters and to Attic Red-Figure Vase Painters*. 2nd ed. Oxford, 1971.
PMG	D. L. Page, ed. *Poetae melici graeci*. Oxford, 1962.
PCG	R. Kassel and C. Austin, eds. *Poetae comici graeci*. Berlin, 1983–.
Pfeiffer	R. Pfeiffer. *Callimachus*. Oxford, 1949–53.
Rabe	H. Rabe. *Commentaria in Aristotelem Graeca*. Berlin, 1896.
RE	A. Pauly, G. Wissowa, and W. Knoll, eds. *Real-Encyclopädie der classischen Altertumswissenschaft*. Stuttgart, 1893–1972.
SEG	*Supplementum epigraphicum graecum*. Amsterdam, 1923–.
SIG	W. Dittenberger. *Sylloge inscriptionum graecarum*, 3rd ed. Leipzig, 1915–.
Spengel	L. Spengel. *Rhetores graeci*. Leipzig, 1854–85.
Suidas	A. Adler. *Suidae Lexicon*. Munich, 2001–4.
TLG	*Thesaurus linguae graecae*. http://www.tlg.uci.edu.
Traill	J. Traill. *Persons of Ancient Athens*. Toronto, 1994–2008.
Vels.	V. Velsen, ed. *Tryphonis grammatici alexandrini fragmenta*. Berlin, 1854.
von Arnim	H. F. von Arnim. *Stoicorum veterum fragmenta*. Leipzig, 1903.
West	M. L. West, ed. *Iambi et elegi graeci*. Oxford, 1971–72.

Greek Prostitutes in the Ancient Mediterranean, 800 BCE–200 CE

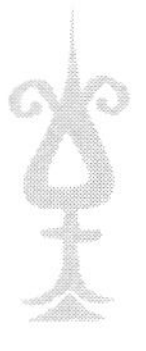

Introduction

Why Prostitutes? Why Greek? Why Now?

ALLISON GLAZEBROOK and

MADELEINE M. HENRY

Our topic is part of a larger scholarly trend. In the last two decades research into prostitution has become mainstream, rescued "from the literature of deviancy and crime" (Gilfoyle 1999).[1] Scholars now recognize that the study of prostitution richly enhances our understanding of political, economic, and cultural history. More specifically, studies on prostitution cut to the core of societal attitude towards gender and to social constructions of sexuality.

Important work in the last fifteen years has considered how the manipulation of the image of the prostitute in rhetoric, poetry, and other discourses helps construct male identity within the Greek polis. Such scholarship treats prostitution in ancient Hellas as a sequela to other social practices involving exchange, aesthetics, and status display. For Leslie Kurke, the creation of the category *hetaira* by male aristocrats in the archaic period is a function of those men's identity formation (1997). In this view, elite men needed specifically to distance themselves from the *pornē*, whom they associated with the emerging middle class. David Halperin has argued that prostitution was essential to the Athenian understanding of male citizenship. In contrast to the prostitute's penetrated body, the male body was sacrosanct (1990). James Davidson describes *hetairai*, along with food, as part of the appetites of Athenian men of the classical period (1998). Other scholars examine exchange systems that categorize prostituted females as one of many objects of exchange in a society (von Reden 2003).

More work needs to be done not only on the cultural construction of the prostitute but also on the social and economic history of prostitution, and closer attention paid to the evidence for prostitution outside of classical Athens and in the archaeological record. Davidson refocused this discussion early on. He complicated the picture of ancient prostitution by acknowledging various types of prostitutes from streetwalkers, to brothel workers, to entertainers to *hetairai*, but his main interest remained the *hetaira* and classical Athens (1998). Edward Cohen followed suit by looking at prostitution from the perspective of the marketplace, arguing that what distinguished a prostitute in Athens was whether or not he or she was working under a contract. He examines prostitution in the context of the Athenian economy and concludes that the Athenians had no moral aversion to prostitution or prostitutes per se but that a conservative ideology existed that frowned on working for another (2000b and 2006). Cohen's interest is the free prostitute and still Athens. The 2006 publication of *Prostitutes and Courtesans in the Ancient World* brought renewed interest to the topic in the field of classics. It broadened the focus of prostitution in ancient Greece to prostitutes themselves—as dedicators at sanctuaries (Keesling), as laborers (Cohen), as owners of prostitutes (Faraone)—and began to look at the effect of prostitution on women more generally (Glazebrook).

The work in this volume builds on the recent scholarship by Hellenists by focusing on the brothel, the *pornē*, the male prostitute, and the trafficking backgrounds of prostitutes, areas underexplored even in the case of Athens. Visual representations of prostitutes and their interpretation also feature. Finally, the volume includes discussion of the Greek prostitute in the Roman context, in the plays of Plautus and the speeches of Cicero. Until we better comprehend such issues we cannot hope to understand prostitution in ancient Greece and the attitudes toward it more generally.

We do not claim to present a unified or unitary point of view. Some contributors definitely see prostitution as an unalloyed form of social oppression; others consider the theoretical aspects more than the experiential. The span of time and space and the nature of the evidence do not permit a grand synthesis. We trust that our differences show the vitality of the problems and hope that the reader's occasional disagreement will provoke further study.

Hetaira versus *Pornē*

Much of what we think we know about prostitution originates in Hans Licht's *Sexual Life in Ancient Athens* (1932), whose focus, supported by mainly literary texts, was on what a customer could get for what price. That focus has resulted in a deceptively helpful taxonomy of prostitution, with the term *pornē* (literally, "woman for sale"; see Konstantinos Kapparis in this volume) signifying the lowest class of woman and *hetaira* (literally, "companion") signifying the highest and most elegant class. As a result, scholars tend to view the *hetaira* and *pornē* as distinct, the former serving the elite in the symposium and the latter, as enslaved, serving the poor in the brothel. This dichotomy, however, is a false one when we consider prostitution from different perspectives. For example, the status of women who worked as prostitutes could be fluid rather than fixed. A woman could move from the status of enslaved prostitute to that of a concubine of one man (*pallakē*) or to that of free agent (and even become wealthy, as commonly understood by the use of the term *hetaira*), and back again. The fourth-century orator Antiphon's first speech recounts events in the life of a *pallakē* whose lover is planning to hand her off to a brothel (Antiph. 1.14–15). Menander's comedy *The Woman from Samos* recounts the misadventures of Chrysis, who is currently a *pallakē* but whose status can tip back to that of streetwalker the instant her lover wants it to (M. Henry 1985, 61–73). In a corollary example from oratory, Alce begins her career working as a slave in a brothel, but is eventually freed and becomes the favorite of a wealthy Athenian (Isae. 6.19–20).

Furthermore, ancient authors use the terms *hetaira* and *pornē* interchangeably. The woman Neaira, in the most extensive account of a prostituted woman of the classical period, is most frequently referred to as a *hetaira* but also at times as a *pornē*. Clearly in the latter case the term is meant to be derogatory rather than to denote a specific and unchanging status (Kurke 1997; Kapparis 1999; Glazebrook 2005a). Plutarch comments that the term *hetaira* was simply an Athenian euphemism for *pornē*, just as the term *syntaxeis* (contributions) was for tribute and *phylakes* (protectors) was for garrisons posted in cities (*Sol.* 15). This volume challenges the polarization of *hetaira* and *pornē*, which creates oversimplified categories that are not accurate in all contexts (see further the contributions of Allison Glazebrook, Sean Corner, and Clare Kelly Blazeby in this volume).

Besides accepting the notions that the term *hetaira* inevitably referred to the upper tier of prostitutes and that the status of prostitutes was fixed, scholars have also tended to focus more on this perceived top category at the cost of expanding our knowledge about the variety of prostitutes available and the *porneion* (brothel). Although one might be tempted to think that this discrepancy is due to a lack of evidence regarding these other women, in fact it is explained by a fascination with the *hetaira* and the correspondingly negative attitude about the brothel and those who staff such places. *Pornai* are considered "lowbrow" and thus not worthy of scholarly attention. Licht, for example, gives ten pages to prostitutes and prostitution in general, spending four on the *pornē* and Hellenic brothel, while devoting forty pages to the *hetaira*, twenty-three pages of which attend to the anecdotes about prostitutes that are recorded in Athenaeus and other writers. In one such anecdote we are told:

> They say that once upon a time when Phryne asked Praxiteles to give her the most beautiful of his works, he agreed, as her lover, to do so, but refused to tell her which he thought was the finest. So when one of Phryne's slaves rushed in, claiming that a fire had broken out in Praxiteles's establishment, and that most but not all of his works had perished, Praxiteles immediately started running through the door, lamenting that his labor was not in vain if only the Satyr and the Eros were all right. Phryne ordered him to take courage and stay; for he had suffered no great loss, but had been trapped into agreeing which were his most beautiful works. And so Phryne chose the statue of Eros. (Paus. 1.20.1–2)

In another story, a lover once sent his seal to the *hetaira* Lais and commanded her to come to his side. But she responded she could not, since "pēlos esti"—"it's mud/there's mud"—punning on the clay material of the seal, and hinting that he should have sent something of more value. The association of the word with mud and mire further implies she cannot go to him because he is lowly (Ath. 13.585d). Such stories have led to an image of the *hetaira* as witty, mercenary, and autonomous, in addition to exceptionally beautiful. Out of this image of the *hetaira* has grown the idea that *hetairai* were, as a group, quite learned and powerful, influencing Athenian politicians, and enjoying the most comfortable status of all women in classical Athens:

> The Athenian women with the most exalted position and the most freedom were . . . the hetaerae. They were intelligent, witty, articulate and educated, the only women in Athenian society allowed to manage their own financial affairs, stroll through the streets anywhere at any time. They were free to attend plays, ceremonies and speeches, to speak with whomever, whenever they pleased, to share the intellectual activities of Greece. They could take the sexual or romantic initiative with men [and] . . . were accomplished conversationalists, the intellectual equals of the men they entertained. (Wells 1982)

Although clearly an exaggeration, this image of the prostitute in ancient Greece circulates to varying degrees in any general account of prostitution (Blundell 1995; Fantham et al. 1994; Dimakis 1988; Cantarella 1987), and novels about ancient Greece typically represent the elegant *hetaira* rather than the brothel inmate or streetwalker (M. Henry 1995, 57–67).

While anecdotes such as Pausanias's are entertaining, tantalizing, and even titillating, they really tell us very little about prostitution in ancient Athens and Greece more generally. Laura McClure argues that Athenaeus, one collector of such stories writing in the second century CE, cannot be trusted as a source for prostitution. She finds that Athenaeus's work *Deipnosophistae* (*Sophists at Dinner*) provides little evidence of actual prostitution in classical Athens, since he makes the *hetaira* into a fetish (an object of irrational reverence that arouses libidinal interest), which tells us more about the Second Sophistic's idealized view of the past than it does about the lived experience of the prostitute in classical Athens (2003). In fact, a trajectory of treatises on learned and witty prostitutes began in the fourth century BCE and continued into late antiquity; the fragmentary remains of these, combined with the work of lexicographers and the comic fragments used by Athenaeus, constitute most of the written information used by historians of prostitution in the Hellenic world. Such treatises have been shown to distort what little evidence there is for women who may have moved between the roles of concubine, pimped prostitute, and brothel prostitute (M. Henry 1995).

Most of the recent specialized studies of prostitutes in the Hellenic world are devoted to the notorious or named prostitutes who consort with Hellenistic kings (e.g., Kurke 2002; Ogden 1999). Catherine Keesling (2006) finds that many of the monuments allegedly dedicated to or by famous prostitutes in the Hellenic world were not only authentic but also, owing to their placement, varyingly transgressive, normative, or liminal; the monuments are a kind of analogue to the singularity of the women themselves. The *hetaira* Phryne's monument at Delphi, for example, provides her patronymic and ethnic. She, or her lovers on her behalf, erected her monument to stand proud and high, but most other women, for example, Neaira, were treated less grandly. The prosecutor in [Dem.] 59.35 describes Neaira as being rubbed in the mud (*proupēlakizeto*) by her lover and later claims that the law will have been rubbed in the mud (*propēlakisthentos*) if the laws are not upheld (59.113). As Kapparis shows in this volume, many terms used to describe prostitutes associate them with filth and dross (e.g., *chamaitypē*, a thing pounded into the dirt, and *spodēsilaura*, heap of ashes, dross). A handful of female prostitutes from the preclassical period, most notably Rhodopis, are often cited in discussions of Greek prostitutes. Acceptance of the ahistorical composite portrait of "the courtesan" has led scholars to treat Rhodopis/Doricha, whom John Boardman (1994) calls "an old man's darling," as if she belonged to a social milieu identical with that of the world Athenaeus creates in his *Deipnosophistae*. Just as scholarship dissects the idealized composite portrait of the polis, so too must we dissect "the courtesan." While some women will have had and taken opportunities to better their lot by prostitution, surely fewer of them became early Grand Horizontals or Gigis. Athenaeus's *Deipnosophistae* and other literary products of the Roman Empire cast long shadows both back and forward in time (M. Henry 1990, 2000). Popular scholarship still paints a homogeneous portrait of "the courtesan" in ancient Greece, and scholarly books continue, visually, this practice of homogenization by using titillating nineteenth-century orientalizing academic paintings of odalisques, courtesans, and the like, as the cover illustrations for books concerned with sexuality or women's history in Greece and Rome.

Visual evidence, while difficult to interpret, does suggest that the image of the elegant *hetaira* is idealized. Vase paintings that depict scenes of revelry, often at the symposium (drinking party), which is the setting of a number of Athenaean anecdotes and a sphere normally associated with the *hetaira*, make it clear that scintillating conversation is not the most important reason for having these women around, nor are such women necessarily richly adorned. We see nude females, without even jewelry, playing the game of *kottabos* (Tarquinia Painter, red-figure *kylix*, 460–450 BCE, Basel 415, Keuls 1985, 169 figs. 143–44). The object of the game is to hit a target by flinging wine at it. The target is a small saucer, which the thrower must sink in the basin of water in which it is floating, or perhaps a disk that must be knocked off from its position atop a pole or lamp stand. Before throwing, the player declares for whom he or she is playing, thereby dedicating the turn to a lover (this flirtatious and erotic game is reconstructed by Lissarrague 1990a). Vase paintings also represent nude women in sympotic or other interior settings who suffer physical abuse and degradation (Antiphon Painter, red-figure *kylix*, ca. 500–450 BCE, Once Munich, Arndt collection, ARV 339.55, Keuls 1985, 183 fig. 164; see also Keuls 1985, 184–86 figs. 165–70). From their study of such images, Eva Keuls (1985) and Carola Reinsberg (1989) conclude that there was very little distinction between *pornai* and *hetairai*. Still, it would be going too far to suggest that there were no differences among prostitutes. A prostitute could be slave or free, be a citizen or noncitizen, work in a brothel, or serve under a contractual arrangement with one or more men. Some were paid more and some were paid less. Some were trained and gifted dancers, flautists, or harpists, while others were not. The heroism, notoriety, or wealth of women like Leaina, Phryne, and Pythionike are at the apex of a pyramid whose lower tiers are established by the poverty and despair of women far more numerous but less well known: those who, likely foreign slaves or free poor, remain unremembered as individuals.

Prostitution's Utopia

Male fantasy has fueled ideas and scenarios about prostitution, prostitutes, and the venues in which prostitution is found. These repay our study, for brothels and other spaces in which men can buy sexual gratification have become a *locus amoenus* of male fantasy in the West. Cities and districts within cities, starting with

Athens, have constructed utopian sites of beautiful courtesans, as McClure has shown in her study of Athenaeus and his fetching courtesans who banter and give erotic tutelage (2003). A space is built and populated within the imaginary (see also Judith Hallett's chapter in this volume); to determine where it touches the historical place and where it diverges is part of this book's task. The buildings are constructed or dreamed of. The French utopianist Restif de la Bretonne (1734–1806) proposed civic brothels as part of an ideal community in a treatise of 1769, and Claude-Nicolas Ledoux (1736–1806) designed fantasy buildings, among them a state brothel, called an *oikēma* ("establishment," one of the ancient Greek terms for brothel), the phallic architecture of which he based on the Forum of Augustus and Temple of Mars Ultor (Marder 1979; Kellum 1996). The places are legion: Venice, Paris, and New Orleans are the setting for mythicized narratives about beautiful prostitutes, some of whom are lowborn but who rise to wealth and power. The Wild West has a full complement of local histories of places whose brothels and brothel keepers helped build the American frontier; auteur Robert Altman's "antiwestern" *McCabe and Mrs. Miller* (1971) focuses on the brothel in the fictional community of Presbyterian Church. The myth of New Orleans' Storyville continues to grow nearly a century after the demise of that fabled district. Louis Malle's 1978 film *Pretty Baby* about a prostitute's daughter's entry into "the life" in Storyville has been called "an almost incredibly romantic, autumnally beautiful movie" (Canby 1978). The review does not address that, among other things, the film is about child prostitution.

The male-centered narrative of prostitution is essential to masculinity itself. A boy's first trip to the brothel—often with his father—becomes a rite of manhood, and the memory of adolescent trips evokes fond memories (Gustave Flaubert's *Sentimental Education* [1869]). Even more, a ninety-year-old man can discover pure love in repeatedly visiting but not deflowering a fourteen-year-old virgin in a brothel in a nameless city (Gabriel Garcia Marquez's *Memories of my Melancholy Whores* [2004]). Athenian youths sometimes got carried away with prostitutes (Isae. 3.17), but such behavior was acceptable and expected for youths (Lys. 3.4) as long as it did not end in marriage. Current media draw attention to the plight of girls and young women literally trafficked and sold to brothel keepers. These women are a modern counterpart to the dross of antiquity. Some young women in Southeast Asia are respected as local heroines for prostituting themselves elsewhere in order to support their aged parents (T. L. Brown 2001; Kristof 2006). The persistence of both the utopian fantasy of elegant brothels and of the reality of "low-end" prostitution requires us to examine and historicize the construction of the brothel. Indeed, the *pornē* (purchased foreign woman) is the mud from which the *hetaira* was formed in the preclassical period. What is her relationship to the trafficked women seen in Homer, to prostitutional scenarios in preclassical texts and in later texts that refer to the preclassical period, and to the ideology of the polis in Athens and elsewhere?

Sex Trafficking

There is evidence, though scant, of the trafficking of women in the archaic and classical period, whether for the sole purpose of prostituting them or for the opportunity to use them in other ways as well. The occupants of Building Z in the Kerameikos (discussed by Glazebrook in this volume) were likely Thracian slaves employed as both textile workers and prostitutes. Archaic and classical sources refer to raiding as a means of obtaining women, and Solon's biographical tradition supports the view that he encouraged the prostitution of women. The alleged connection of one of the seven sages of antiquity with institutionalized brothel prostitution is not a trivial matter. This connection—though it may not have been made before the late classical period—helps construct the brothel as a legitimate fantasy space in the masculine state. This fantasy space is retrojected as well as projected. We should try to determine where, if anywhere, it existed in real space and time. The ideal city, in which brothel girls are available to all, may begin as early as the age of Solon—or perhaps only in the imagined world of a fantasy Solon.

Such traffic in women as may have existed is best examined in connection with the colonization process, the growth of trade, and the development of the polis. Colonization in the Hellenic world has been associated with an increase in population. As warriors became traders, regulation and codification emerged. Conditions conducive to trafficking include the behaviorally driven definition of masculinity in the Homeric poems, the likelihood that women were "the first slaves," and the perception that men needed sexual outlets (Tandy 1997; Madeleine Henry's chapter in this volume). We might ask whether there specifically was sexual trafficking of women, and if so, what the sources and destinations were. Studies of contemporary sexual trafficking have identified specific, at times seasonally operative, sending, transit, and receiving locales (T. L. Brown 2001, 23ff.; Human Rights Watch Asia 1995, 25). Thrace, a source for many slaves later, may be a good place to look. The first historical woman who seems to have been trafficked was from Thrace. Rhodopis/Doricha is identified by Herodotus as "a *hetaira* woman" (*hetairē gynē*). She is an example of Greeks trafficking a non-Greek female among themselves.

Prostitution as Commerce

The commonest semantic field for words we translate as "brothel" is that of words referring to dwellings. Moreover these Greek words can also mean something other than "brothel" (see Glazebrook and Kapparis in this volume). Two difficulties emerge when we begin to look for physical spaces identifiable as brothels. First, if brothels are considered a constitutive element of the polis, then, like other definitive structures or spatial arrangements such as council houses, mints, and agoras, we might expect brothels to conform to a particular plan, but no conclusive evidence of such structures exists in the archaeological record. Second, buildings could well have had multiple uses (Aeschin. 1.24), making them difficult to identify, just as their enslaved occupants had multiple occupations (see further Glazebrook's chapter in this volume, as well that of T. Davina McClain and Nicholas K. Rauh). Some vase paintings show sexual activity that was likely commercialized, but we cannot tell whether the interior spaces in which these sexual events take place were actually dedicated to prostitution, whether the buildings had been built for that sole purpose, or whether they were domestic spaces into which prostituted females were sometimes brought, or commercial spaces sometimes used for prostitutional activities and sometimes for other kinds of work (e.g., textile production). Almost any structure could be used to prostitute women, as long as it had appropriate space for customers and as long as the women, when not servicing men sexually, could be employed at other activities. A list of female brothel keepers from fourteenth-century England shows that all had occupations in addition to that of brothel keeping (Karras 1996, 45). Some brothel regulations in World War I Belgium specify open hours of 5:30 to 9 p.m. (Friedrich 1924). One wonders whether other work was done on the premises before 5:30 or whether the women were employed elsewhere.

In Archilochus (fl. ca. 750 BCE) and Hipponax (fl. 510 BCE) we see glimpses of commercial sexual activity. Fragments that contain the word *pornē* are among those challenged by scholars as post-Archilochan. But genuine and unequivocally showing commercial sexual activity is his fr. 42W: "Just as a Thracian or Phrygian man sucks barley beer through a straw, she was bent over, toiling." The woman's sexual labor is likened to the way foreign men drink beer, and she is attributed with an almost addictive hunger for fellatio and ejaculate. She does her work in a demeaning anatomical position. She, like Phrygian and Thracian men (groups that might be enslaved for labor), could be a foreign slave. Her nourishment is not beer but ejaculate. Some of the sexual activities described in written texts by Archilochus on are also represented on noncontemporaneous vase paintings (Brygos Painter, forced fellatio with multiple partners, 490–465 BCE, Florence 3921, Kilmer 1993, figs. R518A (ii), R518A (iii), and R158B (ii); Pedieus Painter, forced fellatio with multiple partners, 520–505 BCE, Paris G13, Kilmer 1993, figs. R156A and R156B, Kilmer 1993, figs. R152A and R152B [see Henry's contribution to this volume]).

Prostitutes as Uncontrolled and Uncontrollable

The Archilochus fragment compares a fellatrix to a thirsty man; other archaic poetry refers to prostitutes drinking. Later written texts describe prostitutes getting drunk and having intercourse with many men ([Dem.] 59.33); these stories emphasize the excessive nature of the prostitute, who, like the satyr figure, represents behavior that should not be emulated. A red-figure *kylix* decorated with a prostitute drinking from an amphora, the storage vessel for wine, rather than a drinking cup supports the idea that the images of the prostitute were used at symposia as a reminder to behave (525–475 BCE, New York 56.171.61, Peschel 1987, fig. 46; see the chapters by Clare Kelly Blazeby, Helene Coggagna, and Nancy Sorkin Rabinowitz in this volume on the labeling of such women). Such behavior is the equivalent of drinking directly from a bottle of wine in the modern day. It highlights the figure's lack of control and her deviant excess. In a society like ancient Athens where *sōphrosynē* (moderation) and *enkrateia* (self-control) were important aspects of masculinity, such reminders had social importance. Doing anything in excess was looked down on and reflected badly on the doer's masculinity. The *hetaira* came to embody such excess as representatives of the uncontrolled female body (see Coggagna's chapter in this volume).

The prostitute is also a locus of male anxiety. Her affinity for adorning herself and adapting her appearance made her untrustworthy. The fourth-century comic poet Alexis talks of how high heels, padding of the hips and bust, and makeup were used to make the prostitute seem more appealing than she really was (Ath. 13.568a–d). Trickery with her appearance came to suggest a deceitful nature, and thus she came to be seen as a threat to men. Prostitutes as schemers that work against society and men are present in the orators. According to Isaeus, the prostitute Alce, possibly through *pharmaka* (drugs), gained control of her lover Euctemon and convinced him to acknowledge one of her children as his own, thereby securing Athenian status for one of her sons (6.21). The trouble with prostitutes, then, was not just that they victimized lovers but that they aimed to take advantage of all of society. Their paradoxical civic marginality, combined with physical and sometimes emotional proximity, could make them threats to social stability. This fear of the prostitute that is apparent in Hellenic sources became stronger during the Roman Republic (see Rauh's chapter in this volume).

Work on prostitution in ancient Rome has shown how prostitution is connected to larger social issues such as women's place in society, laws relating to marriage and sexuality more generally, and ideas of social privilege. The study of prostitution in ancient Rome, particularly the social context of prostitution, has advanced more quickly than has its study in ancient Greece. One reason is that the Romanists have more archaeological evidence to hand from such sites as Pompeii. But another is the willingness of Romanists to use comparative material in an effort to understand prostitution in Rome. Such a framework grounds Thomas A. J. McGinn's investigations into Roman prostitution and the brothel (1998; 2004). Our better knowledge of Roman prostitution has further shown, however, that we cannot, as Hans Licht did back in 1932, simply use what we know about Rome to fill in the gaps for ancient Greece and Athens (there were, for example, no purpose-built brothels in the Hellenic world, so far as we know, as there were in Pompeii).[2] Rather we need to consider how measured comparisons with Rome and other cultures in various historical periods can be fruitful (see McGinn's contribution to this volume). But before such measured comparisons are possible, we need to understand the Hellenic evidence and the Roman response to the Hellenic prostitute.

We hope that this volume will encourage further exploration of prostitution in the Hellenic world, diversify the approaches to the topic, and demonstrate the complexity and variability of ancient prostitution.

NOTES

1. "Sex work" and "sex worker" have become the accepted value-free terms for this profession and those working in it. We avoid the terms in this study because they refer to more than just prostitutes, and imply further that prostitution is just a job and the prostitute free to choose his or her profession—none of which were true for the majority of prostitutes in the ancient world.

2. On possible difference between the practices of Greek and Roman prostitution, see Glazebrook (forthcoming).

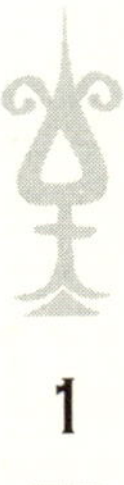

1 The Traffic in Women

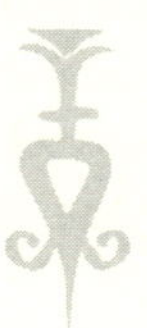

From Homer to Hipponax, from War to Commerce

MADELEINE M. HENRY

Much of the scholarship on women and the female in Homer has examined elite women and goddesses. But if we gaze with a steady eye, we see lowly women everywhere. These women are the precursors of sexually disposable females in lyric poetry, most obvious and evident as slave prostitutes, necessary for patriarchal state formation and state maintenance. These are women who are available for sexual gratification and for other work, to whom and to whose children no obligations are owed, through whom property is not transmitted, and whose virginity has value only as something that can be purchased and destroyed. The so-called aesthetic elements of prostitution within the pornographic scenario are artifacts of the internalized acceptance of this requirement. The development of the *hetaira* out of the substrate *pornē* is proof thereof: the *pornē* is first seen in an urban setting, the nascent polis. I follow Gerda Lerner (1986), Carole Pateman (1988), and Catharine MacKinnon (1989), who posit that the first contract is the sexual-social contract of male sex right. This contract is usually displaced onto marriage, but the prostituted class is equally necessary. I also accept the honor/shame hypothesis, with its emphasis on females as bearers of family and community honor, as broadly applied to Mediterranean societies. Females enact loyalty and disloyalty to the community through their sexual behavior and motherhood.[1]

Classicists who study war, slavery, and systems of exchange often leave women out of the calculus, perhaps unwittingly emulating Thucydides. The effect of war on women receives a short article or perhaps a page. Those who write about slavery usually render the experience of men normative. Scholarship on female slaves has devoted little attention to prostituted female slaves. There is still a resistance to break for the study of prostitution what Graham Shipley calls, regarding war, the illusion of the "watertight compartment" (1993, 1).[2]

Yet in war the connection between prostitution and the state can be seen very clearly, for warfare is a critical phase of state formation and state maintenance. The rape and sexual enslavement of women are frequent consequences of war, however we define it—whether we call it "raiding," "piracy," "war as we know it," or, as Shipley puts it, "organized societal violence" (1993, 6). Violent conflicts between men almost invariably include the doing of sexual violence to women and children. Men's kidnap, seizure, or purchase (with and without their consent) of females for the purpose of sexual and other uses looms large. The Homeric poems, as charter texts of Hellas, provide a functional or performative definition of masculinity that entails male sex right over females; this aspect of the poems deserves as much examination as the poems' long-studied contributions to the evolution of other values of civil society have received. Masculine heroism is enacted in warfare and martial virtue is replicated in peacetime settings.

In Iron Age Greece and in the Homeric poems, no clear distinction was made between war and piracy or raiding (De Souza 2000, 16; Rauh 2003; Tsetskhladze 2000–2001, 11–16; Jackson 1995, 95–99). Despite ample evidence that females were taken in these activities, the political implications of the practice have not been much discussed. Twentieth-century warfare and economic colonizations, which also exhibit the sexual exploitation of women and girls, give us a concept applicable to the Homeric world: the concept of trafficking. Early Hellenic evidence speaks to the trafficking of females from their land of residence or origin to a new place in order to be used for sexual and other labor.[3]

As Moses Finley suggested of slavery, to acknowledge the ubiquity of a practice can make it a starting point of analysis (1982, 11). He invited historians to look with a steady eye at war and unblinkingly asked whether Greek civilization was based on slave labor. Finley paid little attention to female slaves, even though most slave-owning societies have had more female than male slaves, and so his contributions to the study of the ancient economy may not have given the contributions of women's work their due. Even scholars who acknowledge the erasure or lack of visibility of slaves and slavery do not look the one layer down for the female slave. Finley's challenge nonetheless helps generate and inform the question with which this study begins: how did the trafficking in women and girls begin in the ancient Greek world and where can we see the traces that can be so identified?[4]

Orlando Patterson's influential definition of a slave as a socially dead human being meshes well with Lerner's view that slavery could only develop where there existed a concept of otherness (Patterson 1982; Lerner 1986). It has been claimed that the first slaves were female because they could be put to more uses than male slaves; if a prostituted female is someone to whom a male has unrestricted sexual access, then that female is a sort of slave, whether or not a legal construct allows her to be formally "owned" by anyone (Winks 1972, 6). Prostituted females are additionally "socially dead" because their children cannot be acknowledged; that prostitutes are often mothers is not recorded in official sources. That prostitutes in most of the world today lack legal recourse against rape demonstrates the strength of the sexual contract, as does men's ability to sell their wives (Pateman 1988, 120) or even both wives and daughters in the ancient Near East (Hooks 1985, 26 n. 137).[5]

The Homeric poems transmit, in their definitive portrayal of the heroic code, an ideological demand that men capture, rape, and enslave for sexual and other purposes the women of the enemy. The enslavement and sexual use of foreign women in the poems is a poetic analogue of real-life trafficking. The raider ethos of the Homeric poems reflects the raiding and slave trading that was part of colonization and polis formation, and it can be seen in the metaphorical language of later writers. Homer makes it imperative that men rape and enslave the enemy's women, clarifies the shared characteristics of female characters in the poems who meet these fates, and connects masculinity with rape and enslavement. The *Iliad*'s key books—1, 9, and 24—programmatically elaborate the importance of rape and sexual enslavement to masculinity and victory. The *Odyssey*'s central character is known for his raids and for his capture and sexual enslavement of women. Yet the Autolycan trickster calls captive women's woe the most piteous of all. That the "potential fate" (C. Patterson 1985) of all mortal women is capture, rape, and sexual enslavement demonstrates the validity of the sexual contract, and so does the "reverse simile" that likens Odysseus's sorrow to that of a woman on her day of enslavement.

Homer's highly polished representation of historical events and cultural practices shows us the heroic world at war and at peace, when systems of justice begin to become visible. The *Odyssey* concludes with the goddess of war and justice enjoining combatants to oaths, not blows. "War" may be only one manifestation of social conflict (Shipley 1993, 1), in addition to such phenomena as piracy, colonization, and institutionalized slavery, but we can see in the Homeric poems specific and general references to women as a particular kind of booty and to booty as a main purpose of "war." When captured women are brought home or brought to camp, the sexual service they must perform is implicit and explicit. Little distinguishes warring Homeric heroes from pirates (De Souza 2000, 18–19), and the earliest Greek term that parallels the English word and concept of "pirate" is *lēïstēs*, found frequently in Homer (De Souza 2000, 3).

This study focuses not on which layers of historical time are represented in the Homeric poems and how accurately events and material culture are portrayed but rather attempts to establish the value, within the poetic heroic code, of enslaving females for sexual and other labor. I do not indict Homer as endorsing the world he represents. On the contrary, his portrait of the plight of females contains a poignancy that has been underread and undertaught. As A. H. Jackson states, "in the Homeric world and so probably in the early Greek one, one could raid but had to watch very carefully what one raided" (1995, 98); the taken-for-granted sexual enslavement of females—the failure to take note of and to analyze its ubiquity in these poems—is a kind of silent proof of its entrenched nature. As Kurt Raaflaub notes, "the poet does not tell us all he knows . . . not all that the poet does not emphasize is unimportant" (1993, 146).

The *Iliad*

In the Homeric poems and the nascent polis society they reflect, booty, not land, is a major goal of combat (Jackson 1993, 70–71). The combatants' primary goals are to take booty from Troy, to violate and capture the city's women, and to physically despoil the city: Odysseus and the bard Demodocus characterize this goal as rape. Honor is an important component of combat, but that may be due to the literary embellishment of motives (Jackson 1993, 74). Wealth was measured by its tangible presence: "Wealth in the ancient world . . . was generally highly visible and concrete. Wealth consisted of good land, agricultural stores, flocks and cattle, human beings, and precious metals stored in one form or another, all of which were there for the taking by an aggressor" (Austin 1993, 219). Honor gained in combat was made visible with the award or seizure of booty. Booty mainly included livestock and human life, acquired forcibly by piracy or raiding. To raid from others is acceptable behavior but to take from one's own kind is evil (*Il.* 24.253–264, esp. 261; cf. *Od.* 3.74). This "ownership" of objects and people is important in the honor calculus.[6]

War and piracy or raiding flow comfortably together in Homer, in such descriptions as the return of Chryseis by boat (*Il.* 1.430–78), in Tlepolemos's taunt that Heracles came by sea to steal horses and had widowed the city's streets (*Il.* 5.640–42 and *Od.* 14.257–65), in Nestor's prolix recital of youthful raids (*Il.* 11.669–761), in Hecuba's remark that Achilles had sold her sons as slaves (*Il.* 24.751–53), and in Priam's observation that Achilles has either killed his sons or sold them on the far-flung islands (*Il.* 22.44–45). In book 10 of the *Iliad*, Nestor (10.204–17) and Hector (10.299–312.; cf. 10.391–98) both promise booty to the successful spy. In various tales in the *Odyssey*, Odysseus or those who inquire after him hope or state that he is returning with treasure (e.g., 17.527; 19.272). This reaches culmination in the funeral games for Patroclus, where some of the prizes originated as booty and are given various exchange values. Goods and women motivate divine as well as mortal beings. When Hera fails to bribe Sleep with material wealth, she succeeds with the promise of a beautiful woman (*Il.* 14.233–69). The prizes at the funeral games for Patroclus are metals, metal objects, livestock, and women (*Il.* 23.256–70).

Homer's world contains a nascent sexual contract. Books 1, 9, and 24 programmatically elaborate the importance of rape and sexual enslavement to masculinity and victory. In making the sexual enslavement of females in wartime Homeric society an imperative, the *Iliad* shows us a prestate version of the formation of this contract. A crucial component of honor for the Achaioi is to be able to seize women and use them for companionship, labor, and sexual service. Agamemnon states this at the outset when he forecasts Chryseis's future: she will grow old laboring at the loom in Argos and serving him sexually (1.29–31). A woman's sexual attractiveness and ability to perform physical labor make her doubly desirable. Agamemnon knows this when he offers Achilles Lemnian women who are good workers (9.120–32; appending the opportunity to pick from among his own daughters, 9.260–90; cf. 19.243–46; 23.263, 700–705).[7]

Booty is not land but that which comes when a city is sacked. Women are prizes earned with toil and not to be given up easily (1.161–62; 2.689–90; 18.338–41). In the funeral games for Patroclus, themselves a sublimated battle, the prizes are the same as prizes for victorious soldiers. The sacking of cities is mentioned repeatedly in tandem with the enslavement of women and children, both by those who hope to do so (e.g., Agamemnon, offering a tripod, horse, chariot, or female bedmate to Teucer, 8.287–91) and by those who fear that outcome (e.g., the praying Trojans, 6.95, 310, and the Danaans, fighting like wasps or bees for their children, 12.167–72). Hector's words to the dying Patroclus remind him that the Greeks had hoped to destroy Troy and enslave and take away the Trojan women (16.831–33).

Woman is a prize or gift of honor, a *gĕras* (1.118, 120, 133, 135, 138, 161, 163, 167; 9.344; 16.54, 56; 18.444–45; 19.89). *Gĕras,* possibly connected to *gĕrōn* (an elder) or *gēras* (old age), may connote an honor bestowed as a privilege of age; it has nearly the force of a right or an entitlement (e.g., as at *Od.* 24.190, 296) (Chantraine s.v.). Honor resides in having or keeping one's prize, and dishonor in having the prize taken away (1.11, 356, 505–10; cf. 9.109–11, 367–69; 13.111–13, 120–21; 16.52–59). Achilles characterizes as assault Agamemnon's theft of his prize woman (9.367–69). The greatest chieftains decide who gets which woman. In camp, Achilles lies with Phorbas's daughter, the Lesbian Diomede, whom he had taken captive. Patroclus's bedmate, the Scyrian Iphis, was given him by Achilles (9.662–68). Nestor, for his wise counsel, was awarded the divinely lovely Hekamede in the sack of Tenedos (11.624–41). When Agamemnon tries to soften Achilles' wrath he offers him Briseis, seven Lesbian women, twenty Trojan woman, and one of his own daughters (9.120–48; cf. Ajax's reiteration of the offer at 9.260–90 and Achilles' refusal at 9.379–91, as well as Odysseus's false tale to Laertes at *Od.* 24.274–79).

This offer in book 9 effectively recapitulates the equation of victory in combat with the sex right over women that was established in book 1. The loss of Briseis, his captive prize, initiates Achilles' wrath, and Agamemnon's refusal to respect other men's sex right over their women makes Achilles refuse to play the game for the usual stakes (e.g., 9.336–41). When Achilles agrees that Patroclus shall don his armor, he does so in order to regain the girl and to secure additional gifts (16.83–86): he risks his comrade's life on the prize. After Patroclus's death, Achilles blames divinity for his wrath (19.270–75) and wishes Artemis had killed Briseis (19.59–60). He has lost Briseis but can still own many women slaves (9.364–67); the book ends with the mention of numerous women slaves and/or bedmates in his camp (9.658–68; cf. 24.582–90).[8]

Chryseis and Briseis are similar in many ways, most notably in their capacity as prizes. Each is a *kourē*, or girl (Chryseis, 1.111; Briseis, 1.298, 336, 346, 392; 2.689; 9.106, 132, 637; 19.58, 272), and each has lovely cheeks (Chryseis, 1.143, 310, 369; Briseis, 1.184, 323, 346; 9.106; 19.246; 24.676). Chryseis is called her father's child (*pais*) when her father gets her back (1.443–47). Having a living father who can ransom her with countless gifts (1.13) and whose ability to summon a plague from Apollo commands respect from the Achaioi (1.23, 376–77), protects Chryseis, and allows for her return. Briseis, however, had been taken with much toil by Achilles (1.162; 2.690) in the sacks of Lyrnessos and Thebe, bloody engagements in which at least three men had been killed (2.689–93). We learn only later who Briseis's father is (9.131–32, 273–74). As lovely as Aphrodite (19.282), Briseis tells the dead Patroclus that the men were her brothers and that Achilles had killed her husband (19.287–300). Patroclus is feminized here, as a listener and companion who had never abandoned her. Patroclus is like Hector, who was always kind to Helen (24.767–72).

Sacking a city, another constant goal of Homeric conflict, is usually referred to by the verb *perthō* (2.660; cf. 11.625; 12.15; 13.816; 16.57; 18.342; 19.296; 20.92, 192; 21.517, 584; 24.729) and its intensified compounds *ekperthō* (1.19, 125, 164; 2.113; 15.216; 18.283, 327) and *diaperthō* (1.367; 4.53; 7.32; 9.326; 18.511, the last being the description of the shield). Achilles and others are entitled "sacker of cities," or *ptoliporthos* (e.g., Achilles, 8.372; 15.77; 21.550; Odysseus, 10.363; Ares, 20.152; Otrynteus, 20.384). Athena is called *lēïtis*, female raider (10.460), in a description of the theft of Rhesus's horses (cf. 18.327 and 20.188–94 on abducting women). Many descriptions of the sacking of a city also refer to the capture of women and children (2.660, Heracles takes Astyocheia from Ephyra; cf. 9.593–94; 16.831–33). Achilles tauntingly reminds Aeneas that he had sacked Lyrnessos and enslaved women there (20.188–94; cf. 20.89–92).

Book 18 reiterates these themes. Achilles accepts his fate of early death but still seeks renown by capturing Trojan women (18.115–25). Polydamas warns Hector that when Achilles returns, their fight for the city and the women will be desperate (18.254–83, esp. 265; cf. 21.583–88). Achilles' new shield, with its representation of many kinds of human activity, makes siege, sack, rape, and enslavement paradigmatic of human society (18.509–40). To return home without having participated in them would bring warriors ill repute (Agamemnon at 2.112–15) and would be womanish (8.163–66). Hector is feminized in his defeat; stabbed in the neck, he imagines Achilles will kill him without his armor—like a woman (22.123–25). Achaian soldiers repeatedly pierce his corpse and observe how soft he is (22.373–74). Combat and the defense of one's own possessions, parents, wives, and children is emphasized in book 15, where Hector exhorts his men, literally, to be men (*aneres este*) (15.487) and to defend these possessions honorably to the death (15.486–89). Reiterating this imperative, Ajax states that it would be shameful for the Greeks not to fight to the death (15.502–13) and Nestor (15.661–66) supplicates them to remember their wives, children, parents, and possessions, again commanding them to be men (*aneres este*) (15.661). Diomedes makes war the crucible of masculinity when he taunts the roving-eyed, lovely-haired Paris, saying he fears Paris as much as the blows of a woman or half-witted child; when he himself strikes, he makes children orphans and women widows (11.388–95).

The Danaans fight in order to sack Troy and to bring home in ships the wives and children of the slain Trojans (4.238–39). Hector verbalizes that feared outcome by indicating his desire to see his house, his wife, and his child once more (6.366; cf. 8.57, 155; 17.223–24). The drive to gain booty through conflict has imperatival force even for the gods. Zeus himself is overruled when he suggests a compromise that will preserve the city of Priam and return Helen to Menelaus (4.17–19). Because of the constant and reciprocal nature of the raiding mentality, both sides are threatened with the possibility that their women will be kidnapped. Chryseis is no less valued for her attainments than is Clytemnestra (1.113–15), and Helen, Briseis, Chryseis, and Andromache alike occupy the positions of wife or daughter and of "spear wife." Epithets establish the likenesses among the women. Lovely hair characterizes women, especially when their subordinate or captive status is being emphasized (e.g., Briseis, 2.689; Helen, 3.329; 7.355; 8.82; 9.339; Nestor's captive Hekamede, 14.5–8). When thundering Zeus, whom Agamemnon resembles, is described as Hera's lord, she too is figured as having lovely hair (10.5).

Paris can be feminized by reference to his hairdo (11.385) or to his own beauty and his possession of the lovely-haired Helen (13.765–68).

Few characters criticize the raiding mentality. Thersites takes issue with Agamemnon's burgeoning desires for valuable metals and women (2.226–33), but he has an evil character and an ugly body and is most hateful to Agamemnon and Odysseus (2.212–20). His challenge to the system is brief and bathetically ineffectual. Once Odysseus has shamed Thersites, Nestor restates the imperative: the Danaans must not go home until each of them has violated a Trojan woman as vengeance for Helen, here described as a weeping captive (2.354–56). The famous catalogue of ships that directly follows lets us know just how many men, with their waiting ships, are ready to perform this duty. Exceeding Nestor's ferocity, Agamemnon urges Menelaus to order the Danaans to kill even unborn children in the womb (6.57–60).

From book 3 on, the poet develops the terrible equality of both sides' positions. Menelaus characterizes Paris as an outlaw and woman stealer (3.39; cf. 3.46–48). Paris suggests that Helen and her possessions be the prize for the victor and that this one fight might suffice to stop the war (3.67–75; Helen and her possessions are mentioned in 3.91, 93, 254–55, 282–87; 7.350–51; 22.114). Hector, Menelaus, and others consent, whereupon all rejoice that this may end the war (3.111–12). Hector bitterly states the corollary: desire for women causes wars (22.111–18).

Helen and Andromache reflect the vulnerabilities of all women as tokens in the outcomes of conflicts among men. Nestor had represented Helen to the Greeks as a lamenting captive (2.354–56), and she is an unwilling pawn of Aphrodite (3.399–412). She came to Troy on the same voyage that had brought the Sidonian slave women who are expert weavers (6.289–92). In book 3, we first find her weaving (3.125–28), and at the end of the book Paris takes her to bed. We find her again in the *Odyssey*, weaving at home with Menelaus. Helen enacts on a materially grander scale Chryseis's fate of weaving and providing sexual service for her current "master." Nor is her life at Troy serene, for only Hector was unfailingly kind to Helen when others in the palace were harsh (24.767–72).[9]

Homer's Helen, godlike as she is and as capable as she is of seeing through others' disguises, is simultaneously like any wholly mortal woman in martial society—vulnerable always to kidnap and sexual enslavement, a possession herself, allied with and bound up with her possessions, able to start, and stop, wars. Paris separates her from her possessions, yet retains her within the category of "possession." He tells the Trojans he will return all the possessions he took from Argos, except for Helen (7.362–64). The Trojan herald Idaios elaborately tenders the offer to the Achaioi (7.389–93). Helen describes herself to Priam as having followed Paris (*hepomēn*) (3.173–75) but in anger at Aphrodite suggests that the goddess herself go home with Menelaus and become his *alochos* (bedmate) or slave (3.409), as she herself refuses to serve Menelaus's bed. Whatever Helen's motivations for coming to Troy, Paris flatters her by saying he has never desired her so much, and that he desires her more now than he did even on the day he kidnapped her (*harpaxas*) (3.444).

Andromache most poignantly represents the plight of women in wartime society. Asian Thebe is often mentioned in the early books as a source for captive women (2.689–93, on the capture of Briseis by Achilles; he had mentioned this campaign to Thetis at 1.366). Andromache came from Asian Thebe (6.395–98), where Achilles killed her father Eetion and her seven brothers. After Artemis killed her mother, the orphan Andromache becomes Hector's property (6.407–32). He is her last and only "warmth" (*thalpōrē*) (6.412).[10] For Hector, the most grievous consequence of Troy's fall is Andromache's enslavement and her removal to another land, where she is forced to toil at the loom (6.440–65). He does not mention Andromache's inevitable rape and the future of their son. Andromache refers not to her own dismal future but rather to Hector's defilement and their son's unhappy prospects when she learns of her husband's death (22.477–514). This news comes just as she is toiling at her loom (like Helen and Chryseis) and planning to bathe Hector when he returns, battle weary (like Hekamede; 22.437–47). Not until her last speech does Andromache predict that Astyanax will be murdered or enslaved (24.726–38). The constant reference to captured women and to the slaughter of innocents (e.g., 22.60–65), ensures that we are unable to forget them for long. Hekamede (book 11), Briseis (passim), and Diomede and Iphis (book 9) all had had fathers, all came from sacked cities, a few women out of many more who are unnamed.[11]

The women captured on raids and enslaved by Achilles and Patroclus grieve piteously along with Achilles on hearing that Patroclus is dead (18.28–31). When Briseis, as lovely as Aphrodite (19.282), and the other women are brought into Achilles' camp, each mourns her own private woes (19.282–86, 301–2). These women certainly remember their capture, rape, and enslavement or anticipate recapture, more rape, and reenslavement. The laments of Andromache, Hecuba, and Helen close the *Iliad.* Each speaks to the violence and disruption of war and to enslavement and harsh treatment far from home. Andromache forecasts the forced departure of Trojan wives, her own enslavement, the sack of Troy, and her son's death or enslavement (24.725–45). Achilles has either killed or enslaved and sold Hecuba's sons (24.751–53), and only Hector was consistently kind to Helen (24.767–72). The *Iliad* opens with a quarrel over a woman who never speaks in the poem. It ends with women poignantly, albeit briefly, speaking about the fate of women and children in war.

The *Iliad* sketches in shadowy but consistent form a nascent sexual contract. By clearly making the capture and enslavement of females a defining component of masculinity—one that the gods either endorse or cannot forestall—the poet foregrounds women's subordination. The nature of the subordination is clearly founded in women's sexuality. Sexual violence against females is ever-present, and the sexual violence goes unexamined. Thetis, the greatest hero's mother, endorses male sex right when she pleads Achilles' cause before Zeus, when Athena stays Achilles' hand, and when the mother frets that her grieving son has neither eaten, slept, nor engaged in sexual activity with a woman (24.130–31). Once Hector's body is ransomed and Achilles and Priam interrupt their hostilities, Achilles sleeps again, with the lovely-cheeked Briseis at his side (24.676).

The *Odyssey*

> Then he sang how the sons of the Achaeans, streaming down from the horse, went forth from their hollow place of ambush and sacked the city. And he sang how they raped the steep city this way and that, and how Odysseus, like Ares, came to the door of Deiphobos along with the godlike Menelaus. There, he sang, Odysseus braved dreadful war and conquered, with the help of the great-spirited Athena. So the famous minstrel sang these things. And again, Odysseus melted into grief, and his cheeks grew wet with tears. In this way a woman falls down to embrace her beloved husband who has fallen before her eyes among his people, when he wards off the day of no pity from the city and children. She falls, wailing, to embrace him as he shudders and dies. But the men behind her prod her back and shoulders with their spears and lead her off in bondage to toil and woe. Her cheeks are wasted away with a woe most piteous: just so, Odysseus wept. (8.514–31)

It is a commonplace that the *Odyssey* represents the postwar heroic world as the *Iliad* had represented that world at war. This peace is uneasy, and little has changed for women. The *Odyssey* shares the *Iliad*'s values about female sexuality and who owns it but dwells on the extensive hardships faced by enslaved women. They are never free of the possibility of sexual assault (16.108–9; 20.318–19; 22.37, 313–14). Frequent reminders of the piratical Autolycan Odysseus show the sexual contract in all its brutality. Other archaic poets, most notably the mercenary Archilochus, also celebrate this ethos. The *Odyssey*'s central character is acclaimed for raiding and for capturing and enslaving females. But when Demodocus sings of the rape of Troy, Homer makes Odysseus feel the woe of a woman captured by the enemy as she holds her dying husband in her arms. Odysseus weeps like a woman deprived of her freedom when her husband dies in battle (8.520–30)—his cheeks are wet with a most pitiable woe. In fact, Homer calls the woe of captive women the most pitiable in wartime (8.530). This moment of utter truth is the keystone "reverse simile" of the Homeric poems.

Though the war has been over for nearly a decade, a warlike climate prevails. We hear of wanderers who raid and plunder (14.85–87, 229–33, 257–65) and of raiding expeditions prior to the Trojan expedition (21.13–21). Thus the Trojan expedition is merely raiding on a grander scale, one raid among many that may be notable only because, as Helen observes in the *Iliad*, it will be memorialized as art. Odysseus is heroicized as a sacker of cities, in fact programmatically so in the invocation (*eperse*, sacked, 1.2; he knew the minds of men and cities; cf. *ptoliporthos*, city sacker, 8.3), and various characters recall the sack of Troy (Nestor, *diepersamen*, sacked, 3.130; Demodocus sings of the Greeks, *dieprathon*, sacked, 8. 514; Odysseus's crew mentions plunder, *lēïdos*, 10.40–41). Odysseus himself refers often to the sack of Troy (9.265; 11.533; 13.316; 14.241–42) and calls himself a sacker of cities, *ptoliporthios* (9.504), a label also applied to him by the Cyclops (9.530) and assigned to the beggar by the poet (18.356; cf. 16.442). The taking of property and women is part of a sack (Nestor at 3.153–54); Athena bluntly mentions the plunder Odysseus might have taken (5.39–40; cf. Poseidon at 13.138) and reassures Odysseus that she will let him plunder livestock even if he is outnumbered by fifty men (20.49–51). Penelope recalls how Antinoös's father and Taphian raiders (*lēïstersin*) had pillaged Ithaca's allies (16.424–28). Plundering is real toil (8.490). Odysseus promises the herdsmen rewards that are the peacetime equivalents of a general's rewards to his soldiers—wives, property, and houses (21.214–15)—and the poet calls Odysseus *ptoliporthos* (city sacker) during the slaughter of the suitors (22.283). His own home becomes a citadel occupied by an enemy force he must expel. Before engaging in this crucial battle, Odysseus asks Athena to bring back that rapist strength he had when he untied Troy's maiden veil (13.386–91).

Odysseus regales his hosts with tales of plunder. He tells Alkinoös of raids on Ismaros involving sack, looting, and the kidnap of wives (9.39–42). There is a submerged suggestion that Odysseus had coerced Apollo's priest Maron into giving him especially gorgeous wine in return for leaving his wife and children unharmed (9.196–211). Likewise, Odysseus the beggar asks the slave Eumaeus if he had been kidnapped along with sheep or cattle (15.384–88) when his town was sacked. He recapitulates this scenario for the suitor Antinoös, claiming that he himself had owned many male slaves (*dmōes*) (17.422), had gone to Egypt with raiders (*hama lēïstersi*) (17.425), had plundered fields (*portheon*) (17.433), and had kidnapped women and small children (17.432–34). The Greek remnant appear to the Cyclops to be pirates (9.252–55); Odysseus the beggar tells a disguised Athena a yarn about plunder from Troy (13.259–66, 273).

The ubiquity of female slaves reinforces the sense that this is a raiding culture and underscores what becomes of captured females once they have been carried "home." The noun *dmōiai* is related to the verb *damazō* and means "captured, tamed ones," though it is usually translated as "slaves," "serving women," and the like (Cole 1984, 97–113). The *Iliad* refers to individual, pretty female captives by name and calls them *gĕras* (prize), but the *Odyssey* refers frequently to female slaves in the aggregate. *Dmōiai* is not found in the singular; these dehumanized tamed females are no longer unique individuals. Eurycleia informs Odysseus that she and Penelope have taught fifty *dmōiai* to card wool and endure slavery (22.421–23). Penelope refers to them (4.682–83; cf. 2.412), as does Telemachus (20.318). Less frequently mentioned are male slaves, *dmōes*, but Anticleia tells her son that Laertes, grieving and isolated, lies down at night with them (11.190), and Eumaeus refers to their accepted customs (14.59–61). Lowly as Laertes is, there is one more lowly still: the aged Sikel woman who tends him (24.208–12; at 24.365–67 she is called an *amphipolos*, handmaid). Laertes' little house has a few slaves (*dmōessi*) (24.213), where Odysseus tells them and Telemachus that he will test his father.[12]

The *dmōiai* welcome Telemachus home with kisses (17.33–35) and bathe Telemachus and his beggar father (17.88–89). They build up and tend fires (18.308–11; 20.122–23), make up beds for guests (20.138–39), carry buckets heavy with water and axe heads (21.61–62), serve food (5.199), carry lamps, and light passageways (19.24–25; cf. 4.296–301). They bathe and anoint travelers (4.49–51). Even the frailest grinds her quota (20.105–19). They will be ordered by Telemachus to feign a wedding mood so as to deceive wondering passersby (23.130–36). Penelope sits with them (17.505) and is accompanied by them (19.45, 60). These may be the same women referred to as *amphipoloi* (serving maids) (17.91–93; 18.303; 19.317), *gynaikes* (women) (17.75–76), or *amphipoloi gynaikes* (17.49; 19.602; 21.8, 356; 23.364), *akēdēes gynaikes* (uncaring women) (17.319), and *dmōias kynas ouk alegousas* (uncaring dogs) (19.154). Odysseus wonders if Agamemnon had died during a raid for cattle, sheep, or women (11.397–403, esp. 401–3). Menelaus has numerous *dmōiai* (4.49–51, 296–99; 15.93) and fathered his son Megapenthes by a slave woman (*doulēs*) (4.12). Kalypso also has them (5.199), as do the Phaeacians (6.99–100; 7.103, fifty *dmōiai*; 8.433, 454; 13.66–69; very hard work is mentioned at 13.68). Eumaeus's royal family boasted numerous *dmōiai* (15.461). "Tamed" female captives are found most everywhere except the underworld.

Odysseus' Autolycan side has been brilliantly analyzed by Jenny Strauss Clay. Much of this submerged side of Odysseus concerns raids, plunder, and rape. "Mentes" fondly recalls the Odysseus's expedition to Ephyra in search of poisoned arrows (1.255–66). Yearning and lonely, Telemachus informs Antinoös that he will rule the household and the *dmōiai* his father had pirated (*lēïssato*) (1.398). Members of Odysseus's crew recall the plundering of Troy in order to justify their own opening of Aeolus's bag of winds (10.40–41). Places where Odysseus has traveled are often the same places mentioned in both poems as ripe for the plunder of goods and women. He wins a wrestling match at Lesbos (4.342–45; 17.133–36), from whence came the seven Lesbian women offered to Achilles (*Il.* 9.120–48, 270–72). Achilles' slave Diomede came from Lesbos (*Il.* 9.664–65). Heracles captured Astyocheia at Ephyra (*Il.* 2.658–59); at Ephyra Odysseus seeks poison arrows and commerce (1.255–63).

The varied peoples and places Odysseus encounters in his wanderings are alternatives—ultimately inferior—to Ithaca and its work ethic (Redfield 1983). The fairy-tale Phaeacians, protected by Poseidon, can flee the pillaging Cyclopes by moving away (6.4–6); Nausikaa, serene, does not fear Odysseus (6.201–3). She is so carefree that she permits herself and her attendants to remove their *krēdemna* (veils); these are uncivilized and untamed little girls (6.100). This kind of security would not have been an option for many island dwellers. Perhaps the Phaeacians's somewhat sinister inbredness is an apologia to raider culture; the poem may justify the raider mentality by making its opposite a negative. Telemachus, of hardy Ithacan stock and admirer of his father's piratical bent, must be protected from ambush and warned by Athena herself (15.10–55). Disdaining the mercantile and raiding outlook, the aristocratic Euryalos chaffs Odysseus, comparing him not to an athlete but to a greedy grubber (8.163–64). Odysseus proudly claims his grubbiness, and Athena will say that Odysseus is light fingered and seeks gain (13.291–92). But the Phaeacians have the best of both worlds. They have fifty *dmōiai*, whose textiles are a feature of palace luxury (7.103). Nausikaa's nurse, Eurymedousa, a faint double for Eurycleia, was a *gĕras* from a raiding expedition (7.7–10).[13]

Perhaps the harsh life on Ithaca justifies Odysseus's raider bent; Ithaca is rough and poor (4.605–8); many men take to the sea out of hunger (17.473–74); and the diet of male slaves is inadequate (14.80–81). Nonetheless, the movement toward regularization, temperance, and the rule of law in the *Odyssey* is notable. Punishment awaits those who plunder the forbidden (1.7–9; 11.110–18; 12.139–41). The poem ends when Athena herself steps in to prevent bloodshed. In the postwar world, the gravest threats are from within the community. Thus the prominence of the Orestes theme—with its injunction to keep female sexuality under male control—in the *Odyssey*. Those who stay away from home too long are likely to find confusion and rapine there, as Nestor reminds Telemachus (3.313–36; cf. Odysseus at 11.384). Just so does Odysseus find his home: the suitors' *hybris* (arrogance) is noted (16.86; 20.166–71, 366–70; 23.62–64). In fact, it reaches the heavens (15.329), and their wastefulness (17.167–69) and insults to women (16.108–11) are remarked on. The punishment of the sexually unfaithful female house slaves is connected to their misuse of Odysseus's resources, which include their sexed bodies; the barley-grinding woman's weary outrage acts as a token for Odysseus (20.105–21).

Wartime and peacetime meet at the fault line of raiding; the suitors are failed raiders. Like the Iliadic Greeks, the suitors have come from many islands to fight over a woman (1.246–48). The suitors seek marriage with Penelope and the rule this brings, but they will end up, like heroes on both sides in the *Iliad*, as *pikrogamoi* (of bitter marriage, 4.346). Ithaca's female slaves are in a grievous situation. Odysseus and Telemachus are outraged at the suitors' mistreatment of these women yet harshly execute them (16.304, 316–17). Eumaeus sympathetically mentions the fearful mien of male slaves (14.59–61) but has no parallel sympathy for the dilemma of female slaves. As Helene Foley observes, Penelope effectively "stops time" on the island by controlling the mourning schedule with her endlessly woven and unwoven web (2.96–102). Ultimately, a slave woman betrays her to the suitors, and Penelope is on the verge of being forced to marry when Athena brings her husband home. The slave women enjoy no such luck, and they lose all around. Eurycleia is willing to inform on her fellow slaves to the master. All are punished, though it is not clear all were guilty, and they died "most piteously" (22.472).[14]

Homer sees it all. He makes the vanquished city a violated woman. Masculinity depends on the male sexual contract in both war and peace. Commerce begins to replace war as we move from *Iliad* to *Odyssey*. Homer anticipates much of the ideology of masculinity conducive to generating the *pornē*, and the Homeric poems provide a functional or performative definition of masculinity that entails male sex right over women. The raider culture praised in the Homeric poems is also celebrated in archaic lyric poetry, but in an increasingly commercialized context. Women were enslaved and brought to new locales for sexual labor.

Pirates into Pimps

In Iron Age Greece and in the Homeric poems, no clear distinction was made between war and piracy or raiding. There is ample evidence that females were taken in these activities, but less attention has been paid to what happened to them afterward. Certainly there was a slave trade in the eighth century. The Achaeans trade slaves, animals, hides, and metal in return for wine from Lemnos (*Il.* 7.473–75). The Taphians trade in metals (*Od.* 1.182–84) and slaves (*Od.* 14.452; 15.427); the Phoenician woman recounts being kidnapped by "raider men" (*lēïstores andres*)

(*Od.* 15.427). There were also markets in Samothrace and Imbros. Greeks traded slaves in Tyre and helped move textiles, gold, silver, and slaves between Hellas and the Near East.[15]

The first sexually trafficked female in the Greek historical record was from Thrace: Rhodopis/Doricha, called "a hetaira woman" (*hetairē gynē*, 2.134.7) by Herodotus.[16] She was brought as a slave from Thrace, prostituted at the Hellenic *emporion* (trading center) at Naukratis (Kom Gaïf) in Egypt, and later became wealthy and free. The sharp "Egyptian emphasis" to Menelaus's exploits in the *Odyssey* may reflect current interest in renewed contact with Egypt rather than a nostalgic glance at the Bronze Age (*Od.* 4).[17] By the fifth century Naukratis was famed for its alluring *hetairai* (Hdt. 2.134–35). Naukratis may have been a unique trafficking node or only one of several. We should seek evidence for trafficking early on, however difficult this may be; the term *Spuren* (tracks) is apt (Herter 1960, 79 n. 15). To do so is tricky; Greek evidence is late. It is not yet possible to establish a precise continuum along which these bits of evidence are found.

Some trafficked women must have been less valuable than others. Pausanias (second century CE) recounts the horrible assault on an enslaved foreign woman. The bizarre anecdote normalizes and renders invisible the trade in females, making an enslaved barbarian woman more expendable than a nonbarbarian one:

> Euphemus the Carian said that once, when sailing to Italy, he went off course [and] . . . his ship was carried into the outer sea, where no one sails. Many islands there are uninhabited, while on others live savage men. At these the sailors did not want to land. . . . But they were forced to. . . . These islands are called Satyrides. . . . The inhabitants have red hair and tails not much smaller than those of horses. These Satyrs, as soon as they saw the sailors, swept down in silence upon the ship and assaulted the women who were in the ship. At length, the sailors in their fear tossed a barbarian woman out onto the island. The Satyrs committed not just the usual outrage upon her but also ravaged her whole body. (*Description of Greece*, 1.23.5–7)

The eponymously named Beldam vase (fifth century BCE) may represent this event: a woman, possibly African, is sexually tortured by satyr-rapists (see fig. 1.1).

More tenuous and yet more interesting are the hints of prostitutional scenarios and terminology in the archaic poets Archilochus and Hipponax. Their poems may be generic in form and diction, but the experiences, emotions, and locales are presented as quotidian and individual. Archilochus (fl. early seventh century BCE) shows us tantalizing glimpses of island and raider culture.[18] He graphically describes sexual activity in the lowest of mimetic modes. Many fragments and testimonia recount sexual scenarios that may be abusive and that may take place in a

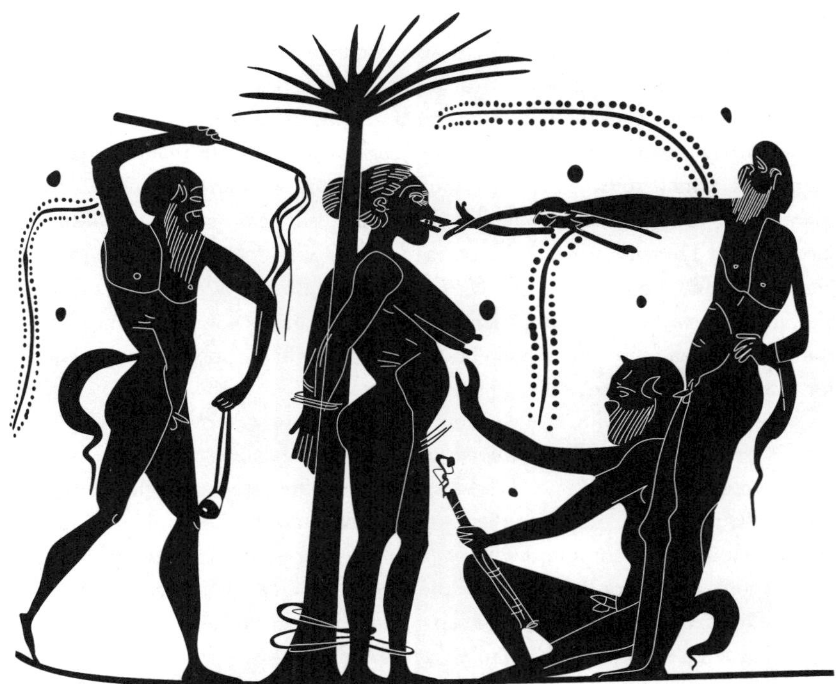

Figure 1.1. Beldam Painter. Attic black-figure *lekythos*, ca. 475–450 BCE. National Archaeological Museum, Athens, NM 1129 = ABVP 149. Drawing by Tina Ross.

commercial setting. Men and women alike are described in specific and degrading anatomical terms (43 West; 189 West; 35 West; 208 West). Archilochus spews venom at the pathic and the *kakē pornē* (evil whore) who think only about being penetrated (328 West), although this fragment and 327 West, which denounces the pathic, are considered to be much later *spuria*. Archilochus states that obol by obol, earned with toil, is poured down the guts of a *pornēs gynaikos* (whore woman, 302 West); if genuine, this is Archilochus's only reference to money.[19] One fragment is paradigmatic for graphic, degrading sexual activity: "Just as a Thracian or Phrygian man sucks barley beer through a straw, she was bent over, toiling" (42 West). This image connects the woman with foreign labor and situates her in a humiliating anatomical position.[20]

Although in Archilochus's poetry we find no mention of commercial sex except in fragments of dubious attribution, Archilochus sketches prostitutional scenarios.[21] Hipponax of Ephesus (fl. 510) provides subject matter and treatment so similar to that of Archilochus that the attribution of some fragments is disputed. Like Archilochus, Hipponax uses abusive language in describing sexual activity with women, but Hipponax's world unequivocally has a money economy and commercial prostitution.[22] Many words and phrases attributed to him suggest prostitutional settings (see Konstantinos Kapparis's chapter in this volume). Two fragments, which some editors combine, refer to a woman clad in a Coraxian mantle and to someone naked to their Sindian "slit" (*diasphax*); the Sindi and Coraxi were Thracian tribes (2 West, 2a West). *Diasphax* is an "opening made by violence, rent . . . gorge . . . cleft" (*LSJ* 9th ed., s.v.). It can also refer to a sluice or cleft in the earth, thus creating a semantic field that allows reference to rape and to the dehumanization of the female body, and from which topographic metaphors for the female body arise.

Hipponax had a wide range of terms for prostitute: *kasoritis* (brothel inmate, 135c West); *pornē* (104 West); *anaseisiphallos* (cock shaker, 135 West). The term *anasyrptolis* (self-exposer, 135a West) is significant. The active meaning of the verb *anasyrō* is "pull up or expose to view"; the reflexive means "to plunder or ravage" (Plut. 2.330d). The compound with *ptolis* (= *polis*) shows that an *anasyrptolis* is one who exposes herself, or is exposed to, the gaze of the city (see Kapparis in this volume). One fragment provides four separate terms that Hipponax uses for newly depilated female genitals (*dorialos*, *myrton*, *choiros*, *kysthos*, 174 West) along with other terms for the genitals.[23] Two fragments certainly refer to commercial sex, something not yet seen in Archilochus: *kasoritis* and *maulistērion* (60 West) refer to Lydian coins of little value and also to a brothel or prostitute's fee; a complex of related classical Greek words includes terms for procuring. *Maulistērion* survives in modern Greek with the same meaning: a brothel fee.

When trying to imagine where the commercial prostitution of trafficked females first occurred, the image of "the brothel" comes to mind, along with a notion of permanence or solidity. However, structures more ephemeral such as "cribs" may have sufficed. The English word "crib" has several meanings: cribs are small, confined spaces of low comfort for animals and small children or the small spaces in which a prostitute works (cf. the English idiom of prostitutes in a "stable"). There are literary references to criblike conditions in Greco-Roman antiquity (Plaut. *Poen.* 268; Plaut. *Pseud.* 178, 214, 229; Prop. 4.5.; see Judith Hallett's chapter in this volume), and one Greek word for pimp was *pornoboskos* (one who keeps prostitutes; the root *bosk-* refers to the feeding of herd animals). The references in Plautus and Propertius imply shedlike or tentlike structures and therefore a lack of permanence. Fifth-century Greek comedy indicates that there were *porneia*, and Solon is credited with having established state brothels. These need not have been substantial in their construction (see Allison Glazebrook's chapter in this volume).

Slave Prostitutes and Solon's City

The biographical tradition of Solon (fl. sixth century BCE) crystallizes and legitimates the existence of a sexually disposable class of women. In a fourth-century comedy, Solon is credited with having established state brothels for young citizen males, using purchased women (Ath. 13.569d3–f4). The "respectable" sources for Solon's laws (*Athenaiōn Politeia*, *Constitution of Athens*, and Plutarch's *Life of Solon*) contain nothing about prostitution, but his alleged brothels are in keeping with prostitutes' association with urbanism in the archaic period. We should not discount the possibility of a "municipal brothel" in sixth-century Athens. Prostitution was lucrative for those who took in the fee, and taxing those who prostituted others would have benefitted the state. The Archive of Zenon in Hellenistic Egypt records that prostituted female slaves commanded the highest prices, and the highest tax was assessed on prostituted women on the Red Sea–Coptos trade route.

Solon may well have provided female sex slaves for Athens' finest youth. Furthermore, his biographical tradition blends the language of plunder with the language of trade and incorporates the theft of women (Plut. *Sol.* 8.5). Solon admired and emulated merchants (Plut. *Sol.* 2.1). He may have considered raiding an acceptable form of commerce (76A Ruschenbusch). Wording in his poetry and in his biographical tradition aligns Solon's language with that of Homer and other early poets (Hesiod *Works and Days* 702 ff.; Semon. fr. 6 West). As Allison Glazebrook observes, Solon's laws "began to distinguish between women who could be prostituted and women who could not be" (pers. comm.; see also 2005b). Men could still be men without having to go to Troy.

NOTES

1. For prostitution and statism, see Stetz and Oh 2001. The U.S. Army made use of the "comfort women" until the spring of 1946 (report, Ibaraki Prefectural Police Department history, quoted in Talmadge 2007). On April 27, 2007, the Supreme Court of Japan rejected compensation claims made by onetime sex slaves and others (Onishi 2007). Walter Burkert (1996, 133) implies that patriarchy requires the prostituted class.

2. For women and girls, sexual violence and warfare, see Gaca 2007. John Evans (1991) devotes one page of a book on war to those demographic and financial imbalances war brought to Roman Italy and which drove many women into prostitution. For historiography, see Tyrell and Bennett 1999, 37–51. Sandra Rae Joshel and Sheila Murnaghan's 1998 collection on women and slaves has nothing on prostituted females.

3. I employ the UN definition of trafficking: "the recruitment, transportation, transfer, harbouring or receipt of persons, by means of the threat or the use of force or other forms of coercion, of abduction, of fraud, of deception, of the abuse of power or of a position of vulnerability, or of the giving or receiving of payments or benefits to achieve the

consent of a person having control over another person, for the purpose of exploitation. Exploitation shall include, at a minimum, the exploitation of the prostitution of others or other forms of sexual exploitation, forced labour or services, slavery or practices similar to slavery, servitude or the removal of organs" ("Protocol to Prevent, Suppress and Punish Trafficking in Persons, Especially Women and Children . . . ," adopted in November 2000 by the UN General Assembly, cited in International Organization for Migration 2001, 17–18).

4. On the invisibility of slaves, see Tandy 1997, 65ff. For critique of Finley on women and the economy, see Pomeroy 1995, 81–195. For contributions made to contemporary economies by women's uncompensated labor, see Waring 1998 and Delphy 1984. For contributions made by women in ancient economies, see Barber 1994 and Ventris and Chadwick 1959.

5. The New Orleans census recorded no children in Storyville, but excavations found incontrovertible evidence that children resided in the brothels (perambulators, feeding bottles, toys, clothing, etc.) (Gray 2003). For wife selling, see Pateman 1988, 120. For wife- and daughter selling in the ancient Near East, see Hooks 1985, 26 n. 137.

6. Aristotle does not condemn raiding, considering it not an illegitimate form of livelihood (*Pol.* 1.1256a35ff.). William Newman (1887, 170) comments that Aristotle conceives of piracy "as he meets with it in the pages of Homer. . . . The Greeks, after all, felt that the robber had something of the warrior about him. . . . Aristotle makes *leisteia* a kind of hunting, and hunting a kind of war."

7. Cf. Hdt. 9.80, 81, on Pausanias's fair distribution of the spoils: Pausanias gets ten apiece of the big items, including women and camels.

8. For Briseis see Dué 2002.

9. For the importance of textiles in the ancient economy and the part played by females, see Barber 1994; Pomeroy 1995, 189–90.

10. Tellingly for the sexual contract, Hector is identified by James Redfield (1975 [1994]) as the representative of civilization.

11. For Andromache, see Nagler 1967, 269–311; C. Segal 1971, 33–57. See Llewellyn-Jones 2003, 130–32, for the throwing down of the headband in this passage.

12. *Dmōiai* are mentioned sparsely in the *Iliad* (e.g., 18.28–31). "The menial tasks that they [the women in the Pylos personnel lists] perform suggest that they were slaves: possibly the labour force for the industry on which the wealth of the Mycenaean kingdoms must at least in part have been built. The casual references to the fathers of the children also seem to indicate that they are not the product of any regular union. . . . It may be suggested that the labour force is in part the product of piratical raids" (Ventris and Chadwick 1959, 156).

13. Thucydides and Herodotus make woman theft an *aitia* for the great wars. David Tandy (1997, 119) observes a suppression of the mercantile in Homer.

14. William Thalmann (1998a) thinks Odysseus and Telemachus are angry with the Ithacan slave women not because they asserted their sexuality with other men but because other men sexually possessed them; Stephanie Budin believes the punishment was so harsh because they did assert their sexuality (pers. comm.). Perhaps Homer shows pity for their

fates. The rare word *oiktista* ("most piteously," *Od.* 22.472) also describes the gobbling of Odysseus's men by Scylla (*Od.* 12.258).

15. Tandy discusses the movement of textiles, gold and silver, and slaves between the Near East and Hellas (65); a one-time market (72–73); markets at Lemnos, Samothrace, and Imbros (74 and nn.); and the Greeks at Tyre (Ezekial 27:13; 120 and n. 33). He accepts the setting of Ezekiel, dated to ca. 630, to the late ninth or early eighth century.

16. For schema on how females can become prostituted, see Schumacher 2001. The sending, transit, and receiving locales for sex trafficking in Asia have been much studied (T. L. Brown 2001, 23). Carpet factories and poor rural communities seasonally send females from Nepal to Mumbai to work in factories, which are main originating nodes. Of three hundred Nepali prostitutes interviewed in Mumbai, 40 percent had been trafficked from carpet factories (Human Rights Watch 1995, 25). For prostituting family members in ancient Athens, see Glazebrook 2005b. On the early enslavement of Thracians, see Rosivach 1999.

17. Heubeck et al. 1988.

18. Mary Lefkowitz notes that "Archilochus appears to be the first real person among Greek poets" (1981, 25) because he describes intense emotions and realistic events but most information thought to be biographical can have come from his poetry (25–31). For influence of other poetic traditions on Archilochus, see Hordern 2001, 39–40.

19. With Valerio Casadio (1996), I accept 302 and 331 as genuine but consider 327 and 328 inauthentic. For 302, see Casadio 1996, 33, 34; for 331, see Casadio 1996, 88–91 and 96; for 327, 328, see Casadio 1996, 78–81. As for 302, Martin West (1974, 138) is skeptical; William Loomis (1998) accepts. I favor early authorship because *pornēs gynaikos* is used to describe the woman rather than just *pornēs.*

20. Beer was foreign, not Greek (Sams 1977, 108–15.) For further discussion of the fragment, see Marzullo 1997, 37–66; Gerber 1976, 7–14.

21. Loomis (1998, 166) claims that Archilochus 328 West is the first textual reference to sex for money. This is followed by a long gap before the next textual reference (Eupolis, *PCG* 247 ca. 420). The first visual reference in an Attic context to commercial sex is dated to 490–475, with Makron's vases of prostitutional scenarios including prices (*ARV* 148, 206).

22. For lexical and literary analysis of Hipponax, see Masson 1962, esp. 31–32; Rosen 1988, 29–41 (see esp. 29 and 30 and n. 4). Hipponax is the first to use *phallos/phalēs* (phallus) in a nontechnical and "obscene" sense (Rosen 1988, 34 and n. 18).

23. For other terms, e.g., *borboropē* (filth opening), see Degani 1984 and Kapparis in this volume. West (1974, 148, 149), discusses alternative spellings of *borboropē*; Olivier Masson (1962, 171, 172) offers more parallels.

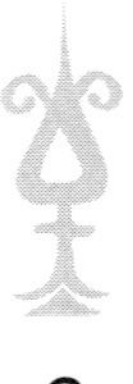

2 *Porneion*

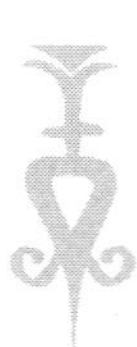

Prostitution in Athenian Civic Space

ALLISON GLAZEBROOK

Social histories of prostitution in ancient Greece have often assumed that what applies to prostitution in Rome applies to Greece—that, for example, we should expect Greek attitudes toward prostitution to be similar to those of the Romans or that prostitution will have taken place in the same venues in Greece as in Rome. But this is not necessarily the case. We should be particularly careful about comparisons with respect to the brothel, broadly defined here as any structure, or space within a structure, where sexual services for pay occur and where more than one prostitute works at the same time.[1] The service providers can be slave or freed, but they must work for pay (that they either keep for themselves or that is given either to a pimp or slave owner) rather than for their own pleasure.[2] Unlike Pompeii, there are no remains of a purpose-built brothel or cribs in archaic and classical Greece. In fact, archaeological remains of spaces of commercial prostitution in all periods of Greece are rare. Possible material evidence of brothels exists for classical Athens and for Roman Greece in Thessaloniki, Mytilene, Ephesus, and Delos.[3] There are, however, textual references to such structures in all periods of the Greek world. Once we have a fuller grasp of such spaces in the ancient city and demes of Athens and the attitudes toward them, we will better understand prostitution and sexuality in archaic and classical Athens. By focusing on spaces of prostitution, prostitutes, regulation of prostitution and customers, I hope to show that the polarized associations of *pornē* (slave prostitute) and brothel with the nonelite and of *hetaira* (slave, freed, or free prostitute) and symposium with the elite are oversimplified.

The Terminology

Porneion is generally translated as "brothel" and is the most specific term we know of for the classical period. Aeschines defines it by the presence of a *pornoboskos* (sex trafficker) and *pornai* (1.124). *Pornai* are technically slave prostitutes.[4] The term likely derives from *pernēmi* (to sell). *Pornoboskoi* (f. *pornoboskousai*) is commonly translated as "brothel keepers" but would be more accurately rendered as "keepers of *pornai*." *Boskoi* relates to *boskein* (to feed, nourish, maintain); it is a term more commonly used in the case of cattle and thus emphasizes the relation of the *pornoboskos* to his prostitutes rather than referring to a particular type of space.[5] The term *porneion* is also connected to *pornē*, literally translating as "the place of the *pornē*," wherever the *pornoboskos* might keep prostitutes and where one goes to find them. It appears in Old Comedy (*Vesp.* 1283; *Ran.* 113), where explicit terminology is common and the translation "whorehouse" perhaps appropriate.[6] It also appears in oratory, suggesting that the term in itself is not overly obscene. Antiphon uses it to refer to where a lover intends to send his *pallakē* (concubine) (1.14). It can, in the right context, shock and induce anger in an audience: Aeschines comments that his political opponent Timarchus has turned many places into *porneia* on account of his licentious behavior (1.124).

Other terminology is somewhat vague and more neutral in tone, since it is also found in contexts not relating to prostitution. *Oikēma*, for example, refers to a dwelling place or a bedroom, but the collocation of *kathēmai* (to be seated) and *oikēma* in phrases such as *kathēsto en oikēmati* (she sat in a little room) (Isae. 6.19) or *epi tōn oikēmatōn kathēmenous* (those seated in little rooms) (Aeschin. 1.74) has the specific meaning of a brothel. It can, however, also appear on its own, where the context makes the meaning of brothel clear (Xen. *Mem.* 2.2.4). *Oikia* (dwelling) is occasionally a euphemism for brothel ([Dem.] 59. 41, 67; Xen. *Mem.* 3.11.4), but again only the context makes this meaning clear. *Ergastērion* appears the most neutral but surprising term, referring simply to a place of business, such as a workshop or a factory. It is perhaps also an official term, since it turns up as a legal idiom for places of prostitution: Apollodoros quotes a law that states that no one is to be seized as an adulterer for having relations with women who sit in an *ergastērion* or openly sell themselves ([Dem.] 59.67).[7] The generic nature of *ergastērion* in particular suggests that prostitution in the brothel was simply viewed as another profession. The suggestion is confirmed by the surprising pairing of *ep'oikēmatos kathēmenos* with "selling salt fish" and "making shoes" in Plato's *Charmides* (163b), making all three occupations parallel. As the context implies, sitting in a brothel was no more despicable to the elite than working in the agora. But it was to be avoided by the elite as all banausic occupations (representing paid labor) were.[8]

The Space

Aeschines informs us that *sunoikiai* (tenement housing) sometimes housed *porneia* but adds that the same space could be a surgery, a smithy, a laundry, a carpenter's shop, or a *porneion*, depending on who was presently working there (1.124). His comment suggests that it is the people occupying the space that identify the purpose of the structure, not the architectural format of the space. What about the visual evidence? Attic vases sometimes depict "brothel" scenes, but, like the archaeological remains, such scenes are often difficult to identify and interpret. The most ambiguous of these scenes are those with a male and female figure and a small pouch.[9] Either figure might hold the pouch or the male figure might even be shown passing it to the female figure. The pouch is commonly supposed to be a money purse, and thus the scene is interpreted as a negotiation between a prostitute and a client in a brothel.[10] Sexual scenes with onlookers are frequently seen as depicting places of prostitution as well (Skinner 2004, 96): a red-figure *hydria* (for holding water) depicts a youth warmly received by a young woman, while another youth and two other female figures look on (see fig. 2.1). The young man's staff indicates he has only just arrived, perhaps coming from a symposium, as suggested by the wreath around his head. The young woman drapes her arms around his neck and is so close to the young man that her nose touches his. She gazes directly into the eyes of this youth, while he reaches his arm down to perhaps grab her buttocks. The intimacy of the central couple suggests all the women are prostitutes.

George Kavvadias (2000, 298) has identified a possible brothel scene on a black-figure *lekythos* (for holding perfumed oil), currently housed in the Kerameikos Museum in Athens. It portrays three male/female couples on a single large couch engaged in various positions of intercourse, either standing, seated, or reclining (see fig. 2.2a). Another couch with three more couples engaged in the same activities crowds the first couch. A pillar separates another couple wrapped in a bedspread and seated on the floor (see fig. 2.2b). Finally, two more couples recline together—also on bedspreads—on the floor. These last three couples do not appear to be engaged in sexual activity but rather converse or watch the couples on the couches. Despite the proximity of the figures in each group, there is no interaction between couples. In contrast to the typical symposium scene in which the common community of the participants is emphasized through the figures' participation in games, music, and physical or visual contact, each couple on the couch is focused on itself, suggesting a context other than the symposium.[11] As is typical in vase painting, architectural details are sparse in these scenes, with furniture, hanging objects, and pillars simply indicating an inside space. The scene on

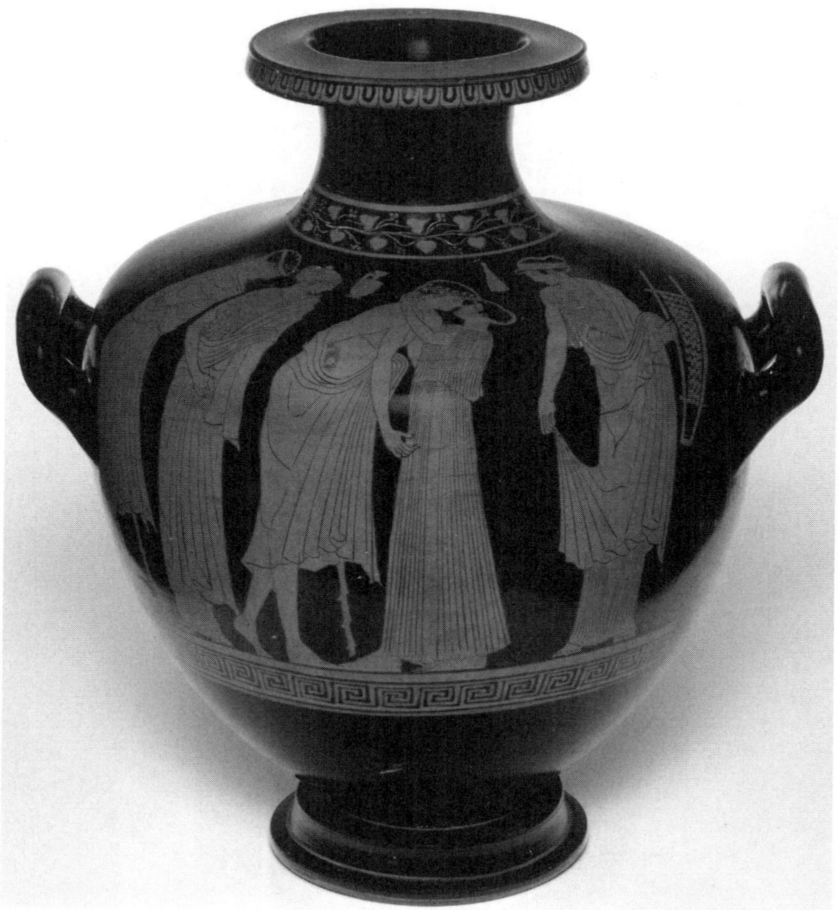

Figure 2.1. Attributed to the Leningrad Painter. Attic red-figure *hydria*, ca. 460–450 BCE. Terracotta, 42.4 x 37.6 x 31.8 cm; D (mouth): 10.3 cm; D (lip): 15.6 cm. Art Institute of Chicago, 1911.456, front (gift of Martin A. Ryerson through the Antiquarian Society). Photo © Art Institute of Chicago.

the *lekythos*, however, suggests a single open room and reinforces Aeschines' point that a unique type of structure or space was not necessary to set up a brothel. A brothel could appear anywhere and even be a temporary setup. The sources do in fact refer to such setups in *sunoikiai* and *oikiai* (Aeschin. 1.124; Isae. 6.19; [Dem.] 59.41, 67; Xen. *Mem.* 3.11.4). *Pornoboskoi* appear to have been mobile and to have gone to customers, even customers in a different city, instead of being permanently

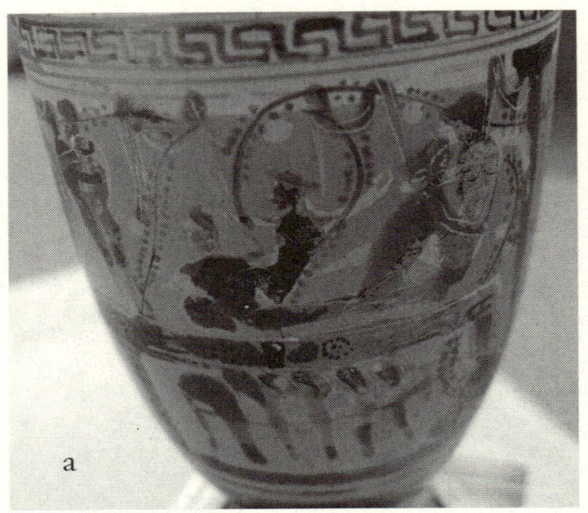

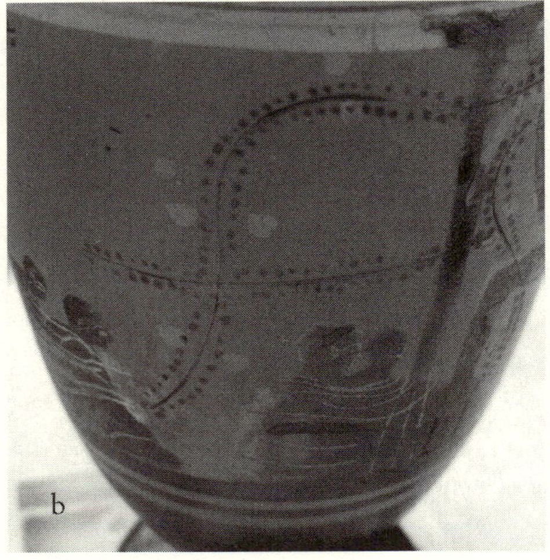

Figures 2.2a–b. Artist unknown. Detail, Attic black-figure *lekythos*, ca. 500–475 BCE. Kerameikos Museum, Athens, A15418. Courtesy of Hellenic Ministry of Culture, Ephorate G (Prehistoric and Classical Antiquities of Athens). Photos by Allison Glazebrook.

stationed in a bawdy house. Nikarete, for example, travels with some of her girls from Corinth to Athens for her customer Lysias and sets up in a house of his friend temporarily ([Dem.] 59.21–22).

Still, an examination of the archaeological remains of Building Z3 in the Kerameikos in Athens reveals that tiny rooms were a possible architectural feature of spaces for prostitution that might help identify brothels in the archaeological record. The site today is unassuming. It is nestled in beside the Sacred Gate in the inner Kerameikos created by the construction of the Themistoklean wall. The structure is rather large (more than 500 square meters) and has five phases dating from the fifth to third centuries BCE. Ursula Knigge identifies the first two phases as private houses (2005, 26, 47) and suggests slave prostitutes worked here in the third phase (2005, 78; 1991, 93) and that fourth and fifth phases were industrial complexes. Hermann Lind states more strongly that phase 3 is a *Hetärenhaus* (house for *hetairai*), and other scholars agree.[12] Bradley Ault suggests further that phases 1 and 2 may also have functioned as brothels or at least *katagōgia* (hostelries), rather than private houses, since the architecture of the structures is unusual for a private dwelling (2005, 149–50). Lind even considers whether or not phase 3 might be the brothel belonging to Euctemon in his *sunoikia* in the Kerameikos (Isae. 6.19). He is unable to come to a firm conclusion since Knigge identifies a gap between phase 2 (destroyed at the beginning of the fourth century BCE) and 3 (built in the early fourth quarter of the fourth century BCE) (2005, 49, 79), the period corresponding to the date of the speech of Isaeus (364 BCE). Still, I am apt to agree with Nick Fisher that "there is no problem in assuming that this area knew many such dwellings" (2001, 261); whether or not Building Z is Euctemon's brothel does not detract from the importance of this site as one of the few remaining structures of prostitution from ancient Greece.

The building possessed at least twenty-two rooms (more than one of which were certainly *andrōnes*, or banquet rooms) and had two courtyards and two entrances, the main of which was located at the northeast corner of the structure.[13] Three large cisterns, a well, and three drains indicate a high level of water consumption. What is most striking about the third phase of Building Z is the large number of small rooms added south of the courtyard, along with a second street entrance on the southeast corner (see fig. 2.3). The rooms range in size from 2 by 3 meters (W, X, Y, Z) to 2.20 by 4 meters (U, V), appearing only large enough for one or perhaps two couches, and may be what *oikēmata* refers to. The location of the new doorway makes these rooms directly accessible from the street, and those entering do not need to pass through the main courtyard to reach this end of the structure. A second door was added at the western end of corridor a, cutting rooms W, X, Y, and Z, along with some larger rooms (L, M, N, P, Bereich Q), off

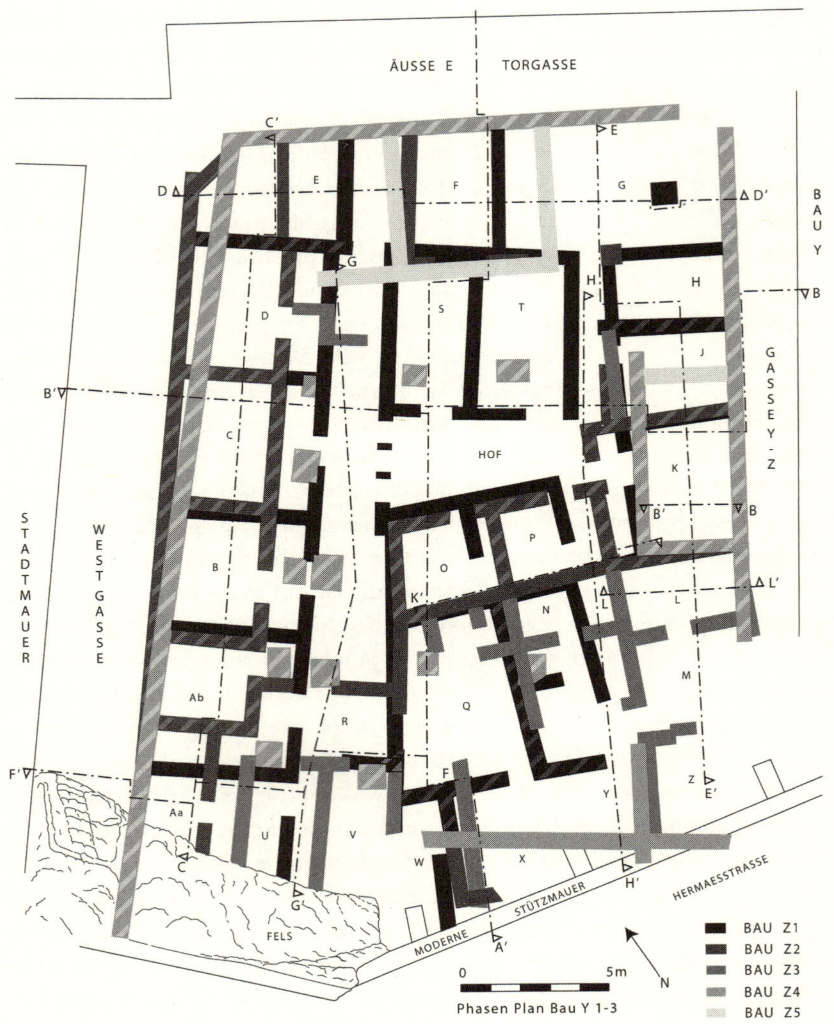

Figure 2.3. Plan of Building Z, blueprint 1, Kerameikos, Athens. Drawing by Tina Ross after Knigge 2005. By permission of German Archaeological Institute in Athens, Kerameikos excavation.

from rooms U and V and the rest of the structure. It is not clear how this might have affected the use of U and V in comparison to W, X, Y, and Z. The excavator simply states they are *kammern* (storerooms/chambers) (Knigge 2005, 61). The finds in W, X, Y, Z, U, and V are few but include drinking cups, a wine *kratēr*, saucers, plates, and coins (rooms V, U, W, Z) (Knigge 2005, 61), finds that do not contradict the interpretation of these rooms as the *oikēmata* in which the prostitutes attended to customers. Lind also suggests the term *oikēmata* for the rooms along the south wall in Building Z3 and cites as further support the fact that the small rooms could be locked (1988, 167). Of further interest, *andrōn* P has two entrances: one from courtyard a and one from a possible antechamber (N) accessed directly from corridor a lined with these *oikēmata*.

James Davidson argues in contrast that the *oikēma* is very different from the *porneion*: *oikēmata* are single rooms opening directly onto the street (1998, 90–91), much like the Roman cribs found in Pompeii.[14] Such an arrangement may be what Aeschines refers to when he points to male prostitutes working close to the agora (1.74). But the fact that there is clearly more than one *oikēma* suggests the rooms are perhaps part of a common establishment easily accessible from the street, as in Building Z. Davidson comments in addition that such "individual cubicles" opening onto the street were more pleasant to work in than the *porneion* and common for male prostitutes.[15] Female prostitutes working in *porneia* were the lowliest of prostitutes (1998, 332 n. 55). While Davidson acknowledges that the term *oikēma* is also used in reference to female prostitution (Isae. 6.19; Din. 1.23; Hdt. 2.121), he argues that a woman working in such a space is a *paidiskē* (a woman who engages in "a more respectable kind of prostitution") and not a *pornē* and that is why she is found in an *oikēma* rather than in a *porneion*. He thus draws a firm distinction between the *porneion* and *oikēma* based on working conditions and gender. But his conclusion is misleading. Aeschines accuses Timarchus of turning many places into *porneia* by means of his licentious behavior (1.24), suggesting that the *porneion* was in fact not restricted to the female gender. The term *paidiskē*, in turn, likely refers to particularly young slave prostitutes who are inexperienced and untrained rather than to a status of prostitute (between the *pornē* and the *hetaira*), since it appears in contexts in which prostitutes are purchased ([Dem.] 59.18; Hyp. *Ath*.).[16] Furthermore, Alce is one of a number of girls who are owned by a freedwoman and working as prostitutes in *oikēmata* (Isae. 6.19). Alce is thus of slave status and subject to this freedwoman. The text indicates that each girl serviced customers in *oikēmata* located in one *sunoikia*. Rather than being distinct from the *porneion*, it represents a *porneion* like Building Z3 where customers had access to individual rooms.

The final scene in Aristophanes' *Assemblywomen*, in which an old woman and a young woman compete for lovers, is also used as evidence for individual *oikēmata* separate from *porneia* as Davidson describes, since both women are in separate structures that open directly onto the street. The women here, however, are not officially prostitutes but likely *astai* (Attic citizen women) trying to exploit or circumvent Praxagora's new law. The scene has overtones of prostitution, certainly, but even so, it is not clear if the structures they run in and out of are single room structures or two-story *oikoi* (dwellings). There is some ambiguity as to where each woman stands, but the structure housing the young woman is usually interpreted as being two-story (Henderson 1996, 181; A. J. Graham 1998, 25), since in lines 960–62 the young man asks the young woman to run down (*katadramousa*) and open the door. The passage more accurately reflects solicitation practices (A. J. Graham 1997, 24–25) than practices associated with the brothel. Opening directly onto the street like the Roman crib is not likely a necessary requirement for an *oikēma*, but *oikēmata* were likely made intentionally visible from the street (as Aeschin. 1.74 suggests) by being constructed so that they would open onto a corridor directly connected with the street (as in Building Z3). Thus *oikēmata*, or little rooms, may be an accurate description of *porneia*, which may explain how "sitting in a little room" (kathēmenos/ē en oikēmati) became a common phrase for referring to prostitutes.

Roman writers critique such spaces of commercial prostitution for lack of cleanliness and indicate that the conditions were not always ideal.[17] The prostitute Adelphasium in Plautus's *Little Carthaginian* perhaps refers to brothel prostitutes when, in a well-known comment, she says she does not want to go near "women who smell of stable and stall, . . . whom hardly any free man has ever touched or taken home, the two obol sluts of dirty little slaves" (268).[18] Although Plautus's plays are based on Greek New Comedy, the attitudes expressed toward prostitutes and prostitution are more likely Roman than Greek, just as comic attitudes toward slaves and slavery in Plautus are Roman. Similar comments in classical Greek texts, for example, are rare. Aristophanes implies that conditions of prostitution in the Piraeus were not ideal. In his comic play *Peace*, Trygaios, flying through the Piraeus on the back of a dung beetle, is alarmed by a man "taking a shit" (houtos ho chezōn) (164–65). *Para tais pornais*, the phrase Aristophanes uses to describe the location of the man, has been translated into English in various ways. Robert Garland translates it as "house of the whores" (1987, 70). Jeffrey Henderson uses the more general phrase "in the whores' quarter" (1998, 447). Given the context and the earlier reference to *laurai*, or back lanes (158), the phrase is likely particular to *pornai* working on the streets, not a *porneion* specifically. Trygaios is not likely to see into a brothel from above. My translation—"Hey man, you there, taking a shit in the Piraeus alongside the prostitutes, what are you doing?"—makes clear it is the district and not the *porneion* in and of itself that is responsible for poor conditions.[19] Antiphon 1, in which a *pallakē* makes a murder attempt on her lover once she discovers he is planning to send her to a *porneion*, is another text often used to support the idea that dire conditions prevailed in brothels. But the *pallakē*, if we are to believe the speaker, is deceived into thinking she is delivering a love potion and not intentionally committing a murder (14–15). Her motivations are likely more complex than simply seeing the brothel as "a fate worse than death" as Davidson comments (1998, 83). Demosthenes uses *kleision* (shed, stable, outhouse) to refer to the place of clandestine meetings of Aeschines' mother with various men (18.129). LSJ suggests its meaning here as "perh. = *brothel*." If so, it perhaps alludes to the poor condition or small size of some brothels. The focus of the passage, however, is clearly the negative reputation of the mother and the implication that she prostituted herself and not the *kleision* as a space of prostitution more generally. The narrative is derogatory to Aeschines and not brothels.

Although the scene portrayed on a black-figure *lekythos* (figs. 2.2a and 2.2b) suggests minimal comfort, the presence of tables with food indicates that clients did not have to rush off. The archaeological evidence in turn confirms that some such spaces hoped to keep clients around and perhaps even catered to wealthier customers. Building Z3 had at least two *andrōnes* and contained much dining and drinking equipment, most of it fine ware, as well as cookware. Room E, area Q, and the second courtyard b had pebble mosaic floors (Knigge 2005, 70). Silver jewelry found in rooms Aa, F, and K hint that brothel prostitutes could be richly adorned.[20] The courtyard areas may have contained a garden, since tools identified for gardening were found by the original excavator in courtyard a, and other metal tools for digging were found in some rooms (K and B). Bradley Ault also argues that Building Z does not resemble a "dark and stinking" hole. It might even be considered "commodious" (2005, 149). James Davidson concedes that not all brothels were necessarily unpleasant: some brothels, "it seems, tried to emulate a sympotic atmosphere if the finds at Building Z are anything to go by" (1998, 94).[21]

Immediately to the southeast of Building Z is another smaller structure (270 square meters) that may be associated with prostitution, Building Y (see fig. 2.4).[22] The building has five phases. Graffito on the wall plaster from room A—*BOUBALION KALĒ* (Boubalion is beautiful) (Knigge 1993, 139)—has led archaeologists to identify phases 2 and 3 as a banquet house or tavern. The female name, Boubalion, is uncommon, making it unclear whether the name is that of a citizen or a *metic*.[23] The context suggests it is the name of a prostitute. Such *kalos/kalē* inscriptions are found on Attic vases used at the symposium and indicate a favorite youth or *hetaira*.[24] The structure is also contemporary with Euctemon's

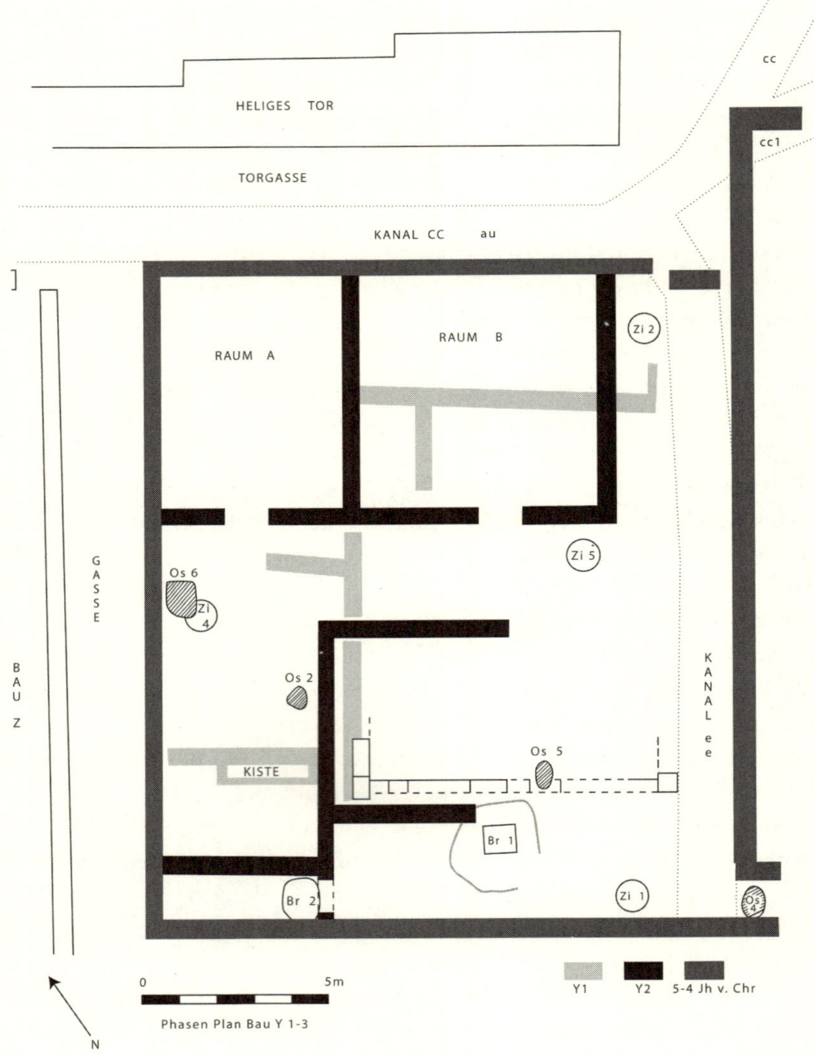

Figure 2.4. Plan of Building Y, blueprint 3, Kerameikos, Athens. Drawing by Tina Ross after Knigge 1993. By permission of German Archaeological Institute in Athens, Kerameikos excavation.

sunoikia mentioned in Isaeus 6.20 and may be the building managed by the ex-prostitute Alce (Knigge 1993, 139). Y2 was built sometime after the start of the fourth century BCE, and when it was destroyed, it was immediately rebuilt as Y3, on the same ground plan as Y2, in the third quarter of the fourth century BCE. Like Building Z3, the structure has two entrances, two *andrōnes* for dining and drinking, multiple cisterns and drains—more than a single dwelling would need and thus suggestive of a nonresidential function. Unlike Building Z3, the current plan provides little evidence of *oikēmata*. The two *andrōnes* open onto a central peristyle courtyard (a courtyard lined with columns). Peristyle courtyards are common in civic and cult buildings in the fifth century BCE. Dining rooms associated with such peristyle courtyards have been found in the Heraion at Argos (sixth century BCE), at the sanctuary of Artemis at Brauron in Attica (ca. 425 BCE), in the Athenian agora (the Tholos, or Skias, ca. 470 BCE), and in the Kerameikos (the Pompeion, ca. 400 BCE), just northeast of Building Y. Knigge stresses the uniqueness of such an arrangement in a nonpublic building at this early date (1993, 138). Such courtyards only begin to appear in private structures in the fourth century BCE, making Building Y an early example of such an arrangement.[25] This peristyle court indicates that Building Y was an elaborate and expensive construction. The entryway and rooms themselves also confirm this lavishness: all three have polished pebble mosaic floors and both banquet rooms had walls decorated with red plaster. The courtyard of Y2 was paved with marble chips (Knigge et al. 1995, 627). If this building was indeed used for prostitution, as the graffito suggests, then it would have been a more upscale sort of brothel.[26] Until the final publication of this building's plan and its assemblage, no firm conclusions can be made about the structure.

In a more recent excavation around the Olympic equestrian center near Athens, an unusual structure that may also be an ancient *porneion* was found. The excavators describe the structure as an Aphrodiseion (a structure sacred to Aphrodite) and identify it as a site of sacred prostitution. The structure, dating to the fourth century BCE, is just beyond the *temenos* (sacred precinct) in Merenda in the ancient deme of Myrrhinous, just off the main road leading to the port.[27] It is rather large (858 square meters) and, like Building Z3, had a garden in the courtyard: holes where trees were planted have been found.[28] Rooms cluster on the eastern and northern sides of the courtyard. It also has a bathing area near the entrance with two baths cut into the ground and lined with plaster. A rectangular cistern was cut into the southwest area of the courtyard. Fine black-glaze drinking vessels (*kantharoi* and *skyphoi*) and storage jars (*pithoi*) were found in the courtyard and cistern. *Pithoi*, saucers, *kantharoi*, *skyphoi*, and fragments from beehives were concentrated in the smaller room on the east side of the structure. These vessels were found in a narrow trench. Many of them are miniature and thus likely cult offerings, but none appear specific to Aphrodite in particular. A small altar was found built into a later structure in the east room on the north side. A simple inscription links the structure to prostitution. A rectangular slab (50 x 35 cm) inscribed with NANNNION (interpreted as Νάνν{ν}ιον [*SEG* liii 223]) in its second use was found just outside the bathing area on the exterior of the structure.[29] Nannion is a well-known *hetaira* from the mid-fourth century.[30] Eubulus wrote a play titled *Nannion* in which the *pornai* were paraded out and put on display for customers.[31] The courtyard of the structure could easily have served such a purpose.[32] The drinking ware found in the area suggest further that customers relaxed and drank during these displays. These finds as well as the ample sources of water do not contradict the use of the structure as a brothel and once again suggest the commodious nature of the *porneion*. Together with the evidence of buildings Z and Y, it further suggests that *porneia* could cultivate a richer clientele and that the more affluent did not rely on the symposium alone for contact with prostitutes. But a pleasant space for the clients does not necessarily mean good treatment of and good working conditions for the prostitutes themselves.

The literary and material evidence suggests further that *porneia* could be shared spaces, and, in fact, space devoted to prostitution alone, such as the Purpose-Built Brothel in Pompeii (more popularly termed the Lupanar), appears nonexistent.[33] The archaeological evidence to date indicates that places of prostitution could be multipurpose and that prostitution may have been a secondary function. For example, Building Z3 seems to have been important for textile production. The large number of loom weights found and the appearance of three large underground cisterns in this phase suggest that it was in fact a textile factory (Knigge 2005, 49, 78). In addition, hundreds of drinking vessels and much dinnerware suggest Building Z3 also served as a tavern (Knigge 2005, 78).[34] There is also the possibility that some *porneia* were part of a sanctuary to Aphrodite and included in her worship (Kakavoyianni and Dovinou 2003, 34–35; Steinhauer 2003, 42–43 n. 31), like at Corinth.[35] Euctemon's brothel in the Piraeus, in turn, which was run by a freedwoman and provided particularly young girls, *paidiskai*, was in his *sunoikia*. It housed prostitutes and ex-prostitutes, such as Alce, along with other tenants (Isae. 6.19–20).

Regulation

The evidence further suggests that *pornoboskoi* and spaces for prostitution were not regulated by the Athenian city-state, unlike in Thasos, where a late archaic/early classical stele, known as the "stèle du port," was found in 1984 (*SEG* xlii 785). A. J.

Graham argues that part of the inscription relates to the regulation of prostitution, particularly solicitation practices (1998, 22–40). He interprets the stele as preventing prostitutes (male and female) from showing themselves to customers by climbing on the roof or by hanging out the windows of the brothel.[36] He uses these Thasian regulations on prostitutes and brothels to suggest that an Athenian restriction on windows opening onto roads (*Ath. Pol.* 50.2) was intended "to prevent the use of windows for purposes of prostitution" (1998, 40) and not to bar "outward-opening window-shutters, which if not secured, might fall down into the street" (Rhodes 1981, 575). But without a direct reference to a brothel, as in the Thasian inscription, and given the immediate context of building, balcony, and canal restrictions designed to ensure the safety, cleanliness, and the width of the road, Peter Rhodes's conclusion is the more convincing one: the regulation is simply about windows and their shutters.[37]

Some scholars argue that the *astunomoi* were involved in regulating prostitution. Aristotle tells us that the city selected ten *astunomoi* (city controllers), five for Piraeus and five for the city of Athens, who set the pay of flute players, harp players, and lyre players: they were not to be paid more than two drachmas (*Ath. Pol.* 50.2). Diognides and Antidoros were impeached for hiring out (*misthountes*) such women for more than the law allowed (Hyp. *Eux.* 19). The *astunomoi* also settled disputes over these women by forcing the parties to cast lots for them (*Ath. Pol.* 50.2). The mention of *aulētrides* (flute players) and other entertainers suggests this law was a law relating to prostitution, since such women usually doubled as prostitutes at symposia (drinking parties) and also, in the case of the *aulētris*, worked the brothels.[38] But there is no specific mention here of brothel workers or prostitutes in general, and so the passage cannot be used as evidence for capping the fees of such women or their pimps. When prostitutes are affected, it is only a secondary consequence of restrictions on female musicians, like the *aulētris*.[39] Such women or their pimp likely negotiated and charged an additional fee for sexual services. William Loomis's catalogue of variable prices for prostitutes and pimps, ranging from a few obols to a drachma to ten thousand drachmae, further supports the idea that how much a prostitute could charge was not regulated but depended on "the attractions of the prostitute and the resources and urgency of the customer" (1998, 184) and also the sexual position desired.[40] Pricing and solicitation practices appear to have been of little concern to the state.

Prostitution does not appear to have been restricted to one particular area in the polis. Xenophon indicates the streets were full of such women and that *oikēmata* were common (*Mem.* 2.2.4). Philemon refers to brothels in "various quarters," implying they could be found in various parts of Athens (Ath. 13.569e).[41] Building Z is located within the city walls in the Kerameikos close to the Sacred Gate. According to Hesychius, the district had numerous brothels of various grades (s.v. *kerameikos*). Yet, the Kerameikos was not a disreputable part of town: Athenians took their evening stroll to the area.[42] Brothels mentioned in the sources were also located in the Piraeus. The Athenian Euctemon had at least two *sunoikiai*, one in each location, that were managed by freedwomen and housed prostitutes (Isae. 6.19, 6.20). There also appear to have been *porneia* within close proximity of the agora. Aeschines points to the *oikēmata* of such an establishment from the law courts (1.74). Nick Fisher comments Aeschines could be pointing to the excavated houses on the south slopes of the Areopagos or even the Kerameikos area, depending on the exact location of the court.[43]

There is not enough evidence to know what the exact distribution of brothels within the city was, but brothels do seem to have occupied space common to other businesses. Once again Aeschines is our source. *Porneia* are not distinguished from the other businesses he notes can be housed in the same space (a surgery, a laundry, a carpenter's workshop) in terms of their locale (1.124). Such sites of business in turn were not segregated from residential areas as they are in North America today. According to Barbara Tsakirgis, "a homeowner could find himself next to a marble worker, or a smith or a dye worker" (2005, 79)—and, I would add, a brothel worker. Renters may have found themselves in the same situation, given that, for example, the *sunoikia* of Euctemon in the Piraeus was a rooming house and also kept working prostitutes in *oikēmata* (Isae. 6.19). Workshop and home could even coexist in the same space (Tsakirgis 2005, 67, 69, 79). Although when Apollodoros implies that Stephanus's home is a brothel, it is more than likely hyperbole ([Dem.] 59.41, 67), the fact that a home could also be a workshop means that in the case of other Athenians it could have been literally true. The evidence suggests, therefore, that brothels were not restricted in terms of locale but that they did collect in certain high traffic areas, like the Piraeus, Kerameikos, and agora. The fact that there was little stigma attached to having prostitutes in one's own *oikos*—at a *symposion* or even for a short-term stay ([Dem.] 59.22)—may explain why brothel spaces were not marginalized in the polis.

Athens did collect a *pornikon telos* (prostitution tax). Aeschines tells us that Demosthenes uses the fact that Timarchus never paid this tax as evidence that Timarchus is not and has never been a prostitute (1.119). But not only would free prostitutes working independently have to have paid this tax; *pornoboskoi* and *pornoboskousai* in charge of prostitutes of slave status must have had to as well. The task of collecting the tax was not performed by the state, however, but farmed out. The comic poet Philonides makes reference to such tax collectors, calling them *pornotelōnai* (fr. 5; Pollux 7.202). We are told in Aeschines 1 that those purchasing the contract do not guess but know exactly (*akribōs*) whom to collect from (119–20).

The comment has suggested to some the existence of a list of those working in the sex trade, but the evidence is not conclusive. If there was such a list, it is not known whether it constituted an official registry of prostitutes and pimps.[44] I suggest not, since the emphasis appears to be on the knowledge of the individual collector and the public nature of prostitution: it is the testimony of the *telōnēs* (tax collector) that is requested and not the production of a list.[45] In addition, although there were likely lists of citizens and of *metics* and of the grain supply, all of which provided information of great importance to the polis, no evidence exists suggesting there were lists for individual professions, and such lists would have been more difficult to maintain.[46] The passage thus more likely hints that the collectors themselves had their own lists, not an official list issued by the state. The existence of a tax legitimizes prostitution as a trade but also recognizes it as unique because most other taxes for Athenians were indirect or took the form of liturgies.

Workers and Customers

Based on the literary evidence, the women and men working in brothels were typically slaves.[47] Phaedo worked in an *oikēma* in his youth after his city, Elis, was captured and he was temporarily enslaved (Diog. Laert. 2.105). These workers likely began practicing at a very young age. The common use of *paidiskē* (young girl) to refer to a female slave prostitute confirms as much. Nikarete purchased seven *paidiskai* and trained them before putting them to work ([Dem.] 59.18). The freedwoman running Euctemon's *sunoikia* in the Piraeus also purchased several *paidiskai* to work in *oikēmata* (Isae. 6.19). Alce was one of these slave girls. Neaira, one of the *paidiskē* of Nikarete, appears to have begun practicing well before puberty, an age even considered young for a Greek ([Dem.] 59.22), suggesting some sort of acceptable age limit to engaging in prostitution did exist (although the speaker, of course, is exaggerating for effect since he accuses Neaira of having a licentious nature).[48] Apollodoros's comment that she "was already working with her body, despite being rather young, since she had not yet reached physical maturity" implies that prostitutes were thought to have a particular sexual nature that predestined them for their profession.[49] But not all such workers had to be young or inexperienced. A bored lover planned to sell his *pallakē* to a *porneion* (Antiph. 1.14–15). Although Nikarete preferred her girls to be youthful, other *pornoboskoi* were not so discriminating. Once Neaira was too old to be of use, Nikarete sold Neaira to some clients, who, in turn, decided to free Neaira once they were ready to be rid of her rather than see her working for another *pornoboskos* ([Dem.] 59.30).

The archaeological evidence appears to support the slave status of those working in *porneia* and *oikēmata* further and provides insight into their daily lives. The women working in Building Z3 appear to have been foreign and thus likely were purchased as slaves. Images of Astarte in statuette form and on jewelry, grasping her breasts, along with the stone *naiskos* (shrine) containing a statutette of Cybele from room Aa attest to an eastern origin for these women and also suggest that these slaves likely lived in the building.[50] Alce too lived in the place she worked and continued to do so long after she was no longer a practicing prostitute. In addition to serving as prostitutes, the women of Building Z3 were expected to work the looms. Knigge believes that weaving and serving were both their main functions (2005, 78). Davidson, however, argues that the female occupants wove while waiting for customers, making prostitution their primary function (1998, 88–89).[51] Red-figure vases adorned with weaving women approached by males carrying money pouches may be illustrative of this practice and give credence to the theory.[52] One interesting find from the Aphrodiseion at Merenda is a loom weight out of lead inscribed with the female name LYSILLA or LYSIMA. This find is especially interesting given the predominance of loom weights (both terracotta and lead) in Building Z3 (Knigge 1991, 93; Knigge 2005, 78) and the associations between weaving and prostitution.[53] Lind also suggests that the *dēmiourgoi* (skilled workers) sold by Euctemon (Isae. 6.33) may have been weavers of cloth who doubled as prostitutes whenever necessary (1988, 166).

It is clear also that the managers of female prostitutes and *porneia* were frequently women (commonly freedwomen).[54] Nikarete is such an example of a *pornoboskousa*. She chose and purchased *paidiskai* and taught them the tricks of the trade ([Dem.] 59.18).[55] Later on in the same speech, Apollodoros claims Neaira pimped Phano ([Dem.] 59.67). Antigone, who worked as a prostitute herself, also appears to have owned and profited from *paidiskai* (Hyp. *Ath.*). An unnamed freedwoman purchased *paidiskai* for a brothel in the Piraeus owned by the Athenian Euctemon (Isae. 6.19). In comic examples, Lysistrata acts as the madam of a brothel, charging Kinesias for a visit with Myrrhine (Ar. *Lys.* 861).[56] Euripides dresses as an old woman with a *pēktis* (a harp) to act as the go-between for a dancer, whom a Scythian archer buys for intercourse at the price of a drachma (Ar. *Thesm.* 1172–1225). The famous Aspasia traffics prostitutes (*laikastriai*, or wenches, is the term used) in a play by Aristophanes (*Ach.* 515–39). While the example of Aspasia cannot be taken to be historically accurate, since there is much doubt as to Aspasia's identity as a *hetaira*, these comic examples suggest that Athenians in general were familiar with freed and free women as owners of and go-betweens for prostitutes.[57]

In some cases, the *pornoboskousa* was a former prostitute herself, even a former brothel worker, backed by her recent master. Upon Alce's retirement from the brothel in the Pireaus, Euctemon freed her and put her in charge of her own *sunoikia* in the Kerameikos (Isae. 6.20).[58] Thus Euctemon had brothels on his property whose management he left in the hands of freedwomen, at least one of whom had previously served as a prostitute in his *sunoikia*. Nikarete's ex-owner (Charisius of Elis) was also likely profiting in the background and providing financial support when necessary, since Nikarete's husband, Hippias, was still his cook ([Dem.] 59.18). Antigone seems to have been connected to Athenogenes (Hyp. *Ath.*), and Neaira had Stephanus as her backer when pimping Phano ([Dem.] 59.67).[59] Two other examples of *pornoboskousai* of possible *porneia* are Theodote (Xen. *Mem.* 3.11) and Nannion (Ath. 13.568f). Despite their own past status as slaves and/or prostitutes, the *pornoboskousai* were not necessarily sympathetic to their workers and did not necessarily guarantee their *pornai* a less exploited existence. Nikarete, for example, appears to have taken possession of gifts given to her girls by an admirer ([Dem.] 59.21).

On occasion these slave workers could end up quite well off. Euctemon must have met Alce when she was working in the brothel in his *sunoikia*. She eventually became a favorite of his. He not only freed her and put her in charge of another of his *sunoikia* but also took most of his meals with her at the *sunoikia* rather than with his wife and family, enrolled one of her children, who may or may not have been his own, in his phratry, and eventually lived full time with her (Isae. 6.21).[60] Neaira in turn became a favorite of two customers, Eukrates and Timanoridas, who purchased her from Nikarete and eventually freed her ([Dem.] 59.29–30). She later became the companion of the Athenian Stephanus and lived with him in his *oikos*. Although her description is idealized, Theodote is likely another *pornoboskousa* and thus further testament to the fact that *porneia* could be run by women and that such women could lead a comfortable life. Theodote and her establishment appear to have been well known in Athens, since this is the reason given as to why Socrates insists he and his young elite followers pay her a visit (Xen. *Mem.* 3.11.1). Her status as free or freed is not explicit, but she and her "mother" are well dressed and adorned with jewelry and inhabit a well-furnished *oikia*.[61] Socrates further observes that the "maids" are beautiful (*eueideis*) and in no way neglected (*oude tautas ēmelēmenōs echousas*) (Xen. *Mem.* 3.11.4). Given the context, *oude ēmelēmenōs* must be understood as referring to the adornment of the female slaves and not simply to their health and general care. His observations suggest they too worked as prostitutes. Carola Reinsberg suggests that most of the sexual services were undertaken by the *therapainai* and only special guests received the attentions of Theodote herself (1989, 121–22). Christopher Faraone also implies that Theodote is a madam in addition to taking customers herself (2005, 218, 220–21). Although the description of her is full of euphemism and innuendo, it is clear that Theodote is a prostitute. I concur that her "maids" were also likely available as sexual partners for her customers and suggest in addition that her "mother" was the previous *pornoboskousa*. The fact that Socrates' group goes to her is further evidence that her establishment may have been a *porneion*. Finally, Nannion, who seems to have been in charge of the Aphrodiseion at Merenda at least at some point during its existence, may be the famous, richly adorned prostitute mentioned by Anaxilas, Antiphanes, Hyperides, Alexis, Timocles, and Menander. Pimping was not a bad business for women to be in, and those who worked in the *porneion* did not necessarily come to a wretched end.

As to customers, evidence suggests that more than simply slaves and the poor utilized brothels and that therefore the often assumed social division between the symposium that *hetairai* frequented and the brothel occupied by *pornai* is a false one. The more wealthy and famous residents of Greece, like the orator Lysias and Simos of Thessaly, as well as Xenocleides the poet and Hipparchus the actor, enjoyed Nikarete's girls ([Dem.] 59.21–26).[62] It is clear that Euctemon came to know Alce when she was working in the *oikēma* in his *sunoikia* (Isae. 6.19). As already mentioned, brothels were not necessarily slum holes but could in fact be commodious, as Ault suggests (2005, 149). Furthermore, nonbrothel prostitutes could be expensive and to spend one's money that way could be seen as frivolous. Comic poets complain of the *hetaira*'s expense. Antiphanes comments that the *hetaira* is a *sumphora* (misfortune) to the one who maintains her. His use of *trephein* (to maintain) emphasizes that it is her upkeep that is the difficulty (Ath. 13.567d).[63] Accusing their opponent of such wasteful spending is a strategy orators use in the hope of tarnishing an opponent. Timarchus is accused of squandering his patrimony on *hetairai*, as well as on gambling and other vices, while not providing for his mother or the city, which would have been a more effective use of his funds (Aeschin. 1.42). Olympiodoros is also critiqued for his supposed spending on a *hetaira*. The speaker of this speech complains that Olympiodoros's *hetaira* walks around bejeweled and with attendants, while his sister and niece live in poverty ([Dem.] 48.53). Mantitheus, in a third speech, also argues that his father spent more money maintaining Plangon, who had a lavish lifestyle and many attendants, than on Mantitheus's upbringing (Dem. 40.50–51).[64] The younger Alcibiades is also reproached for maintaining a *hetaira* (Lys. 14.25). The *porneion* on the other hand can be cheap or at least a more calculable expense, since these prostitutes do not live long term with their lover. The comic writers, for example, claim that this type of prostitute was available for only a little money (Ath. 13.568f).

Visits to the *porneion* might also reduce familial strife and avoid unwanted offspring. Alcibiades' wife seems to have wanted to divorce him because he kept prostitutes at home ([And.] 4.13–15; Plut. *Alc.* 8.3–4), likely using her dowry to maintain them (Cox 1998, 186). Lysias furthermore avoids bringing prostitutes into his home where his wife, niece, and mother reside, even temporarily ([Dem.] 59.22). Since more permanent relations between a prostitute and her client might produce offspring, as in the case of Alcibiades (Davies *APF* 19), visiting the brothel prostitute as one client out of many meant the father of any offspring would remain unknown and thus pose less of a risk to the integrity of the *oikos* and the *polis*. Mantias and Pericles were both criticized for having had children with women of prostitute or concubine status accepted as citizens (Dem. 39.3–4; [Dem.] 40.10–11; Plut. *Per.* 24.5–6, 37.2–5). As Cheryl Cox demonstrates, relations with nonbrothel women could indeed pose an economic and social strain on the household and city-state (1998, 170–89).

Visits to brothels were further a safer alternative to illicit liaisons with *astai*, for which the penalties were steep: fines, corporal punishment at the hands of the injured party, or even death (Lysias 1.32; [Dem.] 59.65–66; Plut. *Sol.* 23). Xenarchus critiques young men who go after freeborn women, when they can find quite decent girls in *porneia* (Ath. 13.569a–c). Eubulus claims that it is possible to purchase pleasure for a small amount in such places and not run the risk of a love carried out in stealth (Ath. 13.568f). Philemon even claims that the lawgiver Solon set up women in *oikēmata* for exactly this purpose (13.569d–f). Although the comment about Solon and brothels is not to be taken overly seriously, it does suggest that brothels and *pornai* were thought useful to more than just slaves and the lowest classes. Brothels were a convenient, cheap, and safe way to access sex. Socrates' young men appear to know of them (Xen. *Mem.* 3.11.1). As noted, orators critique those who spend too much on prostitutes, not simply those who visit prostitutes. Paying for sex is not a problem; paying too much is.

Conclusion

In the important reference work *Brill's New Pauly*, Ines Stahlmann states the following in an entry on the ancient brothel: "We would have to think of typical brothel patrons as being shopkeepers and members of the lower echelons of society, because men of substance would have been able to engage a *hetaira* or would have had slaves as concubines. Brothels were often situated in disreputable parts of town, such as at the port, around the circus or on the arterial roads" (s.v. brothel). I argue instead that Athenian brothels and their clientele were more diverse than previously acknowledged and that those running such places were not socially or legally marginalized—even Athenian citizens owned them. From the evidence available, such spaces do not appear to have been zoned (they appear mixed in with other businesses and residential buildings), but convenience likely made the Piraeus and Kerameikos key areas. Nor do they appear otherwise to have been regulated, aside from being subject to taxes. Although conditions in brothels were not always ideal for either patron or worker, such spaces do not appear to have been restricted to clients of poor, foreign, or slave status or to have necessarily been unsanitary, as sometimes claimed. Rather, they seem to have been a smart and sometimes inviting alternative to expensive nonbrothel prostitutes and *astai*. Some brothels appear to have been rather welcoming for their guests. They kept their clients around with food and possibly other entertainment, indicating that they were not necessarily intended solely for quick visits. The women staffing such facilities, although mostly of slave status, were not necessarily disdained as individuals either and may not have always differed from other prostitutes in dress or expectations. Since prostitutes themselves define brothel-type spaces rather than the spaces defining the brothel, and since brothels could be multipurpose and variable in form, we should not think of the *porneion* as a specific physical space just for sex. *Porneia* are thus very different from the modern conception of "a brothel" as a space designed for sexual activity and reserved primarily for it. "Brothel" is thus a misleading translation of *porneion*, just as I would argue "courtesan" is a misleading translation of *hetaira*. While distinctions between prostitutes, venues, and possibly districts do exist, it is inaccurate to associate the *pornē* and the *porneion* with only slaves and the poor.

NOTES

I am grateful for the comments of audiences at Queen's University, Kingston, and Brock University, who heard earlier versions of this paper. I am also deeply indebted to my coeditor, Madeleine M. Henry, for her valuable suggestions on various drafts. I also wish to acknowledge and thank the Social Sciences and Humanities Research Council of Canada, the Humanities Research Institute of Brock University and the Brock University Advancement Fund for their support for this project through research grants. I would also like to thank the staff of the American School of Classical Studies at Athens for their help with this project in the fall of 2006.

1. Cf. McGinn 2002, 11.

2. This definition does not distinguish between sacred or nonsacred prostitution. The issue of sacred prostitution is a contentious scholarly issue. Stephanie Budin (2006 and 2008) argues against the practice, as do Mary Beard and John Henderson (1998). Rebecca Strong (1997) and Andreas Lentakis (1986) are in favor. We have no written sources attesting to sacred prostitution in Athens, but in recent years archaeologists have identified possible sites of sacred prostitution at Merenda (Kakavoyianni and Dovinou 2003, 34–35) and in the Piraeus (Steinhauer 2003, 42–43). I do not wish to debate the identifications here, since, whether or not a site represents sacred or nonsacred prostitution, it can still shed light on what we can learn about the space of prostitution in the ancient polis and the service providers.

3. The first candidate is a first-century BCE brothel in a bath complex in the agora at Thessaloniki (Adam-Veleni 1997). A peristyle building at Mytilene appears to have functioned as a brothel in the first century CE (H. Williams 1991, 175–91; H. Williams 1989, 167–81). An inscription on an architrave mentions a *paidiskeion/a* at Ephesus (*SEG* xvi 719), but where such a brothel, once thought to be the peristyle house behind the latrine, might have been physically located is currently unknown (see Jobst 1976–77, 63–65, 69; and McGinn 2004, 225, for a summary). Peter Scherrer (2000, 120), argues against the idea that *paidiskeion* refers to a brothel at all, a possibility also entertained by Thomas McGinn (2004, 225). On Delos see Rauh 1993, 206–16, and the chapter by Davina McClain and Nicholas Rauh in this volume.

4. See Kapparis 1999 on the derogatory use of the term in [Dem.] 59.114 (1999, 408–9).

5. Another example of the term used of women is found in Aristophanes (*Lys.* 260).

6. Jeffrey Henderson notes that obscene language is absent in Attic literature outside of Old Comedy. He does not discuss *porneion* specifically but focuses on terms for the "sexual organs, excrement and the acts which involve them" (1975, ix–xi, 11–13, 17, 29, 31–32, 35).

7. But see Steven Johnstone (2002), who argues against [Dem.] 59.67 as a law referring to prostitution. *Oikia dēmosia* (public house) is perhaps another official term for a brothel (*SEG* xlii 785 [late archaic/early classical Thasos]). See also Xen. *Poroi*, 4.49, *IG* I^3 84. French, Italian, Spanish, and German all have such euphemisms (e.g., *maison publique* and *casa pubblica*). See A. J. Graham 1998, 37. See further A. Henry 2002, 219. The ancient term *tegos* also on the "stèle du port" (*SEG* xlii 785) refers to brothels in particular contexts and is "variatio" for *oikēmata*. See A. J. Graham 1998, 29–30. But such terminology does not appear to have been used in Athens.

8. Edward Cohen suggests the prostitute was no more despised than any other individual who had to work for a living. What mattered, he argues, was "the relative degree to which a working individual appear[ed] to be *eleutheros* (free) or *doulos* (*-ē*) (slave)" (2006, 99).

9. See fig. 3.2 and discussion of Corner in this volume. Other examples are: Penthesilea Painter, Attic red-figure *skyphos*, ca. 460 BCE, Hermitage 4224, ARV^2 889.166, S. Lewis 2002, 110 fig. 3.15; Berlin Painter, Attic red-figure *oinochoe*, ca. 525–475 BCE, San Antonio Museum of Art 86.134.59, *Para* 345.184 TER, Reeder 1995, 181 pl. 36; Makron, Attic red-figure *kylix*, ca. 500–450 BCE, Toledo Museum of Art 72.55, Keuls 1985, 167 fig. 141, Reeder 1995, 184–86 and pl. 38; Wedding Cup Painter, tondo of an Attic red-figure *kylix*, ca. 475–425 BCE, Staatlich Münzsammlung Arndt XXXX211241, ARV^2 923.29, Keuls 1985, 181 fig. 162, Peschel 1987, 452 and pl. 186 (1).

10. Sian Lewis (2002), however, argues against the claim that such scenes represent brothels, commenting that the pouch is not necessarily for money (110–11).

11. See, for example, a cup (460–450 BCE, Basel 415, Keuls 1985, 169 figs. 143, 144, S. Lewis 2002, 114 fig. 3.17) and a *stamnos* (510 BCE, Musées Royaux A 717, Keuls 1985, 213 fig. 185, S. Lewis 2002, 108 fig. 3.13).

12. See Ault 2005, 149–50; Younger 2005, 27; Fisher 2001, 261; and J. Davidson 1998, 85. Judith Binder does not interpret this building as a brothel but as the residence for the

girls chosen to weave the *peplos* for Athena (pers. comm., Oct. 2006). Still, most scholars conclude the structure housed prostitutes and was in fact a *porneion*.

13. On *andrōnes* see Corner in this volume.

14. See J. Davidson 1998, 83–90, and J. Davidson 2006, 36–37, for remarks concerning the sad plight of the *pornē* and the conditions of the *porneion*. On Roman cribs see McGinn 2004, 215–17, 291–94.

15. Nick Fisher follows Davidson and sees it as common for male prostitution (2001, 211).

16. The text of Isaeus states "Paidiskas etrephe" ("She reared and kept young girls"), suggesting the freedwoman trained them as well as maintained them. Miner does not discuss the use of *paidiskē* in [Dem.] 59.18 but states "I believe [Neaira] was likely considered a *pornē* when she worked under Nikarete" (2003, 30 n. 35).

17. See Hor. *Sat.* 1.2.30; *Priapeia* 14.9; Sen. *Contr.* 1.2, Juv. 6.131. Also see Kapparis in this volume. On differences between Greek and Roman prostitution practices, see Glazebrook (forthcoming).

18. Trans. J. Davidson 1998, 83.

19. Ἄνθρωπε, τί δρᾷς οὗτος ὁ χέζων / ἐν Πειραιεῖ παρὰ ταῖς πόρναις;

20. J. Davidson 1998, 85–86; Knigge 1991, 93; Knigge 1982.

21. Davidson does not seem overly convinced by this point. He comments that "the brothel, especially a cheap brothel, would have to double as a textile factory" (1998, 83–85, 88), but Building Z certainly seems to have been used for textile production as well.

22. I am grateful to Jutta Stroszeck for bringing this structure and its association with prostitution to my attention.

23. *LGPN* 2, s.v. Boubalion. A marble stele from the Kerameikos dating to the middle of the fourth century BCE also bears the name Boubalion (*IG* 2^2 11611). Kirchner comments, "Nomen servae vel meretriculae."

24. On such inscriptions, see A. Steiner 2007, 65–66, 67–68, 71–72; Lissarrague 1990a, 33; Immerwahr 1990, 56. On the *hetaira* in such inscriptions, see Snodgrass 2000, 27–28; Rotroff and Oakley 1992, 27–28.

25. On the date and use of the peristyle court in residential buildings, see Walter-Karydi 1996.

26. Knigge suggests the structure could have had either a sacred or profane use but favors a profane use given the graffito (1993, 139).

27. The information that follows is from Kakavoyianni and Dovinou 2003, 34–35. I wish to thank Olga Kakavoyianni for her willingness to meet with me and discuss the site in person. Also see the summary in Whitley 2004, 8.

28. A similar structure has been found in the Piraeus (Steinhauer 2003, 42–43 n. 31). Once again I am grateful to Olga Kakavoyianni for sharing what she knows about this structure with me, but its poor condition and few finds make it difficult to invoke as support here.

29. Kakavoyianni and Dovinou 2003, 34–35; Kakavoyianni, pers. comm., Nov. 27, 2006.

30. See Ath. 13. 568f and 587a–b, and Traill 700568. Anaxilas, dated approximately to the mid-fourth century, suggests Nannion is active as a *hetaira* at this time (Ath. 13.558c), and

Timocles, from the second half of the fourth century, ridicules her for being old in his play *Orestautokleides* (Ath. 13.567e). But note: another Nannion is mentioned in connection with Themistocles Phrearios (Ath. 13.576c and Traill 700578). This Nannion is also a *hetaira*, but she dates to the fifth century and thus is too early to be associated with this structure.

31. Athenaeus records two authors: Eubulus and Philippus (13.568f). Breitenbach appears to favor Eubulus as the author (1908, 131). Traill 700568 identifies this Nannion with the fourth-century Nannion.

32. But I do not intend to suggest that this courtyard at Merenda is the actual courtyard Eubulus is referring to.

33. See McGinn 2002, 13–15, 40–41 nos. 26, 27, and McGinn 2004, 220–39.

34. Prostitution, either formally or informally, is a feature of taverns and inns in the ancient world. See McGinn 2002, 11–15; McGinn 2004, 15–20; DeFelice 2001, 92–127, for Rome; and Kelly Blazeby in this volume for Greece.

35. As already mentioned, the topic of sacred prostitution in Greece and elsewhere is highly contentious. See n. 2. On sacred prostitution at Corinth, however, see C. K. Williams 1986 and Strong 1997, 70–105. Unfortunately, there are few architectural remains in which prostitution took place for comparison here. Charles Morgan originally identified Building 3 in the agora as a "Tavern of Aphrodite" (1953, 131–40), but, after further excavation, Williams and Fisher argued against this (1972 and 1973). The South Stoa was perhaps used as a brothel in the Hellenistic period, but this does not appear to have been its original function (Broneer 1954, 99).

36. See also the follow-up by Alan Henry (2002, 217–21). Hervé Duchêne, although toying with the idea of prostitution, concludes that the regulations were for prohibiting access to the roofs of public buildings and for prohibiting women from watching public processions (1992, 50–54). Also see D. M. Lewis's review of Duchêne's book in which he suggests that "women looking out of windows will touch on wider considerations of public order" (1993, 403). A. J. Graham suggests Lewis is hinting at prostitution here (1998, 29).

37. On the inscription, see nn. 7 and 36 above.

38. J. Davidson 1998, 82; Halperin 1990, 110. On entertainers as prostitutes, see, for example, Ath. 13.607d and Theophr. *Char.* 20.10. On entertainers and prostitution in general, see McClure 2003a, 21–22, and her introduction more generally. On flute girls specifically, see Starr 1978, 401–10; J. Davidson 1998, 80–82.

39. J. Davidson (2006, 37) agrees that this price was for "their musical, not their sexual services."

40. Loomis 1998, 166–85. See also J. Davidson 2006, 40. See also David Halperin on the variability of prices (1990, 107–12). In contrast to Loomis, he tends to view type of prostitute as the most important factor in pricing. See for example his comments on flute girls and other musicians (1990, 110).

41. "Various quarters" is Charles Gulick's translation of *kata topous* (1959).

42. Stroszeck lists Dem. 54.7–8 as support and argues further that such walks are the reason that prostitution developed there (2003, 79).

43. On where in the agora this case might have been heard, see Hansen 1991, 191; Boegehold 1995, cited by Fisher 2001, 210–11.

44. E. E. Cohen interprets Aeschines to mean that there was a list provided by the *boulē* (2000b, 131–32; 2000a, 186). Nick Fisher's recent commentary does not interpret Aeschines' comments to imply a list (2001, 258).

45. See McGinn 1998, 256–64, for a comparison with this kind of tax collection under the Romans.

46. The Attic Stelai give the occupation with the names of some slaves, and the Phialai Exeleutherikai inscriptions give the occupation of some manumitted slaves, but in neither case is the inclusion of the occupation necessary information. See Todd 1997, 118–23.

47. See also E. E. Cohen's arguments on this (2006, 101).

48. On the rhetorical aspects of this speech and the representation of Neaira and other women in Greek oratory, see Glazebrook 2005a and 2006.

49. See Carey 1992, 97; cf. Kapparis 1999, 214–15 (but note his translation: "Neaira here accompanied them, already working as a prostitute, though still too young, as she had not yet reached maturity").

50. Knigge 1982, 153–70; J. Davidson 1998, 86; E. E. Cohen 2006, 102; and Kapparis 1999, 228, agree that brothel workers lived in the brothel. The Phoenician goddess Astarte is associated with sexuality, like Aphrodite. Strong argues that "female figures holding their breasts suggest connections with Near Eastern cults which involved prostitution" (1997, 52). Even if such institutionalized prostitution did exist, not every image of the goddess need indicate sacred prostitution, since she and Aphrodite would likely be sacred to all prostitutes just as Hephaistos might be sacred to all smiths. In fact, Building Z3 may be evidence against sacred prostitution since it contains such images but is not in proximity to a sanctuary of Aphrodite. Cybele is a non-Greek female deity associated with Lydia and Phrygia in the eastern Mediterranean. Although known to Greeks by the fifth century BCE, she was not officially worshiped by mainland Greeks. Greeks burned down her sanctuary at Sardis (Hdt. 5.102). For an introduction to Cybele, see Vermaseren 1977.

51. See also E. E. Cohen 2006, 104–8, on prostitutes and weaving more generally.

52. See J. Davidson 1998, 86–89; cf. S. Lewis 2002, 101–12, esp. 110–11.

53. The object was originally interpreted by Kakavoyianni and Dovinou to be a miniature anchor inscribed with the male name ΛΥΣΙΜΑ[ΧΟΥ] (2003, 35), but Kakavoyianni has since suggested it is a loom weight instead (person. comm. Nov. 28, 2006). The idea that it is a loom weight is more convincing, as lead loom weights (typically of the conical or truncated pyramid or equilateral triangle type) have been found at Corinth, Delos, Olynthus, and Priene. See G. R. Davidson 1952, 163; Deonna 1938, 155–59; Robinson 1930, 122 and fig. 287; Robinson, 1941, 471–74; and Wiegand 1904, 393. The one from Merenda is closest to the truncated pyramid. For lead loom weights from Building Z3, see Knigge 2005, 201 (fig. 706), 205 (fig. 745), 208 (fig. 776). Unusual, however, is the inscription on the weight from Merenda, since weights more commonly bear a stamp. The inscription may be a dedication. Loom weights were offered as dedications, but determining whether or not a loom weight is a dedication is often difficult. As Isabelle Raubitschek comments, "Actual weaving would have been done at home, where the lead loom weights 405 and 405A were used, but the weavers who hoped for success in their work were known to have dedicated

loom weights, even terracotta ones, which have been found in large numbers in sanctuaries." Thus 405 and 405A could also be dedications at Isthmia (1998, 111–12). The choice of female names suggested for the inscription on the Merenda loom weight does not require the restoration of more letters after the alpha. In fact, Molly Richardson notes that "the surface to the right of the alpha appears undamaged; never inscribed?" (*SEG* liii 224).

54. See also Kapparis 1999, 207.

55. On the training of prostitutes see J. Davidson 2006, 38–40. See also E. E. Cohen 2006, 103. On Nikarete as a *pornoboskousa* running a brothel at Corinth, see Hamel 2003, 3–4, 24–26.

56. See Faraone 2005, 208, 216, 221, on Lysistrata as a courtesan and madam, as well as Henderson 1987.

57. On Aspasia's identity, see M. Henry 1995, 10–15; and Bicknell 1982, 240–50.

58. It is likely that this *sunoikia* also had a *porneion*, as did the one in the Piraeus. See further Lind 1988, 167.

59. But see E. E. Cohen's arguments (2006, 101).

60. J. Davidson suggests that this relationship with Euctemon proves Alce was never a *pornē* in a *porneion* (1998, 332 n. 55), but the mistake is our assumption that brothels were unsanitary and for customers of low status.

61. C. Cox claims she appears to be a *politis* because Socrates asks if she owns land and because Athenaeus refers to her as *Attikē* (12.535c) (1998, 175 n. 37). E. E. Cohen (2000a, 167 n. 66) agrees.

62. See Hamel 2003, 18–24. Bers notes an inscription recording that Hipparchus was victorious in six competitions (2003, 162 n. 44).

63. On the merits of cheap versus expensive prostitutes in Athenaeus, see M. Henry 1992, 260–63.

64. Although Plangon was not a prostitute, Mantitheus implies Plangon is a *hetaira* in his speech; for this reason I include the example. See Glazebrook 2005a, 178–79; and Glazebrook 2006, 131–32, on her portrait. J. Davidson argues that Athenians were also criticized for being "in the clutches of a strong passion" (2001, 161).

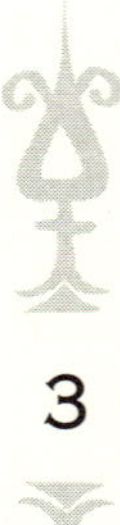

3 Bringing the Outside In

The Andrōn *as Brothel and the Symposium's Civic Sexuality*

SEAN CORNER

According to the view currently prevalent in scholarship, the symposium was an elitist institution at odds with the egalitarian community of the polis. It was an elite "anti-city."[1] Boundaries of gender, sexuality, and space are central to discussion of how the symposium situated itself in society. Occurring behind the closed doors of the *oikos*, as Ian Morris puts it, and further set apart in its own exclusive space within the *oikos*, the symposium is said to be a space of social and political exclusivity (2000, 185).[2] In the elitist privacy of the *andrōn*, the dining group was constituted in opposition to the inclusive public sphere. So, concomitantly, some see the *hetaira*, as the prostitute of the sympotic *andrōn*, as antithetical to the *pornē* of the brothel. The brothel on this view was the venue for an inclusive and egalitarian civic sexuality, while the *andrōn* was home to an exclusive and elitist sexuality.[3] I contend, however, that the space of the symposium was not that of the "inside," exclusively shut off from the "outside" of the city. This is not only literally the case—symposia were held in civic buildings, sanctuaries, and outdoors—but is also true in terms of what the *andrōn* represented as social space.[4] I argue that in certain crucial respects the *hetaira* and the *pornē* were not antithetical but parallel figures, with respect, that is, to a symposium that admitted civic life, including civic sexuality, across the threshold of the *oikos*.

The Space of the Symposium

The Greek house was both the place of all members of the household under the mastery of the husband and the place particularly of women, constituting the female sphere of responsibility. This duality plays out spatially in terms of a division of the interior, where there is an "inside" inside and, concomitantly, an "outside" inside. A man could be outside even in his home, in relation, that is, to the women of his household who belonged in the *muchos*, the innermost place. In Plato's *Symposium*, the women of the household are said to be "inside" (tais gunaixi tais endon) in relation to the male symposiasts who, in the *andrōn*, are by implication "outside" (176e). Nor is this division only figurative. It is a basic trope that the female interior is a place of darkness, in contrast to the bright, exposed male world outside. As Lisa Nevett has elucidated, the house strongly manifested in its architecture the acute concern in Greece for the integrity and inviolability of household and family, turned inward as it was on an interior courtyard that controlled access to the rooms of the house, with no line of sight into the courtyard from the single door that gave access to and from the street.[5] The location of the *andrōn*, however, often just inside the entrance, seems above all to have been determined by a need to provide access to exterior light and air (Jameson 1990, 190; Nevett 1995, 369; Nevett 1999, 164). When women, at the arrival of sympotic guests, withdrew behind a portico, for example, they actually went into darkness, in contrast to the bright *andrōn* with its proximity to the world outside (Nevett 1999, 124). This quality of the *andrōn* as a sort of exterior space by virtue of its being set apart from family and domesticity was commonly given physical expression by means of an antechamber or other architectural device, breaking communication between the dining room and the rest of the house (Nevett 1995, 369–72; Nevett 1999, 124, 155; Jameson 1990, 188).

Yet the relationship of *oikos* and symposium was constituted not in simple terms of opposition but of mediation between household and community. The *andrōn* mediated the worlds of interior and exterior. It is found on the far side of the courtyard as often as by the door, with windows providing sufficient connection to the outside (Jameson 1990, 190; Nevett 1995, 369). Indeed, as Nevett observes, it is striking that, in contrast to houses in many societies, there was no distinct wing for male sociality, separated from the main household (1995, 369). Nothing physically prevented this being the case. Shops, for example, were typically entered by a separate street door and afforded no direct access to the *oikos* proper (Jameson 1990, 185–86). For symposia, however, visitors were often taken to the *andrōn* through the courtyard, the central space of the house (Nevett 1995, 369–72). This interpenetration of two spheres can even be seen in the treatment of walls. The courtyard was commonly the only area other than the *andrōn* to have decorated walls. Thus while it was the place in which much of the household's domestic work was done, it was also, together with the dining room, a place for the unproductive expenditure of household wealth on the entertainment of strangers (Nevett 1995, 372; Nevett 1999, 155).[6]

The *andrōn* was peculiar in the Greek house in being dedicated in its architectural form to a particular function: sympotic dining. Otherwise rooms were flexible in their use and, as Michael Jameson has argued, women's work would have taken them all over the house. The "women's quarters" would seem to have been more an ideal and a matter of behavioral practice than a distinct physical space. The *andrōn*, however, in its narrower sense of dining room, gave concrete expression to the larger sense of the word as "the men's quarters": an actual architectural space of male exclusivity in the *oikos* (Jameson 1990, 172, 183–92; Nevett 1995; Nevett 1999, 123–26, 154–66).[7] And in fact "dining room" can be misleading. While sympotic dining was definitive of the architecture of the *andrōn*, it was not its only use. Rather it was one key instance of the room's general function, which was as the space for receiving outsiders and for conducting the business of the outside, for bringing the relations of male citizen society in. It was, as Cynthia Patterson aptly characterizes it, "the male or 'public' room of the house" (1991b, 51; see also Jameson 1990, 191–93). In this sense, the *andrōn* at home, as in the sanctuary, was a public dining room. In a symposium, then, a man was a man as a member of a community of nonkin male homosociality, apart from the world of his family. He was also a man at the same time as master of his household, protecting the exclusive boundaries of his *oikos* even as he brought the wider world of the outside into his home.[8]

The symposium did not take place "behind . . . closed doors" (Morris 2000, 185 n. 2). It is crucial to its meaning and function that it was an occasion on which the doors of the *oikos* stood open, either quite literally, as during Agathon's symposium in Plato, or in the sense of being open to the passage of nonkin men, including even uninvited visitors (*Symp.* 174e).[9] Sympotic hospitality operated in terms of a fluid and mutable social network rather than of membership in a club. The fluidity of the guest list, the degree of openness, is remarkable even in comparison to a contemporary dinner party, but it is especially so in the context of the closely guarded threshold of the Greek house.[10]

A red-figure scene on a wine jug (*oinochoe*) of the later fifth century provides an instance of iconography reflecting on passage across the threshold and the opening of the house to the world outside (see fig. 3.1). A woman, her hand held to her mouth in a gesture of apprehension, approaches the door of a house by night to open it to a man seeking entry. The scene is striking on account of the prominent role played in it of a doorway. As Jennifer Neils comments, this doorway, with a woman on one side and a man outside, seems to embody "the great divide between the outdoor world of men and the secluded world of women" (2000, 211). Some scholars have taken this to be a wife answering the door to her husband (Neils 2000, 211). Neils argues, however, that this is not a respectable

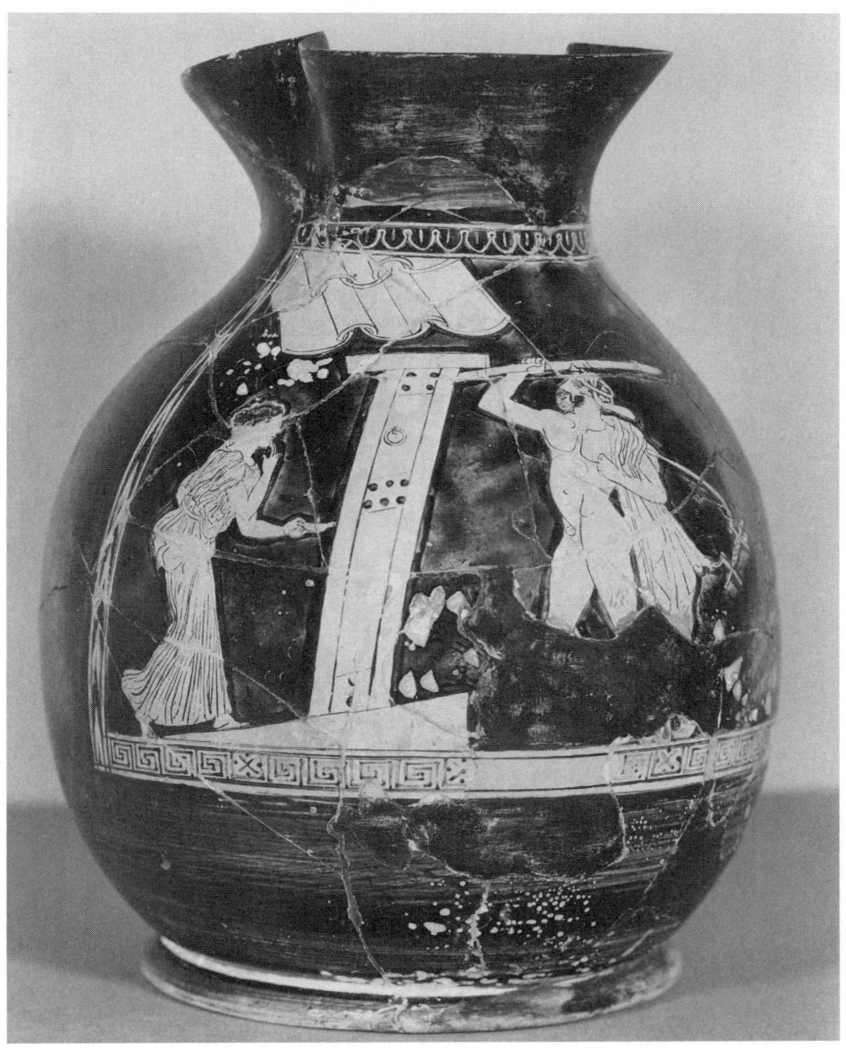

Figure 3.1. Artist unknown. Attic red-figure *oinochoe* (*chous*), ca. 430–420 BCE. Terracotta, H. 23.6 cm. Metropolitan Museum of Art, New York, 37.11.19 (Fletcher Fund, 1937). Photo © Metropolitan Museum of Art.

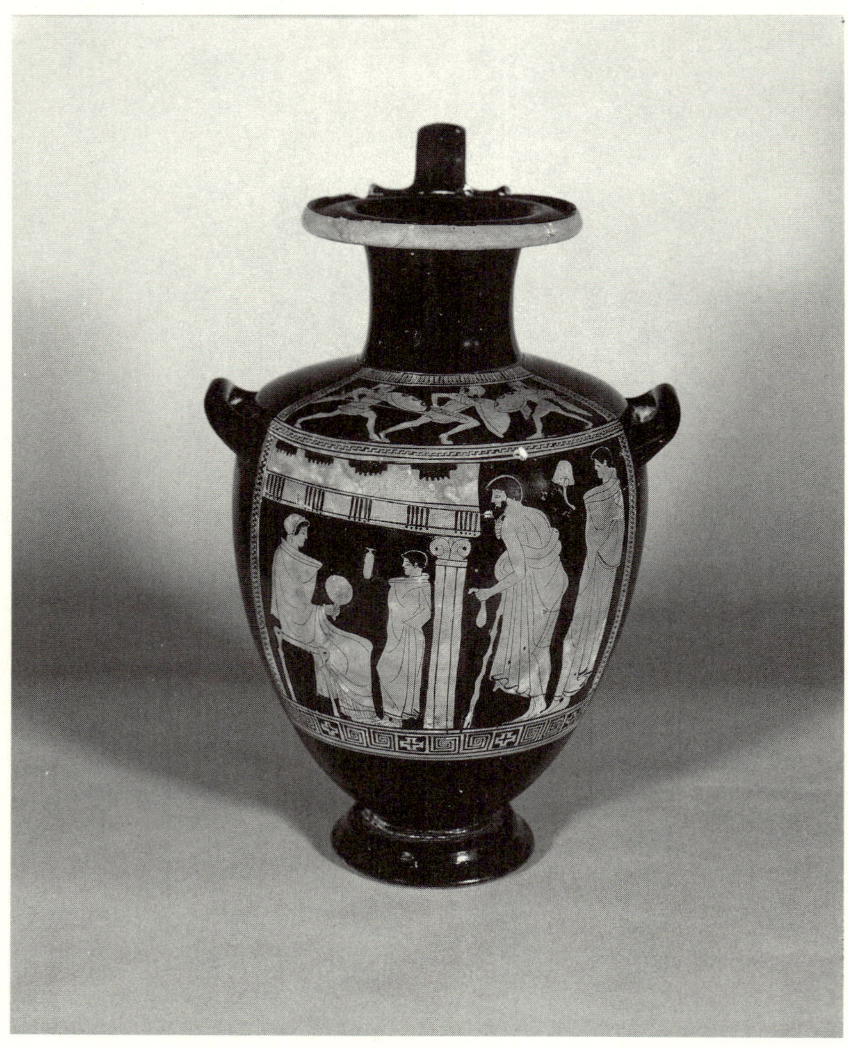

Figure 3.2. Attributed to the Harrow Painter. Attic red-figure *hydria*, ca. 470 BCE. Tampa Museum of Art, 1986.70 (Joseph Veach Noble Collection, purchased in part with funds donated by Mr. and Mrs. James L. Ferman Jr.). Photo © Joe Traina.

woman of the interior but a prostitute. In support of this reading, she points to another image where an unusually prominent architectural setting mediates between a woman inside and a man outside; in this image, however, the depiction of the man proffering money makes it explicit that this woman is a prostitute (see fig. 3.2). Thus Neils argues that what we have in these scenes is a subtle sexual play, proleptically signifying the consummation of the evening at the moment of its start through the trope of sexual penetration as passage through door or gate (2000, 210–13). While I agree with Neils that the scene on the *oinochoe* should be read in these terms, I would argue that the status of the woman—wife or prostitute—is ambiguous and that this ambiguity is intrinsic to the scene's meaning.

Neils argues that the woman can only be a prostitute since respectable women, at least premenopausal women, did not open the door to the street, a proposition that is a priori unlikely (2000, 211).[11] Her only evidence for this is a passage of Theophrastus (*Char.* 28.3) in which aspersions are cast on a woman's faithfulness because she answers her door to strange men. A normal activity, however, might become an object of innuendo and be cast in a disparaging light (and it is the slanderer that Theophrastus is depicting here). Thus the ancient viewer, like the scholars Neils is arguing against, might well take this to be a wife (or other woman of the family) inside her home. The vase, however, gives no indication that the man is her husband. What the passage of Theophrastus and other sources do attest is the anxiety that surrounded a woman's exposure to the outside and to nonkin men and the fact that her presence on the threshold could become a cause for suspicion. Penetration of the household was identified with penetration of the body, and a woman's being seen at the open door could be construed as a sign of adulterous lasciviousness. Adultery overturned the exclusivity of the house and of domestic sexuality and brought the loose, open sexuality of the outside into the home and so could be spoken of as turning the *oikos* into a brothel.[12] Thus the scene is open to being read as one of peril, promising the penetration of wife and household by a stranger.

At the same time, the scene is also open to Neils's reading. That the man carries a torch and lyre identifies him as a *komast*, and he may thus be seen as seeking admission to a symposium.[13] In this reading, rather than a scene of impropriety, the proleptic trajectory of this story resolves itself safely. The man is not in fact passing into the domestic sphere but into the symposium. This woman, in a sympotic scene on a sympotic vase, may be a *hetaira*. Pulled into the sphere of the banquet, the scene conveys not a threat to the productive sexuality of the woman of the household but entry to the antiproductive world of sympotic sexuality. Thus the image, reflecting the symposium to itself, dramatizes the place of the banquet as a singular and highly significant point of intersection, of interpenetration, between inside and outside. Its ambivalence plays on the opposition of symposium and *oikos*, but at the same time its charged ambiguity dramatizes the peculiar and delicate status of the symposium as an occasion when the doors of the *oikos* are opened, when men not of the family may legitimately be let in. Where we regularly see doorways only in wedding scenes, communicating the exogamous integration of a woman into the domestic life of an *oikos*, this vase twists the motif to show the admission into the house of the world outside.[14]

Liberal Pleasures and the Symposium's Civic Sexuality

What we see here is that the symposium brought the brothel into the *oikos*—in the sense, that is, of taking a man out of his family and bringing him into the community of nonkin men who share in the enjoyment of an extramarital, antiproductive, antidomestic sexuality. Michel Foucault has argued, I believe persuasively, that Greek sexual ethics structured a citizen male's sexuality as an experience of civic liberty, whereby so long as a man was free in relation to himself, which is to say exercised control over his desires so as to be rational master of his own actions and consequently able to act responsibly vis-à-vis his obligations as a citizen male, he was free to pursue pleasure as he chose. He experienced freedom in sexual pleasure as the active partner, the autonomous agent in sexual intercourse, where sexual intercourse was conceived as an asymmetrical act done by an active subject to a passive object, the passive role being taken by noncitizen others—women, slaves, and foreigners.[15]

Sex with a wife, however, while an experience for the man of his freedom in his mastery of her as autonomous master of his household, was at the same time thought of as a form of bondage. The household as the sphere of economy was the world of biological and economic necessity, the work of subsistence and sexual reproduction. As Semonides says in his ode on women, "[A wife] makes a man a *philos* by necessity" (anankēi d' andra poieitai philon) (Semon. fr. 7.62 West). Marriage was a condition of natural necessity and exclusive bonds. Wife and husband were yokemates, *suzugoi*. A man was not bound to sexual exclusivity as his wife was, but only she could bear heirs to his patriline, and he was bound to her too in the economic partnership of the *oikos*, which, while certainly not equal, was nevertheless not a relationship of active subject and passive object. She was in her own right free, a member of her free natal *oikos*, and in her marital *oikos* she and her husband were bound in mutual codependence, in the *koinōnia* necessary for the survival and subsistence of the *oikos*.[16] Doubtless people did experience pleasure in marital sex, but this was not its purpose, its defining end. The sphere of the wife was production and reproduction and not the affective and hedonistic bonds of eros. As Morris puts it, "Greek authors regularly spoke of sexual activity between man and wife as 'work' producing legitimate offspring, in contrast with *paidia* or 'play, ' nonprocreative sex. . . . Man's work was to produce food by plowing the land, and woman's to produce children through the *ergon* of legitimate sex, her body sowed through the sexual labour of her husband" (2000, 148).[17]

Play was to be had in the open space of the city, on the streets and in the brothels, not in the closed space of the inside where out of respect for the exclusive claims of his wife a man should not bring his lovers.[18] David Halperin has shown that the freedom to enjoy extramarital sex that licit prostitution afforded to men of all classes was an expression of male civic liberty, a freedom exercised on objectified women whose subordination drew the boundary of citizenship along lines of gender, lines that cut across birth and wealth and united citizens, as men, in equal freedom.[19] I would add to this that civic liberty was experienced not only in the citizen's entitlement to use the bodies of others for the ends of his own pleasure (1990, 101) but also in the fact that having sex for pleasure rather than out of necessity made it a choice, an act of autonomous agency. One chose to have sex with a *pornē* constrained only by oneself, making it truly a choice. So long as one was in control of one's desire for pleasure, pursuing pleasure in a measured and deliberate way, measuring one's interests and obligations rather than being overcome by impulse, one was free to have sex with a *pornē*, where sex with a *pornē*, in contradistinction to sex with a wife, was free in the sense of being purely for the sake of one's own pleasure.[20] It was something one wanted rather than needed to do. Only outside the constraints of marriage in the open, shared space of the city where civic liberty was enjoyed equally and in common by men, outside and apart from their households, could a man partake of what might be called the sexuality of liberal pleasure.[21]

There is an exception, however, to this rule of spatial division, although in fact it is an exception that proves that rule. The symposium is in the house but not of it, setting itself apart as a place of liberal pleasures. It transferred food and drink (and, as we shall see, sex) from the realm of productive household economy to that of unproductive male homosociality. Food and drink are removed from the storeroom and the regime of subsistence and brought into the symposium to be consumed under the rule of isonomic sharing by nonkin men who forge communal bonds in the enjoyment of shared pleasures. Galen glosses *tragēmata* as "that which is eaten succeeding the *deipnon* for the sake of the pleasure [*hēdonēs heneka*] that attends the drinking," and in its poetry and iconography, the symposium contrasts its eating and drinking, for the sake of pleasure, to eating and drinking for subsistence (Gal. 6.550 Kühn). Take, for example, Theognis 467–97, where, as the beginning of the poem makes clear, sympotic society is the society of the free, wherein a free man voluntarily enters into the common rule of the community of the free: "Of those now here with us, do not detain anyone who is unwilling [*aekonta*] to remain, / Nor show the door to anyone who does not wish [*ouk ethelont'*] to go, / Nor wake anyone who is sleeping, Simonides, should one of us, / Well fortified by wine, be gripped by gentle slumber, / Nor bid the wakeful man to sleep against his will [*aekonta*]" (467–71). "For," Theognis says, "everything that is forced [*anankaion*] is by nature painful [*aniēron*]" (472). Necessity is antithetical to the object and defining principle of the symposium: pleasure. One's drinking must be an expression of volition—"For the one who wants [*ethelonti*] to drink, let the boy . . . pour" (473)—free of the compulsion of uncontrolled desire and excessive drunkenness—"Whoever goes beyond the limit of drinking, that man no longer / Is master of his own tongue or of his mind" (479–80). So too one's consumption must be free of the necessity of subsistence, of the economic necessity of poverty and biological necessity of hunger: "don't let your belly / Overpower [*biasthō*] you as if you were a base laborer hired by the day" (485–86). It is thus that "a man feels most pleasure [*chariestatos*] in drinking wine" (477) and thus that the community of the free becomes a community of pleasure: "Conducted in this way, a drinking-party proves far from unpleasant" (496).[22]

The belly, in a long Greek tradition, signified asocial necessity, animal drive, the necessity that reduced a man to dependence and made him servile, placing him on the margins of free society and its relations of convivial sociality.[23] It expressed that mortal side of the human condition that Hesiod identifies with the subsistence economy of the *oikos*, the mortal toil of agricultural production and sexual reproduction (see Vernant 1989a). In Aristotelian terms, the belly belonged to the household as an association whose end was "living," the satisfaction of economic and biological need, rather than to the higher association of polis community whose end was "living well" (*Pol.* 1.1252a–1253b, 1256a–1258a). It was the mark of that internal "other" of the symposium, the parasite, whose condition was to be kept, *trephesthai*—the term for a man's management of his *oikos*, his husbandry of his wife, the keeping of his slaves, and the feeding of his animals—and who could be called by the derogatory nickname Chrēmōn, Needy (Ar. *Vesp.* 401; J. Davidson 1998, 270–72). The parasite was enslaved by his needy belly. As a character in Diphilus's *Parasite* puts it, quoting Euripides, "need and my miserable belly conquer me" (nika de khreia m' hē talaipōros te mou gastēr) (Diphilus fr. 60.2–3 *PCG ap.* Ath. 10.422b–c).[24] Existing on the civic margins between free and slave and between female household and citizen male, nonkin community, he likewise existed on the margin of the convivial community of the symposium.[25] By its exclusion of women of the household and inclusion of nonkin men in the equal enjoyment of liberal pleasures, the symposium brought the world of the city into the house.

It was not only food and drink that were, in the symposium as opposed to the household, objects of liberal pleasure, but also prostitutes.[26] In this sense the *hetaira* and *pornē* were parallel figures, and it is in this sense that the symposium could be said to bring the sexuality of street and brothel into the house. Matro describes the admission of "*pornai*" to the symposium with the bringing in of the second tables, together with the *tragēmata*, as among the tasty morsels to be enjoyed (*ap.* Ath. 4.137b–c). The symposium constructed itself as a sphere of pleasure as opposed to work, and where sex with one's wife was work, sex with a *hetaira* was for the sake of pleasure. As Apollodoros famously puts it, characterizing *hetairai* as Galen characterizes *tragēmata*, "for pleasure's sake [*hēdonēs henek'*] we have *hetairai*, *pallakai* for daily care of our bodies, and wives we have to bear legitimate children and to keep faithful guard inside the house" ([Dem.] 59.122). Significantly, all women of the household, maidservants as well as wives and daughters, were excluded from the symposium (Dalby 1993, 174–75, 187).[27] Thus all productive, domestic femininity was excluded, and productive sexuality was excluded in favor of a sexuality directed to boys and to women outside the *oikos*. It is in this context, I think, that we can best make sense of why prostitution coincided with pederasty in sympotic sexuality and of the *hetaira*'s ambivalent quality as objectified, subordinated woman and yet as quasi-equal "female companion" and honorary male (see Kurke 1997, 118–19, 133; Kurke 1999, 186, 201).

The *Hetaira*: "A Woman Shared in Common by Anyone Who Wishes"

In their aspect as objects of compulsion, commoditized, hired and servile, bound to necessity, *hetairai* represented for the symposiasts the freedom of sexual pleasure for its own sake, just as *pornai* did for their customers.[28] For the men, the *hetaira* represented sexual liberty, as expressed, in Oswyn Murray's words, in "[a] carefree poetry of love of young girls as sexual objects, involving no complications, transient and easily satisfied" (1995c, 230). This was in pointed contradistinction to domesticity centered on a wife whose sexuality was rigorously policed and identified with productive work rather than erotic pleasure.[29] As Isaeus says, "When once they have admitted that the woman [Phile's mother] was shared in common [*koinēn*] by anyone who wished [*tou boulomenou*] to take her, how can it be reasonably conceived that she was also a wedded wife [*gunē enguētē*]?" (3.11; cf. 13–16, 77).[30] The absent wife, as she was the antitype of the *pornē*, was also the antitype of the *hetaira*, removed from the symposium as, ideally, from contact with nonkin men in general, bound in exclusivity (in Athens, by *enguē*) and belonging to the interior of the house. In the black-figure repertoire, for example, the rarity of depictions of women of the household compared to the many depictions of *hetairai* speaks of this distinction of seclusion and availability or exposure. And vase painting also exposed the *hetaira* more directly, commonly depicting her, from the first sympotic scenes, as entirely or partially unclothed in contrast to the wife, who (when she appears) is normally depicted as thoroughly covered up. The *hetaira* could also be pictured naked in the *muchos* of the house, at her toilet and in domestic tasks, stripped of her seclusion and exposed to the male viewer's gaze. As the object of a masculine liberty of pleasure, the *hetaira* represented a transcendence of the exclusive, introverted world of the *oikos*.

As with the other pleasures of the symposium, she represented an expenditure of household capital on nonkin conviviality, a surrender of private wealth in the interests of male egalitarian community.[31] As Isaeus's formulation makes clear, availability to all implied being shared, being a communal object of gratification, an idea reiterated later in the speech: "This woman . . . was common to anyone who wished [*koinē tōi boulomenōi*]" (3.16). She, in opposition to the wife, was shared among men like the food or wine, falling under the sympotic rule of equal shares. The courtesan Gnathaina is said to have written a *Nomos sussitikos* in which this principle is laid down—"The rule here written down is equal and the same for all" (Callimachus fr. 433 Pfeiffer *ap.* Ath. 13.585b)—and Phryne is said to have introduced a new god, Isodaitēs ("Equally Apportioned Feast") (Hyp. fr. 177 Kenyon).[32] In many vase paintings the *hetaira* herself appears as an item of equal distribution: there is one for each man just as their portions of food and drink are identical. In scenes of group sex, a *hetaira* may quite literally be shared by two or more men. As Eva Stehle deftly elucidates in her exegesis of the performative force of sympotic love poetry, "the unindividuated object [boy or girl] becomes the focus of the whole group's feelings of desire. . . . A shared, verbally constituted figure substitutes for the actual individual desires of the symposiasts and creates an experience of collective masculine sexuality" (1997, 253). In Aristophanes' *Wasps*, the symposium is destroyed by Philokleon's transgression of the sympotic rule in carrying off the flute girl for himself (1342–87).

The *hetaira* was part of the symposium's opening up of the household to the community. Isaeus's formulation, "a courtesan at the disposal of anyone who wishes" (hetaira te ēn tou boulomenou) (3.15), appears as a standard gloss for *hetaira*.[33] The echo here, in these Attic speeches, of the Athenian formula for civic participatory entitlement, *ho boulomenos*, is not, I think, without significance.[34] The *hetaira* could represent, as the brothel prostitute could, the open space of civic community in which all citizens could act and, by acting sexually on her, experience their power and freedom as citizens, their prerogative of participation. She did so precisely in the context of and as an artifact of the symposium, which, as an institution of male nonkin conviviality set itself apart from the order of marriage and the *oikos* and brought in the world of the outside:

> That the woman, whom the defendant has deposed that he gave in legal marriage [*enguēsai*] to him [Pyrrhos], was a *hetaira* at the disposal of anyone who wishes and not his wife [*hetaira ēn tōi boulomenōi kai ou gunē*] has been testified to you by his [Pyrrhos's] other acquaintances and by his neighbors, who have given evidence of quarrels, revels [*kōmous*], and licentiousness that the defendant's sister occasioned whenever she was at Pyrrhos's house. Yet no one, I presume, would dare to revel with [*kōmazein*] a married woman, nor do married women [*gametai gunaikes*] accompany their husbands to banquets [*erchontai meta tōn andrōn epi ta deipna*] or think of feasting in the company of strangers [*sundeipnein . . . meta tōn allotriōn*], especially mere chance comers. (Isae. 3.13–14)

The liberty of extramarital sex that the polis afforded to men was normally to be exercised outside the household out of respect for the wife and the proper integrity of the *oikos*. The symposium represented a unique case of legitimately bringing that civic sexuality into the house. We might think here of Agathon's open door and the open door that is a sign of the brothel in Philemon fr. 3 *PCG*. The opening of one's home could be identified with the sexual availability of an adulterous woman's body. Only in a symposium, only in the context, that is, of bringing the outside of male egalitarian community in, could one open one's house to such open female sexuality.[35] And indeed, going in the other direction, when a man visited a brothel he could feel as if he were attending a symposium, since, as James Davidson notes, it seems that some brothels at least "tried to emulate a sympotic atmosphere" (1998, 94; see also J. Davidson 2006, 47). Thus to call a *hetaira* a communal whore (*koinē pornē*) was not merely an insult, nor was it to demote the *hetaira* from her proper status by collapsing her into her "other" (Ath. 13.588f.).[36] It spoke to what she meant and represented in her own right, precisely as a courtesan of the symposium.

This sympotic ethic is well expressed in a passage of Alciphron:

> This Malian soldier . . . is a simple-minded and decent man, and he is so far removed from feeling jealousy about whores [*pornas*] that, when recently, at a drinking-bout [*symposiou*], his conversation ran to this topic, he poured out a great torrent of abuse on people who are subject to such feelings. For, as he said, married women with an inheritance should keep the house and live the respectable life [*gametais epiklērois oikourian prepein kai ton semnon bion*], but courtesans [*hetairas*] must belong to all openly and be accessible to all who wish them [*einai pantōn anaphradon kai pasin ekkeisthai tois boulomenois*]; so then, just as we use

> public baths and their furnishings in common [*koinois*], even though they are held to be the property of an individual, so too, said he, with women who have enrolled for this kind of life. (*Epist.* 3.22.1–2)[37]

Here *hetaira* and *pornē* are used interchangeably; they are represented as constituting a single category in contradistinction to the wife.[38] The convivial ethic constructs the *hetaira* as an object of male civic freedom and equality, open alike to all "who wish." She plays the same role in the symposium as the *pornē* does in the brothel; both venues symbolize the open space of civic community in contradistinction to the private world of the *oikos*. Just as the availability of the *pornē*'s body corresponds to the openness of the brothel, so too the *hetaira*'s accessibility and commonality to all is like a civic building, that is, a public bath, figuring the symposium by implication as a civic space.

Courtesan, Concubine, Wife, and Whore

It is necessary at this point to make distinctions between kinds of *hetaira* and different uses of the term as a designation. Davidson observes that *hetairai* could be treated as wives and that grand *hetairai* appear closer to wives than to *pornai* relative to the poles of protected interior and exposed exterior (1998, 131–33). I do not deny that *hetairai* in the situation of concubines, or grand courtesans with their own establishments, stood in contrast to *pornai* and closer to the wife in terms of exclusivity. Furthermore, any *hetaira* might at a symposium be an object of jealousy as symposiasts competed for her exclusive attentions (in some cases desire might lead to a *hetaira* becoming a concubine) (J. Davidson 1998, 131–33; see also Kapparis 1999, 7–8, 13, 264). Nor do I deny that a *hetaira* would aspire to become a man's mistress or mistress of her own house and to differentiate herself as far as possible from a *pornē* (J. Davidson 1998, 120–36; J. Davidson 2006, 36, 45; see also E. E. Cohen 2006, 108–14). On the other hand, a *hetaira* was a prostitute, and there was always a pull back in the other direction, toward identification with the *pornē*. I agree with those scholars who have argued that even as a *pallakē* the *hetaira* ultimately remained on the other side of a line that divided the wife from other female sexual partners because she was subject to forms of openness to use that were attached to servility and objectification (Kurke 1997, 113, 118–19, 133, 145–56; Kurke 1999, 181, 183, 186–87, 201, 218–19).[39] Moreover, as she moves toward the sphere of marriage, the *hetaira* tends away from the sphere of the symposium.

Neaira, no common *hetaira* but a courtesan from a grand stable, begins her career as a slave hired out to accompany men to symposia ([Dem.] 59.18–20). Indeed, attending symposia is what marks her as a courtesan: "Neaira drank and dined with them [her clients] in the presence of a number of men just as a courtesan would do" ([Dem.] 59.24; cf. 48). She is bought by two men who, although they do not want to see her sold to a brothel and made available to anyone, nevertheless are content to share her between themselves ([Dem.] 59.29–30). Even when she had been set free and had entered into an exclusive relationship with a man named Phrynion,

> he treated her in an outrageous and reckless way; he took her to dinner with him everywhere, wherever he was drinking, she joined in all his carousals, and he had intercourse with her in public whenever and wherever he pleased, making a display of his privilege [*philotimian tēn exousian*] in front of onlookers. He took her to gay parties at many houses and among them to that of Chabrias . . . There were many there [at Chabrias's symposium] who had intercourse with her when she was drunk, while Phrynion was asleep, even the servants. ([Dem.] 59.33)

What is the outrage here? Treating a *hetaira* like a *pornē*?[40] I think not, at least not as a simple binary. Certainly Neaira believes that she is not being "treated with affection" and "prized," as she expects (*ouch hōs ōieto ēgapato*) ([Dem.] 59.35). The expectations she has, however, are those of the free concubine, the *hetaira-pallakē*. Moreover, it would seem that the principal cause of outrage for Apollodoros's audience is Phrynion's violating the sympotic ethic of community by flaunting his exclusive sexual access to Neaira (as Allison Glazebrook [2005a, 170 with n. 28] has observed, eliciting sympathy for Neaira as a wronged woman is hardly consistent with Apollodoros's purpose, and anyway she proves herself undeserving of sympathetic outrage by her own behavior at Chabrias's). One thinks again of Philokleon's transgression in carrying off the flute girl, promising to make her his concubine. At Chabrias's symposium, then, while events certainly go beyond sympotic propriety (and especially in the inclusion of the slaves in the community of pleasure), some just satisfaction is to be felt at Neaira's being shared by the company while Phrynion sleeps, and a drunken Neaira in this convivial atmosphere shows her true prostitute's nature: far from being capable of being a concubine (she who has the gall to pretend to be a wife!), she falls back into the role of *hetaira-pornē*, as the open, shared object of male sexual license. Later in her career, after she flees from Phrynion and takes up with Stephanus as his concubine, Phrynion tries to reclaim her. Even though she is legally adjudged to be free, the arbitrators determine that she should again be shared, belonging to no *oikos*, but shuttling back and forth between the men's houses to serve their pleasure ([Dem.] 59.45–48). It seems that her position was constantly in danger of falling toward that of the flute girl, who also was counted among the *hetairai* and was a prostitute both of the symposium and of the streets.[41]

Another excellent example is afforded us by Chrysis, the Samian woman of Menander's *Samia*. She is a *hetaira-pallakē* and well illustrates the ambiguities of that position. An old man, Demeas, fearing younger rivals, has taken her into his exclusive possession as his concubine (20–28). She is integrated into the household; indeed, she appears in many ways close to a wife. She even visits the neighbor's wife, participating in the society of citizen women (35–38). Nevertheless, she is very definitely not a wife.[42] When Demeas discovers that she, as he believes, has had a child, assuming the reproductive marital role, he declares with bitter irony: "It would seem that I've been keeping a married courtesan without realizing it" (130). His initial response is to expel her from the house rather than suffer the intrusion of a *nothos* (bastard) into his *oikos*, but he is persuaded to relent. When later, however, he comes to believe that Chrysis has been unfaithful to him, violating the concubine's bond of exclusivity, he determines to cast her out into the open, to return her to the condition of a *hetaira*:

> Superstar! In town
> You'll see exactly what you are! The others of
> Your type dash to their parties, where they charge
> A mere ten drachmas and knock back strong wine
> Until they die—or else they starve, if what
> They do's not quick and willing. But I'm sure
> You'll know this just as well as anyone.
> You'll find out what you are and how you blundered!
>
> (390–97)[43]

Here, then, the *hetaira* as concubine is contrasted to the *hetaira* of the symposium. In this configuration of discourse, emphasizing distinction, the latter belongs to the outside world of civic community (*en tēi polei*). Running to and fro to symposia (*trechousin epi ta deipna kai pinous' akraton*), she is a servile object of an open, easy sexuality (*hetoimōs kai tachu*) whose job is men's gratification. Her running assimilates her to the flute girls and *pornai* of the streets, who are nicknamed things like "wanderer," "ground-beater," and runner (*dromas*) (J. Davidson 1998, 78). This is the *hetaira*'s nature, what she truly is (*akribōs hētis ei*).

Being the object of a male liberty of pleasure, however, is only one side of the sympotic *hetaira*. What then of her other side, that aspect of the *hetaira* that, in contrast to the *pornē*, makes her a participant in a social world, someone with whom one enters into the mutual, social bonds represented by the exchange of gifts, someone whose affections and attentions one might seek, vie for, and be jealous of, someone with whom one could forge a personal relationship? How should we make sense of the courtesan as a female *hetairos*, participating in the symposium and competing with the men on equal terms?[44] I suggest that both sides of her status are integrally a function of the transcendent, antidomestic quality of sympotic conviviality. The *hetaira*, in her opposition to the excluded wife and in her role as figure of antiproductive sexuality, brings the sexuality of the brothel into the house, but at the same time she is promoted to a paradoxical reciprocity as a participant in convivial homosociality.

The sexuality of the *hetaira* is, as far as the legitimate *oikos* is concerned, sterile. In Athens, a wife was given to a husband to produce legitimate heirs as her exclusive prerogative. She was given to him, in the words of the ritual of *enguē*, "for the purpose of ploughing legitimate [*gnēsioi*] children."[45] Jean-Pierre Vernant, drawing on Marcel Detienne, observes that in the classical ideology of marriage, the wife belonged, in her function of childbearing, to the sphere of Demeter, in stark contradistinction to the *hetaira*, who belonged to the sphere of Aphrodite, of erotic pleasure, and was "incapable of giving rise to authentic and lasting fruits" (Vernant 1988, 62 n. 25; Detienne 1977). Thus, as Daniel Ogden writes, and as we have seen in the case of Chrysis, "a hetaira is characterized as someone that does not or should not bear children, and it is shameful if she usurps a wife's role in doing so" (1996, 100).[46] Isaeus takes childlessness as evidence of a woman's being a *hetaira* (3.15). In [Demosthenes] 48, the plaintiff laments that Olympiodoros, in taking up with a *hetaira*, has shamefully left the *oikos* barren (and all the while the grasping courtesan ruins it by her extravagance in utter disregard for domestic economy) (52–56). Altogether, then, we can appreciate why Dio Chrysostom calls sex with a prostitute "sterile copulation."[47] Plato in the *Laws* treats sex outside marriage and homosexuality as parallel to one another in being antiproductive (not merely unproductive but at odds with and destructive to domestic reproduction). Both, as he makes clear, were the sexuality of erotic pleasure in contradistinction to the productive sexuality of the household (8.841a–e). It is for this reason, I would argue, that pederastic homosexuality and the heterosexuality of prostitution come together as the hallmark of a distinctively sympotic sexuality. In a number of symposium scenes on vases the male and female participants are assimilated to one another in appearance. In love scenes, this can make it unclear whether homosexual or heterosexual relations are being depicted, blurring the line between the two.[48] It is by her inclusion in this antiproductive world of male homosociality, I suggest, that the *hetaira* assumes her aspect as quasi male.

Shifting Binaries and Categories of Women

I do not deny that *hetaira* and *pornē* represented in crucial ways contrasting, and in some respects antithetical, categories, nor am I seeking to return to that simple dichotomy of the wife and other women that Davidson set out to challenge (1998, 74–76). I find persuasive Davidson's demonstration of systematic contrast between the *hetaira* and *pornē* as defined by a discourse of opposition between gift and commodity exchange, but I also agree with Laura McClure that "an overdetermined dichotomy between the hetaera and the porne . . . has subsequently enmeshed scholarly debate" (2003a, 9). As scholars have long recognized, a systematic distinction seems to elude us since none fits all our sources. At times, contrasts are marked, and at other times *hetaira* and *pornē* appear to overlap, blur, and even become synonymous. This is made more difficult, of course, by the fact that we are not dealing with the definition of and distinction between only two categories but also with the musicienne, the concubine, and the wife, all of which may be compared and contrasted to one another, singly or in a complex.[49] This, indeed, is Davidson's point of departure, and he endeavors to cut the Gordian knot by resorting to the idea of continuum, defined by stable and systematic principles, along which the different categories of women are arranged, but tending to shade into one another and with the possibility of sliding and slippage (1998, 109–36; J. Davidson 2006, 36–39). Thus he hopes to establish stable terms of distinction while preserving the diversity and complexity we see in our sources (1998, 76).

I am not suggesting that we turn our back on this diversity and complexity only to reinstate a single, monolithic binary of wife versus prostitute. Yet Davidson himself seems at points to lean to a vision of an unvarying set of categorical oppositions (albeit with blurred boundaries and slippage from one category to another), as when he criticizes McClure and other scholars for, as he sees it, mistaking denigration for designation when they cite instances of *hetaira* and *pornē* being used synonymously (2004, 170–72).[50] I think he is right to say that this mistake is made in some of these instances. Yet I also think that in some cases they do constitute true synonyms, and, more importantly, I would argue that while *hetaira* and *pornē* stand in some aspects in contradistinction to one another, in other aspects they coincide and can, in contrast to the wife, for example, collapse into one category.

Leslie Kurke's vision, much more than Davidson's, is one of absolutely antithetical categories corresponding to a binary of *hetaira*/gift/symposium/elitist ideology and *pornē*/commodity/city/middling ideology.[51] In her view the ambiguities and slippages we see in the sources are attributable to the internal dynamics of one ideology (the mystification of the *hetaira*'s status), to contradictions internal to that ideology (the *hetaira* providing for in-group bonding as an objectified other and yet providing for separation of group and wider society as a quasi equal), or to conflicts between one ideology and the other (in opposition to elitist ideology, middling writers demystify the *hetaira* and expose her as a common prostitute).[52] I question the idea of a one-to-one binary between civic egalitarianism and commodity exchange on the one hand and elitism and gift exchange on the other. As Dean Hammer argues, the evidence simply does not support the suggestion that the elite systematically shunned commodity exchange, nor does it support a rejection by the city of all aspects of gift exchange or an embrace in all aspects of commodity exchange (2004, 503).[53] I am persuaded by the argument for the use the city makes of the *pornē* as commodified object but not by the idea that the city could not at the same time be averse to monetary transaction in its disembedded individuating and universalizing aspect on the grounds that it was potentially at odds with civic cohesion and community. One cannot, I think, make the one-to-one equation: *pornē* = city.

It does not necessarily follow then that commercial prostitution being deemed unsuitable for sympotic conviviality represented a rejection of the city or that the symposium's mystifying embrace of the *hetaira* as a quasi *philos* represented a rejection of civic bonds of *philia*. Certainly, the wealthy symposiast could take pleasure in his privileged access to glamorous, expensive *hetairai*, but enjoyment of class privilege does not exclude feeling fundamental bonds with one's fellow citizens over and above class at the same time (Hammer 2004, 503).[54] Indeed, the polis was characterized by the accommodation of social difference and socio-economic inequality to civic equality and community.[55] The symposiast's enjoyment of the *hetaira* would better be said to reflect tensions within the city than a rejection of it. Moreover, as I have been arguing here, where the *hetaira* coincided with the *pornē*, the symposiast's experience—of bonding with nonkin males in the enjoyment of liberal pleasures—had something fundamental in common with that of the customer of the brothel. Where Kurke argues that the ambivalence of the *hetaira* is attributable to an ambivalence in elitist ideology that causes instability and "flip-flopping," I hope to have shown how both sides of the *hetaira* are integrally attributable to the orientation of the symposium as an institution of male nonkin homosociality that facilitated a man's integration into civic community.[56] In this view, the symposium socialized a man by detaching him from narrow, private household interest—which is also to say class interest inasmuch as the *oikos* as the unit of economic and biological production and reproduction was also the basic unit of wealth and birth difference—and attaching him to a larger common interest and identity.

Thus, when it comes to thinking about the different categories of women, I agree with Davidson when he says that "while it is true that the Greeks often talked about the world in binary terms as polarized extremes . . . the terms of the opposition might change all the time" (1998, xxv). When the matter at issue is the contrast between the symposium as an institution of sociality, of personal bonds, in contradistinction to the impersonal, socially disembedded relations of the marketplace, the opposition between *hetaira* and *pornē* is marked. When, however, it is a question of the symposium as an institution of male nonkin conviviality as instantiated in liberal pleasure, identifying convivial society with civic community in contradistinction to household interests and identities, the opposition between wife and prostitute is marked, and *hetaira* and *pornē* are collapsed into one category. McClure has argued that "the lack of spatial stability [vis-à-vis the *hetaira* belonging to private space and the *pornē* to public] parallels the unstable social identity of the hetaera and the porne; while the porne inhabited brothels and streets, the hetaera and auletris brought this part of the city into the homes of citizens, but never permanently" (2003a, 16). It has been my purpose not only to bear this claim out but to show how this dynamic worked and with what significance and effect for symposium and city.

Symposium and City

What emerges is a preliminary view of the symposium quite different from that held by many scholars. Yet this is not the only view. Some scholars have been struck by the ways the convivial community of the banquet appears to mirror the larger civic community of the polis. Pauline Schmitt Pantel, with Murray the leading scholar of feasts and banquets in Greek history, questions whether it makes sense to think of the symposium, at least in the archaic period, according to a dichotomy of public and private. She observes the basic ways the archaic symposium was congruent and identified with other collective rituals and institutions, such as the sacrificial feast and phalanx, and argues that these together in fact constituted the public sphere.[57] Florence Dupont has drawn significant analogies between civil law and the laws of the banquet (1977, 21–39). Murray calls the *Theognidea* "vraiment une collection de poèmes qui expriment la voix normative du *symposion*" (1992, 67). Yet Daniel Levine (1985) has pointed to the ways Theognis appears to represent the symposium as a microcosm of the polis. Others have concurred.[58] As I say, the picture I have presented can only be preliminary. To bear it out will require systematic reexamination of what is a very complex institution with a very long history. By exploring how the *hetaira* and *pornē* were in certain respects parallel rather than antithetical figures, and concomitantly how the *andrōn* and brothel were parallel spaces, I hope, however, to have sketched a picture of a symposium that might indeed be understood as microcosm of polis.[59]

I suggest that rather than representing a withdrawal from the agora to the *andrōn*, the symposium brought the outside in. As a function of the symposium's mediation of *oikos* and polis, the *andrōn* mediated between the domestic interior and civic exterior. As a space of male nonkin homosociality, the exclusivity of the *andrōn* within the house respected the seclusion and integrity of the household and the man's role as master of his *oikos*. The life of the polis, however, required the reconciliation of a man's household interests with his place in the civic community. He had to transcend narrow private interest and identify with a larger common, public interest. The symposium's exclusion of the productive world of the *oikos* at once protected the integrity of the household and integrated a man into the reciprocity of an egalitarian nonkin community of liberal pleasures that transcended private household interest. The symposium brought the world of the city, including its antiproductive sexuality, into the house, taking the symposiast in his own dining room out of his household and into the city.

NOTES

1. This view is founded especially on Oswyn Murray's pioneering work on the symposium. It has been taken up in the important and influential work of Ian Morris and Leslie Kurke, for whom Murray's symposium provides the institutional locus for an elitist ideology at odds with the middling ideology of the city. "Anti-city" is Kurke's gloss. See Kurke 1997, 111–12; Kurke 1999, 17–18, 181; Morris 1996, 21, 32–34; and Morris 2000, 178–85. The elitist picture drawn by Murray is also present, *mutatis mutandis*, in many other recent treatments or mentions of the institution. Some prominent examples include Balot 2001, 76–77, 87–89; Burton 1998, 146; Cooper and Morris 1990, 77–81; J. Davidson 1998, esp. 43–53 and 222–27 (although note the important qualifications he introduces at 227–38, with which I am very sympathetic but would take further); Fisher 1988; Luke 1994; Neer 2002; and Stehle 1997, 213–57.

2. See Murray 1983a, 263; Murray 1992, 67–68; and Murray 1995a, 232–33, 239–40.

3. For sympotic sexuality in general as anticivic or anticommunal, see Murray 1994, 48–53; Murray 1995a, 230–31; and Stehle 1997, 250. For the *hetaira* as a creature of the closed and mystified relations of gift exchange, belonging to the private space of the interior, in contradistinction to the *pornē* as belonging to the open and transparent order of commodity exchange and to the public space of the exterior, see J. Davidson 1998, 109–36; and J. Davidson 2006, 36. For this mapping onto a class opposition between exclusive elite society, which is to say sympotic society, and inclusive polis society and hence onto a political opposition between elitist and egalitarian ideologies, see Kurke 1997; Kurke 1999, 175–219; and Morris 2000, 182 (following Kurke).

4. See Corner 2005, 75–76, 250–55, 380–88.

5. On the spatial organization of Greek houses as emphasizing the close sharing of exterior, public space by households but at the same time controlling access to and emphasizing the privacy of the interior space of family life, see Jameson 1990, 179–83. On this, and the concern spatially to control interaction between kin and nonkin, with the *andrōn* serving as the space for receiving outsiders, separate from the space of family, and rigorously separating women of the household from nonkin men, see Nevett 1995; and Nevett 1999,

123–26, 154–66. See also Morris 2000, 125, 147–50, 280–86, on these subjects, including the opposition of male/exterior/light and female/interior/dark and its instantiation in domestic spatial organization. On private and public, and male and female, space and social spheres, see D. J. Cohen 1991, 70–97.

6. Expense could also be lavished on the floor of the *andrōn*. Some of the earliest Greek mosaics, dating to the end of the fifth century, are found in *andrōnes*, and mosaic flooring is found, as it spread through Greece, primarily as decoration for the *andrōn*. See J. W. Graham 1974. See also Jameson 1990, 189; and Nevett 1995, 376–77.

7. On the distinctive form and features of the *andrōn* and their being dictated by the room's function as a sympotic dining room, see Jameson 1990, 188–91; Nevett 1995, 369–72; Nevett 1999, 84–85; Bergquist 1990; and Cahill 2002.

8. Murray and Eva Stehle both put nonkin homosociality, as removed from the world of the *oikos* and invested in building bonds over and across household interests and identity, at the center of their view of the symposium. They regard this as setting sympotic community in opposition to civic community, but I hold that the polis was predicated on exactly this sort of bond, a bond that at once respected the household as the basic unit of society and yet integrated households into society by uniting citizen males outside the *oikos* in a superordinate, common identity to which individual household interests were subordinated (see Corner [forthcoming]).

9. Thus, for example, Aristodemos and Alcibiades are guests who arrive at Agathon's without invitation (174b–e and 212c–e), although they are not *aklētos* in the manner of the parasite, who is of a quite different category and status and who represents an even greater degree of openness in the banquet, although of a highly qualified and compromised sort. They are what Plutarch calls *skias* (*Quaest. conv.* 707a–710a). For different views on the appropriate limits to such openness, see 645f–646a and 678e.

10. This is not to say that all were in practice welcome, that people did not keep at least to the extended circle of their friends and that those circles would not have reflected differences in social milieux including class. My point is that functionally the symposium, as it transcended household interests and built egalitarian community across kinship, served to open otherwise closed spaces and relationships to a wider society. For further discussion of this point and of whether the symposium is rightly thought of as a *hetaireia* (in the sense of a club and further in the sense of a political cabal), see my forthcoming article. On the threshold and the protection of privacy but also on its limits (the opening of the *oikos* to the outside, the integration of the man into nonkin male community, the mediation of public and private interest, and the integration of household into polis), see D. J. Cohen 1991, 70–97.

11. This suggestion is unlikely given the reality that women were not in fact secluded but did go out and that poorer women could not rely on servants to allow them to avoid work and domestic activities that exposed them to nonkin men. For an excellent summary overview of the scholarly debate and the evidence on which it depends, see Kapparis 1999, 16, 217–21.

12. See J. Davidson 1998, 112–13, 128 (also Lycurg. *Leoc.* 40); and Morris 2000, 125 (cf. Lys. 1.4). See also D. J. Cohen 1991, 139–70.

13. Those who have presumed him to be the woman's husband have instead imagined him to be returning home after a revel. See Neils 2000, 211. For the *kōmos* and *komasts*, see n. 35 below.

14. See Neils 2000, 213 and n. 37.

15. Foucault 1990, building on Dover 1978.

16. See C. Patterson 1991b (on being "yokemates," 53; see also LSJ s.v. *suzugos*).

17. See DuBois 1988, 39–85.

18. See Kapparis 1999, 212–13, and the collection of sources cited there.

19. See Halperin 1990. See also Morris 1996, 22–24; Morris 2000, 116–17, 145–46, 149; Kurke 1997, 127–30; and Kurke 1999, 185–99. James Davidson (1998, 77–91, 112–14, 127–31, 237) is sympathetic to the view that the openness and accessibility of street and brothel prostitutes had an equalizing force in making sexual pleasure commonly and easily available, outside of exclusive social and domestic relations. He rejects (1997, 168–82, 253–55, 277, 313–14; also 2001), however, K.J. Dover's view that the Greeks conceived of sex as an asymmetrical act done by an active, penetrating subject to a passive, penetrated object, and so also objects to Foucault's and David Halperin's view that the Greeks thereby experienced sexuality as an expression and enactment of civic status. Davidson argues that sociosexual roles were instead articulated around norms of autonomy in relation to desire. My view is that the evidence supports the idea that both status and self-mastery were at play, and indeed that Foucault has given a convincing account of how they formed an integral complex whereby the freedom of the citizen was experienced both in mastery of oneself and concomitantly in mastery over noncitizen others.

20. For mastery of one's own desire as a condition of freedom, see Foucault 1990, 23, 41–45, 48–50, 69–72, 78–86.

21. On the *pornē* as belonging to the space of the outside, as opposed to the protected world of the interior, see J. Davidson 1998, 77–91, 112–14, 127–31; and J. Davidson 2006, 36. See also Halperin 1990, 102.

22. Trans. Miller 1996, 89. For further exegesis, see Corner (forthcoming).

23. See Svenbro 1976, 50–59; Vernant 1989a, 59–61; Thalmann 1984, 143–46; and Thalmann 1998b, 102–3. I disagree with William Thalmann's claim (1998b, 102) that need and dependence necessarily connote class in a way that implicates a hierarchical, vertically stratified vision of society—a vision at odds with the polis. Rather, I would argue that the opposition we see here is consistent with civic ideology inasmuch as it is (as in the Theognis poem) an opposition to want both in its sense of need and in its sense of desire and so, in terms of normative self-image, positions the symposium "in the middle," as a community of "middling men" between both the needy poor and the greedy rich. This is not to say that need did not allow elite symposiasts to enjoy their wealth and their distance from the poor but rather that it did so in a way that simultaneously allowed for their integration into broader civic society, which is indeed characteristic of how the polis sought (however imperfectly) to avoid *stasis* by accommodating socioeconomic inequality to civic equality and community. See, inter alia, J. Davidson 1998, 232–38; Morris 1996, 22–24; and Morris 2000, 115–16, 138–44, 162–65.

24. Kaibel takes the quotation as beginning with "*khreia*," but I follow *PCG*.

25. I plan on treating the figure of the parasite at length in another essay.

26. For food, drink, and sex as constituting a set, regarded ethically and psychologically as qualitatively equivalent objects of desire (differing only in the intensity, not the kind, of desire they inspired), see Foucault 1990, 50–52.

27. Joan Burton (1998) has challenged the consensus among scholars that citizen women were consistently excluded from symposia, but I do not find her reading of the sources persuasive and would argue that all the contrary examples that she produces are exceptions that prove the rule: see "Appendix: Did 'Respectable' Women Attend *Symposia*? A Response to Joan Burton," in Corner 2005, 474–78.

28. On this aspect of the *hetaira*, in representation and in practice, see Carey 1992, 15–16, 102–3; Kurke 1996, 54–62; Kurke 1997, 137–39; Kurke 1999, 209–11; J. Davidson 1998, 77, 92–93; Kapparis 1999, 7–8; McClure 2003a, 7; and Glazebrook 2005a, 170–71, 178–79, 182. For these traits as establishing a systematic contrast between the *hetaira* and the wife, see also Kurke 1997, 113, 118–19, 133, 145–56; and Kurke 1999, 181, 183, 186–87, 201, 218–19.

29. See C. Patterson 1991a, 284–87; C. Patterson 1998, 200; Ogden 1996, 100–106; Glazebrook 2005a; and Glazebrook 2006.

30. On *enguē*, see C. Patterson 1991a, 51–52; and Ogden 1996, 84. On the exclusion of courtesan and concubine from marriage altogether, not only *enguē*, see C. Patterson 1991a, 56–59; C. Patterson 1998, 199–203; Mossé 1991; and Ogden 1996, 100–106. Patterson and Ogden concentrate on Athens, but for the claim that the same general pattern applies across most of Greece, see Ogden 1996, 277–88. The questions here, about marriage, legitimacy, concubinage, and so forth, are not uncontroversial—they have been the subject of long debate—but I find Patterson's and Ogden's treatments overall convincing and authoritative.

31. For spending on a *hetaira*, as on other convivial pleasures, as being at odds with and potentially destructive of household economy, see J. Davidson 1998, 186–205; McClure 2003b, 264–65; Glazebrook 2005a, 170–71; and Glazebrook 2006, 128–29.

32. On the Callimachus fragment as philosophical parody, see Davidson 1998, 104; and McClure 2003a, 84. Kurke (2002, 57) reads it as a democratic challenge to the order of the banquet, but it is perfectly in keeping with the symposium's isonomic norms of distribution and participation. On Phryne, see J. Davidson 1998, 225; and J. Davidson 2006, 29.

33. Thus compare Isae. 3.11, 13, 15, 16, 77 with [Dem.] 59.19, 20, 23, 41.

34. On *ho boulomenos*, see Hansen [1991] 1999, 71–72.

35. Further to this point, I would observe that in the Isaeus passage quoted in the body of the text, the context is not just of the *symposion* proper but of the *kōmos*, when the fluid network of sympotic society would materialize as symposiasts sallied forth and visited one another, forming a society of the streets, a larger instantiation of the network of male non-kin homosociality mixing across households and through the city. The role of the alleged *hetaira* in this scene is one familiar from many vase paintings: the courtesan orgiastically carousing with the symposiasts in the streets and public spaces, thoroughly blurring the distinction between courtesans and the flute girls and streetwalkers of the outside as the space of the *andrōn* flowed into that of the streets. Murray (1990c) has argued that the *kōmos* was an occasion for symposiasts to cement their bonds by committing outrages against the city

and the general population and so, in fact, going outside only reinforced the separateness and exclusivity of the group. This, I think, depends on an unjustified generalization from the minority of cases, especially in the unusual circumstances of late fifth-century Athens, when the symposium operated as a cabalistic *hetaireia*. Certainly conflict and disorder could attend the *kōmos*, but most of this seems to have occurred between the symposiasts themselves and often played out rivalries within the elite (see Garland 1991 and, for an example of this typical form of drunken dispute, see Dem. 54.). Furthermore, I would observe that one of the transgressive *hetaireiai* that Murray points to (157–60), the Kakodaimonistai, were by their choice of name representing themselves as standing in opposition to sympotic as much as civic norms of piety, moderation, and good order (see Fisher 1992, 146). Sympotic confraternity could be attached to a bid for power within the city, but this is not to say that the symposium was an anti-city. Rather, it is to say that the tensions of the city were also reflected and played out in the symposium.

36. The courtesan in question, moreover, is one of the grand *hetairai*, Lais, and her lover Aristippus does not attempt to deny the characterization; he merely indicates that to have use of a courtesan in common with many others is normal and unproblematic.

37. Trans. Benner and Fobes 1949, 205.

38. *Pornas* is Meiser's emendation of *heortas*, whereas Pierson, as cited in Benner and Fobes 1949, 203 n. 10, provides *hetairas*. If we follow Pierson, then of course no explicit parallel is drawn in the text, but I think that nevertheless the *hetaira*'s correspondence to the *pornē*—as an open object of civic sexuality belonging to public space—is still quite clear.

39. On the *hetaira* as *pallakē*, see M. Henry 1985, 4–5; P. G. McC. Brown 1990, 248–50; C. Patterson 1991a, 283–85; J. Davidson 1998, 101; and Kapparis 1999, 9.

40. As Christopher Carey (1992, 102–3) thinks.

41. See J. Davidson 1998, 80–82; J. Davidson 2004, 170; J. Davidson 2006, 37–39; and McClure 2003a, 21–22.

42. For Chrysis's ambiguous integration into the household, and her definite exclusion from the position of wife, see C. Patterson 1998, 199–203. See also M. Henry 1985, 73 (with n. 123): "This blending of Chrysis' roles may have been indicated by her stage dress. While the mosaic [the Samia mosaic from the series at the House of Menander in Mytilene] shows her wearing the hetaira's diadem, she wears the same garments as do married women in the rest of the series."

43. Trans. Arnott 2000, 97.

44. See J. Davidson 1998, 95–105, 120–27; Kurke 1997, 113–18, 133–37; Kurke 1999, 183–86, 201–9; McClure 2003b; and Faraone 2006.

45. On the formula and its sense, see Gomme and Sandbach 1973 on *Dyskolos* 842; Fantham 1975, 46 n. 6; Vernant 1988, 73; C. Patterson 1990, 56 n. 64, C. Patterson 1991b, 52; and Ogden 1996, 38. On legitimacy and illegitimacy (and the terms can be misleading in their application to Greece), see C. Patterson 1990 and Ogden 1996.

46. See Ogden 1996, 100–106, and the sources cited there.

47. See Krenkel 1988, 1293.

48. On the *hetaira* being assimilated to men in appearance and in sexual role: in vase

painting, see Kurke 1997, 133–37; and Kurke 1999, 201–9; in literature, see McClure 2003b, 272–73, 285.

49. On the instability of reference and on the variety of categories and conditions of prostitutes and scholars' various attempts to make sense of them, see Chantraine s.v. *pernēmi*; Fantham 1975, 51; Vernant 1988; Dover 1978, 20–21; Brown 1990, 247–50; Carey 1992, 1–17; J. Davidson 1998, 73–77; J. Davidson 2006, 31, 36–39; Kurke 1997, 107–9; Kurke 1999, 178–79; Kapparis 1999, 5–8, 422–24; McClure 2003a, 9–22; and E. E. Cohen 2006, 98–99.

50. See McClure 2003a, 9–22; McClure 2006, 7; Dover 1978, 21; P. G. Brown 1990, 247–50; Kapparis 1999, 408–9; Miner 2003.

51. Kurke 1997, 107, 110–13, 115–16, 127, 145–46; Kurke 1999, 180–83, 185–87, 195, 218–19.

52. Kurke 1997, 113, 118–19, 133, 145–56; Kurke 1999, 181, 183, 186–87, 201, 218–19.

53. Hammer's "Ideology, the Symposium, and Archaic Politics" as a whole presents a challenging critique of the kind of polar model employed by Kurke and Morris, and in particular a critique of the conception of the symposium as anti-city, with which I am very sympathetic.

54. "[H]ow does the invention of the *hetaira* in the symposium symbolize an 'anti-city?' The answer, as we have seen, rests upon a conflation of political equality with cultural egalitarianism, a conflation that is dictated by a framework that politicizes and then places into the binaries of *polis*/anti-*polis* every aspect of human life. Absent any limits to what is meant by 'symbolic sameness,' aristocratic efforts at distinction, display, consumption, and even seclusion can be interpreted as politically subversive" (Hammer 2004, 503). See also J. Davidson 1998, 232–38, for ways in which differences of wealth, as experienced in consumption, could coexist with "ideological class blindness."

55. See also n. 23.

56. Kurke 1997, 119, 133, 139, 142–46; Kurke 1999, 187, 201, 213, 218–19.

57. Schmitt Pantel and Schnapp 1982; Schmitt Pantel 1985, 1987, 1990, and 1992, 17–52. As has been indicated here, I do not view this correspondence between symposium and city as limited to the archaic period but as an essential and enduring characteristic of the institution.

58. See Donlan 1985a, 237–38 (I disagree, however, with the limit Donlan sees to the analogy of symposium to city: see Corner [forthcoming]); and Anhalt 1993, 79–101. In Pauline Schmitt Pantel's view, the city to which the symposium corresponds is the "aristocratic city." The potential problem with this characterization, as I see it, is that Schmitt Pantel does not elaborate on or define what she means by "aristocratic," and if aristocratic is construed in a certain way then aristocratic city comes to mean something very like Murray's, Morris's, and Kurke's anti-city. There is a similar and related problem, I think, with Emily Anhalt's claim (81) that while "the *polis* is described in terms of a symposium, and the symposium is described in terms of a *polis*" in the *Theognidea*, for Theognis the polis means only "his political party." I do not object to the view that the symposium sometimes provided a forum for groups pursuing power in the city, nor to the claim that such

groups could be committed to a narrower, more exclusive vision of the polis, but this is not to say that Theognis did not believe in a civic community larger than a particular faction or in a public sphere greater than private party interest. Nor do I think that there was any necessary connection between the symposium and a particular partisan political position. Indeed Morris, while arguing (2000, 161) that the symposium represented in its very form and function an elitist anti-city, seeks to square this with the "middling" commitments of the *Theognidea* by adopting a position similar to Anhalt's but then goes on to argue that there were nevertheless also "middling," antielitist symposia (1996, 27–28; 2000, 163, 169, 191). Kurke instead proposes that the *Theognidea* preserves in one corpus a tradition of contestation between elitist and middling traditions (1999, 28; criticized by Hammer 2004, 490). Here I have suggested a way in which the symposium might be understood to accommodate a sense of elite social difference but nevertheless also give the elite a sense of common identity and interest with other citizen males.

59. See Murray 1992, 66, for the objection to the claim that the symposium was a microcosm of the polis and my response (Corner, forthcoming).

4 Woman + Wine = Prostitute in Classical Athens?

CLARE KELLY BLAZEBY

The image in figure 4.1 depicts two women; one holds a drinking cup to her chest while holding out another to her companion who plays the *aulos*. They recline against cushions and are naked apart from jewelry and headwear. To someone unfamiliar with the scholarship surrounding Attic red-figure pottery, the scene represents nothing more than two women enjoying wine, music, and each other's company. However, the caption below the scene in *Women in the Classical World* explains that this is a drinking cup "with a pair of hetairai amusing themselves as if at a symposium; their nudity and poses, as well as the drinking vessels they hold, make it clear that these are not what the Athenians would consider respectable women" (Fantham et al. 1994, 118). The authors further explain that drinking cups offer "many images of naked hetairai by themselves, which must have functioned like pinups for male consumers" and that on the cup in question, "one pair [of *hetairai*] faces each other, relaxed on pillows, as if having their own private, all-girl symposium, probably a male fantasy" (Fantham et al. 1994, 116–17).

Sarah Pomeroy (2002, 109–10) describes the image on an archaic Laconian cup (see fig. 4.2) as depicting "women and men together at a symposium. Because the woman reclines with the man and doubtless drinks wine as he does, some viewers, perhaps because they are more familiar with the iconography of Athenian vase painting, may deduce that she is a hetaira." The woman is absolved from this charge however with the explanation that "Spartan girls and women regularly drank wine," and the conclusion drawn by Pomeroy is that we must therefore be viewing a religious scene.

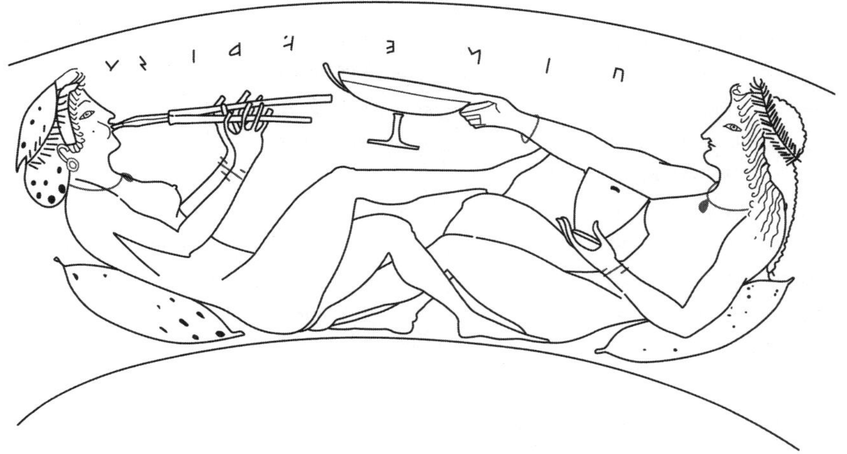

Figure 4.1. Artist unknown. Attic red-figure *kylix*, ca. 520–510 BCE. Museo Arqueológico Nacional, Madrid, 11.267. Drawing by Tina Ross.

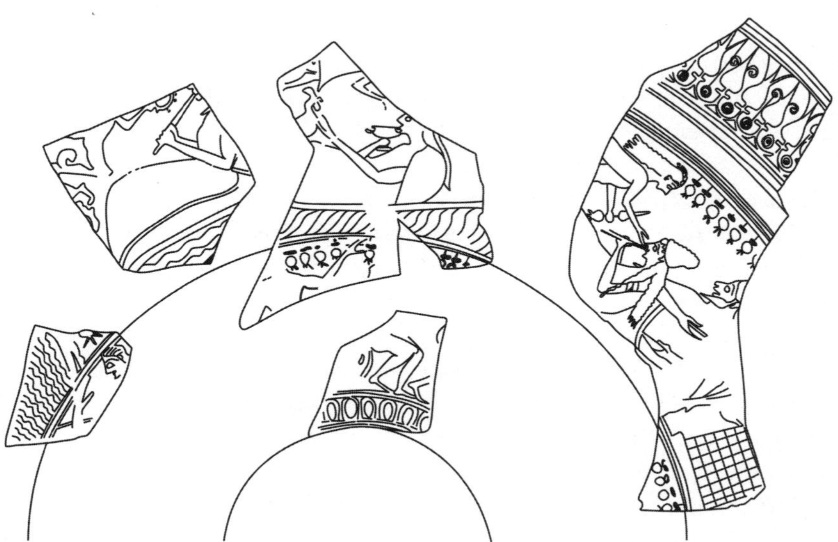

Figure 4.2. Arcesilas painter. Laconian cup fragments, ca. 565 BCE. Samos (Heraion) K1203, K1541, K2402, and Staatliche Museum, Berlin Charlottenburg, 478x, 460x. Drawing by Tina Ross after Maria Pipili in Pomeroy 2002.

Looking more closely at these images, what exactly is it that would have us understand these women as particularly Athenian *hetairai*? The women in figure 4.1 are naked, but there are no men involved, so must nudity automatically be indicative of a sexualized scene involving prostitutes? As Sian Lewis rightly points out, "prostitution is a trade, not an identity" and questions "whether 'hetaira' is something a woman can 'be' on a pot: can there be a prostitute without a customer?" (2002, 99, 101). Lewis cites ten other drinking cups with scenes of women reclining and drinking in the company of other women but without male partners (2002, 113); nudity aside, what else could possibly suggest to scholars that these women are not respectable? The answer lies quite simply in the fact they are drinking wine and that the images are painted on drinking cups.

Wine and Men: Sympotic Tyranny

According to Pomeroy (1975, 143), "wine drinking was an activity ideally reserved for men," and the study of wine drinking of the Greek classical period has almost without exception focused on elite men at play in the symposium. The symposium is the framework around which all studies of classical Greek drinking are built (Dunbabin 1991; Dunbabin 1998; Murray 1990c; Lissarrague 1990a; Murray and Teçuşan 1995; Schmitt Pantel 1997), regardless of a body of archaeological and literary evidence that suggests that this type of drinking was enjoyed primarily by a small minority of wealthy, politically active, elite, and perhaps predominantly Athenian, men and their emulators. The symposium proper would continue to resist widening participation throughout the fifth and fourth centuries BCE and remain a largely private and aristocratic male preserve.

Despite this, any and all contexts for wine consumption have become "symposia," and images of men and women drinking (either together or alone) are described in purely sympotic terms. Since we know that the highly ritualized and religious symposium was a men-only affair, the consequences of all drinking being understood as "sympotic" has tremendous implications for the women in our scenes, as the only women we know who could be present were hired entertainers who may or may not have provided sexual services, as well as the *hetairai* who most certainly did. Thus discussion surrounding the status of Athenian women depicted in red-figure painting polarizes sharply when wine is involved: wine drinking is immediately viewed as the indicator par excellence that a woman has crossed the distinct boundary from decent woman to whore and has transgressed into the world of male drinking, that she is a prostitute attending the symposium.

So was female wine drinking truly only the preserve of prostitutes at the symposium? What of ordinary "decent" women, foreign women, and female slaves? Studies of the symposium overstate what can reasonably be inferred about the drinking habits of everyone who was not a rich citizen male in classical Athens, and in addition to the question of whether "decent" women drank, there is the matter of the drinking habits of nonelite males, non-Greeks, and the inhabitants of *poleis* who did not rely on the symposium to cement political and kinship ties (see esp. Dunbabin 1991; Dunbabin 1998; Murray 1990c; Lissarrague 1990a; Murray and Tecuşan 1995; Schmitt Pantel 1997). What of wine drinking during the day or indeed at any time outside the evening symposium? Can we really believe that the enjoyment of wine was open only to those men eligible for an invitation to an evening drinking party and the prostitutes they took with them? Any reader who relied on the available academic literature to gain insight into classical Greek wine consumption would be forgiven for reaching just such a conclusion.

Wine and Women: *Not* the Sympotic Ideal

The participation of women in Greek drinking parties varied over time and place (Burton 1998, 143). During the classical period, it is taken for granted that when a woman is present at a symposium she is a prostitute ([Dem.] 59.33). But what of feasting and drinking in the home with family and friends or on special occasions? A fragment of Menander describes just such a family gathering of a young man, his father and mother, aunt, aunt's father, and another old woman who drink, eat, and talk together at a dinner party (*thurōros*) (*PCG* 186). Mixed-gender drinking clearly was acceptable in some contexts. Female students of Plato might have attended philosophers' symposia, and the Pythagoreans and Epicureans were remarkably open to women as followers (Burton 1998, 148).

Festivals and meetings with friends and neighbors (Ar. *Thesm.* 348–49) provide by far the greatest opportunities for commensality among the women portrayed in Athenian comedy (Wilkins 2000, 61). On each of these occasions, the humor centers on drinking rather than eating and on the drinking of strong wine in particular. Athenian state religion, with its many cults, festivals, and rituals, was an integral part of everyday life, and women all social positions, both native and foreign, would come together and honor the gods, participating just as much as men. Wine was provided in abundance for the women celebrating the Haloa festival in Eleusis (Fantham et al. 1994, 83, 92), and women would drink together at religious occasions such as the Thesmophoria, a three-day event in honor of Demeter.

Classical Athenian women had ample opportunity to drink wine, so we should not expect that all of those who did were prostitutes. The issue I address here therefore is whether "decent" women were engaged in more wine drinking, and wine retailing, than Athenians writing of the fifth and fourth centuries would have us believe with its "inebriate" female stereotype (Just 1989, 166) and whether images such as those on the vases form a perfectly innocent genre of women engaging in commensal drinking of their own, a genre masked by a need to describe all drinking as "sympotic" and all women reclining and drinking in a "sympotic" manner as prostitutes.

Ancient Wine Drinking: An Anthropological Viewpoint

The classical Greeks would not have enjoyed such a diverse range of liquid consumables as we do today. In addition, owing to the lack of clean, fresh, drinking water, wine—albeit in a weaker form than that consumed in order to become inebriated—could have been drunk continuously throughout the day and would also have provided essential calories. Typhoid and other dangerous microbes rapidly die when mixed with wine (Singleton 1996, 75). Food-poisoning organisms and human pathogens cannot survive and certainly cannot multiply in the acidic, tannic, and alcoholic medium of wine. Whether the ancient Greeks understood its mechanism of action, wine in antiquity promoted health because it could not be the source of microbial health problems, unlike water. Wine, therefore, could have been used to make contaminated water safe, as well as more palatable.

Today in Europe and North America, coffee or tea act as indicators of the time of day, and the switch from nonalcoholic drinks to alcoholic signals the switch from work time to play time. In the past, to drink alcohol for breakfast would not have raised any eyebrows, and consumption of wine would not have signified specific and bounded leisure time, although the strength of the mixture might have varied significantly. Leisure and relaxation are historically emergent terms, dependent on the separation of work from home and of one period of the day from another. The conception of leisure as a definite and bounded period of time is a feature of the industrial and postindustrial world of work. Preindustrial societies would have reckoned their time divisions by rhythms dictated by sunrise and sunset, religious calendars of festival and feast days, and the ebb and flow of bodily energy. However, there is often an intellectualist assumption that leisure, or at least the more "important" elements of a culture's leisure activities, are exclusively the preserve of a "leisured" class (Fisher 1998, 84–88), and this assumption is especially prevalent in studies of classical Greek drinking. At the outbreak of the Peloponnesian War most Athenians were farmers (Thuc. 1.142.1). However, the havoc wrought on the countryside during the war brought a marked demographic shift to the city, where new small shops and workshops began to spring up among the houses. New urban drinking patterns and practices, far removed from the more nourishing and thirst-quenching uses of alcohol followed by agricultural laborers in the countryside, would soon develop. The scene depicted on Achilles' shield is said to have shown farm laborers ploughing a field at each end of which the laborer is handed a mug of "honey-sweet wine" (*Il.* 18.545). In much the same way that British agricultural laborers drank weak beer all day long (as did everyone else in pre-industrial Britain; see Bennett 1996, 16–17), it should not be assumed that there was any prohibition on wine drinking by women.

In many civilizations women are habitually excluded from drinking alcohol, but little is known about the source of such rules (Douglas 1987). According to our Greek sources citizen men, and those whose drinking behavior follows what can be described as a generally inclusive pattern, enjoy their wine in moderation and preferably in the company of other citizen men at the symposium. Ancient Greek written sources represent foreigners, slaves, and women as following a generally exclusive pattern by abusing their drink whenever and wherever they can, whether that be at home or in a *kapēleion* (tavern). Part of the rationale of these perceptions must be that sympotic drinking is kept orderly by the rules of the symposium, where the host regulates the size of the cups, the speed of the drinking, and the number of *kratēres* to be consumed during the evening, whereas other types of casual and nonregulated drinking and the places where such drinking occurs are not moderated by that or by any other principle of order. This is demonstrated beautifully in the image of what is thought to be a domestic storeroom scene (see fig. 4.3) depicting a woman drinking out of a cup bigger than her head, while a young slave girl follows with a wine skin on her shoulder lest her mistress run dry.

Sanctions on women's drinking can be partly explained by classical notions of the physical differences between the sexes. Medical knowledge at the time, based largely on the late classical theories of Aristotle, considered female temperament generally colder and moister than that of men (Mayhew 2004, 40–41).[1] The colder nature of women served as a context for their perceived sensitivity to alcohol, as alcohol was believed to possess a fiery quality that was incompatible with the female temperament. Wine especially was believed to enhance the sanguine nature of men, purging the phlegmatic humors associated with female characteristics. Therefore, when men drank they became more witty, vulgar, sensual, and manly—all characteristics considered completely inappropriate in women or rather completely inappropriate for classical Greek women. What about non-Greek women with different drinking attitudes and practices? According to Julian Reade, in

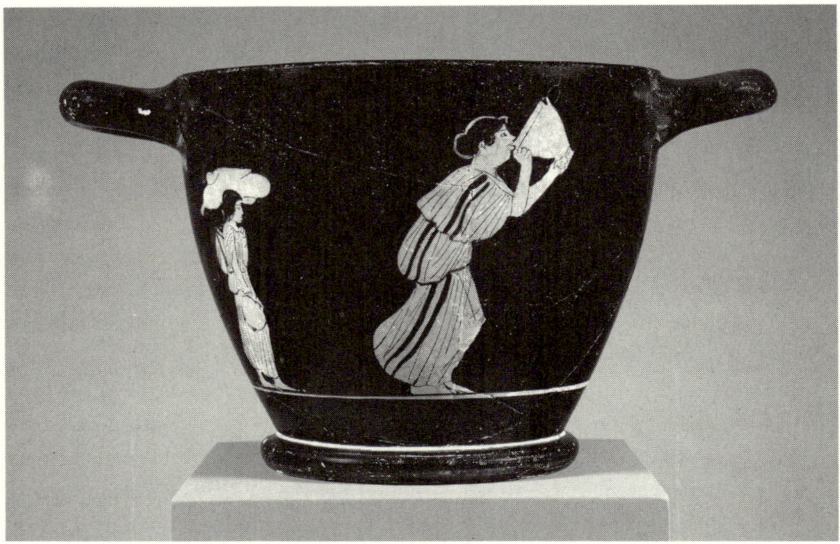

Figure 4.3. Artist unknown. Attic red-figure *skyphos*, ca. 470–460 BCE. J. Paul Getty Museum, Malibu, 86.AE.265 (Villa Collection). Terracotta; body: H: 15.3 x W (with handles): 27.5 x D: 17.9 cm; rim: D: 18.8 cm; foot: D: 12.1 cm.

Mesopotamia, for example, there was a custom of men and women drinking together (1995, 40).

Wine and Non-Greek Women: A Broader Perspective

In Egyptian Eighteenth Dynasty tomb scenes (ca. 1570–1320 BCE), women both offer and are offered alcohol with exhortations to "drink, be happily drunk, and make holiday!" (Poo 1995, 32). Tomb paintings from Beni-Hasan show us that beer and wine were drunk by the Egyptians often to excess, and that the women of the upper classes also partook in this practice; indeed wall paintings from Thebes depict women vomiting out of drunkenness (Lutz 1922, 99). According to an inventory of the income and expenses of the royal court at Thebes from the end of the Middle Kingdom (ca. 1800 BCE), the queen received five jars of beer on one day (Lutz 1922, 86). In an Egyptian bazaar scene dating to the Fifth Dynasty a woman offers a beverage to a prospective buyer. This market scene is significant since it demonstrates that in other Mediterranean countries, alcohol was sold by women in public places: women who may, at a later period, have traveled to work in Greece.

The frequent mention of wine and beer in Sumero-Akkadian documents would suggest that the Babylonians and Assyrians consumed substantial quantities of intoxicating liquors (Lutz 1922, 115). The Babylonians had the reputation of being heavy wine drinkers; apparently, they surpassed even the notorious wine-drinking Persians. Babylonia's wineshops and beer houses are described delightfully by Henry Lutz as "a favorite haunt for all kind of rabble that shunned the light" (1922, 123). According to tradition, Kish owed its existence to Queen Ku-Bau, who was a woman of obscure and humble origin (1922, 128) said to have achieved her initial popularity and influence as the keeper of a wine shop. The Code of Hammurabi devotes four paragraphs to the regulation of inns, which are called "wineshops," and a striking feature of the code is that it speaks only of female taverners. We know that there were near easterners and Egyptians living in Greece because from the late fourth century BCE onward Isis, Serapis, Zeus Ammon, and Baal were worshipped in the Piraeus (Garland 1987, 109), and it would be completely unreasonable to suppose that they did not bring their own customs and traditions with them at an even earlier date, women drinking and selling wine among them.

Women and Wine: Problems with the Literary Evidence

There are no ancient texts directly relating to women's drinking in classical Greece, and we are left to view our information through the filter of red-figure scenes, comic plays, curse tablets, and the works of scholars writing long after the classical period. Our ability to use ancient texts to explore the various aspects of the relationship between the literary and archaeological evidence is severely limited by the orientation of the sources. Our sources, written by literate men of some social standing, are keen to eulogize the ideal state of Athenian affairs, which is exactly what it was: an ideal. In the same way, Pericles idealizes Athenian women: "Not to be worse than your natural condition, such as it is, that is your great glory, and greatest is the reputation of that woman about whom there is least talk among men, whether in praise or in censure" (Thuc. 2.45.2).

Attic comedy shows that drinking by the elites in company is considered good, that drinking by males of lower class is bad, and that drinking by females is truly appalling (though apparently with terrific comic potential), especially the older they are. The desire (and ability) of women to drink in the vicinity of their houses often relates to the local *kapēleion*, and it is a frequent topic among women. In the following example from Antiphanes' *Akontizomenē* (fr. 25), and retold by Athenaeus (10.441b–c), a female drinker suggests that she lives close to a *kapēleion*:

"I have a neighbor who is a taverner; whenever I am thirsty and go to him he knows at once—and he is the only one—how I have it mixed. Never do I remember having drunk it too diluted or too strong."

In Aristophanes, a chorus of women invokes the Olympian gods to "castigate those who harm the feminine community," "worst of all" apparently being the barman or barmaid (*kapēlos ē kapēlis*) "who dares to serve short measure" (*Thesm.* 347–48). In Aristophanes' *Wealth*, women are accused of frequenting the tavern as often as men attend the lawcourts (973–74). In that play, the goddess Poverty is mistaken for a tavern keeper because, according to the character Chremylus, she screams at them "for doing no harm at all" (*Plut.* 457–58). He then asks if Poverty is the "*kapēlis* from round the corner, the one who never serves me a full *kotylē*?" (435–36). Although undoubtedly exaggerating for comic effect, Aristophanes has caricatured the stereotypical attributes of establishments well known to the audience and therefore recognized by all.

Aristotle remarks in the *Politics* that in democracies it is impossible to keep poor women from going out when they wish to (1300a). Demosthenes (57.45) refers to a period when citizen women had been forced to become wet nurses, wool workers, or grape pickers "owing to the misfortunes of the city in those days." In the same speech, a mother's poverty is said to have led her to serve as a nurse and to sell ribbons (57.31–34). Women who were not wealthy, privileged, and closely guarded citizens may not have lost social standing, or suffered a dent in their reputation, by enjoying time and a drink in a bar or, indeed, by working in one. Aristophanes portrays women as inveterate and insatiable drinkers (an impression later perpetuated by Athenaeus), and the women in his plays are not all prostitutes and slaves; many are decent wives.[2] A male character declares, "Women, you overheated dipsomaniacs, never passing up a chance to wangle a drink, a great boon to bartenders [*kapēloi*] but a bane to us—not to mention our crockery and our woollens!" (*Thesm.* 735–38). The word *kapēlos* is often used in its feminine form, *kapēlis*, and the impression given is that more women than men were actually employed as tavern keepers.

Pandokeutriai (female innkeepers) (Ar. *Lys.* 458; Ar. *Ran.* 114, 549–78) and *kapēlides* (female tavern keepers) (Ar. *Thesm.* 347; Ar. *Plut.* 1120–22; Theopompos Com. Fr. 25–29) also made use of skills practiced in the *oikos*, or household, transferring the labor itself to a distinct location (Brock 1994, 340). The milieu is low status; these women, too, had a reputation for bad language as well as dishonesty and are frequent targets of curse tablets. Probably attacked as much by commercial rivals as by customers, they are often associated with low-life figures like pimps and prostitutes (Brock 1994, 341). The two in *Frogs* are *metics* (resident aliens), since they look to their patrons Cleon and Hyperbolus for redress against Heracles-Dionysus (569–71).

A Curse on *Kapēleia*!

Some of the most informative written evidence for bars and their female staff comes from curse tablets (*katadesmoi*). Commissioned by real people and mentioning real businesses (as opposed to theatrical or oratorical constructs), these tablets provide an otherwise unknown glimpse into the world of the *kapēleion*, filling in the archaeological gaps such as the names of these taverns and their staff. All members of ancient society, it seems, used or knew of these tablets, which simply consisted of a thin sheet of folded or rolled lead pierced through by one or more nails (Gager 1992). Their intended function was to bring supernatural power to bear against persons and/or animals by calling on Hermes or Persephone to bring named persons under the control of the individual who commissioned or personally inscribed the tablet. Some of the tablets display the same elegant hand and highly formulaic language suggesting that professional scribes were employed (Gager 1992). Where the tablets were deposited in graves, a professional must surely (to our twenty-first-century sensibilities) have been commissioned, as it is highly unlikely that an ordinary individual would creep into the Kerameikos in the dead of night, open up the grave of a newly buried youth, and place the tablet in the corpse's right hand per requirement. The graves of those who had died young or violently were preferred because their souls were thought to remain in a restless state near their graves (Gager 1992). Wells and crevices were other preferred locations for the depositing of curses, presumably for the squeamish; the curse could simply be inscribed on a pottery shard and dropped down a hole in the ground. Lead seems to have remained the primary medium for wishing ill, as some of the curses testify, requesting that the person become as "cold and useless as this lead" (Gager 1992, 4).

Among the occupations listed in the tablets, the most common is that of taverner (Gager 1992). Who would wish them such extreme ill will, and who would have been prepared to deposit them in such a ghoulish manner, is open to speculation. It was perhaps an impoverished alcoholic refused credit, a less popular or prosperous establishment, or simply a disgruntled and drunken customer. The tablets also confirm that both women and men were proprietors and, as reference to their owners indicate, many were clearly slaves. Female slaves and freedwomen seem to have been particularly active as *kapēloi*, as evidenced by their names: Mania is Phrygian and Thraitta, used so often in the ancient world, simply meant "a [slave] woman from Thrace." However, we cannot discern whether these women were still tied to a master who put them to work in a business for which he was too respectable to be involved with himself or whether they had been freed but continued to work in one of the few professions available to them. That the wives of tavern keepers are included in the curse suggests they worked alongside their husbands and must have been known to the customers by name.

The following texts come from two fourth-century BCE Attic tablets excavated during work on the Athens-Piraeus railway (an exact location is not given) and are quoted in full from *Curse Tablets and Binding Spells from the Ancient World* (Gager 1992, 157–59; *IG* 3:87, 75):

> (*Side A*) I bind Kallias, the shop/tavern keeper who is one of my neighbors and his wife, Thraitta; and the shop/tavern of the bald man and the shop/tavern of Anthemiōn near [?] and Philōn the shop/tavern keeper. Of all of these I bind the soul, the work, the hands, and the feet; and their shops/taverns. I bind Sosimenes, his [?] brother; and Karpos his servant, who is the fabric seller and also Glukanthis, who is called Malthake, and also Agathōn the shop/tavern keeper the servant of Sosimenes: of all of these I bind the soul, the work, the life, the hands, and the feet.
>
> I bind Kittos my neighbor, the maker of wooden
> frames—Kittos's skill and work and soul and mind
> and the tongue of Kittos.
> I bind Mania [feminine] the shop/tavern keeper who is [located]
> near the spring and the tavern of Aristandros of
> Eleusis
> and their work and mind.
> The soul, hands, tongue, feet, and mind: all of these I
> bind to Hermes the Restrainer in the unsealed
> graves
>
> (*Side A*) I bind Anacharsis and I bind his workshop. I bind Artemis, the . . . and I bind the master of Artemis. I bind Humnis. I bind Rhodiōn the shop/tavern keeper. May Rhod[i?]ōn perish along with his workshop . . . [?] who works [there?]. I bind Rhodiōn the shop/tavern keeper, I bind the shop/tavern, and I bind also the store.
>
> (*Side B*) I bind Artemis and . . . and . . . may [?] gain power over Artemis . . . I bind the work . . . and the tongue. I bind Theodotus and the/this workshop. I bind Artemis and Philōn, his works . . . sister . . . friend . . .

Women and Bars: Beyond the Symposium

Although the majority of incomers to the city of Athens would be regarded as Athenian, coming as they did from Attica, over time resident aliens or *metics* who arrived to take advantage of new and expanding job opportunities would become a highly visible group within the polis; perhaps Thraitta and her husband referred to in the first curse tablet were such immigrants. The Piraeus had expanded to become a major Mediterranean harbor by the fourth century BCE and would have attracted individuals and social groups who would have been regarded as marginal to mainstream Athenian society. *Metics* fell into two distinct groups: aliens who arrived in Athens as artisans and tradesmen or political refugees and manumitted slaves who had achieved the status of *metic*, their former master standing as guardian (Isager and Hansen 1975, 69).

Many of these *metics* were barbarians from Lydia, Phrygia, Syria, and other remote regions (Xen. *Vect.* 2.3); however, grave markers from Athens demonstrate that freeborn *metics* were primarily Greeks from the Aegean and the colonies (Isager and Hansen 1975, 69). Non-Athenians (even other Greeks) were not allowed to own property in Athens and as a result would have formed a highly itinerant workforce forced to share rooms in *sunoikiai* (multioccupancy houses), take lodgings in inns, or sleep in the open. The development of new styles of drinking more appropriate to (or representative of) the increasing proportion of people moving to the new growing urban centers meant not just the emergence of traditional contexts for drinking but also the formation of new ones more appropriate to this new urban lifestyle and more representative of the diverse nationalities arriving to take advantage of the employment opportunities Athens and Attica had to offer.

In the *Gorgias*, Socrates describes the Athenian polis as reduced to "a swollen and pustular condition" on account of its being filled "with harbours and docks and walls and all that kind of silliness, thereby leaving no space for temperance and justice" (519a). In such a time of social dislocation in classical Attica the *kapēleion* may have evolved from its traditional function of grocer selling wine to the domestic market into a dedicated wineshop or tavern providing an essential center of light, warmth, and social interaction for lower-class itinerant workers newly arrived from the countryside. In the Piraeus especially, these shops would be places where the disoriented and lonely newcomer could meet and talk with his or her fellow country folk and gather information, such as where to find accommodation or work, and all of this in a place where others who spoke the same language might have gathered. For a newly arrived foreigner who was forced to sleep out in the open or who simply was unable to afford fuel to heat his or her living space, the tavern would have been an invaluable source of light and warmth. For those in shared lodgings or in shared accommodations the bar could be an escape from less desirable company.

In the classical aristocratic and literary tradition, the tavern and its proprietor were treated with disdain as the very embodiment of the disorderly and dishonest lowlife in the newly democratic city (J. Davidson 2007, 57–60). However, for the ordinary patrons of a local *kapēleion*, the institution must have served a whole range of functions that outside observers were simply incapable of understanding.

The *kapēleion* sits at the opposite end of the spectrum from the Greek idea of formal and organized commensality inherent in the symposium. Although some *kapēleia* would have functioned more as social clubs than as commercial wine dispensaries, in the tavern there would be none of the ordered drinking of the strictly regulated symposium, and individuals, men and women, would have felt no need to socialize or converse if they did not want to. According to François Lissarrague, the Greeks were not solitary drinkers; the consumption of wine was seen as a communal act (1990a, 19). However, an assertion such as this, which would appear, on the surface, to embrace Greek drinkers in their entirety, in fact really only refers to aristocratic men drinking at the symposium, a fact made clear by Lissarrague's use of the word "communal." Groups of friends, bands of thieves, gatherings of tradesmen, workmates, gossips, drunks, slaves, solitary drinkers, women—whoever felt able to drink in their local *kapēleion*—may well have shared a bond with other individuals choosing to drink in the same "local," but commensality was not what defined tavern drinking.

In opposition to the symposium, where drinking was characterized by shared pleasure, reciprocity, and mutual benefit for the participants, the kind of groups that may have formed in a *kapēleion* would have been bound more by friendship than by purely political affiliation or kinship ties, and commensality in the tavern was entirely incidental and unforced. Anonymous drinkers, such as travelers, foreigners, and transients, could find nonjudgmental company in a tavern along with warmth and light. Conversely, this nonjudgmental anonymity could also prove dangerous to democracy by allowing conspirators and outlaws to gather (Fisher 1999). Excessive alcohol consumption can undoubtedly induce antisocial and immoral behavior, and prostitutes would likely linger around taverns to capitalize on any loss of sexual inhibition or desire for company, but this does not mean that all women found at taverns were prostitutes. Foreign slaves and *metic* women who, as we already know, may not have shared the moralistic classical Greek notion that "decent" women should not drink in the company of men, may have used taverns as places to gather and meet friends or to drink alongside men from their own countries, who likewise saw no harm in women enjoying wine. *Kapēleia* could therefore be regarded as vital social spaces for the ordinary inhabitants of the Greek city. Indispensable social agencies, they were focal meeting places where business (not necessarily honest) and trade could be conducted, information exchanged, political issues debated, and social rituals performed. Taverns in the new and expanding Greek polis would have had an important role to play.

Perhaps with the slow and relentless adoption of democratic ideals throughout the classical period, the tables were being turned, and it was the aristocratic elites who now, consciously or unconsciously, considered themselves to be excluded, a dwindling band of nobility desperately clinging to the good old days when a man could wear his hair long and flaunt his wealth openly. Cultural groups can only survive insofar as their cultural differences persist, but since differences tend to diminish as groups interact, a strong mechanism must be at work to maintain any cultural distinctiveness in an environment in which there is significant intermixing (Wilson 2005). The symposium therefore should be viewed as an act of cultural preservation through boundary maintenance: a barrier erected between the "them" the symposium excluded, who now have access to wine whenever they wish in the *kapēleion*, and the "us" the symposium included, who might no longer have the time and money needed in order to enjoy alcohol at lavish dinner parties but who do at least know how to drink it properly and in the proper context.

Oswyn Murray described the symposium as "the organising principle of Greek life" (1995b, 7), and Joan Burton joins him in describing the symposium as one of the "central institutions" of ancient Greece (1998, 143). The symposium was undeniably important to a select circle, but Murray effectively discounts the lifestyle of the vast majority of the populace who would not, under normal circumstances, be considered for invitation. It was, throughout all of its history, part of the life of a minority of people in the classical Greek polis. In Sparta's communal messes, for example, a very different type of "democratic"' drinking took place. The Athenian symposium was never intended to be an "all-inclusive" affair. Its very exclusivity marked it, and its participants, as a cut above the ordinary populace—or at least, it did in theory. The majority of our evidence for the symposium comes from Athens, and there is no real evidence that the Athenian symposium was adopted with such enthusiasm elsewhere within Greece. Scholars have too often mistaken separation of spheres and roles for seclusion and isolation, and it does not follow that women, *metics*, and slaves did not have social and economic spheres of their own that centered around wine drinking. We must learn to distinguish between ideology and (sometimes conflicting) normative ideals if we are to truly understand the lives of classical Athenians.

Wine Drinking: Physical and Spatial Context

Studies of both the *kapēleion* and the symposium miss an engagement with the actual physical archaeological or spatial context. Studies of drinking carried out by classicists and philologists deal only with the written and iconographic evidence, and the tendency has been to take a wholly uncritical approach. For example, the Beazley Archive (online) refers only to the symposium as a context for drinking, and all scenes of drinking whether they involve men or women are described in sympotic terms (see also Osborne 1998). James Davidson (1998) was the first scholar to attempt to work with both the literary and the archaeological evidence, but in the same way that the literary sources are taken at face value, he simply relies on the excavators' interpretations of the archaeological material. He adds nothing new to our understanding of the archaeological context or physical setting of either the *kapēleion* or the symposium; there is no interrogation of the archaeological or the literary evidence (see Kelly Blazeby 2000; Kelly Blazeby 2006 for analysis and discussion of the archaeological evidence for "casual" and commercial drinking in classical Greece).

Without an understanding of the spatial context in which drinking took place, any attempt to laminate the textual evidence directly to the archaeological is doomed to failure. For example, Davidson describes the setting for the symposium as "the 'mens' room,' the *andrōn*, a small room with a slightly raised floor on all sides, which makes it one of the most easily identified spaces in the archaeology of the Greek house" (1998, 43), an understanding shared by Murray (1990c, 7). Katherine Dunbabin goes further, stating that "we are better informed about the physical environment of dining in classical antiquity than about almost any other activity. Written descriptions of dinners and symposia can be compared with illustrations, often detailed, in all the major media; these in turn can be used to complement the archaeological record" (1991, 121). Dunbabin also believes that a "Greek could go from Olynthus to Eretria, from Athens to Kassope, and find himself in familiar surroundings when invited to a symposium" (1998, 82) even though we have no evidence to suggest that the Athenian model of the ritualistic symposium was enjoyed anywhere other than Athens.

Wine and the *Andrōn*: A Return to the Symposium?

According to Murray "Greek commensality was essentially an all-male activity: it normally took place in the *andrōn*, the 'men's room'" (1990c, 6). *Andrōn* has come to describe what Janett Morgan (2005) calls simply a function-neutral "bordered room," which is fundamentally all that they are: rooms with raised borders around three sides on which couches could have been placed. Bordered rooms do exist outside Athens, but no written evidence supports any claim that they were used and experienced in like ways. Even the "illustrations of symposia" that Dunbabin (1991, 121) believes to be detailed do not actually refer directly to the symposium; it is merely assumed that because the figures involved are reclining with drinking cups they must be attending symposia. The exact context for the drinking taking place is never explicitly stated and could relate to any all-male or all-female drinking occasion in any location.

Archaeologists occasionally need to explain the layout of rooms in Greece that look like *andrōnes* but are found in religious sanctuaries at Perachora, Brauron, and Acrocorinth. Nancy Bookidis excavated the "*andrōnes*" at the Sanctuary of Demeter and Kore in Acrocorinth, a site of female religious cult (Bookidis and Fisher 1969; 1972; 1974; Bookidis and Stroud 1997; Bookidis, Hansen, Snyder, and Goldberg 1999). Burton considers the subject of women's commensality and their supposed exclusion from symposia and states that "the participation of women in the history of Greek commensality does not depend solely on female presence at male-defined symposia. Just as men had a wide range of venues in which they might socialize with one another, so too women" (1998, 143–44). Were, then, the so-called Demeter and Kore *andrōnes* places where women gathered to enjoy wine, their function masked by overzealous sympotic scholarship? What we encounter on pottery is not a photographic representation and cannot be reduced to the attribution of roles. The painters were not aiming to depict sisters, aunts, cousins, or friends, and hence our interpretations of relationships between the figures in all-female drinking scenes are merely speculative, but to call them all prostitutes is a gross oversimplification. Such an interpretation relies implicitly on the belief that these cups were for men to drink out of at the symposium, and again we fall victim to sympotic scholarship that interprets these scenes from a masculine perspective that sees women solely as sex objects (Lewis 2002). Such a sympotic interpretation, however, relies implicitly on the concept of a male Athenian viewer, but can we be sure that this is the context of use of these cups? Although they may be "symposium shapes" in origin, there is no evidence that they ever went near a symposium, and the reality is that the majority of intact cups were discovered overseas in Etrurian graves (see Stansbury-O'Donnell 2006 for data on the findspots of archaic black-figure pottery).

Wine and Religion: Female Worshippers

Scenes of women worshipping on drinking cups highlights in an interesting way the use of the *kylix* as a cult object: these cups were not just made solely for use at symposia but were used in religious practice too.[3] The prevalence of religious themes depicted on various types of drinking cup and the *kratēr* shows that these shapes cannot be defined in a meaningful way as "drinking vessels" or "symposium ware" because the reality is that they could have been utilized in any context in which a container to hold, pour, or drink liquid (not necessarily alcoholic) was required.[4]

Wine and wine drinking were explicitly celebrated in Athens during the festival of the Anthesteria in honor of the god Dionysus (Burkert 1985, 237). The festival lasted three days: on the first day (*pithoigia*) the jars of new wine were opened for the first time and the contents tasted. Samples of the wine were taken to the sanctuary of Dionysus "in the marshes," where they were mixed with water. After this, the worshippers were free to taste the wine themselves, and it is reasonable to assume that the rest of the day was spent in drinking.

The second day was the feast of the *choes* (Burkert 1985, 237), the *chous* being a type of wine jug with a round belly, short neck, and trefoil mouth; as wine could be bought by the *chous*, it may have represented a standard measure containing twelve *kotylai*.[5] Large numbers of this type of jug survive in miniature from Athens, seemingly because it was the custom to give them to children on the second day, though whether they contained wine for the children to drink is unknown. On the night of the second day it was traditional to revel with friends, and guests brought their own wine and cup to drink it from, apparently in silence (Parke 1977, 113).

The third and final day was the day of the pots (*chytrai*) in which vegetables were boiled and offered to Hermes in the underworld on behalf of the dead (Burkert 1985, 240). On the surface, it appears strange that the Athenians changed the focus for their worship on the third day of this festival from Dionysus and wine to boiled vegetables and Hermes, but the classical Greeks used boiled cabbage as an everyday hangover cure (Stafford 2001, 11). Might this be the practical origin of the ritual of eating boiled vegetables on the third day? Perhaps we can also detect some irony in their choice of Hermes in his role as guide to the underworld, as that might have been exactly where they felt they were heading after two days of heavy alcohol consumption.

Stafford describes the scene on the jug in figure 4.4 as the personification of a hangover. The woman in the center is Kraipalē, which translates as "hangover," and the female figure to her right is Thymēdia, translated by Stafford as "heart's delight" (2001, 10). Thymēdia holds a cup containing something that gives off steam. The shape of the jug (*chous*) suggests drinking at the Anthesteria, but the *kantharos* that "Hangover" holds is an attribute of Dionysus and so may allude to the Athenian Dionysia festival. Both involve wine drinking and overindulgence; the image depicted on the vase informs us that the classical Greeks were all too aware of the consequences and also that they knew of ways to alleviate the effects of too much wine.[6]

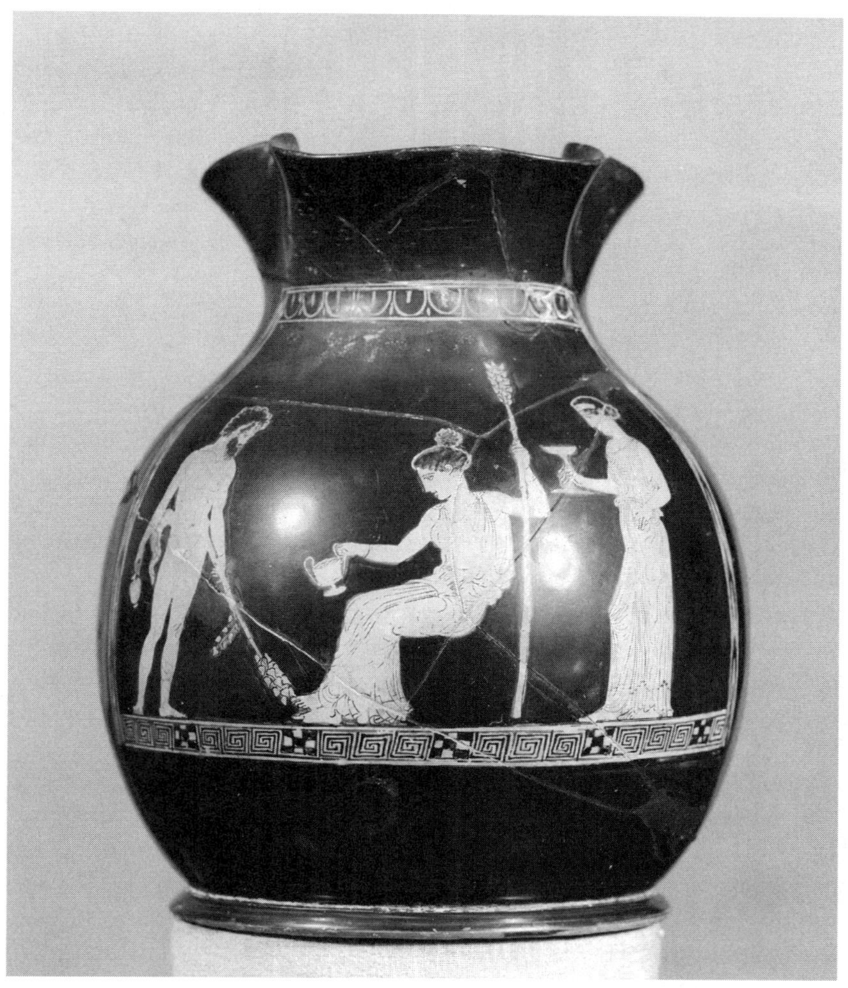

Figure 4.4. Kraipale Painter. Attic red-figure *oinochoe* (*chous*), ca. 430–425 BCE. H: 21.2 cm; D: 17.25 cm. Museum of Fine Arts, Boston, 00.352 (Henry Lillie Pierce Fund). Photo © 2011 Museum of Fine Arts, Boston.

The most numerous drinking shapes recorded from the Sanctuary of Demeter and Kore were *kotylai*, *oinochoai*, and *skyphoi*, the last having been discovered in "staggering" numbers, according to Elizabeth Pemberton (1989, 15), with no *kylikes* documented.[7] *Kratēres* were present for wine mixing but not in large numbers. In the Sanctuary of Demeter and Kore here we find so-called *andrōnes* but no *kylikes* and few *kratēres* (see Kelly Blazeby 2006 for a more detailed analysis of shapes and quantities of drinking cups from this site). Therefore it could be argued that drinking in these spaces was not understood as sympotic. Women attending the Sanctuary of Demeter and Kore celebrated in rooms identical to *andrōnes*, so clearly women could and did recline and drink wine. Whether it took place in the company of men we cannot know, but the practice was obviously not alien to them.

Conclusion: Moving Beyond the Symposium

Lewis sees the response to images of women "symposiasts" as divided: "Some scholars are convinced that the scenes cannot represent reality, that they must be fantasy, designed to appeal to male users of the cups; others accept the scenes of images of real women on real occasions, drinking toasts to their chosen partners" (2002, 114). I hope here to have demonstrated that by describing all drinking in sympotic terms we effectually deny that there was any other location where or type of occasion on which men and women in classical Greece could drink wine either together or in same-sex groups. The implications of such a blinkered approach are enormous and result in iconographic, archaeological, and textual evidence being constantly misunderstood. Future scholarship on the subject of women and wine needs to extend beyond the symposium and take a more critical approach to the evidence. That drinking cups should place women at the center of a drinking occasion, as actors and not just objects, is surprising only if the point of reference is attitudes expressed in Athenian literature. Insofar as generalized social norms posit males as sexual initiators, women may be construed as objects of sexual conquest, and when alone in public situations they are likely to be regarded as open to sexual encounters. In classical Greece, and especially in Athens, where women were strictly censored and ranked, the tavern, which is of its very nature a place of open group interaction, must have been perceived as a threatening context for the "decent" citizen woman, as it poses for the lone female the contradiction of deregulated social norms defining appropriate behavior and male expectations of female sexual availability (Smith 1983). Even nudity, which might appear to be an obvious indication of a woman's status, marking her as a prostitute or sexually available, is challenged by Lewis and she describes the assumption as "untenable"

(2002, 102). It may seem to be a flip observation, but it is hot in Greece, so why not shed some clothes in the company of other women while drinking in a hot stuffy room? Some contemporary cultures, nationalities, and individuals experience unease with communal nudity while others do not, so do we really know how classical Greek women behaved together behind closed doors? Lewis cites religious, marriage, and mourning scenes devoid of any sexual content in which the main protagonists are naked women and concludes that clothing does not equate with a set idea of "respectability" (2002, 102). Men and women must have come together to drink in nonsexualized situations and certainly drank alone, but scholars' insistence on interpreting the imagery through the expectation generated by literature, which would have no "decent" Athenian women drinking wine, means that they construct a scenario (woman + wine = prostitute) around a scene for which literary evidence is vague (women reclining and drinking in a sympotic manner), making 2 + 2 = 5 instead of considering the possibility of women as wine drinkers in their own right, regardless of status.

NOTES

1. Hippocrates, more interested in disease and pathology, is generally silent on the subject of women's drinking.

2. See Ath. 10.440d–442a: "That the race of women love their wine is commonplace."

3. Although there are three types, the *kylix* in general terms was a two-handled cup with a wide, shallow bowl and stemmed foot. One of the most common drinking cups produced in Attic workshops, it remains instantly recognizable.

4. A *kratēr* is a vessel with a deep, broad body and wide mouth, used for mixing wine with water. The wine-mixing bowl was indispensable during the symposium proper.

5. Although probably originally a generic term for a cup, the use of *kotylai* as a unit of measurement may indicate a cup of a certain size and capacity rather than a fixed shape.

6. Ps-Aristotle *Queries*, Q. 17. According to Pete Brown (2003, 25–26), cabbage contains chemicals that help neutralize acetaldehydes, an unpleasant by-product of the liver's attempts to metabolize alcohol. See also Ath. 1.34c–e; Alexis fr. 287; Eubulus fr. 124; Anaxandrides fr. 59; Nichochares fr. 18; Amphis fr. 37; and Apollodoros of Carystos fr. 32.

7. A *skyphos* is a deep cup with a low foot, two handles, and no distinct lip. Often appearing in scenes of revelry, this is the shape to drink from when all pretension to sobriety is lost.

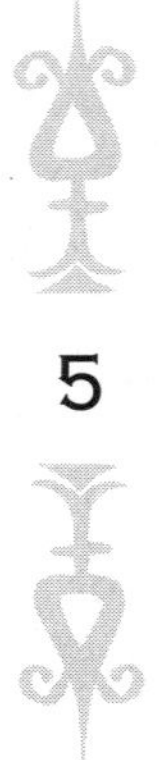

5 Embodying Sympotic Pleasure

A Visual Pun on the Body of an Aulētris

HELENE A. COCCAGNA

In the tondo of a late sixth-century BCE red-figure cup attributed to Oltos, now unfortunately lost, a naked woman, depicted frontally, straddles an overturned pointed amphora, its toe disappearing into her body (see fig. 5.1).[1] John Beazley describes the image as a "naked flute-girl raping a pointed amphora" (*ARV*[2] 66), and subsequent scholars have viewed it as a masturbation scene and have offered little further analysis aside from raising the question of whether it reflects an actual performance or simply a fantasy.[2] In this essay, I offer a new interpretation of this vase, as well as other scenes that treat amphorae in a similar, sexual manner. Arguing that potters and painters employed rhetorical strategies analogous to those of sympotic poets such as riddling and punning, I claim that these images enact visual puns that evoke parallels between the amphora and the female body by focusing on the *stoma* (mouth) and *gastēr* (belly) of each. In this essay I explore the lexical fields of *stoma* and *gastēr* and show how the ambiguities common to both anatomical features are explored in vase painting. In so doing, I reveal the lexical and visual games that hinge on the body parts common to women and vases and that invite the viewer to compare the female body and the body of the vase.

Vases in Context: Iconography and the Symposium

Both the shape and decoration of the cup by Oltos suggest that it was originally created for the symposium context. The vessel is described by Beazley as the

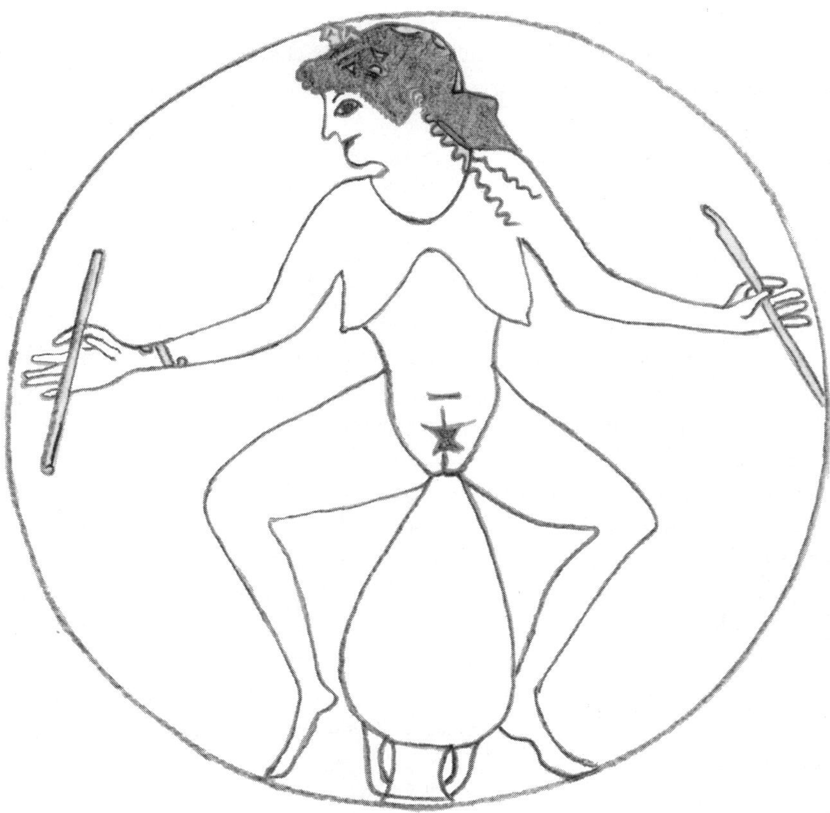

Figure 5.1. Attributed to Oltos. Attic red-figure cup, late sixth century BCE. Location unknown. Drawing by Tarah Csaszar.

fragment of a cup that was likely close in shape to the *kylix*—a two-handled, shallow cup with a high foot, which is one of the most common types of drinking cups in symposium and *kōmos* scenes in both black- and red-figure vase paintings (Richter and Milne 1935, 24–25). In such banqueting scenes, the *kylix* is one of several different types of cups used by both men and women and even doubles as a game piece in the sympotic game of *kottabos* (Richter and Milne 1935, 25). It is not just the form of the vessel that locates the woman in the context of the symposium; her appearance does as well. Her nudity, the wreath on her head, her snake bracelets, and the *aulos* (flute) in each of her hands accord with her role as an *aulētris*.[3]

A specialized form of banquet or ritualized drinking party, the symposium was the prerogative of adult male citizens. It was characterized by specific elements including libation and purification rituals, prayers, communal dining, the regulated consumption of wine, as determined by the *symposiarch*, performances, including music and dance, and contests among the participants.[4] The event usually took place in the *andrōn*, or men's room, and was attended by a small group of men who reclined as they drank, dined, sang, and conversed. Hired performers of both sexes provided entertainment and sometimes served as prostitutes (Neer 2002, 9).

Because such an array of potted vessels was used in the symposium, I work from the assumption that this specialized banquet served as an important market for a significant portion of Attic pottery produced in the late archaic and early classical periods, the periods to which the vases discussed in this essay date.[5] In response to this demand for symposium ware, I believe that potters and painters would have crafted some of their products for this specific milieu and can be shown to have explored many of the themes that characterized the event when choosing what to represent in their shapes and images (Neer 2002, 2). François Lissarrague has explored how the symposium had an impact on the iconography produced for it (1990a). Emphasizing the role the vases played beyond their functional purpose, he describes these vessels as not just mere containers but as vehicles for images (1990a, 11). He points out that they are "reconsiderations in another medium" that play an important role in establishing and reinforcing the setting of the symposium (1990a, 106).

From the poetry performed at the symposium, Richard Neer extracts a set of terms that he uses to interpret the material culture of the symposium. Drawing from the language, forms, and motifs of sympotic poetry, which is replete with puns, riddles, and metaphors, he argues that potters and painters deploy these same methods as "a pictorial counterpart to poetry" (2002, 10). That is, the predominating sentiments of deliberate ambiguity and evasiveness that characterized much of sympotic literature sometimes also led to an ironic playfulness in the production of these craftsmen. Thus, these characteristic literary elements of the symposium typified some of its visual aspects as well (Neer 2002, 23).[6]

Sympotic Games: Evoking Anatomical Parallels

Potters and painters both drew parallels between the human body and the body of the vase.[7] As we still do today, ancient Greeks assigned anatomical terminology to the various parts of the vase. The pot's handles were its "ears" or *ōta*, the mouth was its *stoma*, and its foot was a *pous*.[8] Lissarrague describes this toying with anatomical substitutions as one of the "less complex games" played by potters and painters (1990a, 56). However, these games reflect the craftsmen's awareness of the conceptual parallels between the vase and body. Moreover, such manipulations, however playful, allude to the potential for more complicated, and rather clever, puns and riddles.

In addition to cases of vases that evoke anatomical parallels through plastic attachments or the incorporation of human attributes, there are also instances where the shared conceptual frameworks of vases and bodies are manipulated. In some scenes we find vases being handled in a similar way to how a body might be treated. For example, satyrs engage in sexual intercourse with such objects. The common vessel utilized in this way is the amphora. Amphorae were characterized by two handles stretching from the mouth or neck to the body of the vase (Richter and Milne 1935, 3–4). They had a variety of shapes and sizes and fulfilled various functions, from utilitarian to decorative and commemorative. The amphora with a pointed base was depicted often in scenes on Attic vases (Richter and Milne 1935, 4). In these images, the amphora most often serves as a storage vessel for wine, as indicated by scenes of wine being poured from the amphora into a more proper serving vessel, such as a *kratēr*.[9] This shape of amphora also appears in every instance of intercourse with this type of vessel. For example, in the tondo of a red-figure *kylix* in Kassel, a satyr bends forward, in profile, with his broadly smiling face confronting the viewer (see fig. 5.2).[10] The satyr's eyes do not meet the viewer's gaze, however, but are directed downward, at the amphora he holds in both his arms. With its pointed foot positioned away from his body, the satyr grasps the pot around its center as he penetrates its mouth.

Such an image is not particularly surprising or even uncommon in the repertoire of satyr scenes.[11] In fact, one of the most distinctive features of these wild creatures is their insatiable sexual appetite, evident in their ithyphallic appearance (Lissarrague 1990c, 57).[12] In the iconographic tradition, satyrs are indiscriminate in their choice of sexual partners, not even limiting themselves to a specific species. They appear in an array of erotic scenarios, including those depicting intercourse with animals and each other (Lissarrague 1990c, 61–64). The satyr's decision to penetrate amphorae is not accidental, according to Lissarrague, who calls the vase "the essential accessory of the *kōmos* and the symposium, and sufficiently capacious for a satyr" (1990c, 61). Such behavior is typical of these creatures, who tend to confuse and conflate the realms of Aphrodite and Dionysus, or eros and wine (Lissarrague 1990c, 61).

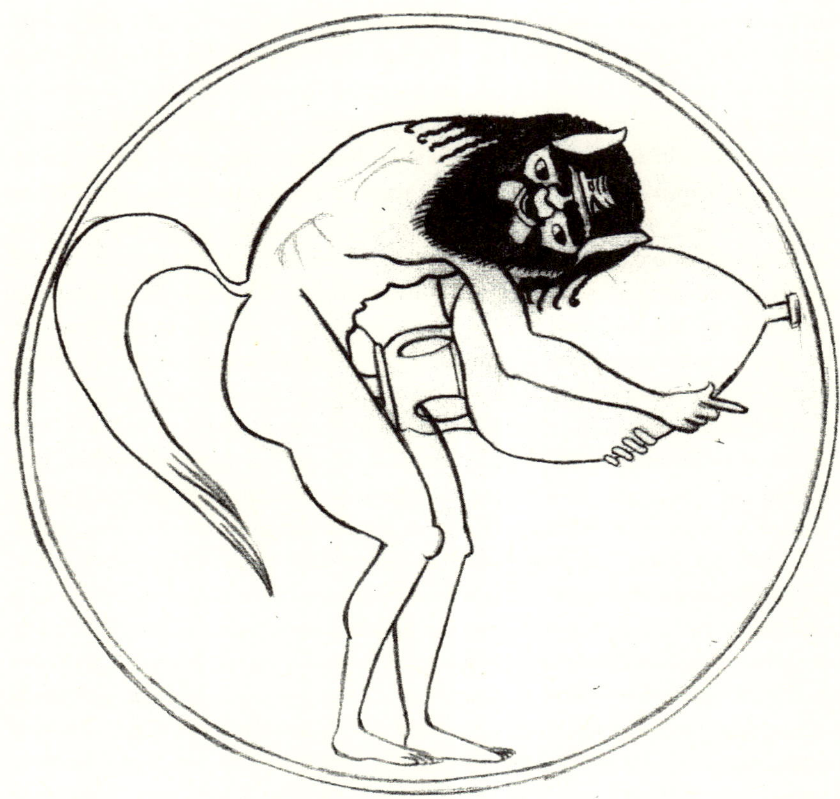

Figure 5.2. Attributed to the Nikosthenes Painter, signed by Pamphaios as potter. Attic red-figure *kylix*, ca. 520. Museumslandschaft Hessen Kassel, Kassel, ALg 214. Drawing by Tarah Csaszar.

Allusions to the Appetite: Highlighting the *Stoma* and *Gastēr*

While the amphora may seem a natural choice of sexual partner for satyrs, the language used to describe the components of this vessel suggests that the image in the Kassel cup may have had further implications for the ancient viewer. The *stoma* and the *gastēr*, the two main features of the amphora that take anatomical names, have much in common as interdependent anatomical features of the digestive system with respect to their broader lexical fields.[13] In literature, we find these two organs closely associated not only in descriptive anatomical discussions, as we might expect, but also in moralistic discussions of their functions, both real and perceived. An examination of the semantic fields of these two words reveals that they are marked terms that have connotations extending beyond mere anatomical labeling, particularly when used to refer to the female body.

The term *stoma* can be translated most simply as "mouth." This primary definition concentrates on the physical aspect of the *stoma*, serving to label an anatomical feature. However, just as in English when a person is described as "mouthing off," the term can also be used to describe products of, or actions performed by, the mouth, thus broadening the term's lexical field beyond its literal sense. Examining instances of the *stoma*'s wider lexical field, Nancy Worman (2004) has explored the *stoma*'s metonymical function in disputes between Aeschines and Demosthenes, citing examples wherein a lack of moderation is closely associated with the *stoma*, effectively focusing a moralizing discourse on this body part.[14] Worman explains how the mouth was conceptualized and what functions were attributed to it as well as the negative associations that were assigned to it. Citing examples of insults and accusations of oral excess in these works, she highlights tropes focusing on the mouth that had their roots much earlier, in claims of excessive consumption from lyric poetry to comedy. For example, in Aristophanes' *Frogs*, Euripides is characterized as a *stomaourgos*, or "mouth worker," connoting his style, which was perceived of as "too glib and finely wrought" (2004, 5). The choice of a compound form that uses the word *stoma* is common and localizes this criticism in the mouth. Worman argues that "the caricaturish details that the orators offer as proof of each other's failings reveal that the mouth is a central metonymy for distinguishing between the upstanding Athenian citizen and the mercenary excess of brutal or craven sophistic types" (2004, 8). That Athenians favored comparisons that pitted their strengths against the perceived weaknesses of an "other," be it foreigner, woman, or another social class, has been extensively discussed in recent scholarship.[15] In the course of employing such binary oppositions, Greeks in the archaic and classical periods ended up devoting a great deal of attention to the appetite and its moderation.[16] Worman's observations highlight the frequency with which the mouth was focused on in Greek culture as an organ to be either praised or faulted. More than a mere body part, the *stoma* was at the center of moralizing language used to accuse and condemn those perceived as having an unrestrained appetite.

From this exploration of the metonymical functions of *stoma*, let us now consider its other usages. *Stoma* is also applied more broadly in describing a variety of openings, such as the mouth of a river or the opening of a jar.[17] In Aristophanes' *Frogs*, a diminutive form of the word is used to denote the "little mouth" of a vase (185). Discussing the function of a vase's mouth, Froehner points out that "l'orifice du vase est une de ses parties essentielles; par la place qu'il occupe, le service qu'il rend, il provoque pour ainsi dire la comparaison avec la bouche humaine." He goes on to cite examples of the various descriptive epithets a vase might assume based on the characteristics of its mouth (1876, 12).

Finally, we turn to another important function of the term *stoma*, namely, its use in relation to the woman's body. Giulia Sissa points out that, in the case of the female body, "the upper and lower portions [of the body] . . . are shown to be symmetrical through the use of identical terms to describe the parts of both. The mouth (*stoma*) through which food is ingested and from which speech emanates corresponds to the 'mouth' (*stoma*) of the uterus" (1990, 53).[18] From the Hippocratic Corpus, we see that *stoma* refers to the vagina, in addition to the mouth of the uterus (King 1998, 35). In fact, early medical writers likened the female sexual organs to an overturned jug, with its bottom facing upward, its *auchēn*, or neck, and *stoma* facing downward. This assimilation to a container for liquid is made more significant when we consider, as Ann Hanson points out, that the chief concern with the female reproductive system was with the management of liquids (1990, 317).

Let us now consider the other, closely associated anatomical feature of the amphora, its *gastēr*, or belly. The human *gastēr* becomes an extended metaphor, as we can see from the application of terms for it to parts of vases and associated apparatus. The bulging portion of the amphora was its *gastēr* (Froehner 1876, 16–17), and the portion of a tripod placed on a fire was called *gastrē* (Hom. *Il.* 18.348; Hom. *Od.* 8.437). In further analogy to the human abdomen, some vase forms were said to have an *omphalos*, or navel, as with the *phialē mesomphalos*.[19] Just as the *stoma* evoked analogies between the vase and body, so too did the vase's *gastēr* provide fodder for jokes and parallels on this shared body part. From early sources, we see that this word refers to an individual's stomach, often described as very demanding, as when Odysseus bemoans the effects of hunger on a human being: "The belly's [*gastēr*] a shameless dog [*kunteron*], there's nothing worse. Always insisting, pressing, it never lets us forget—destroyed as I am . . . still it keeps demanding, 'Eat, drink!' It blots out all the memory of my pain, commanding, 'Fill me up!'" (*Od.* 7.216–21).[20] In fact, the stomach enjoys a particular prominence throughout the *Odyssey*, appearing repeatedly as a primary motivating factor for the hero's actions. Much like the *stoma*, the *gastēr* also bears a wealth of connotations extending beyond its primary use as an anatomical label. The *gastēr* almost always brought negative associations, many of them extensions of the faults attributed to the *stoma*. In Hesiod's *Theogony*, the Muses evoke the pessimistic connotations that accompany the *gastēr* when they hurl blame at the poet, referring to "shepherds who dwell in the fields, worthy of reproach, mere bellies [*gasteres oion*]" (27). A great deal of scholarly discussion has focused on this passage, with many suggestions made as to why and how the belly is invoked.[21] What is clear is that here, once again, we witness an organ metonymized to represent an entire person, with negative undertones about the nature of the person labeled with the term. In a comparison of the Iliadic heart, or *thumos*, to the Odyssean belly, *gastēr*, Pietro Pucci points out that the former emphasizes the bold heart that motivates the hero, while the latter reflects sheer necessity as the incentive for the hero's actions (1987, 158–59). Furthermore, throughout the *Odyssey*, the term *gastēr* is frequently accompanied by blame epithets, associated with evil, greed, and destruction.[22] Nor is it only in the *Odyssey* that the *gastēr* bears such associations. In discussing the belly's defining characteristics, Jasper Svenbro argues that in Homer, Hesiod, and Epimenides the *gastēr* connotes laziness, dependency, susceptibility to abuse, and a disposition that is quick to resort to lies, suggesting that, on the discursive level, the *gastēr* produces lies (1976, 50–70).[23]

There is another important application of this term to the human body. In the case of women, the *gastēr* takes on a more complicated signification, where the term refers not only to the digestive tract but also to the womb.[24] In both medical and nonmedical texts, "to take something into the *gastēr*" meant "to be pregnant."[25] Helen King points out that "one should perhaps think of the *gastēr* as a single organ," since the delineation between stomach and womb is a more modern concept (1998, 25). Thus, the female *gastēr* is undifferentiated and the term is used indiscriminately to identify the stomach and the womb (1998, 25). Surveying the broader literary record for evidence of how ancient Greeks perceived the internal organs of the female body, King employs the myth of Pandora to demonstrate that the model seen in the Hippocratic Corpus presents views that predate these medical writings and reflect ideas that were commonly held by the nonspecialist public (1998, 23). She points out that in Hesiod's *Works and Days*, Pandora is described as having ravenous "insides" (1998, 24). Female nature shares a common feature, then, with the *gastēr* described by Odysseus. Both are ravenous and drive the individual they control to engage in inexplicable behavior. Hesiod draws this comparison more explicitly when, calling women "no helpmeets in hateful poverty, but only in wealth," he likens women to drones in the race of bees, stating:

> And as in thatched hives bees feed the drones whose nature is to do mischief—by day and throughout the day until the sun goes down the bees are busy and lay the white combs, while the drones stay at home in the covered hives and reap the toil of others into their own bellies [*allotrion kamaton spheterēn es gaster 'amōntai*]. (*Theog.* 594–99)[26]

Women not only have large appetites, according to this analogy, but they are also lazy and thus rely on the efforts of others to fulfill their needs and desires.

The *gastēr* is presented as an evildoer when it is described in the *Odyssey* as bringing "many *kaka* into the world" (17.284). King suggests that "as a manufactured *kakon* [evil or bad], and as bringer of *kaka* [the plural of *kakon*], . . . Pandora is . . . a *gastēr*" (1998, 26). Her observations on the Pandora myth demonstrate not only that the model of the female body in the Hippocratic Corpus predates these medical writings but also that negative views of the female and the ways these views tied into how the body was conceptualized can be found very early in Greek literature. This belief that the woman's *gastēr* left her insatiable, both alimentarily and sexually, proved to be a persistent trope in subsequent centuries.

From a consideration of the lexical fields of the *stoma* and *gastēr*, we see that they are far more than mere anatomical features of human bodies. Rather, they are points around which tension, debate, and judgments are formed concerning the contentious issue of moderation. Deborah Steiner, discussing Pindar's audiences, neatly summarizes the stress placed on the importance of self-control when she says "allowing one's appetites, whether gastric or sexual, free rein constitutes an obvious violation of the self-control that Greek thinking from the archaic period on constantly advocates and that the select, elite subjects and audiences for Pindar's songs are notoriously supposed to exercise—and nowhere more than at the symposium, which supplies such abundant opportunities for indulgence in food, drink and sexual pleasures" (2002, 311). By focusing on these two anatomical features, the *stoma* and *gastēr*—loci of tension on both the physical and the discursive levels—a vase painter could comment on issues of the unrestrained appetite in the sympotic setting through allusions to a vase's mouth and stomach.

A perceived lack of self-control among barbarians, satyrs, and women served to differentiate these groups from citizen men.[27] As noted above, in the sympotic context, moderation and self-control were deemed male virtues and were major themes of the symposium.[28] We have seen that the descriptions of woman's "ravenous nature" are important early examples of women being negatively viewed on account of their appetites. One need only look to Aristophanes' *Lysistrata* for the comic representation of women's difficulty controlling their sexual appetites or to the *Thesmophoriazusae* for women portrayed as being in constant pursuit of wine.[29] Nor is it only in literature that we find these stereotypes about the female appetite expressed. As Marjorie Venit has demonstrated, these sentiments also appear in Attic vase painting. From her analysis of scenes of women who drink from very large *skyphoi*, Venit has demonstrated that Athenian vase painters represent women as more bibulous than male symposiasts (1998, 125). She adds that while literature generally focuses on the appetites of wives, vase paintings focus on the drinking habits of *hetairai* (1998, 126).[30] While literature furnishes ample evidence of "respectable" women being faulted for their inappropriately large appetites, vase painting reveals that "nonrespectable" women in the sympotic setting were subjected to these same criticisms.

As my exploration of the lexical fields of the *stoma* and *gastēr* shows, these words were polysemous, applied to inanimate objects and human bodies alike. Returning to the discussion of the amphora's anatomy, we see that the anatomical components of the amphora are subject to multiple manipulations in its comparison to the human body. When the amphora is set upright, on its foot, the viewer might see a limbless torso, the neck of the vase leading to its mouth. Moved into another position, however, as in the satyr scenes, the painter plays with the viewer's understanding of shared features of the vase and the body. By having the satyr penetrate the vase, the painter makes allusions to far more than simply the mouth of the amphora as an opening available to a satyr who will take advantage of the first available object at hand to pleasure himself. Rather, in such scenes, a series of anatomical parallels is evoked. First, a viewer might recognize the shared features of the vase and human body—both male and female—and see the satyr penetrate the mouth of this "body." According to this interpretation, the amphora should be seen as performing fellatio on the satyr. On this level, the visual pun plays on both the male and female body, since both sexes possess a *stoma* and *gastēr.* On another level, however, the painter suggests that the viewer should no longer see the upper *stoma*, or mouth, common to both men and women, but rather another human anatomical feature with the same name—the vagina. Consequently, when we reexamine scenes of satyrs masturbating with amphorae, such as that in the tondo of the Kassel *kylix* (fig. 5.2), we are able to detect a pun on the terminology of the vase and the human body. In fact, it can even be said that such scenes go even further and make a comment on the nature of the female body to the effect that a woman's body is perceived as being just a belly and a mouth. To further support my argument for this visual parallel to the female body, I point out that the particular posture assumed by the satyr in the Kassel cup is reminiscent of other contemporary images of sexual intercourse in which a symposiast bends over and penetrates a woman from behind (see fig. 5.3). While similarities in pose can be attributed to a variety of factors, the Kassel satyr's pose is so similar to such images that it is safe to say it was likely a deliberate imitation on the part of the painter. Another example of an amphora appearing where we might expect to see a woman is shown on a vase in a private collection.[31] On this early fifth-century black-figure *oinochoe*, a satyr raises a sandal in his right hand, prepared to strike the amphora beneath him. Once again, this image borrows from a well-known scene type, where a man uses a sandal to spank his sexual partner, most often a woman. In a period when it was popular to represent satyrs as symposiasts in vase painting, it would have been appropriate to imitate a popular scene type and comically alter a crucial factor,

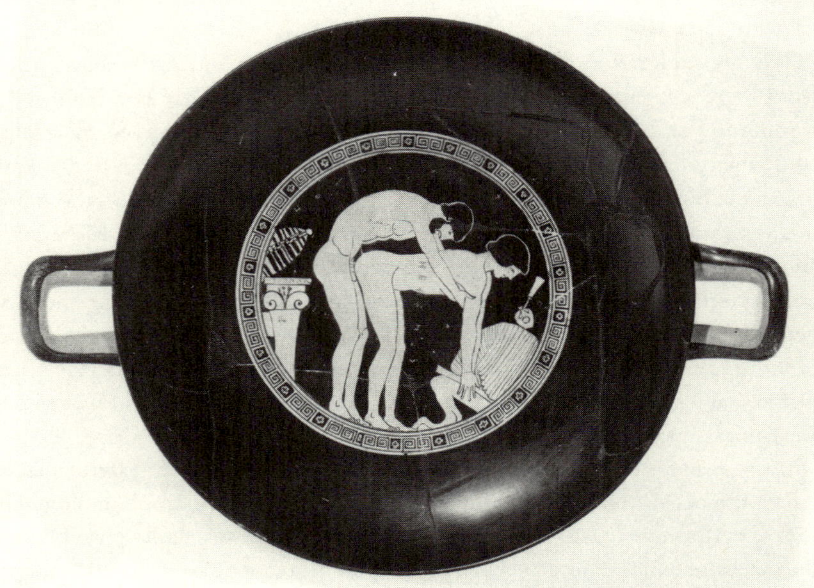

Figure 5.3. Douris Painter. Attic red-figure *kylix* with erotic scene, ca. 480 BCE. H: 7.8 cm; D: 21.2 cm. Museum of Fine Arts, Boston, 1970.233 (gift of Landon T. Clay). Photo © 2011 Museum of Fine Arts, Boston.

such as the sexual partner, to emphasize where the satyr falls short of being a true symposiast.[32]

Seeing Double: Oltos's Visual Pun

Returning now to the Oltos vase, let us consider how these observations impact our interpretation of the image of an *aulētris* astride an amphora. In his discussion of this cup, Martin Kilmer states that this scene should be viewed as a counterpart to depictions of satyr-amphora-masturbation (1993, 65). Undoubtedly, the viewer would initially have been struck by the *aulētris*'s actions and might have made the association with the wild sympotic creatures and their behavior. Such observations might incite the viewer to draw comparisons between the natures of these creatures and prostitutes. In fact, we have instances of similar visual comparisons, wherein satyrs and maenads are juxtaposed with prostitutes and satyrs (Neils 2000). In the case of the Oltos cup scene, the choice to masturbate with the foot of an amphora puts emphasis on the huge sexual capacity of the woman, a trait that women are perceived as sharing with satyrs.

Beyond allowing us to compare the masturbatory practices of prostitutes and satyrs, what do the observations made in this essay concerning the conceptualization of the body as vase and vase as body contribute to the analysis of the scene in this cup? First, as we have seen, the idea that women possessed two *stomata* was a common one in Greek culture. In the Oltos cup, the *aulētris*'s *stomata* are altered by the painter, who, by inserting an amphora into her body, replaces her vaginal *stoma* with that of the inverted amphora. In effect, Oltos replaces one source of sympotic pleasure, the female sexual organs, with another source of pleasure, the mouth of the amphora, which pours forth wine. By doing so, Oltos treats the amphora's *stoma* as an equivalent to the biological *stomata* of the *aulētris*. The woman is seriously altered and yet, technically, lacks nothing. Through the amphora's placement, the *aulētris* acquires not only a new *stoma* but an additional *gastēr* as well. As noted, this ambiguous term can refer to both the stomach and womb and, at times, to the entire woman (King 1998, 25). The question then arises: if one *gastēr* brings with it such negative associations, what are the implications of an *aulētris* who now has two? There is no simple answer to this question, but, based on what we know about the lexical field of the *gastēr*, we are able to make some inferences. First, the *gastēr* was the seat of the appetite for both food and sex and, as such, its doubling would have undoubtedly been intended to evoke unease among men who already perceived women as insatiable. As a representation of the womb, perhaps we might also detect here not only a fear of the woman's sexual appetite but also an anxiety at the risk of her becoming pregnant.[33] Complicating the interpretation of this scene even further is the fact that one of these bellies belongs to the vase and surely has positive connotations as the container of wine. Sympotic ambiguity pervades these two "stomachs," offering a visual contemplation of the positive and negative aspects of both woman and vase.

One might further observe that the visual comments Oltos makes about the female body are by no means restricted to the *aulētris* or even to prostitutes. Women of all social positions are subject to such comparisons, as is made clear in the literary sources, which do not limit their discussion of women's insatiability to prostitutes. Rather, the unrestrained appetite is a feature of every woman, and within the realm of vase painting, representations of prostitutes serve to highlight this perceived flaw.[34] The prostitute's body is thus a manifestation of the uncontrolled female appetite and reflects a negative trait believed to be common to all women. Just as a satyr's wild antics could serve as a visual reminder of the potential loss of control risked by a man who does not practice self-restraint, the *aulētris*'s body in this scene reminds symposiasts of the potential excesses of a woman's appetites when they are not kept in check. Images of insatiable prostitutes thus serve not just to entertain male symposiasts but also to allude to the volatile nature of all women, including their wives.[35]

The scene in the cup's tondo carries to a new level a well-established tendency to objectify women visually in sympotic iconography. Leslie Kurke discusses an example of such imagery in her analysis of a cup by the Pedieus Painter dating to circa 510 BCE (1999, 209–11 figs. 5–6). On the exterior of the cup, symposiasts penetrate women at both ends of their bodies. Several of these men also prepare to strike the women. In her analysis of these images, Kurke concludes that male dominance is emphasized and that "the result . . . is to unite the male komasts through the humiliation and objectification of the women" (1999, 211). Oltos's image similarly objectifies the woman's body, but in a different way, by equating it with an inanimate object commonly found in the symposium setting.

Oltos compels us to make observations about the amphora in this scene as well. First, we might notice that, unlike the woman's body, the amphora does not have two *stomata*. We are not intended, then, to see the amphora as figuring the complete female body but rather only part of it. This echoes the scenes of satyr-amphora-masturbation and visually comments on the perceived function of the woman's body in the sympotic context. To an extent, the amphora represents a simplification of the woman as a participant in the symposium. However, the scene is more than a mere boiled-down presentation of the female body, for the *aulētris*'s action in the Oltos tondo emphasizes the vase's *male* sexual role in her straddling of it and in her being penetrated by its foot. The term for the vase's foot, *pous*, is also used euphemistically of male genitals (Oikonomides 1988, 45).[36] Are we, perhaps, to view the amphora as hermaphroditic? This is possible, since it is a parallel to human sexual organs that is made in both types of scenes. In light of this, we might say that the amphora is the implement of sympotic pleasure par excellence. This wine-transporting vessel provides endless pleasures; it furnishes wine and has the ability to penetrate and be penetrated.[37] In this, the amphora enters into the discourse concerning both the male and female participants at the symposium with regard to what was deemed acceptable sexual behavior.

Conclusion

As we have seen, Oltos's attribution of human qualities to the amphora fits within an established, broader tradition of anatomical manipulations of vases for the ancient Greek symposium. Often these allusions were made through straightforward parallels, such as the cup turned into mask in the form of the eyecup. Close examination of Oltos's *aulētris* with an amphora reveals a more nuanced understanding of the similarities between the human body and vase. In addition to evoking anatomical parallels, Attic vases were also animated by the use of inscriptions, which at times were meant to sound like the voice of the vase.[38]

By drawing on contemporary perceptions of the female body and concepts of the anatomized vase, Oltos is able to replace the *aulētris*'s genitals with the mouth of the amphora while simultaneously replicating her *gastēr*. Intended as a clever and entertaining image suited to the riddling ethos of the symposium, the image in Oltos's cup reveals much about the rhetoric surrounding the female body and how it was conceptualized in the sympotic setting.[39] By uniting two pleasure-giving elements of the symposium, Oltos equates these two "bodies," simultaneously promoting the amphora to the level of a living being and reducing the body of the *aulētris* to the equivalent of sympotic furniture.

NOTES

1. I know of no other examples of this pose in Greek iconography. However, it should be noted that a woman in a strikingly similar position appears on the Egyptian Turin papyrus, which dates to circa 1150 BCE and is without provenance but may come from Deir el-Medina (Omlin 1973). The interpretation of the erotic scenes on this papyrus is much debated. Among the current arguments are claims that this is an image of a brothel, as Lisa Manniche (1987, 107) states: "When one considers the fact that almost all of those present are . . . engaged in various forms of intercourse there can hardly be any doubt that we are experiencing a unique glimpse behind the screen in a whorehouse at Deir el-Medina." However, Lynn Meskell (2002, 136–37) counters this claim, pointing out "there is no physical evidence for such establishments." She stresses, rather, that the images in the Turin papyrus present a series of stereotypes that sexually objectify women. See also Toivari-Viitala 2001, 147–53. I am grateful to Elizabeth Waraksa for pointing out this parallel to me and for directing me to the relevant bibliography.

2. See caption for Keuls 1985a fig. 75; Kilmer 1993, 65.

3. On *aulētrides*, see J. Davidson 1998, 80–82; McClure 2003a, 21. The identification of the status of women in Attic vase painting has been the subject of extensive scholarly debate. While no individual, undeniable identifying element can be singled out that always indicates that a woman is a prostitute, it is generally agreed that a combination of factors such as nudity, *auloi*, and a sympotic context makes the identification as a prostitute secure. For recent discussion of this issue, see E. E. Cohen 2006, 95–96; S. Lewis 2002, 98–117; Neils 2000, 204–5. For the iconography of the *hetaira*, see Peschel 1987 and Reinsberg 1989. For recent discussion of the *hetaira* in literature in general, see Faraone and McClure 2006.

4. On the characteristics of the symposium, see Pellizer 1990; Neer 2002, 9–26.

5. In arguing for the interpretation of Greek vase iconography as a reflection of the Greek imaginary, I align myself with Neer 2002 and Lissarrague 1990a, among many others,

but recognize that not all scholars agree that the imagery reflects Athenian views, with many arguing that the iconography was created with an Etruscan clientele in mind. I believe that the arguments I make in this paper adequately substantiate my reasons for approaching Attic vases as reflections of an Athenian viewpoint. See Lewis 2002 for a contrasting opinion.

6. For examples of riddles, see Ath. 10.448b–459c. For Plato's displeasure at these ambiguities, see *Resp.* 5.479a–480a.

7. See Lissarrague 1990a, 56–57, for brief discussion. For a longer discussion of the phenomenon, see Froehner 1876.

8. These terms represent only a small sample of the rich vocabulary of vase anatomy as collected by Froehner.

9. The pointed amphora's status as a storage vessel allows us to assign it a utilitarian function. Furthermore, a pointed amphora would have contained unmixed wine, not yet diluted in the *kratēr* and therefore not yet suitable to be drunk. Consequently, scenes such as a reclining satyr who drinks straight from an amphora in the tondo of a cup by Epiktetos (ca. 520–510 BC, Archaeological Collection of Johns Hopkins University, Baltimore, AIA B3, *ARV*[2] 75, 56) highlight the satyr's lack of refinement and attention to socially appropriate drinking behavior.

10. For discussion of these scenes of satyrs with amphorae, see Kilmer 1993, 65.

11. For discussion and other instances of this scene, see Lissarrague 1990c, 61.

12. For a more recent discussion of satyrs in Attic vase painting, see Hedreen 2006.

13. Compare Aeschylus (fr. 108): *stenostomon* (narrow mouthed). For *gastra,* see *Il.* 18.348. For *gastēr*, see Cratin. fr. 202 *PCG.*

14. See also Worman 2002.

15. For recent scholarship on this topic, see B. Cohen 2000.

16. For discussion with citations of numerous primary sources, see index of Foucault 1990.

17. Artem. 1.66; Ar. *Ran.* 185. Herodotus repeatedly uses the term to refer to the mouths of rivers, as when he describes the geographical boundaries created by the course of the Nile (2.17).

18. Sissa (1990, 53) argues that by the time of the writing of the Hippocratic Corpus, this concept of the female body as having two *stomata* had crystallized.

19. Froehner 1876, 17; Richter and Milne 1935, 29. The *phialē mesomphalos*, with its raised central medallion, is an object primarily used in a ritual context to pour libations.

20. Trans. Fagles 1996, 186.

21. See Katz and Volk 2000 for a recent discussion and bibliography.

22. See Arthur 1983, 102, for a list of epithets. See also Pucci 1987.

23. See also Pucci 1987, 191.

24. King 1998, 25; Sissa 1990, 63.

25. Thgn. 305. For further discussion, see Sissa 1990, 63.

26. Trans. Evelyn-White 1920, 123.

27. For discussion, see Venit 1998, 126; Lissarrague 1990a, 57–59.

28. See Kurke 1997, 140 n. 103, for examples of praise for moderation in Alcaeus, Anacreon, and Theognis.

29. In Aristophanes's *Thesmophoriazusae*, woman's deception to ensure access to wine is comically portrayed at 765–69, when the kinsman abducts Mika's "baby" only to learn that it is a swaddled wineskin when he unwraps it, which Mika persists in defending as if it were her child.

30. Venit's observations are important in that they suggest that overindulgence by *hetairai* was a theme explored by Attic vase painters.

31. See Padgett 2003, cat. no. 61.

32. Shapiro 2004, 10. See also Carpenter 1997, 27–28; Lissarrague 1998, 187–93.

33. Further supporting this claim is the fact that taking something into the *gastēr* connoted pregnancy, as I already mentioned. See n. 25 above.

34. Allison Glazebrook (2005c, 5, 36) and Gloria Ferrari (2002, 21) also emphasize female figures as female rather than as of a particular status, such as wife or prostitute.

35. Oltos's visual commentary on the nature of the female body is an early example of what Mikhail Bakhtin describes as grotesque imagery in his discussion of folk humor (1984, 30–31). The image's concentration on the mouth and stomach comes early in a long tradition of comedic concentration on bodily orifices Bakhtin finds in Rabelais. See, for example, Bakhtin 1984, chaps. 4 and 5.

36. See also D. B. Levine 2005, 57–59. See Henderson 1974, 129, 219, 130, 138, 161, for examples of the euphemism in Attic comedy.

37. Of course, the *eromenos* would have been capable of both active and passive penetration, but a passive sexual role for men was deemed inappropriate and was instead assigned to the realm of the male prostitute. See Shapiro 1992, 56–57.

38. For example, Little Master cups are frequently inscribed with drinking inscriptions that greet the cup's user and exhort them to drink well. See Wachter 2003 for examples.

39. One might argue that the sort of playful punning I propose here is too nuanced and subtle to have actually occurred in vase painting. On the contrary, puns and jokes of a sort generally viewed as belonging to a later period, such as in Old Comedy, do occur in vase painting of the late archaic period, as Alan Shapiro has argued: "[We] must credit the painters of the late sixth century BCE with a subtle brand of humor that is more often associated with a much later period" (2004, 10).

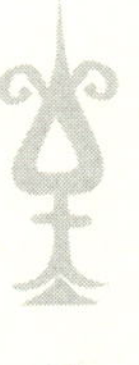

6 Sex for Sale?

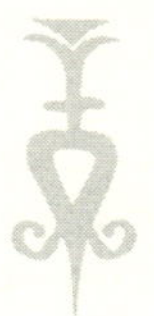

Interpreting Erotica in the Havana Collection

NANCY SORKIN RABINOWITZ

This essay is located at the crossroads of some very thorny paths—debates about the status of women in ancient Greece, male homoeroticism, and the status of vase painting as evidence. Earlier research on women in antiquity was often framed as the question of the "status of women" and has only recently been redefined as the study of sex and gender (Katz 1992, 71). From the eighteenth century to the middle of the twentieth, the idea that male and female spheres were separate as well as the idea that women were secluded in Athens was for the most part accepted; scholars even talked about the "oriental" seclusion of respectable Greek women.[1] The much vaunted public/private dichotomy led to a related question about the status of (especially naked) women on painted pots—were the women on drinking cups by definition "in public" and therefore "not respectable"? Elements of the "orthodox" view have been challenged—first, as to whether separation equals seclusion equals oppression (e.g., D. J. Cohen 1996) and second, as to whether the archaeological evidence supports the existence of a well-defined female space. We can see remains of an *andrōn*, a male banqueting space with signs of couches, but a specified female corollary is not obvious (Nevett 1999, 4–20; Jameson 1990, esp. 172).[2] Nonetheless, the ideology of separate spheres has affected the interpretation of women on pots, and given the concern for status, that interpretation often rests on the question of what kind of women they were—were they respectable women or not?[3]

The question of status, of course, is only one of the many questions surrounding the study of Greek vase painting and especially the study of women on Greek vases (see, for instance, D. Williams 1985, Harvey 1988, Petersen 1997, S. Lewis 2006). Who bought the pots? What were they used for? By whom were they used? Were cups used by men at the symposium, and were small pots used by women as cosmetic containers? It is customary to distinguish between scenes of myth and scenes of everyday life. That notion implies that we can simply take the latter as evidence about Greek life. But we must continue to remind ourselves that there is no one-to-one correspondence between the vases and objective reality; as with any art form, there is considerable room for interpretation of what it is that we are seeing. Vase painting is not primarily naturalistic in technique; it is a highly conventional form, and an archive of images and ideas was available to painters who were painting bodies, for instance.[4] The images on vases are determined to some extent by technical and aesthetic considerations; for instance the space available for decoration may dictate how many figures are shown. Moreover, the vessels were functional objects (Neer 2002, 3–4), and that context contributes to iconography and meaning as well.

There is inevitably an ideological component to vase painting's depictions of people interacting with one another and to our response as we examine them. In the preface to *A City of Images*, which is to a certain extent programmatic for iconographic approaches, Jean-Pierre Vernant says: "The authors, instead, emphasize the difficulties, the obstacles, the necessary uncertainties of deciphering. In doing so, they stress a fundamental point, that no figurative system is constituted as a simple illustration of discourse, oral or written, nor the exact photographic reproduction of reality. The imagery is a construct, not a carbon copy; it is a work of culture, the creation of a language that like all other languages contains an element of arbitrariness" (1989b, 8). We can learn about antiquity from these images if we exercise caution and look more broadly at the social construction they offer—but we learn as much about what the ancients thought as we do about what actually went on in antiquity. As Sian Lewis (2002, 91) points out, women as workers in commerce are underrepresented on pots compared to literature, while prostitutes are overrepresented. Why is that? Is it a result of the selection process of history? Or were there actually more representations of prostitution? We also read them through our own ideas. Perhaps we take scenes to be erotic because of our contemporary interests.

Even the objects that appear in the background of pots are not available for simple consumption. While these items might have been identified (if not entirely grasped) without explanation in antiquity, they would also have had connotations and cultural meanings for ancient viewers. In contrast, we have to decode them explicitly, and we interpret them on the basis of our own assumptions as well as on the basis of what we know from Greek textual evidence.[5] To take an example that

I explore in this essay, what are we to make of the small bags that men hold in many scenes? Would the ancient viewer have known what they meant, or would they have found them ambiguous?

These material objects are only one part of the ambiguity that surrounds interpretation. It is now generally acknowledged that we *read* the images, whether as metaphors (Ferrari 2002, esp. 7–8), as naturalistic reflections of reality (Neer 2002, 4–5, 27–86), or as elements of ideology (Neer 2002, esp. 2–3, 7; Keuls 1985, 1–15). Most recently, Mark Stansbury-O'Donnell (2006) and Ann Steiner (2007) have applied narrative theory, originally developed for reading literary texts, to the reading of archaic and early classical vases. Such notions of narrative implicate viewers as readers who have to interpret what they are seeing. The reader constructs a text based to some extent on preconceptions, which may or may not be conscious; thus our own biases come into play. This is particularly complicated when we come to questions of desire. As Robin Osborne (1996, 77) points out in an essay on female desire, "what the viewer makes of women's desire depends on the viewer." Whatever our strategy, the images have to be read, and the interplay of ancient intentions and current beliefs leaves us with certain fundamental ambiguities.[6]

In what follows I primarily raise questions about how we describe and label figures on Greek vases; my point is that with the labels and language come ideology. The need for captions derives from the fact that we are not seeing these objects in their native habitat but in museums or books; they have indeed achieved status through age.[7] The labels of course shift, as do museum practices in general. The kinds of exhibits we see now, for instance, in archaeological museums reflect not only changes in the field but also political changes. To give one example, Chicago has a large immigrant population from Latin America. The Chicago Field Museum is involved with the community, and in its permanent exhibit about the ancient Americas self-consciously changed the structure of the viewing experience: "To tell that story, the galleries of *The Ancient Americas* are organized in a uniquely revealing way: not in chronological order around isolated cultures, as in traditional museum exhibitions, but around the diverse approaches people have developed to meet the challenges they face" (http://www.fieldmuseum.org/ancient americas/exhibition.asp). The staff wants the audience, made up primarily but not exclusively of young people, to understand that different peoples have had different ways of solving problems; they are countering the notion of "Western progress," which would seem to imply that people in other times and places had no culture. In art museums as well as in texts, the labels direct our attention, if they do not actually control the viewing experience.

My main focus here is on four examples from the Lagunillas Collection in Havana, but one can find such examples in other museums. My main intention is to use this collection as a case study to explore some of the ambiguities between courtship and negotiation, between male and female sexuality, and between classes of women—between so-called respectable women, prostitutes, and *hetairai*.[8] The collection was acquired with consummate care; the collector, Joaquín Gumà y Herrera, Conde de Lagunillas (1909–80), was a member of a wealthy Creole family (Olmos 1993, 31); he worked closely with Dietrich von Bothmer of the Metropolitan Museum of Art for more than twenty years to acquire representative pieces that spanned a wide period of time and that embraced different styles and material (www.museonacional.cult.cu; von Bothmer 1990, 6–7). The building for the Museo Nacional de Bellas Artes was opened in 1955, and Lagunillas gave his entire collection to the museum in 1956 on permanent loan. At the time of the 1959 Cuban Revolution, the rest of his family fled, but he remained in Havana with his collection and was regarded as something of a hero (Blundell 2009). I was introduced to the collection by the antiquities curator, Maria Castro Miranda, when I was in Havana in 2005 on a trip organized by the Women's Studies Department at Hamilton, and I owe her an enormous debt of gratitude for her generosity. This collection is small and somewhat isolated, and as a result it is little known, but it repays close attention. Its size and compact display were an advantage to me; putting the pots in close proximity to one another heightens their relationship to one another and brings out the ambiguities that interest me.

Textual Ambiguity

The famous lines from Apollodoros in the law suit *Against Neaira* make it seem as if there were clear categories of women, based on male needs: men have "female companions [*hetairai*] for pleasure, the concubines [*pallakai*] for attending day by day to the body and wives for producing heirs, and for standing trusty guard on our household property" ([Dem.] 59.112). Apollodoros does not mention prostitutes other than *hetairai*, perhaps subsuming them under the term, but it is a distinction that is commonly made, both in ancient texts and later scholarship (McClure 2003a, 9).[9] *Pornos* or *pornē* comes from the verb *pernēmi* (to buy), while *hetaira* is the feminine form of a male companion.[10] Thus there seems to be a difference at least in how the two kinds of women are conceptualized, whether in terms of a price or company. It seems that the *hetaira*'s work is not explicitly sexual and payment is not made in cash, while the *pornē* performs specific acts for specific prices. Xenophon (*Mem.* 3.11.1) recounts a visit Socrates makes to see Theodote, a woman famed for her beauty and who is willing to go with anyone who can persuade her (*hoias suneinai tōi peithonti*); she lives in a lavish home with an unnamed source of income. Socrates cannot get her to say anything more concrete about her finances than that her comfortable surroundings come from her friends and the gifts that they give her (cf. the wealth of Rhodopis in Hdt. 2.134).[11] The later discussions of *hetairai*, for example, of Aspasia in Plutarch (*Per.* 24) or in Athenaeus (e.g., 13.583a, 583f; McClure 2003a, 51–57), convey a sense that they are witty, worldly, and powerful women, often associated with philosophers and political leaders; scholars have accepted that view (see, e.g., Licht 1932, 339).[12] These women are distinguished from *pornai*, who were paid to perform particular sexual acts. One word for brothel (*ergastērion*) was the same as the word for any other kind of factory, so the prostitute was literally a working girl, an American term for a whore. In a comic fragment from Philemon's *Brothers*, the prostitutes "stand there naked, lest you be deceived: look everything over. . . . The door's open. [Price] one obol; jump right in. There's no coyness, no nonsense, she doesn't snatch [herself] away, but straightaway whichever one you want and in whatever position you want" (fr. 3 *PCG*).[13] Other comic writers similarly give the impression that women stand about naked or in transparent garb and can be bought cheaply (Eub. *Pannuchis* fr. 82 *PCG*; Ath. 568e).

It is easy to say that *hetaira* is the feminine form of *hetairos*, a male companion, but it is not easy to translate it.[14] Does it resemble our words "mistress," "call girl," or "courtesan"? Courtesan, a frequent choice, has connotations of court and therefore status.[15] As a result of these implications, Allison Glazebrook (2006, 135 n. 1) prefers the term "sexual companion." The difference between *hetaira* and *pornē* is often taken to be a matter of status, gift exchange vs. commodification (Kurke 1999, 176–77, 181; McClure 2003a, 11–18; E. E. Cohen 2006, 95–97; J. Davidson 1998, 77, 109–12). This distinction, however, has also been well analyzed as a discursive effect and not just a reflection of empirical reality—it was doing cultural work of various sorts (Kurke 1999, 178–219; J. Davidson 1998, 139–42). For instance, in *Acharnians* (527), Aristophanes associates Aspasia, typically thought of as a courtesan or mistress to Pericles, with prostitutes, saying that two *pornai* were stolen from her. And as we can see in the rest of Apollodoros's case against Neaira, an individual woman might go from one status to another, and/or she might be *called* one or the other (Plut. *Sol.* 15.3). Neaira was brought up in a house run by Nikarete, who had bought several girls to train as prostitutes. Nikarete called them her daughters, so that she could pass them off as freeborn and thus get more money for them (18–20). In order to prove his claim that Neaira was an alien, Apollodoros shows that she made her living from her body (*ergazeto tōi somati* [20]; *ergazomenē . . . tōi sōmati* [22]; *sōmatos ergasia* [36]) and was a slave of Nikarete (23). It would seem that Nikarete ran a brothel, profiting by selling the sexual services of children. There is already some ambiguity of language, however, as another woman is said to have a lover (*erastēs*) (21). Later, however, we learn that

Neaira was purchased from Nikarete; she lived with two men in sequence and was supported by them; she was also their slave (*doulēn*) (29). Eventually she arranged to buy her freedom with the help of other lovers. She has moved up in status and is living with Stephanus at the time of the trial, but she still allegedly follows her old line of work (41). Apollodoros on numerous occasions calls her a *hetaira* (24, 30, 37, 48), but he also uses that phrase "worked with her body," and when he wants to malign her, he accuses her of going with whatever man approached her (20); in his summation, he uses the phrases *hetaira* and "working with her body" together (49). Were all *hetairai* simply prostitutes who liked or needed to give themselves airs?

It is not quite that simple. The case against Neaira was prompted by the instability of status: Apollodoros claims that after having prostituted her daughter Phano in a scheme to blackmail citizens, Neaira has passed her off as a woman of citizen class and married her to a citizen. To make matters worse, the girl as wife of the royal archon even served as the Queen in the ritual of sacred union to Dionysus (*hieros gamos*).[16] Thus, the Neaira case identifies the *hetaira* with the prostitute in order to strengthen the difference between the *hetaira* and the wife. Apollodoros asks the jurors who make up his audience to think what they will say to their wives when they go home if they vote to acquit. Acquittal will insult the institution of marriage by association (C. Patterson 1994; Glazebrook 2006, 129; Glazebrook 2005a, 164). Of course, we cannot take what Apollodoros says at face value; he is trying to make a winning argument in a court case. Nonetheless, as others have noted, the slipperiness of the categories remains; it is part of the plaintiff's problem, and it plagues us still as scholars and critics (Dover 1978, 21).[17]

Female prostitution was arguably part and parcel of democracy (Halperin 1990, 98–101; Kurke 1999, 195–97). For instance, Philemon embeds his statement about prostitutes in his account of Solon's legislations, alleging that Solon saw in them a solution both "democratic" and "saving" since with access to prostitutes young men would not go astray, "in the urgency of their nature, after what didn't belong to them" (fr. 3 *PCG*; cf. Nicander *FGrH* 271/72 F9). While this may be a comic misappropriation from the worship of Aphrodite Pandemos and thus apocryphal (Rosivach 1995), the coincidence of democracy and prostitution obviously made sense to the comic audience; it also fits with what we learn from Plutarch, namely, that Solon not only regulated such public matters as debt slavery but also the proper behavior of youth (*Sol.* 1).

Male prostitution, on the other hand, was anathema to the democracy because the man who so sold himself might later in life take a political bribe (Aeschin. 1.27–29; Plut. *Sol.* 21 [allowable gifts]; Fisher 2001, 39–41; Winkler 1990, 54–64; Dover 1978, 19–57).[18] Aeschines, in *Against Timarchus*, seeks to distinguish between (praiseworthy) male homosocial relationships in politics and homoerotic courtship with the giving of gifts, on the one hand, and the (blameworthy) sale of the citizen body on the other (esp. 1.134–37, 141, 155–58). There is no clear evidence relating Timarchus to a brothel, as Aeschines admits. Therefore, Aeschines faces serious problems in making his case and has to base his argument on rumor and common knowledge about Timarchus, who stayed with many men in their houses and therefore *must* have given favors in exchange (1.75–76).[19] In *Wealth*, Aristophanes compares *hetairai* and boys (149–54) and calls our attention to the possible interchangeability of objects and money: "It is said that the boys do this, and not out of gratitude for their lovers but for money [*ou tōn erastōn alla t'arguriou charin*]." "Those are not the trusty ones, but the whores [*pornous*]; the trusty boys never ask for money." "What then?" "A good horse or a pack of hunting dogs." The reply to the suggestions that they ask for a horse or dogs is that "they are ashamed to demand money and dress up their wickedness with words" (*Plu.* 153–59).

Visual Ambiguity/Labeling Clarity

Thus while the existence of different words to indicate different forms of sexual labor might seem to offer a clear distinction between those forms, the slippage between their meanings and usage indicates that the demarcations do not hold true for all cases. There is a similar instability in the visual imagery. In this case, however, our habit of labeling (in catalogues and in museum cases) masks the fluidity as secure knowledge.[20] Walking through a gallery, the casual observer in particular often cannot identify objects and figures without a caption or legend. Moreover, the pots frequently contain inscriptions that may be difficult for even the classicist who lacks archaeological training to see and decipher, although once recognized they are helpful in that they sometimes name figures from mythology. While Dionysus is readily identified from his attributes and Heracles from his, others are more ambiguous. In the scenes of everyday life, where there are no divine attributes, the caption seems helpfully to tell the viewer what she is seeing—but in the process it controls the viewing experience. Walter Benjamin once said about photography that in the future, "the caption [will become] the most important part of the shot" (1972, 25); I would argue that the caption is very influential in the viewing of any ancient art work, whether in a book (as Benjamin was arguing) or in a museum display. The drive to label overlaps in its effects with the discourse on women that has focused on defining women's status (M. Katz 1992). That is, scholars have felt motivated to define the female figures in vase painting as either respectable or not. The resulting descriptions of visual imagery suggest that any woman receiving a gift is a prostitute of some sort and not a potential or actual wife.[21] The terms *hetairai* and prostitute are both used but mostly the former. In contrast, the labels make it appear that a male who receives gifts, no matter what their value, is always being courted, never being purchased.

The images that initially caught my attention in the Havana collection decorate vessels for drinking and carrying liquid: wine cups (*kylikes*), which were associated with the symposium, and water jugs (*hydriai*), which were used more generally.[22] The symposium setting leads to multiple ways of reading and viewing. First, the vessels were placed in a context of revelry, music, drinking, and sexual activity; women at the symposium were presumably hired, either as musicians or prostitutes (either *hetairai* or *pornai*); second, different people would have had different views of a cup; third, the drinker would see the bottom of the cup, the tondo (or inside circle), after the vessel was drained.[23] The normative ancient viewer for such a cup, especially at the symposium, was male. It is worth noting again that our viewing context is entirely different: we are typically walking through a museum or looking at a book (or, increasingly, online) and can often view only one side of a three-dimensional vessel. We rarely if ever touch these pottery artifacts meant to be handled. And, relevant to my concerns, the cups are often labeled for our edification.

Gift-Giving—Male and Female

An early fifth-century red-figure wine cup in the Havana collection is useful as a starting point, because it suggests many significant themes in the discussion of sexuality and vase painting (see figs. 6.1a–c). It presents a young man holding a lyre on the inside and scenes of youths (or boys) and men on the outside. The youth on the interior of the vase is filleted and chastely attired; he is ready to play or in the midst of playing; he faces a seat; behind him hangs a case for the pipes known as an *aulos* (see fig. 6.1c). Thus, the viewer is placed in the realm of music.

The catalogue refers to the pederastic world of Athens and labels the outside scenes "courtship" (Olmos 1993, 166), a word we have inherited from John Beazley (1948), who characterizes several different kinds of scenes showing men and boys with this term, further categorizing them according to type of image.[24] If we read the inside and the outside together, we see that music is connected to the courtship of boys.[25] The outside of the cup displays adult men looking intently at youths or boys. On one side (see fig. 6.1a), the standing youth holds his arm out under his cloak (see Aeschin. 1.32), drawing the viewer's attention to the degree that he is wrapped up and protected from improper attention; his body is hidden from the men. As in other examples of this type of scene, a standing man (with full beard) leans forward on his staff and seems to hold out a wreath, while a seated man holds his staff and has a flower (?) in his hand. The extended arms of boy and

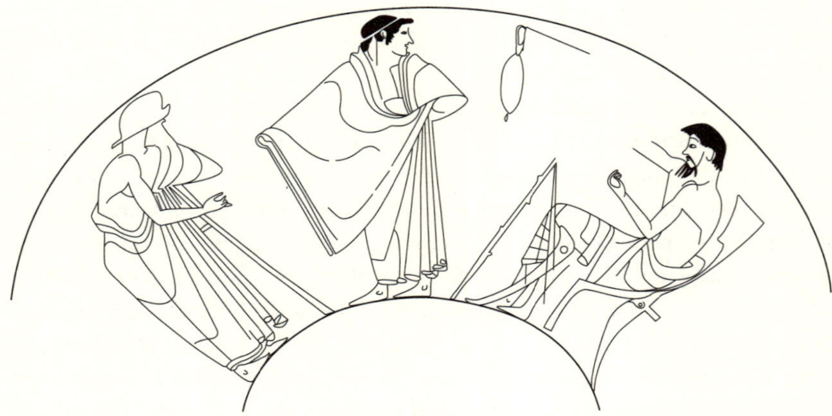

Figure 6.1a. Attributed to the Clinic Painter, or follower of Makron. Exterior, Attic red-figure cup, ca. 480–470 BCE. Museo Nacional de Bellas Artes, Havana, 165 (Lagunillas Collection). Drawing by Tina Ross.

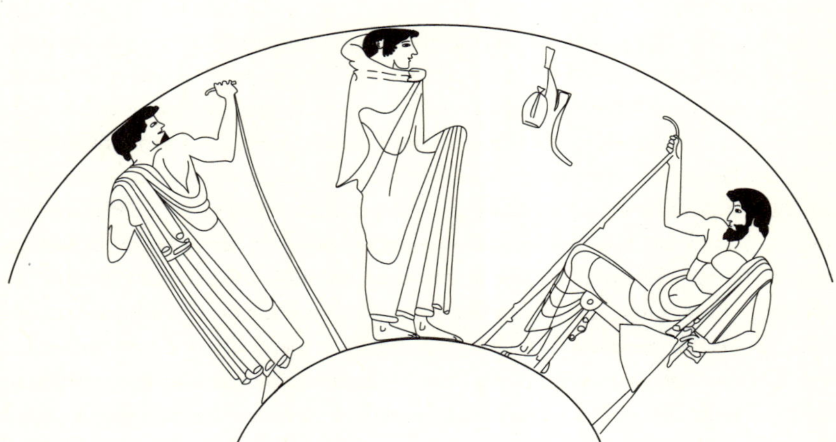

Figure 6.1b. Exterior, red-figure cup. Lagunillas 165. Drawing by Tina Ross.

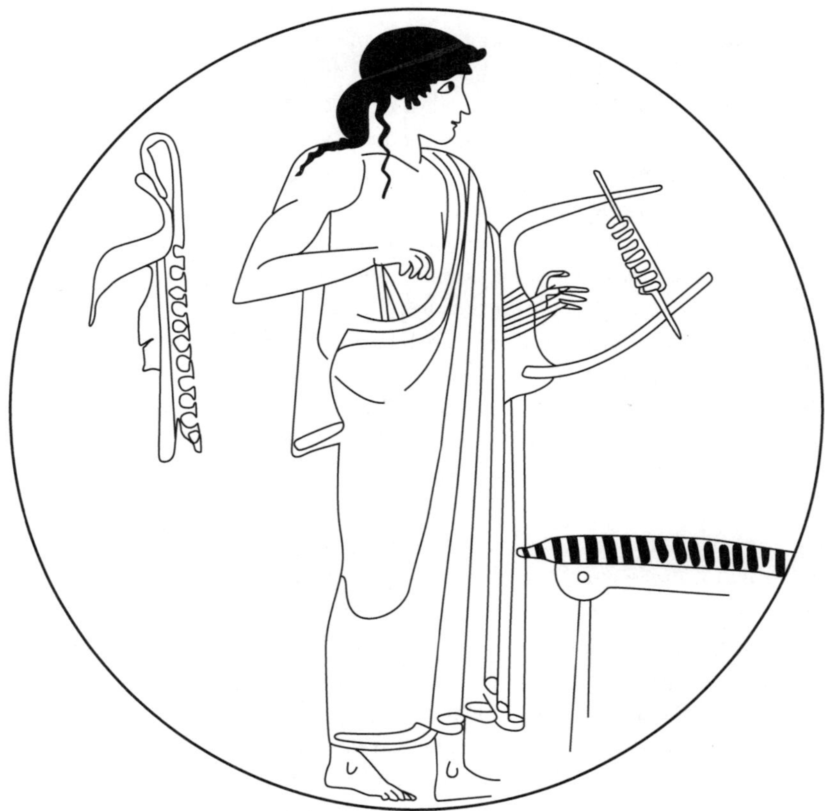

Figure 6.1c. Interior, red-figure cup. Lagunillas 165. Drawing by Tina Ross.

man lead the viewer's eye to the eager man on the left, yet the boy faces the man on the right. This position may simply be conventional, following a common way of posing bodies (looking one way, with feet pointing the other way), or we can read it as indicating the boy's conflict between two men who are seeking his favors. In the background is a net bag, which might have held a gift; it is identified in the catalogue as holding knucklebones, for playing a game of chance (also a love token).

On the other side (see fig. 6.1b), the boy is again fully cloaked; here the man on the left does not lean over, and the man on the right does not extend his hand. This scene is much more restrained than the reverse. The strigil and oil jar, nonetheless, suggest athletic competition and the gymnasium, also sites of homoeroticism and pederasty; they justify interpreting this scene as one of "courtship" as well. From this pot, we can infer an erotic component to music and a pedagogical component to sexual attraction.[26] If we read the individual decorative fields as constructing a narrative, we can perhaps argue that all three views are about what makes the *eromenos* desirable and worthy of gifts or even money.

The cup represents acceptable desire for a respectable youth, and it does not seem to differ from the textual evidence about the upbringing of a virtuous boy. But attention to or courtship of boys may also slip into something closer to a bargaining process. One of the younger men or boys in the Havana vase is receiving a flower, and on other pots beardless youths do receive gifts of small flowers, reticules, or valuable animals, and even small bags, which may or may not have contained money. The relationship between the *erastēs/eromenos* (lover/beloved) and gifts of animals, such as the hare, cock, or deer, has been well examined, most recently by Andrew Lear. For instance, in a *kylix* by Douris, the inside of the cup shows a seated youth with a hare on his lap; the outside shows pairs of seated boys and standing men, three of whom are giving hares to the boys.[27] Lear says that "the hare marks the youth as an *eromenos* just as the gym-kit of sponge and *arybal-los* (oil-flask), hanging on 'the wall' to the right, marks him as an athlete" (Lear and Cantarella 2008, 34). In light of my earlier discussion of ideology, we can say that we are predisposed to recognize gift giving as part of the *eromenos/erastēs* scenario because we have the category of pederasty or courtship in place. But it is an inference, and we might be wrong; moreover, there might have been other signs available to the ancient viewer that we miss entirely (cf. Lear and Cantarella 2008, 38). On another pot attributed to the Dokimasia Painter, a reticule is conflated with hare, cock, and bird in a cage; Martin Kilmer labels this as follows: "Youth offers reticule to boy, who already carries cockerel; the bird in the cage and the hare are also courting-gifts—though we do not know whose."[28] A smaller, closed bag appears in the hand of a youth with an incipient beard inside a *kylix* by Makron; a hare hangs on the imaginary wall beside him.[29] In this instance, we have no idea if the youth has been given the animal, if he is planning to give it to someone else, or if it was a gift at all. Lear (Lear and Cantarella 2008, 35–36) assumes that he is an *erastēs*, but the outside of the cup shows a group of fully bearded men, also with hares; they are distinguished from him by conventional signs of age. It seems that the youth might have been the recipient not the donor.

The correlation of bag and hare clearly puts us in the realm of "courtship," but it raises further questions of interpretation. Another *kylix* by Douris depicts a seated youth with a slender staff facing a standing man who extends a small bag toward him; the hands of each gesture toward the genitals of the other, and a reticule is in the field as well.[30] What is in this bag and others like it? It and its contents remain ambiguous. It might have held money (see Lear and Cantarella 2008,

85–86, 119; Shapiro 2003; Ferrari 1986; von Reden 2003 [1995], 197–202; Keuls 1983a, 226).[31] Gloria Ferrari (1986) has argued that such bags might contain knucklebones (as they are often taken to do when shown with men), while Sian Lewis argues that they contain money but that it is not necessarily sex itself that is being purchased (2002, 110–11, cf. 93–94). Given the opacity of the bag, we will never know its contents with certainty; moreover, the bag does not need to have held the same thing in every image.

If it did contain coins, should we think of this as a purchase or price, not a gift? When boys are shown receiving such sacks the captions do not typically call them prostitutes. Eva Keuls refers to the image in the text as negotiation, but she captions it as a scene of "erastes and eromenos discussing money" (1983a, 226 fig. 14.35) even though we know there were male prostitutes in Athens. Aeschines calls Timarchus a whore with less evidence than the bags would provide, if they contained money. Lear entertains the hypothesis that this scene is "prostitution or improper pederasty" and is "an exception" to the pederastic protocol (Lear and Cantarella 2008, 85). Remembering the lines from Aristophanes, perhaps we should be more alert to the possible slippage between gifts and payment especially in a culture that had only recently moved to a money economy (Sutton 1981, 279; von Reden 2003 [1995], 195).

Two pots in the Havana collection represent women receiving gifts. In the cup (see figs. 6.2a–c) attributed to the Penthesilea Painter (Olmos 1993, 170–72), the inside (fig. 6.2c) shows a beardless youth giving a fillet to a woman, who is called a *hetaira* in the catalogue. Thus, the assumption is made that this is not an innocent or virtuous gift; Robert Sutton is not expressing an idiosyncratic opinion when he says that gift giving was "not possible," citing the absence of literary evidence for such practices in heterosexual relationships leading to marriage (1981, 280).[32] It would make a huge difference in our reception of the image if it were simply labeled "lovers." We would see display of affection, not payment, as the action imitated.

But perhaps the scenes on the outside shape our interpretation of the image as a representation of sexual companionship for hire, for there we have two scenes of several youths (with an inscription reading *kalos pais* on both sides) approaching women (figs. 6.2a–b); these are also referred to as *hetairai* in the catalogue (Olmos 1993, 179–80; Olmos 1990, 127–31). Two standing women, one on each side, serve to divide the seated pairs. Nothing in the women's attire or behavior makes them particularly sexy. The dresses of the women on the left and far right are transparent (see fig. 6.2a), but the others are quite modestly covered up, as were the modest boys in the first vase. Though scholars have tried to find a visual marker that clearly distinguishes representations of women on the basis of their sexual labor, none has been successful. In the past, female nakedness has been taken to be such an indicator, but Andrew Dalby points out that lavish dress, not nudity, is the

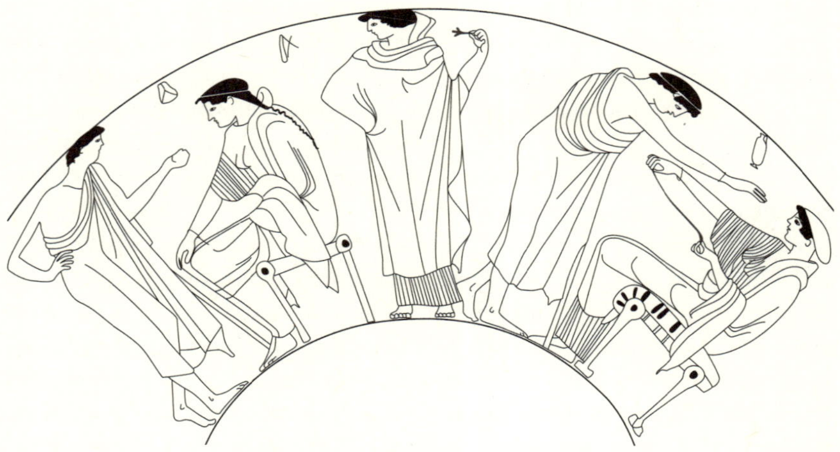

Figure 6.2a. Attributed to the Penthesilea Painter. Exterior, Attic red-figure cup, ca. 475–450 BCE. Museo Nacional de Bellas Artes, Havana, 163 (Lagunillas Collection). Drawing by Tina Ross.

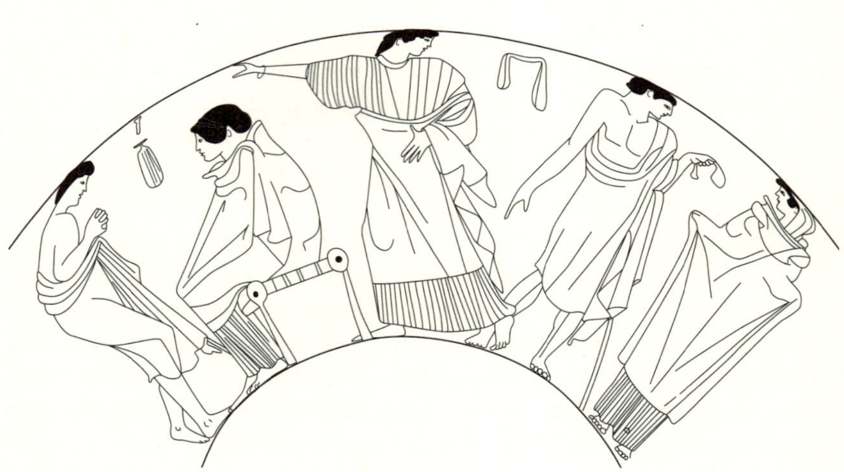

Figure 6.2b. Exterior, red-figure cup. Lagunillas 163. Drawing by Tina Ross.

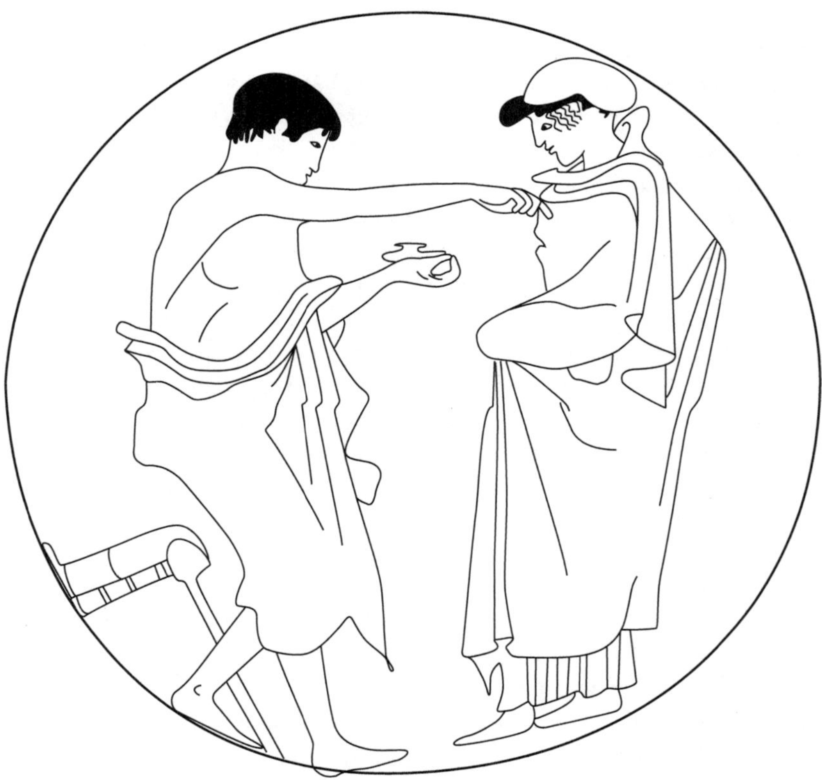

Figure 6.2c. Interior, red-figure cup. Lagunillas 163. Drawing by Tina Ross.

more reliable indicator, at least in the texts (2002, 112, 114), perhaps because the women needed to catch the eye. This is consistent with the literary interpretation of the *hetaira* as a mystified prostitute.[33]

The note of prostitution is introduced most particularly by the presence of the small bag we see in scenes depicting the courtship of boys (on the overlap, see von Reden 2003 [1995], 206–9). In heterosexual scenes, it is generally taken to hold money, though Lewis debates whether even so we need to assume that it is sex that was for sale (2002, 93, 110–11); in this painting (see fig. 6.2b), however, it is hard to imagine what else might be on offer. On the right, a young man holds out a bag to a fully cloaked, standing woman who makes an indeterminate gesture with her arms. One woman in particular seems in control of the situation—her arm stretches out energetically to her right, while she looks left. The most amazing figure is the young man on the far left, who has a pleading expression and has his hands in a position we now associate with prayer. He seems to be imploring the woman: is it for her affection or for her sexual services, even though he does not have a bag, presumably full of money, as the other does?[34] Lewis (2002, 197) might interpret this image as a sign of the woman's power—after all she is being courted. Perhaps these are *pornai* seated in the same room for the sale of sex, with a madam in charge; the women would have no choice, then, and would presumably not respond to begging.[35] If we take these women to be *hetairai*, the figure could be being supplicated and could have some degree of choice of partner, but such women presumably would not be seated in a group in this way. Neither of our ideologies can lead us to a consistent interpretation of what actually happened or what is being represented as happening in this image. Perhaps a man could go to a brothel and purchase a companion for an evening on the analogy of modern call girls.[36]

A number of problems are illustrated as we try to interpret this pot by creating narrative scenarios. From the speech against Neaira, it is clear that there were agents selling these women, but the use of the term "madam" indicates our modern point of view. However, such an implicit comparison may not be inappropriate. How do we know when we are justified in assuming a similarity between past and present? I am not arguing that we should never make such connections but rather that we need to be aware of what values we unconsciously import or express when we do so. As I pointed out earlier, the very word "courtesan," often used for *hetaira*, indicates class. It might also indicate a glorification of the sex trade, for instance, which is also seen in the contemporary fascination with geishas.[37] We may be led astray here by our need to establish a narrative and assign a specific status to the women, based on implied sexual behavior. They might simply be marked as desirable. The bag in the end may be more a signifier of the power of the man holding it than of the status of the woman facing him (von Reden 2003 [1995], 208; Shapiro 2003; Keuls 1983a, 229, "economic phallus" [cf. Keuls 1985, 264]).

In the background of this vessel we have sashes and a small loom as well as an *alabastron*, all of which might put the women in a domestic space as well as in an erotic situation. The loom seems to mark the women as weavers, and thus brings us to another vexed topic in the study of the iconography, the so-called spinning *hetaira*. When a spinning woman sits facing a man holding a bag, presumably of money, Beazley (1931) argued that the spindle or yarn basket signifies that the woman is a wife; others argue that the bag makes her a prostitute (Rodenwaldt 1932).[38] Keuls shows two images on a *hydria* by the Pig Painter that seem to reveal considerable overlap between prostitute and housewife.[39] Each woman faces a man who is holding a pouch. Keuls calls one figure a wife because she stands behind a wool receptacle and the other a *hetaira* because she lacks that sign of

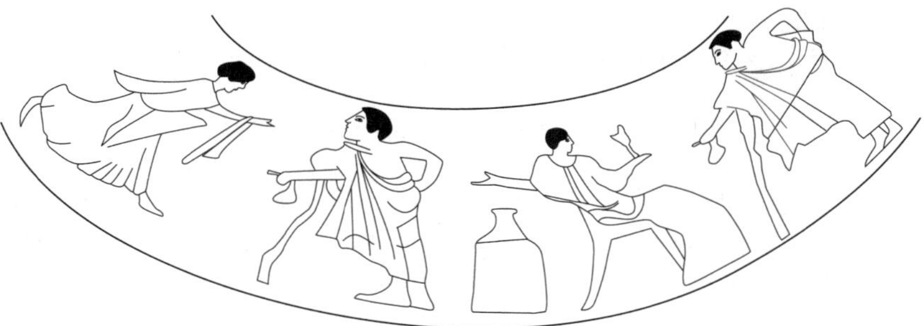

Figure 6.3. Attributed to the Hephaistos Painter. Detail, Attic red-figure *hydria* or *kalpis*, ca. 460–450 BCE. Museo Nacional de Bellas Artes, Havana, 155 (Lagunillas Collection). Drawing by Tina Ross.

marital status, while the man has a walking stick (1985, 228 figs. 205, 206). Keuls points to the antithesis (1985, 224), but she does not see a discrepancy of power in the two images; on the contrary, she highlights the similarity: both men hold the purse strings; both women are objects but they are used for different purposes (1985, 224).[40] To return to the Havana cup after this long detour: given the extensive debate, it is worthwhile considering whether this vessel actually represents women who are meant to be perceived as *hetairai*. The labels that are used give the appearance of stability to concepts that are in fact fluid.

In another Havana *hydria* (see fig. 6.3), we see two women, one seated and one standing, with two standing beardless men or youths, both leaning on staffs and both presenting bags to the women.[41] The woman on the left extends a sash and almost runs to the right. Is she giving or perhaps selling the sash to the youth? Lewis has analyzed scenes of vending, and we know women did work in textiles (2002, 91–94; cf. Keuls 1983a). The museum catalogue calls this "scenes of courtship" and identifies the couple on the left as engaging in courtship by exchanging gifts (Olmos 1993, 181). In between the two pairs is an object that looks like a bird cage, which we also see in vessels depicting male lovers, where it is generally taken to be a gift. The man on the right is described as engaged in "a transaction with a *hetaira*" because of the bag, which presumably contains money.

If we accept the likelihood that the bag contains money and that it is sometimes used to purchase sexual favors, are we then romanticizing exchange or business transactions when we use words like *hetaira* and courtship, perhaps on the basis of the elite atmosphere of the seat and attire of the women? In this, we may be following the wishes of the ancient women themselves, who perhaps sought to obscure the economic transaction, as James Davidson (1998, 126) argues, or perhaps the wishes of the men who painted these pots. When modern scholars adopt this language, it may be on the basis of our own desire to avoid the implication of commercial sex, at least in the context of our research projects.

Music Making—Male and Female

The first vase I discussed (fig. 6.1) featured a male musician, but women as well as men were depicted playing music. Music making was considered high status for men but not for women.[42] Since the female musicians who entertained at the symposium were mostly slaves, critics argue that they would have been sexually available to citizen men; *aulētrides* in particular are often specifically identified as prostitutes. In one relief on the Ludovisi throne, we see a girl who plays a flute; she seems to be a prostitute.[43] Jennifer Neils asserts that "she is certainly a flute girl and so by definition a highly prized evening entertainer. Thus a priestess and a prostitute appear in parallel positions" (2000, 214–15). Lewis (2002, 97) and Sheramy Bundrick (2005, 96), however, convincingly unsettle this commonplace about the interrelationship between pipes and sex, pointing out that the woman could simply be a professional musician.

In any case, when we see women enjoying music together, we do not need to assume that they are representing women who could be hired for sex. There are images of seemingly respectable women on their own with musical instruments; women may have enjoyed concerts, too (Bérard 1989, 91). Groups of musical women are sometimes labeled muses in catalogues or in museums, perhaps indicating learnedness or their ability to inspire men; they are sometimes labeled Sappho (in four examples according to Sutton 1981, 50, 69 n. 165), perhaps also indicating desire for other women.[44] In two red-figure *kratēres*, one at the Metropolitan Museum in New York and one at the British Museum, we have two standing women facing a seated woman.[45] The Danae Painter shows affection between the two standing women by their physical closeness: one rests her head on the shoulder of the other and has her arms around her. They look intently at the seated woman. In the pot by the Niobid Painter, the figures are less close, but the woman to the left has both arms clasped around the shoulder and neck of the other. The affection between the standing women and their attentive gaze at the musician shed an aura of longing over the whole.[46]

What about women musicians in the company of men? In a *kalpis* or *hydria* from Havana attributed to the Nausicaa Painter, beardless men or youths and women (see fig. 6.4) occupy the shoulder. The two men are wreathed and stand facing a seated woman with stringed instrument. Both the seated women have elaborate hair styles and decorated *chitones*. Are these *hetairai*, as one iteration of the catalogue states (Olmos 1990, 143; cf. Olmos 1993, 188, which simply calls

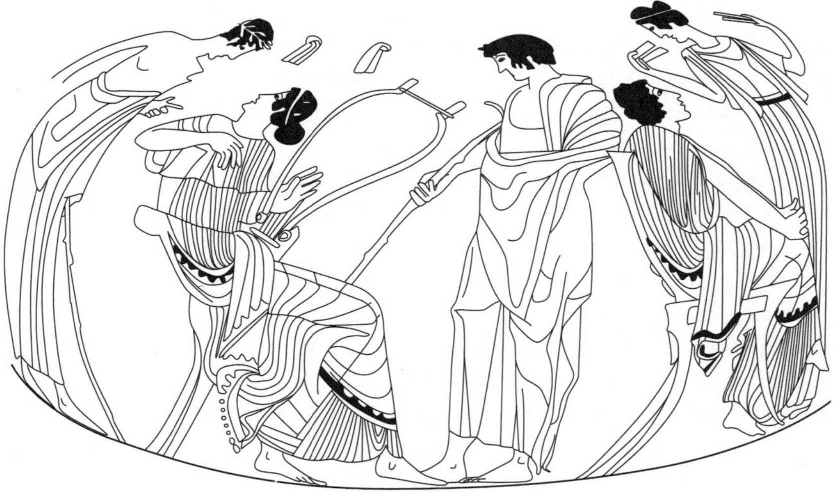

Figure 6.4. Attributed to the Nausicaa Painter. Attic red-figure *kalpis* or *hydria*, ca. 450 BCE. Museo Nacional de Bellas Artes, Havana, 166 (Lagunillas Collection). Drawing by Tina Ross.

them women [*mujeres*])? What marks them as such? Is it simply because men are present? I admit that the *krotala* might mark the woman on the right as a prostitute, but the wreaths may indicate that the men have been involved in a contest (musical or athletic), and perhaps the women have as well. The wreaths and *krotala* might suggest a dionysiac setting, as well.[47] The women on the right, like figures in some of our other musical images, seem only interested in one another (though it might be the music that moves the seated woman). Only if we assume that the image is realistic *and* that respectable women never interacted with men do we need to label the women *hetairai*. But neither is necessarily the case (S. Lewis 2002, 101–29, 172–75).

Desire vs. Rape

Sometimes the desire associated with music *is* heterosexual. A girl with a lyre on the tondo of an often-reproduced cup attributed to the Pedieus Painter in the Louvre seems to be the loving companion of the young man with her; he stands behind her, with his arm around her. She holds a lyre, while he has a *kylix* and a walking stick in his other hand. She is well dressed and attractive. We might think the inner scene represented courtship or affection, but a different context is provided by the outside of the cup. There we have an orgiastic scene with women performing fellatio and being penetrated from the front and the rear by naked men with exaggeratedly large penises.[48] These women seem older, and they are definitely heavier, than the beauty on the inside. Lines around the women's mouths suggest that the fellatio is uncomfortable for them. There is no consistency in the way the figures are referred to in the literature on the vase, but sometimes they are all called *hetairai*. There seems to be a difference, however: the inner scene represents companionship, as both figures are smiling; on the outside of the cup, force is indicated not only by the lines around the women's mouths but also by the fact that one man has a sandal raised to strike and that multiple penetrations are taking place. When Sutton (2000) discusses the outside, he ignores the inside, but we ought to take the two scenes together (Kurke 1999, 209–13 figs. 5, 6, 7). It helps to take this, as Kurke does, as "an oscillation between identification and difference, companionability and humiliation" (1999, 213).[49] The drinker would have been forced to take in both sets of images. When we do the same, we are warned not to make too much of the difference between *hetaira* and prostitute. We may perhaps see two sides of prostitution.

In the end, the imagery is as ambiguous as the words in the textual tradition, and our preconceptions and desires come into play as we describe them. When I presented this as a paper, I realized that I did not want to conclude with the explicit and quasi-pornographic images of the exterior of the Pedieus *kylix*; it was less embarrassing to end with the image in the tondo on screen. It is much more pleasant for me to think of the women not as slaves but as *hetairai*, elegant female companions. As a classicist, I too am invested in the Greeks. The figure of the *hetaira* makes us feel better about our idealized Greek men, since it allows us to obscure the fact of slavery and its involvement in the sale of sex. Feminist critics like myself may also be reluctant to dismiss these women as imaginary because to do so eliminates one source of powerful females from antiquity.

If we emphasize the differences between the prostitute and the *hetaira*, stressing the courtship of the *hetaira*, we risk ignoring how she came into the business—perhaps as a prostitute. *Hetairai* often seem to have started off as slaves even if they bought their freedom. They were paid for sex, whatever they wanted to call it. *Hetairai* like Rhodopis and Theodote, even if they were historical women, did not come into the world fully formed with their great wealth; they were produced by training and effort. None of this means, however, that the *hetaira* was no different from any other prostitute; if we say that, we minimize what might have been real differences in conditions of employment. A comparison to our own day might be in order; there are differences between the enslaved girl in sex tourism and the woman hired for five thousand dollars an hour by a politician. Moreover, some of these differences may result from the ways we talk to one another depending on who and where we are.[50] Similar differences might have held in antiquity.

The asymmetry in labeling male and female figures also has its effects. When we label any woman who is represented receiving a gift as a *hetaira*, we eliminate the possibility that wives or respectable women received gifts and played music. Thus, women on vases can only be purchased. At the same time, by implying that boys only receive gifts, we privilege male-male relations as less materialistic than heterosexual ones and eliminate women's erotic relationships to women entirely (Petersen 1997, Rabinowitz 2002a). In the end, I have to come back to the importance of reading strategies. I have not sought to argue for a single point of view here—I am not saying either that the wife is just a legal *hetaira* and the *hetaira* a glorified whore or that those boys are really being paid. Rather, I wish to point out that our values are implicated in the way that we label Greek vases and interpret the scenes depicted on them. We must be careful lest we create the impression of a reality that might not have been there in the past and perpetuate ideas in the minds of the general public that the scholarship has left behind.

NOTES

This essay began its life at a colloquium organized at the Museo Nacional de Bellas Artes to celebrate the fiftieth anniversary of the Havana Collection (July 17–19, 2006); I am very grateful to the museum and especially to curator Maria Castro. Versions were also presented at the 2008 Classical Association meeting, the 2008 Feminism and Classics conference at the University of Michigan, and the Institute of Classical Studies in London. Thanks also to Sue Blundell, Robin Osborne, Walter Penrose, Alan Shapiro, and the editors and anonymous readers for their advice. My student Michael Harwick was very helpful in the final stages of editing. I of course take full responsibility for any errors or infelicities that remain.

1. Others disputed this view of the oppression of women in ancient Greece; some went so far as to assume that ancient Greek men treated their women much as they themselves did in modern Europe, for instance (Gomme 1925, 25; cf. Kitto 1951, 219–31, 235; Rabinowitz 2002b, 7–8, 10–12).

2. There has also been a great deal of work hypothesizing that women had more power than had been thought, especially priestesses and women engaging in rituals, and contesting the notion of seclusion as being unrealistic for nonelite women (Sourvinou-Inwood 1995, 111–18; Reeder 1995, 22–23). James Davidson (2006) and Christopher Faraone (2006) also stress agency. I (2002a and 2008) see women's relationships to women as a source of strength.

3. The traditional view of the subjection of respectable Greek wives includes a rationale for men's recourse to *hetairai*, who were thought to be witty and sophisticated, and boys (Symonds 1970 [1901], 33, 63; cf. J. Davidson 1998, 73–77). As a result of a burgeoning interest in sex and gender studies, new and more sophisticated attention has been given to the topic of prostitution. We are now aware of what has been missing. In 1932 Hans Licht felt that the subject was well studied (1932, 329), but in 2003 Laura McClure could say with

reason that there had been no "comprehensive modern study" of courtesans in ancient Greece (2003a, 2).

4. On conventions of the representation of courtship, see Lear and Cantarella 2008, 24–26. In his section of the introduction to *Images of Greek Pederasty*, Lear points out the lack of realism in the portrayal of genitalia, for instance, and the use of synecdoche—taking the items used, say, in the gymnasium to signify that space. For a sophisticated consideration of naturalistic elements within ideology, see Neer 2002.

5. Certain objects, like the spindle and the mirror, may be confused because they are both associated with women and their shape is similar (Frontisi-Ducroux and Vernant 1996; Keuls 1983a, 219; Wasowicz 1989).

6. François Lissarrague and Françoise Frontisi-Ducroux offer a view of the relevance of Dionysian imagery to the interpretation of the so-called Anakreontic vases; they end by saying that "they are ambiguous to our eyes, but in their time they bore a clearly defined ideological message" (1990, 232). Lauren Petersen (1997) analyzes shifting audience perceptions at length.

7. Sitta von Reden argues that the pots must have had value in antiquity, even though they were not precious metals, given that they were dedicated to gods and placed in graves "in honor of the deceased"; she furthermore points out that "this means that we are confronted with an idealized rhetoric about reality, rather than with images of reality itself" (1995, 196).

8. The ambiguity about this term is the point of the essay, so I leave it undefined for the time being.

9. Diphilus fr. 75 *PCG* uses both terms in the same line.

10. There are many other terms for the common prostitute or streetwalker: bridge woman (*gephuris*), runner (*dromas*), wanderer (*peripolas*) (J. Davidson 1997, 78, 328 n. 15); other names come from animals; Eubulus (*Pannuchis* 82) uses the word foal.

11. Given the issues surrounding the interpretation of vase imagery, it is interesting that this meeting is described in the context of Socrates' trips to learn from others, implying that Theodote's beauty and practice of gift exchange could be educational. On Theodote, see Goldhill 1998, 114 (who emphasizes the fact that Theodote is dressed to attract, not naked); Davidson 2006, 46–47; Faraone 2006, 210 (on Theodote and the power of some wealthy courtesans.)

12. Allison Glazebrook (2006, 125, 135 n. 2) cites other scholars who have embraced this position. The association of Aspasia with both Pericles and Socrates does give some credence to this view of *hetairai*, though as the work of Glazebrook (2005a), Laura McClure (2003a), and Madeleine Henry (1995), among others, demonstrates, all these references are parts of discursive constructions and not necessarily evidence about historical women's lives (cf. J. Davidson 2006, who insists on at least some historical accuracy).

13. Trans. Kurke 1999, 197.

14. Because of the difficulty of translation, some authors simply leave the word in Greek (the two catalogues of the Havana collection generally do so), while others put the word "prostitute" in parentheses.

15. "1607 E. SHARPHAM *Fleire* Dijb, Your whore is for euery rascall, but your Curtizan is for your Courtier" (*OED*).

16. As Debra Hamel (2003, 103–6) emphasizes; see also J. Davidson 1998, 73, 326 n. 1.

17. Leslie Kurke (1999, esp. 181, 182) argues for the invention of the *hetaira*, accepting that the opposition does exist in antiquity.

18. For a convenient collection of the documents on homosexuality, see Hubbard 2003.

19. Aeschines also makes use of arguments based on appearance: we know what such men look like (1.189).

20. Scholars in art history have debated the issues surrounding representation of these categories (e.g., S. Lewis 2002, 101; Kilmer 1993, 159–69). S. Lewis (2006, 32–34) discusses the problems that arise for the study of iconography when critics accept the categories from textual study without questioning them.

21. In the abstract to his dissertation, Robert Sutton asserts that "the interaction shown ranges from prostitution, signified by the gift of a purse or other valuables from male to woman, to true romance, seen in the gifts of flowers and the like which are given by members of both sexes" (1981, iv). In the dissertation itself, he says that the "the material is more ambiguous and difficult" than he had initially allowed and that he is "not entirely satisfied with the conclusions" (1981, 277). He gives a more complicated reading, allowing for attempted seduction and fantasy, as well as prostitution as the explanation of the gift (1981, 281).

22. There is a problem about how to interpret cups in particular. S. Lewis (2002, esp. 118) has argued strongly that the fact that most cups were found in Etruria means that we cannot take them as evidence for Athenian life. Though we cannot in any case take the vessels as documentary evidence, I disagree with this position. Obviously, there are difficulties about provenance, but even if the pots were primarily exported, they could have reflected the ideology and values of the producing society. For a cogent statement, see Stansbury-O'Donnell 2006, 36–42.

23. See S. Lewis 2002, 95–97, 112, on the nonidentity of the categories *hetairai* and *pornai*.

24. Andrew Lear and Eva Cantarella (2008, xv) point out that "Sir John Beazley published a typology of these scenes in his tactfully titled *Some Attic Vases in the Cyprus Museum*. Beazley made it clear, perhaps for the first time in English, that pederasty was a common subject of vase-painting." Gift giving is the most common image-set associated with Greek classical pederasty that we have.

25. Aeschines argues that Timarchus was a prostitute to Misgolas, who "has a phenomenal passion for this activity and is always in the habit of having male singers and lyre-players" (1.41). In his footnote, Chris Carey notes the analogy to "females in this category, [where] the borderline between musician and prostitute was fluid" (1992, 38 n. 46).

26. Toward the end of the speech *Against Timarchus*, Aeschines mentions Alexander as a ten-year-old playing the lyre; he says, "Of course, I didn't address him because of his age" (1.168–69). On music and gym, see Bundrick 2005, 62. Aeschines (1.7–10) sets out the

protocols surrounding respectable boys at the gymnasium, making it clear that it was a dangerous site for male virtue. The instruction in choral dance was also strictly controlled (1.10–11). See Koch-Harnack 1983, 54–58, and Lear and Cantarella 2008, esp. 77, for the relationship of pedagogy and pederasty in representations of the hunt in vase painting.

27. Douris Painter, red-figure *kylix*, 500–450 BCE, Louvre, G 121, *ARV*^{2} 434.78, Add. 238, Lear and Cantarella 2008, 33 fig. 0.5 A.

28. Dokimasia Painter, red-figure *kylix*, 480–465 BCE, Museo Civico, Bologna, 365, *ARV* 415.7, Kilmer 1993, pl. R546.1. Lear and Cantarella believe that the strigil could be a gift in a courtship (2008, 48–49 fig. 1.8).

29. Makron, red-figure *kylix*, 490–470 BCE, Antikensammlung, Staatliche Museen, Berlin, F 2292, *ARV*^{2} 471.195, Lear and Cantarella, 2008, 35–36 figs. 0.7, 0.8.

30. Douris Painter, red-figure cup, 500–450 BCE, Metropolitan Museum of Art, New York, 52.11.4, *ARV*^{2} 437.114, 1653, Lear and Cantarella 2008, 85 fig. 2.12.

31. Of course, even if the bag held money, it does not prove that the boy's favors were being purchased. As Alan Shapiro (1992) points out, the bag can be a sign of male authority, like the walking stick. Lewis (2002, 93–94) argues that the money can be purchasing something other than sex.

32. When I delivered this as a paper at the Feminism and Classics V conference, members of the audience dismissed Sutton's point, but in truth people could come up with very little by way of specific examples of such gifts.

33. S. Lewis 2002, 101–11, 115; Kilmer 1993, 164. On slave status, see Oakley 2002 with bibliography; on dress, see Glazebrook 2005a, 170–71. Keuls speculates that "high-class professionals adopted the appearance and mannerisms of ladies" (1983a, 225).

34. Cf. Makron, red-figure kylix, ca. 500–450 BCE, Toledo Museum of Art 72.55, ca. 500–450 BCE, Keuls 1985, figs. 141, 142; Reeder 1995, 184–86 pl. 38. Here we see two men with and two men without pouches, facing four women.

35. Maria Castro suggested to me the idea that these are *pornai* seated before a madam. See Dyfri Williams's use of the term "madam" (1985, 99 fig. 7.6); Keuls (1983a, 228 fig. 14.41, 229) and J. Davidson (2006) would demur. In this case the room would be a brothel (according to the ideology sketched out earlier). See S. Lewis 2002, 115, on faulty brothel ascriptions.

36. Although this may be an unforgivable anachronism, I am reminded of Nately and Nately's whore in *Catch-22*. He is regularly begging her to love him, even though he has plenty of money.

37. Lesley Downer discusses this interest, as it affects Japanese geishas, saying that "the West, meanwhile, had been swept by geisha fervor" (2001, 4). Her informants say that "geisha were dancers, musicians, entertainers, and conversationalists who filled a specific niche at the highest levels of Japanese society. They were absolutely not prostitutes, high class or otherwise" (2001, 5, cf. 21). She speculates that the geisha "were the original liberated women" (2001, 20), as classicists have emphasized the education and opportunities of *hetairai*. We should not, however, overemphasize the similarities to *hetairai*; Downer notes that "their whole profession depends on their ability to keep secrets" (2001, 6).

38. Keuls (1983a, 227–29) opposes the dogmatism of the two positions; Sutton argues that "vase painters of the period made no sharp distinction between the domestic lives of respectable and non-respectable women except in terms of their dealings with men" (1981, 358). The archaeological discovery of many loom weights in Building Z in the Kerameikos (along with statuettes of foreign goddesses) as well as extensive deposits of pottery for drinking and dining, seems to indicate that the building was used for textile work by day and drinking by night (Rosenzweig 2004, 69; J. Davidson 2006), and further that prostitutes also did textile work. Rachel Rosenzweig (2004, 69, 128 n. 65) accepts Davidson's view (1998, 89) that these red-figure scenes of *hetairai* spinning and receiving customers represent "the precise moment when one kind of work is put aside and an altogether different labor is taken up." On other similarities of wives and *hetairai*, who both worshipped Aphrodite, see Rosenzweig 2004, 77.

39. Pig Painter, red-figure *hydria*, 500–450 BCE, Adolphseck, Schloss Fasanerie 41, *ARV*2 566.6, *CVA* Adolphseck, Schloss Fasanerie, 1:20 pl. 509; Keuls 1983a, 228 figs. 14.43a, 14.43b, 229.

40. One aspect of the traditional view of respectable women has maintained that the *hetairai* actually had more independence than married women, who had no say about who her husband would be (Licht 1932, 339, cf. 28; S. Lewis 2002, 197; Cantarella 1987, 49–50).

41. This pot has been extensively repainted; the woman on the right seems to hold a bird, but it is not very clear.

42. Sutton 1981, 44. See Glazebrook 2005c, 26, on music and education, citing Ar. *Vesp.* 859–61, 987; *Eq.* 188–89; *Ran.* 727–29; *Nub.* 961–63. But see nn. 25–26 above on the dangers of excessive attraction to male musicians (Aeschin. 1.49).

43. Marble Ludovisi throne, ca. 460, Palazzo Altemps, Rome, Ludovisi collection 8570, Neils 2000, fig. 8.5 and 214–15 n. 44.

44. Muses inspire poets but do not possess an active voice themselves (Glazebrook 2005c, 34).

45. Danae Painter, red-figure column *kratēr*, Metropolitan Museum of Art, New York, 23.160.80, Add. 326, Rabinowitz 2002a, fig. 5.3; Niobid Painter, red-figure *kratēr*, British Museum E 461, *ARV*2 601.20, Rabinowitz 2002a, fig. 5.4.

46. The potential linkage between *hetairai* and *hetairistria* (Aristophanes' term for women who are only attracted to other women in Plato's *Symposium* 191e) is not made much of, but I'd like to add it to the mix here (Rabinowitz 2002a, 134). We might also think of the connection between women's music and dance and lesbianism in the imagery of armed dancers (on Pyrrhic Dancers, see Liventhal 1985; Bérard 1989, 91–92). Sappho's intimate friends are also called *hetairai* (McClure 2003a, 204 n. 20; on *hetairai* and poetry, including Sappho, see Faraone 2006, 217–18).

47. Glazebrook, pers. comm.

48. Pedieus Painter, red-figure *kylix*, 525–475 BCE, Louvre G 13, *ARV*2 86, Reeder 1995, 109 fig. 10 (A), Kilmer 1993, R 156.

49. Sian Lewis notes that our interest in these explicit scenes leads to their overrepresentation in books: there are only five such examples (2002, 4–5, 124, 295 n. 106).

50. As Robin Osborne pointed out after reading this essay, conversation varies "just as in modern society it varies a lot from situation to situation (rugby club talk goes down badly at Oxford high tables . . .)."

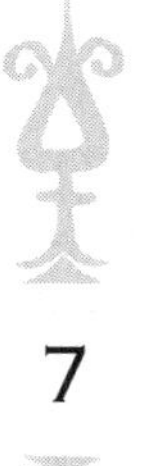

7 The Brothels at Delos

The Evidence for Prostitution in the Maritime World

T. DAVINA MCCLAIN and

NICHOLAS K. RAUH

Few suggestions about the identification of functional space in the remains of ancient "domestic quarters" have generated as much controversy as Nicholas Rauh's hypothesis that the House of the Lake in the harbor district of Delos was a *tabernaria deversoria*, a tavern-inn that incorporated prostitution as a component commercial enterprise.[1] The argument is based on some eccentricities about the building, most particularly three large reliefs carved into exterior wall blocks and located in situ at opposite ends of the house.[2] Here we examine the character of these reliefs within the context not only of their placement on the building but also their positioning throughout the wider "district" of the Sacred Lake. We conclude that the clustering of these and similar reliefs, when combined with what we know about the associated building complexes, point to this neighborhood as a place of male recreational pursuits such as prostitution. The evidence demonstrates that the timing of the development of this neighborhood coincided with that of the notorious Delian slave trade (ca. 139–88 BCE), when the island was presumably frequented during summer sailing season by droves of rootless, unattached males—sailors, merchants, pirates, and soldiers.

Identifying Locations of Prostitution

Any attempt to identify the functional space of prostitution remains extremely controversial. Some locations, such as the Purpose-Built Brothel at Pompeii, are unambiguous as to their function, but such clarity is rare where places of prostitution generally are concerned.[3] More often than not, utilitarian structures leave few indicators of the activities that occurred within them. It becomes necessary, accordingly, to look for additional clues that might indicate the emergence and integration of venues of prostitution in the remains of ancient urban landscapes. The problem in determining the identity of locations of prostitution comes in constructing too narrow or limiting guidelines. Andrew Wallace-Hadrill, for example, has argued that three elements are needed to prove that a building or space was dedicated to prostitution: graffiti that explicitly identifies sexual activity, a masonry bed, and sexually explicit artwork (1995, 52). Although requiring these three elements may make sense when seeking to establish the use of a structure such as Pompeii's Purpose-Built Brothel, the realities of prostitution in the ancient Greco-Roman world were far too complex for one such example to serve as a universal template. Textual evidence for Greco-Roman prostitution argues that venues of prostitution served multiple functions and that the prostitutes worked in a variety of "urban environments" on a regular basis.[4] Indeed, the wide variety of names for prostitutes and for brothels suggests that the concepts of prostitute and prostitution were as multifaceted in the ancient world as they are today, if not more so (Adams 1983).[5]

Harbors and Prostitution: The Sacred Lake "District" at Delos

With these challenges to identifying places of prostitution in mind, we consider the development of the "district" or neighborhood of the Sacred Lake at Delos. Typically, ancient harbor towns were notorious for prostitution. The liminality of ancient Mediterranean harbors—spatially, socially, economically—encumbered these settlements with advantages and disadvantages that made places like Corinth, the Piraeus, Pompeii, Puteoli, Ostia, and Delos notable. Transient populations, the prevalence of money economies, and the predominance of young, male, unattached, nonagricultural, wage laborers combined to encourage the development of commercial prostitution alongside other recreational outlets.[6] Delos in the late second/early first centuries BCE was probably exemplary in this regard. After favoring Macedonia during Rome's war with King Perseus, the island's inhabitants were expelled by Rome and replaced by an Athenian cleruchy (166 BCE). The Roman Senate granted Athens control of the island on condition that its harbor remain a "duty-free" zone for all transit cargoes. This unique advantage transformed the island into a major hub of the trans-Mediterranean slave and luxury trade. The island quickly assumed the appearance of an international "boomtown" as wealthy foreign merchants relocated from Italy and Syria, Phoenicia, Palestine, and Egypt. Whole neighborhoods such as the "district" of the Sacred Lake underwent "remodeling" to accommodate the demand.[7] Remains of edifices designed to offer recreational activities to the milling crowd of merchants and sailors who frequented the island during the summer sailing season ought to be visible in the archaeological landscape. Because of the "absentee-landlord" character of Athenian authority on the island, however, the design and scale of commercial facilities for prostitution need not necessarily present themselves according to the template established by Wallace-Hadrill, nor in any other uniform or easily recognizable manner. Many of these establishments were likely indistinguishable from ordinary houses, reflecting the tendency of the industry to develop piecemeal as pimps and patrons acquired or constructed houses in areas of high-volume foot traffic (cf. McGinn 2004, 15–17).[8] Certain establishments possibly gained notoriety as venues of male entertainment, thus attracting foot traffic; other establishments might then have relocated to the immediate vicinity to profit from the gathering population. Eventually salient features, commercial signage, aligned commercial establishments, and streets leading inextricably to commercial doorways ought to reveal themselves. The district of the Sacred Lake at Delos presents itself as something of a "red-light district" from this perspective.

The Sacred Lake region was largely developed during the era of Athenian suzerainty in Delos (ca. 150–88 BCE) (Bruneau 1968, 668–71; Siebert 2001).[9] Apart from a few venerable religious monuments, specifically the Temple of the Dodecatheon (*GD* 51), the Letoön (*GD* 53), and the Terrace of the Naxian Lions (*GD* 55) along with the two Hellenistic-era gymnasia (the Palaestra of the Lake and the Granite Palaestra), the terrain was largely vacant until this time (Bruneau 1968, 635–36; *GD* 171).[10] Men's clubs, such as the Establishment of the Beirut Poseidonists (*GD* 57), established by 153 or 152 BCE, the so-called Agora of the Italians (*GD* 52), begun after 110 BCE, and possibly the House of the Diadumenus (*GD* 61) quickly transformed the neighborhood (see Rauh 1993, 30–31).[11] A large two-story *insula*-like commercial structure, the Monument of Granite (*GD* 54), went up directly opposite the Agora of the Italians (*GD* 171).[12] Together these two complexes framed a narrowed entrance to a pedestrian "boulevard" extending from the intersection with the north road of the Sanctuary of Apollo, past the Letoön, the Agora of the Italians, and the Sacred Lake on the east and the Monument of Granite, the Naxian Lions, and the Establishment of the Beirut Poseidonists on the west. Originally the road probably extended past the two palaestrae toward the harbor at the Bay of Skardhana. Panajotis Hatzidakis, who has recently reexcavated an area opened earlier by the French, has demonstrated, however, that its progress was soon obstructed by a cluster of menial shops and storefronts directly west of the

Palaestra of the Lake.[13] The artifacts found in these structures demonstrate that they mark the culmination of the cluttered, seemingly uncontrolled development of the Sacred Lake district. By this time (before the outbreak of the First Mithridatic War in 88 BCE) houses encroached on the sloping terrain west of the Naxian Lions. At first these were arranged along straight paths characteristic of Delian development elsewhere during this era, but eventually they became arranged along increasingly irregular paths designed to utilize in any way possible the diminishing available space in this neighborhood.[14]

Although imperfectly understood, the history of the development of the Sacred Lake district sets it apart from that of other excavated neighborhoods at Delos, particularly the theater district and the stadium district. Although houses in these two other areas were also remodeled, adapted, and expanded to accommodate the housing crunch that occurred at Delos during this era, the fact remains that these neighborhoods were older and more extensively developed prior to the expulsion of the Delian inhabitants in 166 BCE (Bruneau 1968; Trümper 1998). Everything observed about the district of the Sacred Lake indicates that its development as a "domestic quarter" coincided precisely with the era of the Delian slave trade. Amphorae discovered in the House of the Comedians, the House of the Seal Stamps, the House of the Sword, and at a large warehouse bordering the east bank of the Sacred Lake, for example, all date precisely to the late second/early first centuries BCE.[15] Obviously one must avoid exaggerating this point: evidence of habitation and extensive remodeling at the time of the slave trade survives in all excavated neighborhoods at Delos, and had the amphora remains been examined as carefully in the other districts as they were in the district of the Sacred Lake they would probably have revealed similar chronological results.[16] Nevertheless, the accumulated evidence suggesting that the development of the Sacred Lake district occurred largely between 150 and 88 BCE makes it a useful proving ground for habitation patterns during the peak era of the Delian slave trade.

The Reliefs: Phalli, *Piloi*, and the Club of Heracles

All of this has direct bearing on the clustered presence of exterior wall reliefs found in this neighborhood. The fact that the reliefs were concentrated largely in this district and not in the older ones of the theater and the stadium suggests that they represent a significant component of the development that occurred here at this particular juncture, just as their near dearth elsewhere on Delos indicates that they played little role in those localities. Indeed, given the remodeling that is known to have occurred concurrently elsewhere, the absence of these reliefs in these other

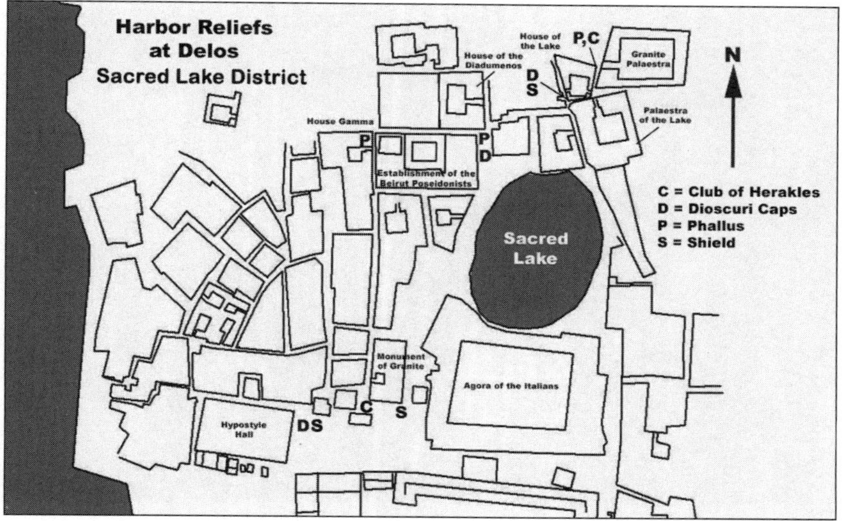

Figure 7.1. Plan of the Sacred Lake area showing reliefs of Heracles' clubs, *piloi*, shields, and phalli. Drawing by Nicholas K. Rauh.

neighborhoods makes their presence in the district of the Sacred Lake all the more striking. The reliefs come in three forms: reliefs of horizontally pointing phalli, reliefs of oblong objects identified by Philippe Bruneau as clubs of Heracles, and reliefs of twin caps emblazoned with stars, identified as the *piloi* (caps) of the Dioscuri, the twin-brother patrons of sailors, Castor and Pollux. In two instances the caps frame a round object identified as a shield (or moon) at the center; in two other examples the cap and shield motifs appear in separate reliefs.[17] With few exceptions the wall blocks exhibiting the reliefs are very large—greater than 1 meter—and furnished permanent, patently visible ornamentation to building exteriors in the neighborhood.[18] Some reliefs survive in situ while others were deposited in the vicinity of their original findspots. Those surviving in situ tend to be situated at corners of the buildings in question, at or near doorways (though rarely above them), or otherwise at eye level at street intersections where they would undoubtedly have caught the attention of passersby.

As the map shows (see fig. 7.1), these reliefs appear to be clustered in three particular street intersections of the Sacred Lake district. One group survives near the southern entrance to the "boulevard" framed by the Agora of the Italians and the Monument of Granite. Slightly removed, limestone blocks (*voussoirs*) that form the key to a doorway arch exhibit twin *piloi* capped with stars set to either side of

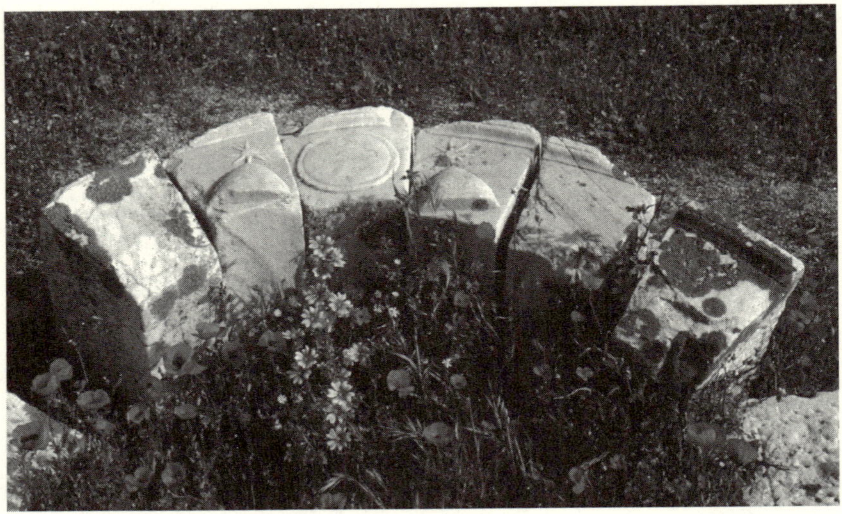

Figure 7.2. Relief of *piloi* flanking a shield. From a no-longer-extant structure near the Hypostyle Hall. Photo by Nicholas K. Rauh.

a central shield (see fig. 7.2). According to Bruneau, the *voussoir* blocks were found in a ruined structure behind the Hypostyle Hall and deposited within the remains of the hall for safe keeping (1964, 160; 1970, 398, 643).[19] Closer to the Agora of the Italians, the relief of a circular shield appears on a granite block found at the southeast corner of the Monument of Granite, while a relief representing the club of Heracles was found on a similar wall block at the building's southwest corner. Presumably both of these would have been placed somewhere high along the exterior walls of the Monument of Granite so that they would confront pedestrians turning onto the "boulevard" of the Sacred Lake from the avenue bordering the northern perimeter of the Sanctuary of Apollo. Progressing northward along the boulevard one would have encountered a second cluster of reliefs at its northern end, precisely where it was interrupted by an intersection formed by menial shops in the vicinity of the Establishment of the Beirut Poseidonists and the House of the Diadumenus. A relief of twin *piloi* devoid of central shield was also discovered in the vicinity of the House of the Diadumenus (Bruneau 1964, 161 fig. 12; Bruneau 1970, 398 pl. 16, fig. 3).[20] Along the street that separates this establishment from that of the Beirut Poseidonists, archaeologists found a relief of a club of Heracles (Bruneau 1970, 404 pl. 16, fig. 1). At the corner of the very same intersection on the south-facing wall of the House of the Diadumenus, the excavators recorded in situ a stuccoed wall relief of two feet tentatively identified as the legs of a phallus

(Chamonard 1922, 106 fig. 47). The published photograph indicates that the phallus faced left (west) pointing up the street (street C) that passed along the north side of the Establishment of the Beirut Poseidonists. If one were to proceed in this direction and turn left (south) at the end of the Poseidonists' complex, one would have encountered a quick succession of doorways in the "houses" that faced directly opposite from across the narrow street (houses B, C, and D). The entrance to house C in particular began as a short alleyway leading to the recessed doorway of a partially excavated house slightly set back from the street. The excavated marble posts of the doorway, in situ, exhibit small reliefs set high on their inner faces above the doorsill. To the right stands a graffito-like phallus with a "smiley face" and sticklike legs recalling the stuccoed feet of the phallus relief at the House of the Diadumenus; to the left a skeletal human figure appears to be slaying a small animal with a large knife.[21] The similarity of the phallus reliefs and the fact that the stuccoed relief seemingly drew passersby away from the boulevard into the narrow streets and to this doorway suggests that their implantation was coordinated. Had one ignored the stuccoed phallus and proceeded right (east) along the boulevard toward the two palaestrae (Palaestra of the Lake and Granite Palaestra), one would have encountered three additional reliefs at the House of the Lake. Directly beside the door at the southwest side of the house, a long block of granite in situ exhibits the twin *piloi* flanking a central rounded shield. Passing the House of the Lake and turning north along the street that separates it from the Granite Palaestra, one encounters two additional reliefs at the northeast corner of the house. These very large reliefs stand directly opposite the west side entrance to the palaestra and were intended to be viewed by those exiting the complex. On granite blocks set diagonally from each other in the wall, one relief exhibits a club of Heracles and the other a long, arching, horizontal phallus, both pointing unmistakably back along the street toward the door at the southeast corner of the House of the Lake (see fig. 7.3). Although Bruneau and others interpret all of these reliefs as apotropaic devices, the combinations of the reliefs, their arrangements in specific localities, and the identification of some of the adjoining complexes suggests that there are other ways to interpret them. At the very least it is possible to suggest that the location of these reliefs in or near doorways or at street intersections was too deliberate to have been a coincidence.

As Bruneau himself once suggested, the phalli and Heracles' clubs at the northeast corner of the House of the Lake point sideways in a manner resembling that of direction indicators (1978, 165). However, important caveats must be reiterated here. As Hatzidakis demonstrates, numerous additional phallus reliefs and terracottas have been found in the remains at Delos, revealing their rich and varied use in Delian popular culture (2003, 289). The fact that several phalli, such

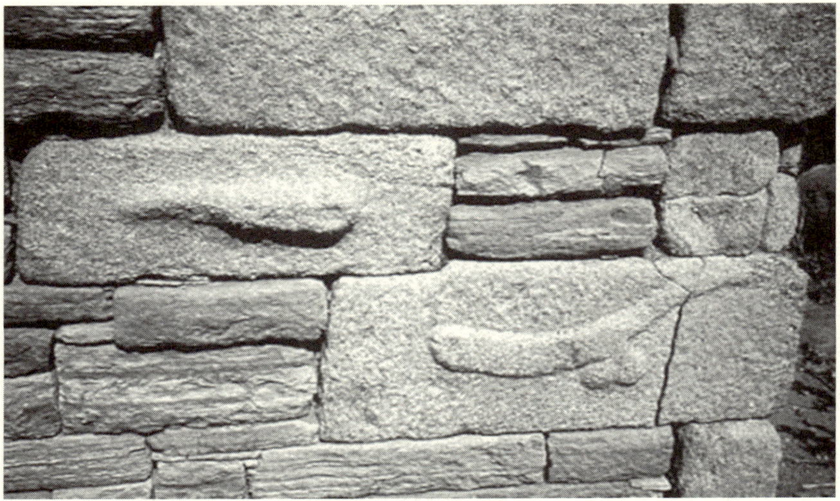

Figure 7.3. Relief of phallus and Heracles' club directing the viewer to the door of the House of the Lake. Photo by Nicholas K. Rauh.

as those found at the House of Skardhana and the House of the Inopus, were not found in situ and do not resemble in form those found in the Sacred Lake district complicates matters immensely (Bruneau 1964, 162; Bruneau 1970, 643 pl. 16, fig. 5; Hatzidakis 2003, 289 fig. 513). At least two additional phallus reliefs do survive in situ, however. One stands at the intersection of road 5 behind the Sacred Harbor and an alley leading to a doorway on the side wall of warehouse alpha in the Agora of the Competaliasts.[22] Another phallus relief sits high on a wall at the intersection of the Road of the Theater and a small street labeled "alley delta" and points sideways into the alley. This particular passageway ends in a cul-de-sac consisting of a small cluster of menial habitations too modest to qualify as houses. These two in-situ phallus reliefs closely resemble in design and setting the phallus relief at the House of the Lake. In view of the nondescript character of the localities of these two reliefs (one along an alley leading between two harbor warehouses, the other pointing to a short cul-de-sac framed by menial structures), we have connected these two phalli with likely venues of prostitution in the past. Further up the Road of the Theater, however, a relief of a club of Heracles survives in situ at the exterior wall of the celebrated House of Dionysus. In other words, a handful of the reliefs in question are found in neighborhoods beyond the Sacred Lake district, rendering their interpretation more difficult. One must also acknowledge that the motif of Heracles bearing his club figured in stuccoed wall paintings on the exterior walls of several houses excavated at Delos, including two in the district of the Sacred Lake, which complicates matters further.[23] One has to allow for the possibility, therefore, that the wall paintings and the in-situ exterior reliefs of phalli, Dioscuri caps, and clubs of Heracles were somehow intended to form a combined decorative program of ancient popular culture whose import eludes us today. Still, the fact remains that the bulk of the exterior wall reliefs of phalli, clubs, and *piloi* occurred in concentrated clusters in the district of the Sacred Lake where an unmistakable array of men's clubs and palaestrae were situated. Several of these reliefs appear to have been positioned to alert passersby to the character of this district, almost as if they were intended to "mark the territory" of a men's club region on the island. If our reconstruction is correct, the reliefs tend to confront passersby at eye level at intersections where a choice in direction had to be made, and they potentially aid in that decision by pointing toward doorways along narrowing streets. With respect to the stuccoed phallus feet on the south wall of the House of the Diadumenus, the relief seems to mark a deliberate attempt to redirect passersby away from the more natural route leading in the direction of the palaestrae by the Sacred Lake toward the narrow street leading eventually to houses along the back side of the Establishment of the Beirut Poseidonists. Although one must resist the urge to exaggerate these findings, the clusters of reliefs representing the Dioscuri caps, Heracles' clubs, and horizontally pointing phalli appear to designate the district of the Sacred Lake as an area of male recreation or entertainment. And, as noted, their placement and arrangement appear to have been contemporary with the historical development of this neighborhood and more specifically with the emergence of a number of men's clubs, palaestrae, and clustered food and wine shops in the immediate vicinity of the Sacred Lake. The presence of a handful of these reliefs in other areas of the island indicates that the district of the Sacred Lake was not the only such district, but it would seem to have been the main center at Delos.

Prostitution and Delos

First, however, it will help to say a little more about suggested areas of prostitution on Delos. Rauh has previously argued that the rather strangely designed residence, the House of the Lake, tucked away at the northern end of the Sacred Lake at a fork in the road leading from the Sanctuary of Apollo to the Bay of Skardhana offers features that suggest that it may have housed prostitution (see Couve 1895; Chamonard 1922, 417–25; *GD* 64; Kreeb 1988, 40, 162–66; Rauh 1993, 206–7). The angular location forced its architect to adapt the design of a two-story, rectangular, peristyle structure to a more or less triangular plot of land. Additional peculiarities include the division of the northern side of the house into three large, distinct "suites" of rooms. In the larger geographical context, the exterior walls of this house contribute to the reliefs of the large curved phallus and club of Heracles that are set low on the wall directly opposite the entrance to the Granite Palaestra at the northeast corner of the house. The symbols face left and are arranged diagonally to one another. Although the standard interpretation identifies these reliefs as apotropaic devices, given their distance from the doorways to the house, this function seems unlikely (Bruneau 1964; Bruneau 1970, 643–45; Bruneau 1979, 104–5).[24] Secondly, the Dioscuri and shield reliefs on the southwestern corner also mark the house; they perhaps indicate that the house is a place safe for sailors but perhaps also suggest that it is located in an area where recreation could be found, such as boxing, for which the Dioscuri, in particular, were known.

Phallic Markers: A Reinterpretation

Challenging the interpretation of the phallus reliefs, which have long been labeled almost exclusively as apotropaic devices, will provoke further controversy (Slane and Dickie 1993). Yet, as has been shown, some of the phalli appear to point toward locations of commercial prostitution, just as the other reliefs appear to be clustered near the other men's clubs. In challenging the strictly apotropaic label, we follow and expand on the suggestion of both Thomas McGinn and Wilhelmina Jashemski that a phallus relief marks a place of prostitution. McGinn identifies as a place of prostitution the structure located in Pompeii's *regio* 1 outside *insulae* 17–19, on the basis of the phallus on the exterior wall, the sleeping rooms in the back, and the "Hic futui" (I fucked here) graffiti (2004, 270). Similarly, Jashemski states that a phallus over a doorway marked a crib for prostitution (1977, 220 with n. 19). In light of the multiple interpretations of phallus reliefs in the Greco-Roman world, we propose that the apotropaic-only interpretation offers too limited a view of the function of phallic images generally and that it fails, accordingly, to furnish an adequate explanation for the images found in clusters in the Sacred Lake district on Delos.

Phallus reliefs have been found in other Italian cities such as Ostia, Alba Fucens, and Pompeii. Archaeologists typically believe that they functioned as apotropaic devices, warning passersby of the "particularly dangerous" nature of these locales (Jashemski 1979, 353 with nn. 18–20; G. Picard 1969, 223; Hatzidakis 2003, 287, 290).[25] Certainly, some phalli, when accompanied by a threatening inscription, are clearly meant as a warning (see Clarke 2003, 108–9 fig. 76). Kathleen Slane and Matthew Dickie cite several phalli with inscriptions from the outskirts of the Roman Empire (Themetra in Africa Proconsularis, northern England, and Dalmatia) that make statements in the vein of "Hoc invidiis" (This is for the envious) (1993, 488–92). They note examples only from the edges of the empire, however, and none from the Roman world proper. A mosaic from Antioch from the House of the Evil Eye shows a clear example of a phallus as part of a series of weapons or attackers aimed at warding off the evil eye: prominent in the mosaic is an eye that is impaled by both a trident and a sword and that is being attacked by a cat, a centipede, a scorpion, a dog, a bird, and a snake. To the left of the eye is a figure, perhaps a dwarf, wearing a mask and clicking sticks in front of him with his back to the eye. His phallus points backward between his legs at the eye. Although the image is unambiguous, the artist added the inscription to confirm the threat *kai su* (and you). The image of an eye possibly being impaled by a phallus in a relief found at the House of the Inopus may likewise have been apotropaic.[26] However, the horizontally pointing phallus reliefs found elsewhere at Delos and at other places appear to be different.[27] Unlike the Antioch mosaic, the other combined reliefs of the phallus and Heracles' club do not protect the opening to a specific dwelling but rather seem subtly to direct those who exit the Granite Palaestra to the door at the southeast corner of the House of the Lake.

Phallus reliefs in other areas of Delos appear to have a similar effect. The two phallus reliefs in situ on external walls along road 5 on the wall of Magasin Alpha some distance from the corner and along the Road of the Theater on the wall of Magasin 49 are also located near the port but are not accompanied by other reliefs. Both are set high on the wall and both appear to direct the viewer down narrow alleyways: the one leads to a side door on Warehouse Alpha (see fig. 7.4); the other points down a cul-de-sac that leads to a cluster of small structures (see Bruneau 1979, 104–5; Rauh 1993, 211; Rauh, Dillon, and McClain 2008, 202–3).

It seems possible, then, that these phalli served as directional indicators, a function that even scholars who argue for the strictly apotropaic interpretation of phallic images sometimes acknowledge: for example, in their article on a phallic Knidian vase, Slane and Dickie describe a number of phallic images, including "a badly preserved painting below the stairs of a shop in Pompeii (1, 6, 12) [that] shows a male figure with one phallus coming from his groin, which points towards the Via dell' Abbondanza, and another emerging from his buttocks, which is directed at the door leading in the back of the shop" (1993, 10 with n. 53). The two phalli in this image thus encourage even the skeptical viewer to look in the directions in which they are pointing. Likewise, in discussing mosaics of bath attendants, John Clarke points out the directional function of two images. The first figure is that of the Ethiopian in the entry to the caldarium of the House of Menander at Pompeii, who strides from left to right: the "active figure appears just as the spectator

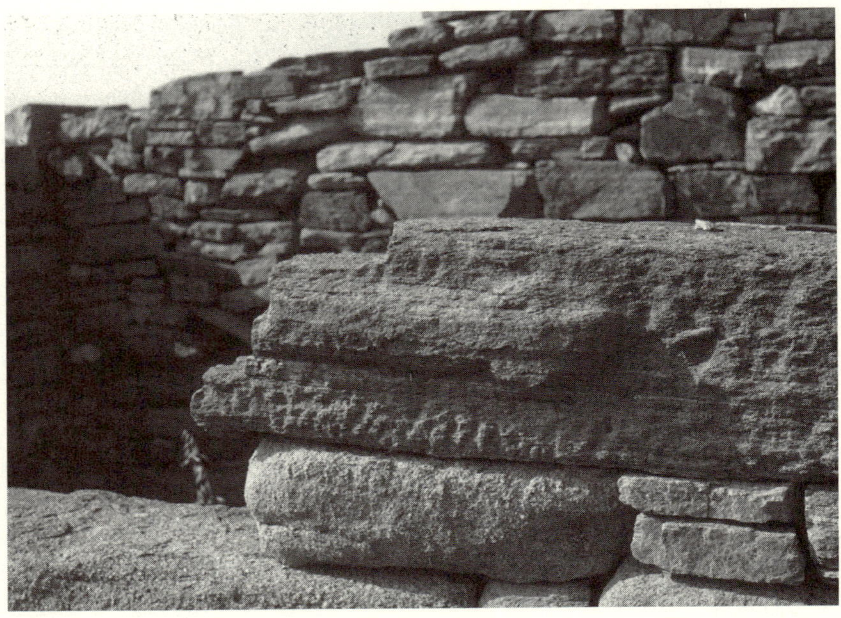

Figure 7.4. Relief of phallus pointing down an alley along Warehouse Alpha. Photo by Nicholas K. Rauh.

is about to enter the caldarium, and he [the spectator] will certainly follow the left-to-right direction of the *unguentarius'* stride (and erection). . . ." (1979, 13). A second is the figure of Buticosus, which greets the visitor to the Baths of Buticosus in Ostia Antica: "It is clear from his stance and his directional erection that we are meant to follow him into room C" (1979, 25–26). Although in his earlier work on black-and-white mosaics (1979) Clarke focuses on the directional nature of these two images and phalli, in *Looking at Lovemaking* (1998) he argues at length that these and other ithyphallic images of bath attendants are apotropaic (1998, 129–36), and relegates to a footnote the statement that "the figure of Buticosus also shares with the House of Menander bath attendant the function of directing the viewer to the most important doorway; the *Aethiops* with his left-to-right stride, Buticosus with his 'directional' erection, pointing to the viewer's right" (1998, 303 n. 52). As Clarke shows, the two ideas need not be contradictory or mutually exclusive: phallic images in mosaics and phallic reliefs on walls may have served to direct the eye of the viewer as well as offer some protection or comfort to the traveler.[28]

Herms

The relationship between phalli and doorways is complicated. Consider for a moment the development of one of the most well-known images of phalli in the Greek world: herms. The basic function of a herm was to mark boundaries and then after 520 BCE specifically to mark the halfway points between the Athenian Agora and other Attic towns (Goldman 1942).[29] If, as Hetty Goldman argues, the development of the image was influenced by the rituals of the rural Dionysia, which celebrated the images of Dionysus set up to protect the crops and make them fertile, herms then were multipurposed: marking boundaries, offering protection, and ensuring fertility and prosperity. The ones set up along the roads—in addition to specifying the midpoint between Athens and the next town—reportedly offered bits of wisdom from Hipparchus (son of Pisistratus, murdered in 514 BCE) in the hope of convincing country travelers of the greatness of Hipparchus and Athens (Pl. [Hipparch.] 228c–229b). For comparison, the herm of Plato at the University of California-Berkeley Museum, recently declared an ancient creation and not a modern copy, offers quotations that reflect Platonic philosophy.[30] One quotation inscribed on its base states, "Every soul is immortal."[31] The other quotation advises caution in choosing one's next soul: "Blame the one who makes the choice; God is blameless" (Pl. *Resp.* 10.617e).

The development of the herm form into a more anthropomorphic image—a human head, usually but not always male, normally bearded, with male genitalia either flat against or protruding from the square pillar—can be attributed to the Athenians who used them to mark important public and private spaces in the city, particularly doorways or gates. In her detailed study of archaic and archaistic statuary in the Athenian Agora, Evelyn B. Harrison catalogues herms that individuals set up as memorials and commemorations of victories.[32] Nothing suggests that these herms had an apotropaic purpose. Why, then, if the primary function seems to be marking boundaries and doorways and as conveyors of Athenian propaganda, has the term apotropaic become so synonymous with the herm and other phallic images? Walter Burkert, in discussing herms and Hermes, sheds light on the evolution of this idea when he states that the "modern history of religion has coined a convenient term to cover this and related phenomena, from Babylonian phallus-shaped boundary stones to phallus pictures in doorways at Pompeii: the phallus is 'apotropaic,' besides having its obvious fertilizing function" (1979, 40). In *Greek Religion*, Burkert explicitly connects herms with marking territory: "Another form of territorial demarcation, older than man himself, is phallic display, which is then symbolically replaced by erected stones or stakes" (1985, 156). He then also expresses his own discomfort with the phallic images: "The obscenity [of the erect *membrum virile*] is caught up in the geometric form and somehow neutralized" (1985, 156).

Lumping all these images together under a "convenient term" does not make the assertion an accurate description of their function. And "obscene" is a modern—not an ancient—judgment of phallic images. The suggestion, therefore, that this most prevalent of phallic images did not have a strictly apotropaic function is also consistent with Slane and Dickie's own rather inconsistent statement about the history of apotropaic images:

> Both the phallus and the motif of self-strangulation or choking are used to avert the Evil Eye of Envy. The phallus in particular was the most widely used means of warding it off. In Greece its use is attested from the sixth century BC onwards, although there is much less evidence for its employment against the Evil Eye in the Greek-speaking world and especially in Greece itself than there is in the Latin-speaking world. The phallus as an *apotropaeum* against the Evil Eye was known in the Roman world from at least the second century BC. (1993, 486)

So the phallus is apotropaic but not in Greece, and such a use is not even documented in the Roman world until the second century BCE. This assessment of the function of the phallus suggests that its purpose and meaning needs more study. In addition, it is worth remembering, as Christopher Faraone points out, that "the adjective *apotropaios*, although it is regularly used as an epithet of protective gods or to describe a form of 'averting' sacrifice, does not appear to have been used to refer to a stationary object that performs a similar function" (1992, 4–5).

Phallus Reliefs at Delos

A pair of phallus reliefs, each displaying the twin phalli discovered at the House of Fourni near the Bay of Skardhana, also calls into question the assumption that phallus reliefs always serve as apotropaic devices (Marcadé 1969, 329–30; Bruneau 1970, 633). The House of Fourni complex, isolated on the far southern side of the island, with its enclosed courtyard and raised Rhodian portico on the east side, includes a row of shops at the front and a large reservoir for water behind the structure near a rock outcrop at the back of the building. The plaques with the phalli were found in the rubble before what were the entrances of the building (see Roes 1935; Marcadé 1969). Unlike the smiling phallus at house C that has no inscription, the phrases *Touto emoi, kai touto soi* (This one's mine/for me, and this one's yours/for you) and *Touto soi, kai touto emoi* (This one's yours/for you, and this one's mine/for me) appear between the winged dancing Fourni phalli (for photographs, see Hatzidakis 2003, 287 figs. 507–8).

This pairing of phalli raises new questions. Slane and Dickie call these reliefs "phallic monsters" and argue that they belong in the category of "Hoc invidiis" (This is for the envious) phallic markers and inscriptions (1993, 492). Their explanation is challenged by the mutuality of the threat. Why would the person setting up the inscription propose a threat to himself? One point of comparison comes from the hundreds of images in Greek and Roman art that are not apotropaic in nature. The numerous images of sexual acts in vase paintings, in statuary, and in wall paintings, most of which present images that focus on penetration or the moment before penetration or offer images of one man fondling another, usually younger, man's penis have nothing to do with warding off danger. Nor do the images of men, women, and satyrs using phalli or about to use phalli for anal or vaginal penetration appear to have an apotropaic function, so the argument that disembodied or fake phalli serve a different function from those attached to male bodies should not necessarily be a given. Note that even herms are represented as options for sexual penetration: an Arretine bowl fragment shows an ithyphallic herm surrounded by images of homosexual and heterosexual intercourse, and a marble sarcophagus in the National Archaeological Museum at Naples shows a young satyr mounting a smiling herm (see fig. 7.5).[33] For two phalli, in particular, consider also a wall painting from the Suburban Baths of Pompeii (room 7, scene 6)—a woman is being penetrated by a man who is himself at the same time being penetrated by a man—could a hypothetical inscription inscribed below this scene not read "This one's for you, this one's for me"?

One phallic monument on Delos clearly is not apotropaic. The Stoibadeion or Sanctuary of Dionysus includes two giant phalli on tall column bases (see Bruneau 1970, 296–304). These monuments commemorate the theater and Dionysus, perhaps reminding viewers of the phalli worn by comic actors but more likely invoking Dionysus's associations with fertility and sexuality. Similarly, the association with Hermes may add a guardian aspect to the herms, but the negative aspect of an apotropaic device with its focus on harm should not overshadow the positive elements of prosperity and fertility and sexuality that the phallus represents. We compare two phallus reliefs from Pompeii: in a bakery on the wall above the oven, there was a relief of a phallus in a vertical position with the inscription "Hic habitat felicitas" (Here dwells happiness) (see fig. 7.6.).[34] The message of this phallus relief is not one of danger; rather the image and its message emphasize or encourage the prosperity of the place of business. This sentiment is exactly the opposite of that of "Hoc invidiis," since it might, in fact, encourage envy in those less fortunate. Similarly, two phalli on a vat at the door of a fuller's

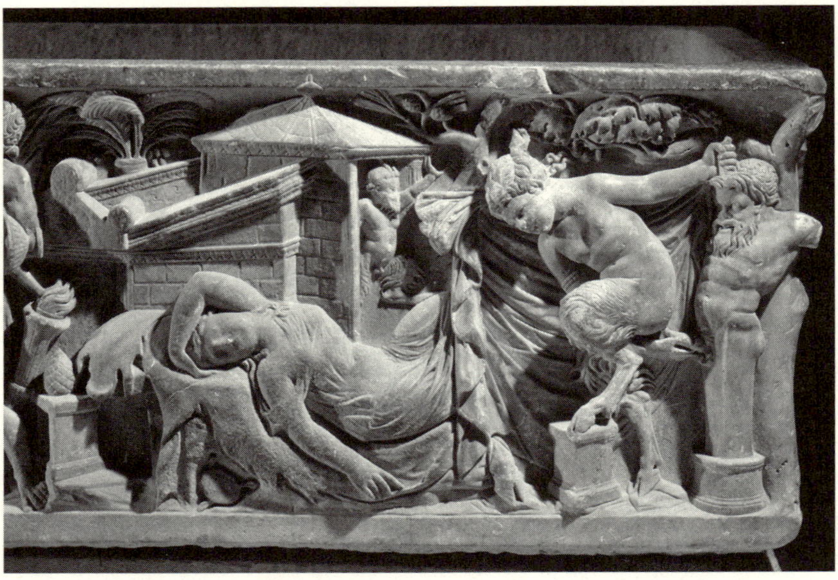

Figure 7.5. Roman sarcophagus with bacchanalia relief (detail), late second century CE. Museo Archeologico Nazionale, Naples [ART174433]. Photo © Scala / Art Resource, New York.

shop in Pompeii also suggest prosperity: one phallus on the side of the fuller's vat, with a horizontal orientation leading the viewer in the direction of what appears to be a step, is swollen and ready to burst, suggesting an invitation to the passerby to make a contribution; the second phallus is framed in a small shrine relief. This winged phallus, presented vertically and on the other side of the step, faces the sidewalk and seems also to encourage or direct viewers to contribute to the fuller's prosperity. The variety of phallic images and the different message associated with them suggest that there is more to learn about how these and other reliefs functioned in the Greco-Roman world.

Male Prostitution at Delos

The connection between some phallic reliefs and locations of prostitution appears secure. What is less certain is the evidence for male prostitution in concert with female prostitution in Delos. In other harbors, evidence does exist suggesting that male prostitutes worked in brothels, or *oikēmata*—Aeschines 1.40 mentions Timarchus's sexual activities at the Piraeus; in Athenaeus's *Deipnosophistae*, Stratonicus calls Heraclea "Andro-Corinth" and is afraid of being seen coming out

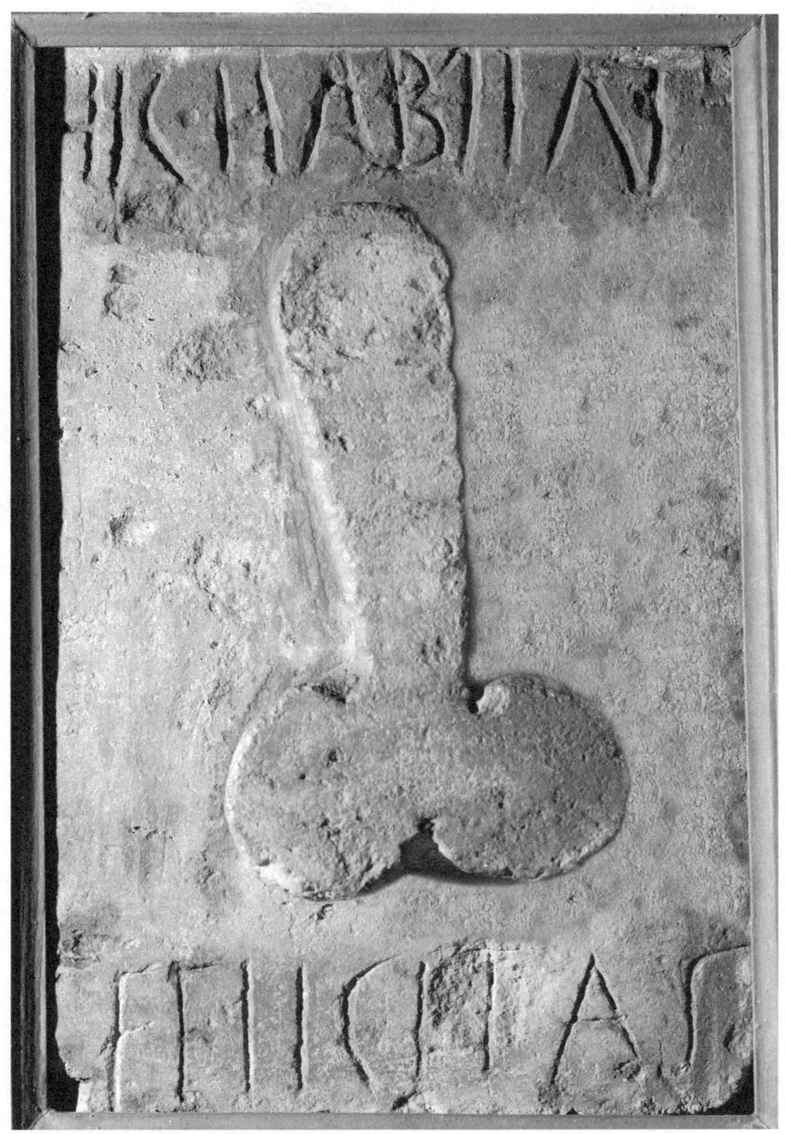

Figure 7.6. Phallus, stone relief from Pompeii, first century CE. Museo Archeolgico Nazionale, Naples [ART63529]. Photo © Erich Lessing / Art Resource, New York.

of the city as if he were coming out of a brothel (8.352d)—and this may establish a similar pattern for Delos. Although most references to male prostitutes indicate that they were slaves (e.g., Trimalchio in the *Satyricon* and Phaedo in Diog. Laert. 2.105), the comic reference in Theopompos to a possible boys' brothel on Mt. Lycabettus (fr. 29 *PCG*; Halperin 1990, 91) and a comic lament about boys called *pornoi*, because they demand payment for services (Ar. *Plut.* 153–56) point to the availability of male prostitutes in other cities. Ostia offers the House of Jupiter and Ganymede, once called by Clarke a hotel for homosexual lovers but suggested by McGinn to be a men's brothel (Clarke 1991, 89–104; McGinn 2004, 226–31). In Rome, Plautus's *Curculio* identifies the Tuscan Alley through the Velabrum as a place where "there are men who themselves sell themselves" and where there are "those who themselves turn and those who offer to others to be turned" (482–84).[35] The possibility that phalli mark sites of male prostitution helps explain a wall sculpture that has long perplexed scholars. A plaque in Pompeii exhibits a phallus protruding from the wall with the inscription "Hanc ego cacavi" (I shat this). In his study *Roman Sex*, Clarke seems at a loss and states that "no scholar has been able to offer an explanation for this strangely permanent record of a good-luck bowel movement" (2003, 990). But the sculpture is not a piece of excrement; it is a phallus, so perhaps the interpretation should take more account of the phallus. Could the withdrawal of the penis after anal sex be likened to "shitting" a phallus? Although the feminine gender of the pronoun *hanc* appears to pose a problem at first, as J. N. Adams points out, the feminine noun *mentula* was the more common term for penis (1982, 9–13). A. E. Housman connects this particular image and inscription with one of the Priapic poems in which Priapus threatens a would-be fig thief: "Look at me, thief and, once you have determined how great the weight is, (look at) the penis you will have to shit" (ad me respice, fur, et aestimato / quot pondo est tibi mentulam cacandum) (Housman 1931a, 405). As the poem suggests, the phallus on the plaque does not refer to a bowel movement but rather to anal penetration and withdrawal. Even so, it is unclear why someone would announce that he has been penetrated anally, although the emphasis is more on expelling the penis than on the penetration. While a relief on Delos, found to the southwest of the Agora of the Italians, near the Agora of Theophrastus, of a winged phallus attempting to penetrate a cupid who has his hand over his buttocks in protest, expresses a certain objection to anal penetration, could the unusual exterior phallus reliefs at the House of Fourni, the two phalli that proclaim such reciprocity, suggest the activity and availability of male prostitutes and the possibility, therefore, of anal penetration (Marcadé 1969, 401 with n. 4; Hatzidakis 2003, 286 fig. 506)? Although this interpretation does not furnish conclusive evidence for the existence of male prostitution at Delos, the unusual offer presented by the inscriptions at the House of Fourni, combined with the existence of establishments for male prostitution in other harbor cities, at least suggests that a homosexual sex trade may have been available at Delos as well. Since, according to Jashemski, a phallus above a doorway on an exterior wall marks a *cella meretricia* at Pompeii, the inscribed phallus reliefs above the entrances to the House of Fourni may mark the availability of male prostitutes (1977, 220 with n. 19).

Delos's "Red-Light District"

We return to the clusters of reliefs north and south of the Sacred Lake. The location of the House of the Lake at the intersection of streets leading to the Palaestra of the Lake, the Palaestra of Granite, and the Bay of Skardhana, surrounded by shops and a number of "men's clubs," rendered it the center of what might be called an unofficial ancient "red-light district."[36] Although McGinn has objected to the use of the term "red-light district" to refer to the area around the Sacred Lake, his description of the area around Pompeii's Purpose-Built Brothel sounds very much like a red-light district:

> We can safely conclude that not only the Purpose-Built Brothel itself, but the immediate neighborhood around it was an *unofficial* center of sexual activity. The presence of one crib virtually across the street, another down the block, the largest hotel in town across the way, a sizable tavern facing one entrance, and an important bath complex a few steps away are all evidence of this. Sex might have been for sale in any or all of these places, and they might have helped generate business for the brothel. (2004, 238–39)[37]

Although there was certainly no such thing as an officially designated area for recreational establishments, some locations did clearly lend themselves to becoming areas that we would now define as a red-light district: a place where a man could expect to find prostitution and other recreational opportunities. The district of the Sacred Lake seems to have been developed to fulfill just such a purpose. In the absence of red lights, the reliefs on the walls of buildings throughout the neighborhood might have served to advertise and direct passersby to recreational opportunities.

The function of the buildings in the area south of the Sacred Lake is less certain. One location, the Agora of the Italians (see fig. 7.7), offers numerous features that suggest recreational possibilities. The spacious courtyard surrounded by two-story porticoes provided a palaestra-like area. The large doorway offered a grand entrance for the important men who left their mark through statue groups commemorating their generosity. A smaller doorway allowed service personnel to

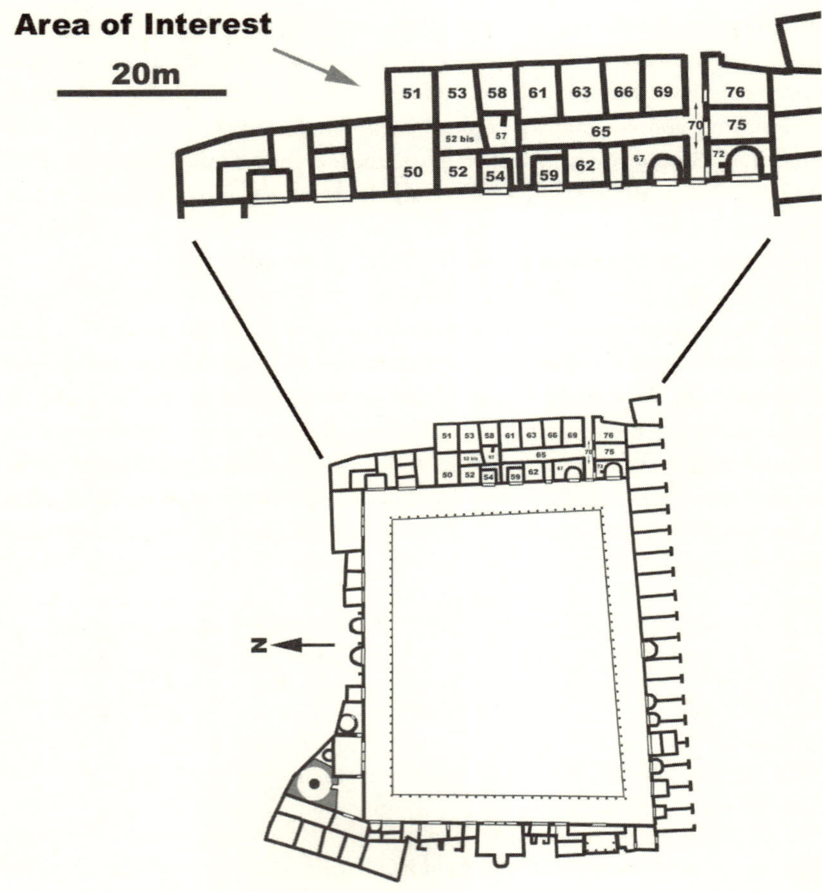

Figure 7.7. Plan of the Agora of the Italians. Drawing by Nicholas K. Rauh.

provide refreshments and carry messages for the guests. The bath complex offered relaxation and exercise for those who chose to take advantage of its proximity. These features are components of the sort of complex that may have existed in southern Italian communities at the end of the second century BCE, where a good percentage of the merchants frequenting Delos originated.[38] Epigraphical evidence suggests that the building was constructed by a wide array of benefactors, including the *magistri* (leaders) and members of the Italian religious fraternities on the island (the Hermesists, the Apollonists, and the Poseidonists), wealthy individual Italian merchants such as C. Ofellius L. f. Ferus and M. Orbius L. f. Hor., and even wealthier near eastern friends such as Philostratos Philostratou of Ascalon (Rauh 1993, 295–96).[39] Additional inscriptions on a column at the entrance to the building's bath complex record the performance of *ludi* (games) and suggest that the building functioned as a "men's club" for the large population of Italian merchants and traders that frequented the island. Otherwise, as Jean Delorme has observed in his study of Greek palaestrae, the wealthy Italian merchants would have had no place of assembly commensurate with their status as international businessmen (1960, 453–55, 493–95).

The function of the attached "outbuilding" with the narrow, transverse corridor sheltering approximately thirteen small cells or cubicles on the building's east side remains disputed (Lapalus 1939, 75 n. 3; Rauh 1992, 293 n. 2; Rauh 1993, 333).[40] Although Rauh at one point suggested that the small rooms might have served as *carceres* (cells) for gladiators and animals, another possibility exists. The key to the function of this outbuilding lies in its role as a service element to the attached "men's club" of the Agora of the Italians.[41] It is likely that this series of small cubicles served as *cellae meretriciae* and thus provided a brothel for the men's club within (see Rauh, Dillon, and McClain 2008, 207–8). The overall design is consistent with descriptions of brothels elsewhere: small dark rooms with no windows that could be screened by curtained doorways and accessible through a single entrance that could easily be monitored (Bloch 1912, 326, 43 with n. 102; cf. McGinn 2004). Such an establishment would have provided a necessary source of income for the maintenance of the men's club and provided an additional draw to merchants passing through Delos's harbor. And just as the *piloi* and shield, club of Heracles, and the phallus reliefs possibly marked the area around the Establishment of the Beirut Poseidonists and the House of the Lake as one of male recreation, so also here the existence of shield and club of Heracles reliefs across the boulevard at the Monument of Granite conceivably highlight the Agora of the Italians as another, similar establishment of male entertainment.[42]

Admittedly, the nature of the archaeological record will continue to pose challenges to the identification of areas of entertainment and prostitution, and the possibilities offered here are by no means devoid of controversy. Yet, if we are to understand the culture and society of the unique environment of maritime cities in general, and on Delos in particular, we have to ask new questions and reexamine past assumptions. There has to be a reason for the clustering of these reliefs in the areas north and south of the Sacred Lake, in association with the House of the Lake, the two palaestrae, the Establishment of the Beruit Poseidonists, the House of the Diadumenus, the Monument of Granite, and the Agora of the Italians. Accumulated evidence points to the harbor at Delos as a thriving and cosmopolitan district with its own version of red lights drawing in the island's transient population of unattached males to areas of entertainment and prostitution, such as that which appears to have emerged on the banks of the Sacred Lake.

NOTES

1. First raised by Rauh 1993, 213; revisited by Rauh, Dillon, and McClain 2008.

2. The other arguments have been presented earlier: multiple wells and cisterns suggest a consumption of water exceeding the requirements of an ordinary domicile; the location of the house at a fork in the road leading from the Sanctuary of Apollo past the west bank of the Sacred Lake indicates that its builder intended it to benefit from heavy foot traffic. The west fork of the road led to the harbor at the Bay of Skardhana; the east fork led past the Granite Palaestra to neighborhoods on the north side of the island. In addition, the house was near two gymnasia and other large complexes tentatively identified as men's clubs and was designed in a trapezoidal fashion to fit within this awkward space—a clear indication that the road system preexisted the house itself. Rauh has attempted to argue as well that the layout of interior rooms, particularly the suite of rooms on the east side of the house, was designed to accommodate privacy. Although the surviving walls of this portion are 3 meters in height, there is no evidence of windows, lending considerable darkness to the rooms. Nonetheless, in all other respects the design of the House of the Lake does not differ radically from that of a dozen other excavated houses on the island. The arrangement of rooms around an interior peristyle court can be found in numerous Delian houses, making any attempt to identify functionality of space exceedingly difficult.

3. Thomas McGinn (2004, 232) offers a compelling argument for this designation for the large brothel or Lupanar in Pompeii.

4. How would Wallace-Hadrill (1995) categorize the spatial requirements for streetwalkers, who, the sources make clear, were commonplace in ancient cities?

5. Thomas McGinn addresses the different venues for prostitution and some of the terminology (2004, 15–30), questioning the idea that prostitution regularly took place in other commercial locations, like bakeries and barbershops (2004, 28–29). He does, however, acknowledge that *alicaria* (one who grinds spelt) may have been used as a slang term for prostitute. Lewis and Short, s.v. *alicarius*, suggest it is because of the presence of prostitutes around spelt mills, but McGinn argues it is the action of grinding that connects the term with prostitution (2004, 28 n. 106; see also Adams 1983, 335–37). For recent studies of prostitution in the modern world, see Farley 2007; Frances 2007; Della Giusta, Tommaso, and Strøm 2008; Kelly 2008; and Warren 2008.

6. Cf. Timothy Gilfoyle (1994) for an account of the development of prostitution in New York City.

7. For a discussion, see Bruneau 1968; Rauh 1993; Müller and Hasenoh 2002; Duchêne and Girerd 2001; and Siebert 2001.

8. On the lack of differences between these establishments and ordinary houses, see Plaut. *Poen.* 302f; Plaut. *Men.* 354f; Cat. 32; Prop. 2.6.27; Bloch 1912, 329.

9. Below the foundations of houses constructed in this era (e.g., Island of the Jewels), there is some evidence of earlier structures, possibly from the beginning of the third century BCE.

10. The Sacred Lake region was partially occupied by gardens during Delos's independence; see *ID* 1417, B II, 11. 110–11, for the garden attached to the Letoön, mentioned epigraphically as late as 157 or 156 BCE. The Palaestra of the Lake was constructed during the third century BCE and remodeled at mid-second century BCE; the Granite Palaestra was constructed by mid-second century BCE atop an earlier structure.

11. Philippe Bruneau (*GD* 189) suggests that the House of the Diadumenus was a "men's club." His arguments focus on the complex's large size (36 x 26 meters) and elaborate water storage capacity (decanting tank, cistern, and separate well). Cf. Chamonard 1922, 426–31; Hatzidakis 1997.

12. Fifteen shops are on the ground floor; the second floor enjoyed some monumentality, suggesting that it functioned as the headquarters of Italian *collegia*. Reliefs include the dancing Lares, Heracles holding a *phialē* above an altar, and a winged human being chased by a birdlike phallus (reproduced in Gallet de Santerre 1959, pl. 75; Bruneau 1970, pls. 12, 14, X15, with Bruneau's interpretation of the building and its reliefs at 633–38).

13. Remains include a circular stone-paved treadmill for a grain mill and stacked assemblages of Lamboglia 2 (Will Type 10), Italian amphorae of the early first century BCE. Similar shops aligned the street abutting the east bank of the Sacred Lake. The work is based on a test trench conducted by Jean-Yves Empereur (1983).

14. For a reconstructive drawing and discussion of the Sacred Lake district, see Duchêne and Girerd 2001, 65–85, and doc. 35.1. See also Bruneau 1968, 667; and Siebert 2001.

15. Grace and Savvatianou-Pétropoulakou 1970, 282–83. Virginia Grace and Elizabeth Will examined 284 stamped amphora fragments in the House of the Comedian; 27 of these were Roman, largely Lamboglia 2 (Will Type 10) (early first century BCE [1970, 383]); of the Greek-stamped amphora remains, 70 percent date to the end of the second/early first centuries BCE. For similar amphorae stored in the House of the Seals, generally believed to have been the residence and office of a Roman banker, in which again mostly Lamboglia 2s are on display, see Siebert 1975, 722; Siebert 1987, 636; and Siebert 1988, 758, 761, 777. In the House of the Sword, there are two Dressel 1Bs on view (see Siebert 1988, 777). Remains of fifty-nine Koan amphora handles of the same era were recovered in the house directly north of the Island of Bronzes; see Empereur 1982, 233 (first published by Siebert 1976). For the amphora remains investigated in the warehouse east of the Sacred Lake, see Empereur 1983.

16. For Roman habitation in the stadium and theater districts, see Chamonard 1922; Bruneau 1968; Rauh 1993; and Trümper 1998.

17. For the reliefs, see Bruneau 1964, 160–61; revised in Bruneau 1970, 398, 404, 643–44. Bruneau reidentifies the shield reliefs as images of the moon (1970, 398).

18. Most probably they were stuccoed over, evident in relief and painted over in profile.

19. Their original location thus bordered the district's south side.

20. Bruneau identifies the garland draped between the twin caps as a crescent moon.

21. For line drawings, see Rauh 1993; for photos, see Hatzidakis 2003.

22. In other words, this crude (broken) relief was situated directly behind the harbor. Bruneau noticed it (1978, 165).

23. The remains of multiple layers of plaster demonstrate that these wall paintings were repeatedly restored by the inhabitants. For a list, see Bruneau 1970, 404–5, recorded in the stadium district, the theater district, and the Inopus district, as well as in the Sacred Lake district. See Rauh 1993, 200–205, for the layers of stuccoed wall painting at the house of the "Granii" in the stadium district. The wall paintings were revealed during excavation and photographed. Most have since disintegrated. Nonetheless, the number of houses with recorded exterior wall paintings remains limited to eight.

24. For an earlier discussion, see Chamonard 1922, 105.

25. Street corner locations in Pompeii are 3.4.3 and 9.5.1.

26. Possibly being impaled by a protruding lower phallus in the relief; see Bruneau 1970, pl. 16, fig. 5; Hatzidakis 2003, 289 fig. 513.

27. For other examples of phallus sculpture and relief stored in the Delos Museum, see Hatzidakis 2003, 286–89.

28. All travelers, especially when coming to a place for the first time, feel some comfort and relief when they see a sign that tells them which direction they should go.

29. Consider the giant phalli dedicated to Dionysus in the forum at Delos. For Dionysus's representation as a pillar, see Csapo 1997, 255.

30. See http://www.berkeley.edu/news/media/releases/2003/04/09_plato.shtml (with flash slideshow of herm).

31. This statement reflects the general belief of Plato in the immortality of the soul, especially prevalent in book 10 of *The Republic.*

32. See Harrison 1965, 110–16, for a discussion of three herms set up to commemorate the victory at Eion.

33. The bowl fragment is part of the collection of the Museum of Fine Arts in Boston.

34. The plaque now resides in the Pornographic Collection in the National Archaeological Museum, Naples. In 1814 Sir William Gell made a drawing of the bakery with the plaque in situ. See Clarke 2003, pls. 68–69.

35. See Williams 1999, 15–20, for references to Roman male prostitutes.

36. The Establishment of the Beirut Poseidonists, the House of the Diadumenus, and the Agora of the Italians all functioned as something other than private residences. But despite Hatzidakis's discovery of a cluster of small shoplike structures directly south of the House of the Lake, the fact needs to be stressed that the interior décor of the House of the Lake emits nothing specifically "brothel-like" to reinforce this argument. The statue of the woman in exedra "e" provides no obvious clue, despite its arrangement for optimum visibility from the street, nor does any of the rest of the interior statuary.

37. The term "red-light district" dates to 1894 and may have developed from the practice of signalmen on the railway who used red lanterns and left those lanterns on the doorstep of a prostitute's house to indicate that she was busy. At the 2007 annual meeting of the Archaeological Institute of America, McGinn served as the respondent to a panel called

"The Hellenic Brothel as Space, Place, and Idea," in which a version of this essay was delivered. In his comments, he expressed concern about the use of the term "red-light district," perhaps thinking of the more modern, officially zoned areas such as Storyville in New Orleans or the red-light districts in Amsterdam rather than of the earlier unofficial development of such areas of prostitution. In China, for example, red lanterns appear to have been used to identify brothels, a practice that suggests that brothels had to do something to make themselves stand out from the other buildings in the area.

38. The building exhibits important similarities with the Pompeian Ludus, for example (Rauh 1993, 326).

39. Cf. *ID* 2612 for contributions made by returning visitors from Italy, the Aegean, Pamphylia, Cilicia, Cyprus, and Syria, presumably to restore the complex after 86 BCE.

40. These structures are too ruined to determine whether they even had doorways. If so, they possibly stood several centimeters above the level of the corridor itself.

41. As proposed for the outbuildings attached to the front of the complex; see Lapalus 1939, 75; Rauh 1992. Bruneau's observation (1995, 51) that these elements postdate the initial construction of the complex (ca. 120–110 BCE) in no way eliminates the possibility that they were added prior to its destruction in 86 and 69 BCE. As he notes, the building underwent constant remodeling before these events.

42. For the widespread locales of prostitution in Rome, see McGinn 2004, 15–21.

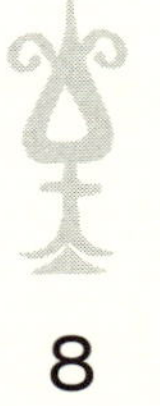

8 Ballio's Brothel, Phoenicium's Letter, and the Literary Education of Greco-Roman Prostitutes

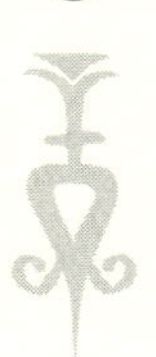

The Evidence of Plautus's Pseudolus

JUDITH P. HALLETT

My essay initially adopts a philological approach to the topic of ancient Greek prostitution by focusing on the language associated with sex work at an ancient commercial establishment in Hellenistic Athens. It also views Hellenistic Greek prostitution through a later, fictionalizing Roman lens by analyzing the language employed by both the labor and management of Ballio's imaginary brothel in Plautus's *Pseudolus*. First staged in 191 BCE, the *Pseudolus*—like all of Plautus's comedies—is Greek in location and Latin in locution.[1] Consequently, in exploring some similarities among the words that Plautus assigns the pimp Ballio when he speaks to and about his female brothel slave Phoenicium, the words that he attributes to Phoenicium in her correspondence with her elite young male lover Calidorus, and the words he places in the mouth of the play's title character—Calidorus's slave Pseudolus—I primarily examine them, their style, and their sentiments from Latin linguistic and literary and from Roman rhetorical and cultural perspectives.

I contend that Pseudolus does not assess Phoenicium's use of language fairly. I contend as well that the resemblances between Phoenicium's language and that of Ballio prove her an apt, and successful, pupil of the controlling, linguistically inventive, materially obsessed and socially astute brothel keeper. I also look closely at language used by Pseudolus himself and argue that Plautus, ironically, portrays Pseudolus as taking literary lessons from Phoenicium herself, and ultimately from her pimp Ballio himself, during a linguistic and dramatic process that has been impressively analyzed by Niall Slater and others in which Pseudolus outwits Ballio by assuming the role of a comic playwright (1985, 118–46).[2]

My essay also adopts a philological approach because the cultures of both ancient Greece and ancient Rome were highly oral, rendering a close focus on Greco-Roman linguistic expression and literary representation not only valid but also vital. Plautus's distinctive brand of linguistic expression and literary representation, moreover, make him a particularly valuable source on the contemporary reactions of mid-Republican Romans to peoples and practices from elsewhere in the Mediterranean world. Chief among these peoples are the Carthaginians that Rome conquered in the Second Punic War (218–201 BCE) and the Greeks that Rome vanquished in the First and Second Macedonian wars (214–205 and 200–196 BCE). Plautus's comedies derive from earlier Greek models and feature stock Greek characters, such as the parasite, a man who persistently dines at the expense of others, on which he places a strong Roman imprint. His dramatic scenarios, which are likewise of Greek derivation, have strong affinities to what took place at the Roman winter festival known as the Saturnalia. Many of them portray clever slaves, such as Pseudolus himself, who reverse roles with their masters, taking control of social situations in adverse circumstances to accomplish their masters' goals, as Pseudolus does by finding funds to wrest Phoenicium from her owner Ballio.[3]

Yet in addition to engaging in Latin linguistic and literary analysis, my discussion raises questions about both the Greek and the Roman social and material realities supposedly reflected and gently mocked in this Plautine comedy.[4] Plautus's portrayal of the brothel slave Phoenicium as endowed with persuasive speech resembles those of eloquent female prostitutes in earlier Greek literary and philosophical texts. At *Wasps* 1015–32, for example, Aristophanes associates the verbally skilled demagogue Cleon with the prostitute Kynna; Plato's *Menexenus* represents the *hetaira* Aspasia as delivering a funeral speech honoring the men of Athens who died during the war between Samos and Athens to Socrates (see M. Henry 1995, 27–28, 32–40).

These questions thus concern the representation of Ballio's brothel as an "educational institution," a rhetorical site that imparts the skills of effective speaking and writing to those interacting with literarily educated customers. Among them are whether, and how, verbally talented brothel keepers catering to a lettered clientele, in ancient Rome as well as Greece, may have provided models of public communication for the female and male slaves under their legal control and in their sphere of influence. Significant, too, is how literacy, and specifically the acquisition of elite male modes of expression, oral and written, may have functioned as a valuable social commodity for those who enslaved female prostitutes, and indeed for these enslaved workers themselves.

Phoenicium's Letter and Pseudolus's Response

The opening scene of the *Pseudolus*—in which the title character reads aloud for the audience a letter written to his young master Calidorus by the female brothel slave Phoenicium—launches its plot without benefit of a traditional expository prologue.[5] Here Plautus highlights, and exploits for comic effect, the different reactions of both men to her amorous and importuning words. In so doing, he furnishes evidence on how men, in his Roman as well as in earlier Greek society, may have assessed women's writings, evidence that strongly suggests that these assessments depended on the men's social status generally and on their personal relationship with the individual woman writer in particular.[6]

Let us look first at the opening scene of the comedy.

PSEUDOLUS
Si ex te tacente fieri possem certior,
Ere, quae miseriae te tam misere macerent,
Duorum labori ego hominum parsissem lubens
Mei te rogandi et tui respondendi mihi;
Nunc, quoniam id fieri non potest, necessitas
Me subigit ut te rogitem. Responde mihi:
Quid est quod tu examinatus iam hos multos dies
Gestas tabellas tecum, eas lacrumis lavis,
Neque tui participem consili quemquam facis?
Eloquere, ut quod ego nescio id tecum sciam.
CALIDORUS
Misere miser sum, Pseudole. **PS.** Id te Iuppiter
Prohibessit. **CA.** Nihil hoc Iovis ad iudicium attinet:
Sub Veneris regno vapulo, non sub Iovis.
PS. Licet me id scire quid sit? Nam tu me antidhac
Supremum habuisti comitem consiliis tuis.
CA. Idem animum nunc est. **PS.** Face me certum quid tibist;
Iuvabo aut re aut opera aut consilio bono.
CA. Cape has tabellas; tute hinc narrato tibi
Quae me miseria et cura contabefacit.

PS. Mos tibi geretur, sed quid hoc, quaeso? CA. Quid est?
PS. Ut opinor, quaerunt litterae hae sibi liberos:
Alia aliam scandit. CA. Ludis iam ludo tuo.
PS. Has quidem pol credo, nisi Sibulla legerit,
Interpretari alium posse neminem.
CA. Cur inclementer dicis lepidis litteris,
Lepidis tabellis lepida conscripta manu?
PS. An, opsecro hercle, habent quas gallinae manus?
Nam has quidam gallina scripsit. CA. Odiosus mihi es.
Lege, vel tabellas redde. PS. Immo enim pellegam,
Advortito animam. CA. Non adest. PS. At tu cita.
CA. Immo ego tacebo. Tu istinc ex cera cita;
Nam istic meus animus nunc est, non in pectore.
PS. Tuam amicam video, Calidore. CA. Ubi ea est, opsecro?
PS. Eccam in tabellis porrectam: in cera cubat.
CA. At te di deaeque quantumst. PS. Servassint quidem.
CA. Quasi solstitialis herba paulisper fui:
Repente exortus sum, repentino occidi.
PS. Tace, dum tabellas pellego. CA. Ergo quin legis?
PS. "Phoenicium Calidoro amatori suo
Per ceram et lignum litterasque interpretes
Salutem mittit et salutem abs te expetit,
Lacrumans titubanti animo, corde et pectore?"
CA. Perii! Salutem nusquam invenio, Pseudole,
Quam illi remittam. PS. Quam salutem? CA. Argenteam.
PS. Pro lignean salute vis argenteam
Remittere illi? Vide sis quam tu rem geras.
CA. Recita modo; ex tabellis iam faxo scies
Quam subito argento mi usus invento siet.
PS. "Leno me peregre mittit Macedonio
Minis viginti vendidit, voluptas mea.
Et priusquam hinc abiit quindecim miles minas.
Dederat; nunc unae quinque remorantur minae.
Ea causa miles hic reliquit symbolum,
Expressam in cera ex anulo suam imaginem,
Et qui huc afferret eius similem symbolum
Cum eo simul me mitteret, et rei dies
Haec praestita est, proxuma Dionysia."
Cras, ea quidem sunt. CA. Prope adest exitium mihi,
Nisi quid mihi in test auxilii. PS. Sine pellegam.

CA. Sino, nam mihi videor cum ea fabularier,
Lege: dulce amarumque una nunc misces mihi.
PS. "Nunc nostri amores, mores, consuetudines,
Iocus, ludus, sermo, suavisaviatio,
Compressiones artae amantum corporum,
Teneris labellis molles morsiunculae,
+Nostrorum orgiorum os . . . nculae+
Papillarum horridularum oppressiunculae
Harunc voluptatum mi omnium atque itidem tibi
Distractio discidium vastities venit,
Nisi quae mihi in test aut tibist in me salus
Haec quae ego scivi ut scires curavi omnia;
Nunc ego te experiar quid ames, quid simules. Vale."
CA. Est misere scriptum, Pseudole. PS. Oh! Miserrume.
CA. Quin fles? PS. Pumiceos oculos habeo: non queo
Lacrumam exorare ut expuant unam modo.
CA. Quid ita? PS. Genus nostrum semper siccoculum fuit.

[PSEUDOLUS. If I could have gotten a better idea from you with your mouth shut, master, what sorrows hurt you so wretchedly, I would gladly have saved the effort of two men—of me asking you and you answering me. Since that cannot happen now, obligation forces me to ask you. Answer me: what's the reason that you, after being a virtual vegetable for many days now, keep carrying these writing tablets with you, wash them with your tears, and don't let anyone in on what you're thinking? Speak up, so that I might know as well as you know what I don't know.

CALIDORUS. Pseudolus, I am wretchedly wretched.

PS. May Jupiter keep you from that condition.

CA. This has no relevance to Jupiter's sphere of judgment. I am suffering under the reign of Venus, not Jupiter.

PS. Is it allowed for me to know what the problem is? In the past you considered me your closest consultant in your thinking processes.

CA. That's my intention now.

PS. Give me an idea of what's bothering you. I will help—with money or work or good thinking.

CA. Take these writing tablets and from reading them tell yourself what unhappiness and concern make me waste away!

PS. Your wish will be my command. But what's this, I ask you?

CA. What's this?

PS. As I ascertain, these letters are seeking to produce children; since they climb on top of each other.

CA. Are you now joking with a joke?

PS. Indeed by Pollux I believe that unless the Sibyl manages to read these letters, no one is able to make sense out of them.

CA. Why do you speak disparagingly of charming letters on charming tablets, written by a charming hand?

PS. By Hercules I plead, what hands do hens have? For a hen has certainly written these letters.

CA. You are annoying to me. Read the tablets or hand them back.

PS. Why, I'll read them through. Pay attention in my direction.

CA. It's not here.

PS. Then you summon it.

CA. Why I will keep my mouth shut, you summon it from the wax; for my attention is now there, and not inside of me.

PS. I see your girlfriend for hire, Calidorus.

CA. Where is she? I appeal to you.

PS. Fully stretched out, on the tablets and lying as if in bed on the wax.

CA. May the gods and goddesses to you with all in their power—

PS. Be protectors of course.

CA. Just like grass of midsummer I stood tall for a while: suddenly I rose up, suddenly I withered.

PS. Keep your mouth shut while I read the tablets.

CA. Fine, why don't you read, then?

PS. "Phoenicium sends good wishes to her lover Calidorus, through wax and wood and letters as intermediaries, and seeks good wishes from you, as she is weeping, with trembling mind, heart, and breast."

CA. I'm done for, Pseudolus, nowhere do I find good wishes of the kind I can send back.

PS. What good wishes do you mean?

CA. Of a moneyed persuasion.

PS. Do you want to send her good wishes in the form of money in return for good wishes on a wooden tablet? Please consider what kind of business you're doing.

CA. Just read the text: now I'll arrange for you to know, from the tablets, how suddenly I need to have money found.

PS. "A pimp has sold me, abroad, to a Macedonian soldier for twenty *minae*, my darling: and before he departed from here, this soldier had given fifteen *minae*: now only five *minae* hold up the sale. For that reason the soldier left a pledge, his own portrait from his ring stamped in wax so that whoever might bring him a pledge resembling his might at the same time send me with it, and the day for this transaction has been appointed beforehand, the very next festival of Dionysus." Why, that's tomorrow!

CA. My day of destruction is almost here, unless there's some kind of help for me in you.

PS. Let me read the words through.

CA. Fine with me, for I seem to myself to be having a conversation with her; read: now you mix sweet and bitter together for me.

PS. "Now our love affairs, ways, routines, joking, playing, talking, sweet conversation, close cuddlings of loving bodies, on delicate little lips soft little bites . . . of our secret passionate rites, little squeezing of slightly stiffening nipples, a dragging apart, a tearing apart, a devastation of all these pleasures for me and likewise for you is coming, unless there are good wishes for me toward you or for you toward me. I have taken care that you may know all of these matters I have known of: now I will try to determine what you do by way of loving and what you do by way of pretending. Farewell."

CA. That's wretchedly written, Pseudolus.

PS. O, most wretchedly.

CA. Why aren't you weeping, then?

PS. I have eyes made of pumice stone: I am not able to beg them to trickle even one single tear.

CA. What's the problem?

PS. Our race has always been dry eyed.[7]]

As the language of the passage attests, Calidorus appears to find everything about Phoenicium's letter appealing and affecting: its physical appearance, its sentiments, and its style. He describes it as "charming letters on charming tablets written by a charming hand" (lepidis litteris, / lepidis tabellis lepida conscripta manu) (lines 27–28). He evokes Sappho's love lyrics in likening his response to that of withering grass in midsummer.[8] He claims that reading her letter is like conversing with her face to face, mixing the sweet and bitter (nam mihi videor cum ea fabularier, / Lege: dulce amarumque una nunc misces mihi) (62–63). Most important, he initially refers to the contents of the letter as causing him "unhappiness and concern" (quae me miseria et cura contabefacit) (21). So, too, once the entire letter has been read aloud, Calidorus characterizes how it is written in line 75 with the adverb *misere*, investing the word with the sense of "painfully unhappy," "emotionally wrenching."

Pseudolus, however, is explicitly and vocally critical of the letter's physical appearance before he even reads it. He is more implicitly but no less vehemently dismissive of its content once he does. He mocks the letter's looks, and its author's erotic propensities, with a string of sexual and sexist insults. Not only does he liken the collocation of the individual letters on their tablets to a position taken in sexual coupling (Ut opinor, quaerunt litterae hae sibi liberos, / alia aliam scandit) (23–24) and the letters themselves to scratching by hens (an, opsecro hercle, habent quae gallinae manus? / Nam has quidem gallina scripsit) (29–30). He also claims that only the female Sibyl could make sense of the writing (Has quidem pol credo, nisi Sibulla legerit / interpretari alium posse neminem) (25–26). He even identifies Phoenicium's words with her physical presence and sexual availability by remarking "[I see your girlfriend for hire] fully stretched out, on the tablets and lying in as if in bed on the wax" (Tuam amicam video, Calidore . . . / Eccam in tabellis porrectam: in cera cubat) (35–36).[9]

Most important, after Pseudolus reads the entire letter, he characterizes how it is written in line 75 with the superlative adverb *miserrume* (wretchedly), evidently investing the word with the sense of "most dreadfully," and faulting its style and content as well as its physical appearance.[10] After all, Calidorus immediately observes with surprise, in line 76, that Phoenicium's words have failed to bring tears to Pseudolus's eyes. Pseudolus must resort to a feeble joke—itself a literary allusion to the editing functions of pumice stone—in self-exculpation (Pumiceos oculos habeo: non queo / Lacrumam exorare ut expuant una modo) (76–77).[11] When that excuse fails to placate Calidorus, Pseudolus then invokes *genus nostrum*, "our kind of people," as *semper siccoculum*, "always dry eyed," unsusceptible to such writing.[12]

To judge from Pseudolus's reactions to reading the letter itself—a process that the two men interrupt twice—Pseudolus evidently finds fault with two aspects of Phoenicium's writing. One is her mercenary motives that are revealed not only in her declaring her deep affections for Calidorus but also in her enumerating, graphically, the physical pleasures they have shared. In the second epistolary segment that Pseudolus reads, Phoenicium discloses at once, in lines 51–54, that a pimp has sold her for twenty *minae* to a Macedonian soldier, who is going to pay the final financial installment the next day. It causes Calidorus to realize, quite rightly, that he must come up with the funds to purchase Phoenicium himself if he wants their affair to continue.

Yet in line 46, immediately after Pseudolus reads the first segment of Phoenicium's letter, Calidorus acknowledges that the kind of *salus*, good wishes, she seeks from him is *argentea*, "of a moneyed persuasion." In lines 99–102, moreover, Pseudolus provides his own interpretation of the letter, referring to its message with the word *sermo* (speech, conversation):

PS. Ut litterarum ego harum sermonem audio,
Nisi tu illi drachumis fleveris argenteis,

Quod tu istis lacrumis te probare postulas,
Non pluris refert quam si imbrem in cribrum geras.

[**PS**. As I understand what this letter has to say [*litterarum ego harum sermonem*], unless [*nisi*] you will have wept for her with money-coated tears [*lacrimis argenteis*], your effort to make yourself loveworthy with these tears will not matter any more than if you were to pour a torrent of rain into a sieve.]

Pseudolus's use of a conditional introduced by the negative conjunction *nisi* to describe the consequences of failing to do what Phoenicium has demanded warrants notice. This statement recalls Phoenicium's own earlier words in line 71–73, where she claims that the many sensual joys she and Calidorus experience will come to an end unless (*nisi*) there is *salus*, good wishes, toward her from him and vice versa—presumably *salus* "of a moneyed persuasion." As we will see, it foreshadows Ballio's own words, in which he issues various *ultimata* with this same construction.

Pseudolus, though, also seems to find fault with Phoenicium's writing in the final epistolary segment: lines 64 through 73, which immediately precede Calidorus's assessment of the letter as *misere* and Pseudolus's assessment of it as *miserrume scriptum* (wretchedly written). If Pseudolus is criticizing this part of the letter on stylistic grounds, several of its features seem liable to have prompted his criticism. The most eye catching and ear catching is the whopping abundance of nouns, a few of them evidently *hapax legomena*, words evidently coined for the occasion and never attested anywhere else in extant Latin literature. Some are abstract, others concrete. Several of them, such as *morsiunculae* (soft little bites) and *oppressiunculae* (close cuddlings), are diminutives. Most are, repetitively, in the nominative case.[13]

Another stylistic feature of this passage likely to incur Pseudolus's disapproval is its frequent omission of connective words (asyndeton). Yet another is its extremely generous use of alliteration, the repetition of initial or medial consonants in two or more adjacent words, in such phrases as *sermo, suavisaviatio* in line 65 and *distractio discidium* in 70.[14] The prominence of rhyming, illustrated by the final syllables of *amores, mores, consuetudines* in line 64 and *papillarum horridularum* in 68, merits mention as possibly objectionable, too: both verbal collocations are examples of homoeoptoton, words in the same case with the same terminations.[15] Finally, we might note the pairs of abstract terms that are fairly close in meaning to one another, if not precise synonyms, a stylistic peculiarity known as "padding": *mores* and *consuetudine*s in 64 and *distractio*, *discidium*, and *vastatio* in 70.[16]

To be sure, the style of Phoenicium's letter is closely linked to its content. The words detailing the erotic joys that she and Calidorus share, however incongruously assembled, disclose a great deal of personal information about her. Similarly, the words in the final five lines of the letter, 70–74, which issue her lover a pointed ultimatum, reveal her mercenary motives. As just noted, they employ the negative conditional conjunction *nisi* (unless)—along with the emphatic alliterative, triple noun phrase *distractio discidium vastities venit*—to remind Calidorus that if the two of them do not have her monetary brand of *salus*, "good wishes," toward one another, all of the pleasures detailed in the first six lines will cease.

Furthermore, Phoenicium here underscores that she and Calidorus share a bond of mutual interest by, again, noting that "I have taken care that you may know all of these matters I have known of" (and repeating the verb *scio* in the phrase *scivi ut scires*). In this connection, she threatens to ascertain where Calidorus has been acting truthfully and where he has been deceitful, differentiating the trustworthy from the untrustworthy aspects of his conduct. She does so with the verb *experiar* (I will try) followed by an indirect question: "Now I will try to determine what you do by way of loving and what you do by way of pretending."

If, as I am inferring, Pseudolus finds Phoenicium's style of writing problematic, he is obviously judging it by a higher standard than that which is applied by others to speeches by males—whether of lowly or of lofty station—elsewhere in both Plautine comedy and contemporary Roman oratory. Consider, for example, the style and content of lines 131 through 142 of Plautus's own *Casina*, written approximately eight years after the *Pseudolus*.[17] The context is a conversation between two male slaves, Olympio and Chalinus, sexual rivals for the female slave Casina. In these lines, Olympio fantasizes about what Casina will say when he and she make love. Like the final ten lines of Phoenicium's letter, this passage also features a massive piling up of nouns, alliterative and diminutive, abstract and concrete. She will say to him, he imagines,

OLYMPIO
Mi animule, mi Olympio,
Mea vita, mea melilla, mea festivitas,
Sine tuos ocellos deosculer, voluptas mea,
Sine amabo ted amari, meu' festus dies,
Meu' pullus passer, mea columba, mi lepus.

[OLYMPIO. My little soul, my Olympio, my life, my little honey, my holiday spirit, let me kiss your little eyes, my delight, please let yourself be loved, my day of vacation, my sparrow chick, my dove, my bunny rabbit.]

Some of these nouns are virtual synonyms. One of them, *deosculor* (kiss), seems to be a new coinage; several are asyndetically linked.[18] Some also carry strong erotic connotations, such as *passer*, sparrow, a lovebird linked elsewhere with the male organ.[19] Whereas Pseudolus does not acknowledge any physical attraction to Phoenicium, Chalinus is pursuing Casina, albeit under orders from his mistress; Olympio's fantasizing rendition of her words is meant to taunt him. But unlike Pseudolus, Chalinus does not criticize the style or content of what Olympio imagines will be Casina's love talk, only Olympio's insufferable attitude.[20]

It warrants major emphasis that ancient rhetorical authorities react quite positively when linguistic embellishments of the sort figuring bountifully in Phoenicium's letter adorn, to the point of excess, speeches delivered by male politicians: alliteration and rhymed endings, the coinage of new words such as *oppressiuncula*, and "padding" through the use of synonyms. Had Pseudolus judged Phoenicium's language according to the criteria prized by Roman oratory, an elite and masculine domain of public activity, he could have viewed her writing, in spite of its apparent excesses, approvingly, as testimony to her linguistic ingenuity and acumen.

At *Noctes Atticae* 13.25.12–15, Aulus Gellius quotes some interminably long sentences from two orations by one of Plautus's contemporaries, the elder Cato, prefacing and illuminating Cato's words with laudatory remarks by his contemporary Favorinus about how the use of multiple synonyms enriches meaning, because they are heard multiple times.

> Inquit Favorinus. . . . Sed quia cum dignitate orationis et cum gravi verborum copia dicuntur, quamquam eadem fere sint et ex una sententia cooriantur, plura tamen esse existimantur, quoniam et aures et animum saepius feriunt.
>
> Hos ornatus genus in crimine uno vocibus multis aeque saevis extruendo ille tam tunc M. Cato antiquissimus in orationibus suis celebravit, sicuti in illa, quae inscripta est *De decem hominibus*, cum Thermum accusavit quod decem liberos homines eodem tempore interfecisset, hisce verbis eandem omnibus rem significationibus usus est, quae quoniam sunt eloquentiae Latinae tunc primum exorientis lumina quaedam sublustria, libitum est ea mihi *apomnemoneuein*; "Tum nefarium facinus peiore facinore operire postulas, succidias humanas facis, tantam trucidationem facis, decem funera facis, decem capita libera interficis, decem hominibus vitam eripis, indicta causa, iniudicatis, incondemnatis." Item M. Cato in orationis principio, quam dixit in senatu pro Rhodiensibus, cum vellet res nimis prosperas dicere, tribus vocabulis idem sentientibus dixit. Verba eius haec sunt: "Scio solere plerisque hominibus in rebus secundis atque prolixis atque prosperis animum excellere atque superbiam atque ferociam augescere."

> [Favorinus says. . . . that because they are uttered in conjunction with the worthiness of the speech and the weighty abundance of its words, although they are almost the same and arise from one idea, they are thought to be richer in meaning, since they strike the ears and attention more frequently.
>
> M[arcus Porcius] Cato, that most ancient orator of ours, even in his day often employed this kind of embellishment, by heaping up in one charge many and harsh terms, in his speeches, as in that speech entitled "About the Ten Men" [190 BCE], when he accused [Quintus Minucius] Thermus of killing ten free men at the same time. Cato used all of these words meaning the same thing, words that—since they are some bright lights of Latin eloquence, then coming into being for the first time—it is my pleasure to recall: "Then you demand to cover up an appalling deed with a worse deed, you commit so great a slaughter, you cause ten deaths, you kill ten free heads, you take away the life from ten men, with a case untried, unjudged, uncondemned." Likewise M. Cato, in the beginning of the oration he delivered in the Senate on behalf of the Rhodians (167 BCE), when he wanted to say that things were extremely prosperous, he said it in three words that mean the same thing "I know that where most men are concerned, in circumstances favorable and successful and prosperous the spirit soars, and pride and arrogance increase."[21]]

Cato's words display many of these same features, in both combination and abundance: alliteration (*tantam trucidationem*, *scio solere*), rhymed phrase endings (*excellere . . . augescere*), new coinages (*incomdemnatis*; see *OLD* s.v.), and above all "padding." A double standard for assessing men's and women's words evinces itself yet again.

While Gellius and Favorinus write several centuries after Cato and Plautus, Roman writings from the first century BCE onward indicate that they derived their favorable views of such stylistic overembellishment from a generation of predecessors: these linguistic refinements are an enduring feature of Roman rhetoric and Latin style. For example, at *Rhetorica ad Herennium* 4.38, after referring to the use of synonyms as *interpretatio* (explanation) and offering two illustrations, the unnamed author claims that "the reader cannot help be intellectually impressed when the force of the earlier expression is renewed by the explanation of words" (necessum est eius qui audit animum commoveri cum gravitas prioris dicti renovatur interpretatione verborum).

What is more, despite his objections to Phoenicium's writing, apparently stemming from the materialistic motives and particularly the stylistic excesses of her lively love talk, Pseudolus strives mightily and cleverly to aid Calidorus in finding the funds to retain Phoenicium's favors. So, too, when Pseudolus reports on the joyful reunion of the couple at lines 1246 and following, near the end of the play, his own, inebriated, words have much in common with those of Phoenicium's letter; indeed some, such as *voluptas* (pleasure) and *labellum* (lip), are Phoenicium's own. Consider, for example, 1259–62:

PS. Nam ubi amans complexust amantem, ubi ad labra labella adiungit,
Ubi alter alterum bilingui manifesto inter se prehendunt,
Ubi mamma mammicula opprimitur aut, si lubet, corpora conduplicant,
Manu candida cantharum dulciferum +propinare amicissimam+ amicitiam.

[PS. For when a loving man squeezes a loving woman, when he joins little lips to lips, when they clutch one another, each probing the other in an unmistakable double tonguing kiss, when a breast is crushed by a little breast or, if they desire, when they double up their bodies and a tankard full of sweet-tasting wine, poured with a dazzling hand, toasts their most affectionate affection.]

Pseudolus's language here displays the same stylistic excesses in describing the same pleasurable, body-merging activities as does that of Phoenicium. The passage teems with diminutive nouns, alliterative phrases, and *hapax legomena* such as *mammicula* (little breast).[22] By having Pseudolus speak in this way on this topic, of course, Plautus renders him a hypocritical critic of Phoenicium's letter, compromised by both his own language and his insistence on holding her writing to a higher standard than that applied to men.

In view of Pseudolus's dismissive attitude toward Phoenicium's mode of literary expression in her letter to Calidorus, the stylistic resemblances between these two passages, over a thousand lines apart, require explanation. To be sure, Phoenicium herself finally appears on the stage at line 1038, not long before Pseudolus delivers this speech.

Yet she exits thirteen lines later and is silent for her entire time onstage. By the same token Plautus assigns Pseudolus exuberant, extravagant language of the kind he employs in lines 1246 and following far earlier in the play. The first such passage occurs in lines 574–585a, where he describes, gleefully and in an extended military metaphor, his plans for outwitting his adversaries with a plan he has just devised:

PS. Pro Iuppiter, ut mihi, quidquid ago, lepide omnia prospereque eveniunt!

Neque quod dubitem neque quod timeam, meo in
    pectore conditumst consilium
Nam ea stultitiast, facinus magnum timido corde credere,
Nam omnes res perinde sunt
Ut agas, ut eas magni facias, nam ego in meo pectore prius
Ita paravi copias
Duplicis triplicis dolos perfidias, ut, ubiquomque hostibus
    congrediar
(maiorum meum fretus virtute dicam, mea industria
    et malitia fraudulenta).
Facile ut vincam, facile ut spoliem meos perduellis meis
    perfidiis.
Nunc inimicum ego hunc communem meum atque
    vostrum omnium
Ballionem exballistabo lepide; date operam modo.

[PS. By Jupiter, how all things, whatever I perform, come out charmingly and successfully for me. Nor do I have anything to doubt or anything to fear, there is a plan stored up in my mind. For it's stupidity to entrust a great deed to a fearful heart, for all things are just as you may perform them, as you may consider them important, for I have already prepared troops in my mind in such a way—double, triple, schemes, treacheries—that wherever I encounter the enemy, I may say that I have relied on the courage of my ancestors, my energy, and deceiving wickedness, that I may conquer easily, that I may easily despoil my adversaries with my deceits. Now I will ballificistically besiege Ballio, our shared enemy, foe of mine and of you all, and do so charmingly, just pay attention.]

Not only does Pseudolus rely heavily on alliteration (*conditumst consilium*, *corde credere*, *pectore prius*), asyndeton (*duplicis triplicis dolos perfidias*), rhyming (*agas*, *facias*, *copias*, *perfidias*), and padding (*dolos perfidias*, *perduellis perfidiis*). He even employs a new coinage based on the name of Ballio himself, punning on *ballista* (siege engine) in vowing to overcome the pimp.

The Language of Ballio's Brothel

I would attribute Pseudolus's change in speaking habits once he decides, in lines 574 and following, to best Ballio, to the encounter that he and Calidorus have with Ballio from lines 133 through 303. This encounter begins with a spirited speech by the pimp, to which Calidorus and Pseudolus listen and on which they comment, in asides, to the audience. Here Ballio harangues and intimidates the prostitutes of both sexes in his brothel, in words featuring a massive amount of alliteration, anaphora, asyndeton, *hapax legomena*, and padding.[23]

BALLIO
Exite, agite exite, ignavi, male habiti et male conciliati,
Quorum numquam quicquam quoiquam venit in mentem ut recte faciant,
Quibus, nisi ad hoc exemplum experior, non potest usura usurpari.
Neque ego homines magis asinos numquam vidi, ita plagis costae callent;
Quos quom ferias, tibi plus noceas, eo enim ingenio hi sunt flagitribae,
Qui haec habent consilia: uti data occasiost, rape clepe tene harpaga bibe es fuge.

[**BALLIO**. Come out, start acting, come out, you lazy losers, not worth having, not worth getting, not one of whom has ever had the slightest idea of how to do anything right, and from whom there can be no productivity produced unless I make trial of you in this whipping way. Nor have I ever seen men that were more like asses, their ribs are so stiff with lashings, the sort of men whom, when you beat them, you would harm yourself more: with their talent, these men are whip-wearer-outers, who have these items on their agenda, whenever the opportunity arises: grab steal hold snatch drink eat flee.]

BA. Nunc adeo hanc edictionem nisi animum advortetis omnes,
Nisi somnum socordiamque ex pectore oculisque exmovetis,
Ita ego extra latera loris faciam ut valide varia sint,
Ut ne peristromata quidem aeque picta sint Campanica
Neque Alexandrina beluata tonsilia tappetia.

[**BA**. Now unless you all should pay attention to this pronouncement, unless you should shake the sleep and exhaustion off your heart and eyes, with whippings I will make sure that your torsos are markedly multihued, that not even Campanian coverlets are comparably colored nor Alexandrian close-cropped carpets, embroidered with beasts.]

BA. Nam mi hodie natalis dies est; decet omnis
vos concelebrare
Pernam, callum, glandium, sumen facito in aqua
iaceant. Satin audis?
Magnifice volo me summos viros accipere, ut mihi
rem esse reantur.

[BA. For today is my birthday, and it behooves all of you to make merry. See to it that the ham, pork rind, tenderloin, sow's udder soak in water. Do you hear loud and clear? I want to welcome top-drawer men splendidly, so that they may think I am worth something.]

BA. Vos, qui in munditiis, mollitiis deliciisque
aetatulam agitis,
Viris cum summis, inclutae amicae, nunc ego
scibo atque hodie experiar,
Quae capiti, quae ventri operam det, quae suae rei,
quae somno studeat;
Quam libertam fore mi credam et quam venalem,
hodie experiar.
Facite hodie ut mihi munera multa huc ab amatoribus
conveniant.
Nam nisi penus annuos hodie convenit, cras populo
prostituam vos.
Natalem scitis mi esse diem hunc; ubi isti sunt quibus
vos oculi estis,
Quibus vitae, quibus deliciae estis, quibus savia,
mammia, mellillae?

[BA. You who act out your tender years in elegances, luxuries, and pleasures, celebrity girlfriends with top-drawer men, now I will know and I will make trial today, to determine who pays attention to obtaining her freedom and who to filling her belly, who is focused on her own advantage and who on her beauty sleep, who I will believe is going to be my freedwoman and who is going up for sale, today I will make trial. Bring it about today that many presents assemble for me from your lover men. For unless a year's worth of provisions gets assembled today, tomorrow I will sell your bodies on the street to all takers. You know that this is my birthday; where are those men to whom you are darlings, life's treasures, precious pets, sweet kisses, sugarpies, honeybunches?]

BA. Principio, Hedylium, tecum ago, quae amica es frumentariis,
Quibus cunctis +montes maxumi, frumenti acervi sunt domi:
Fac sis delatum huc mihi frumentum, hunc annum quod satis
Mi et familiae omni sit meae. . . .
Aeschrodora, tu quae amicos tibi habes lenonum aemulos
Lanios, qui item ut nos iurando, iure malo male quaerunt rem, audi:
Nisi carnaria tria gravida tergoribus onere uberi hodie
Mihi erunt, cras te quasi Dircam olim, ut memorant, duo gnati Iovis
Devinxere ad taurum, item ego te distringam ad carnarium;
Id tibi profecto taurus fiet
CA. Nimis sermone huius ira incendor
PS. Huncine hic hominem pati
Colere iuventutem Atticam!
Ubi sunt, ubi latent, quibus aetas integra est, qui amant a lenone?
Quin conveniunt, quin una omnes peste hac populum hunc liberant?
Sed vah!
Nimis sum stultus, nimis fui
Indoctus; illine audeant
Id facere, quibus ut serviant
Suos amor cogit.

[BA. First of all, Hedylium, I perform with you, who are the girlfriend of the grain dealers, all who have most massive mounds, heaps of grain in their possession, make sure that grain has been brought to me, in an amount that is sufficient for me and my whole household this year. . . .

Aeschrodora, you who have butchers, rivals of pimps, as our male friends, men who just like us, by sauciness, by wicked transgression, wickedly seek their fortune, listen up: unless there will be three meat racks heavy with carcasses of huge size, in my possession today, tomorrow, just as two of Jupiter's sons, as they recall, once tied up Dirce to a bull, likewise I will tie you up to a meat rack: it will surely become a bull for you.

CALIDORUS. I am extremely disturbed by this man's words.[24]

PSEUDOLUS. That the young men of Athens allow this man to reside here! Where are they, where do they hide, those of ripe young age, who love from this pimp's establishment? Why don't they assemble, why don't they together free this community from this disease? But I am excessively stupid, I am excessively short on learning; would they dare to do this, those whose passion forces them to be enslaved?]

BA. Xystilis, fac ut animum advortas, quoius amatores olivi
Dunamin domi habeant maxumam.
Si mihi non iam huc culleis
Oleum deportatum erit,
Te ipsam culleo ego cras faciam ut deportere in pergulam. . . .
Tu autem, quae pro capite argentum mihi iam iamque semper numeras,
Ea pacisci modo scis, sed quod pacta est non scis solvere,
Phoenicium, tibi ego haec loquor, deliciae summatum virum:
Nisi hodie mi ex fundis tuorum amicorum omne huc penus adfertur,
Cras Phoenicium poeniceo corio invises pergulam.

[BA. Xystilis, make sure you pay attention, you whose lovers have the greatest power of olive oil in their possession. If oil will not have been trucked in to me in leather sacks, tomorrow I will see to it that you yourself, in a leather sack, are trucked out into the brothel shed. . . .

You moreover, who always are on the point of counting up money to pay for your freedom, you only know how to make an arrangement, but you do not know how to pay what has been arranged, Phoenicium. I say these things to you, the darling of the top-drawer men: unless today the entire store of household provisions is brought to me from the estates of your male friends, tomorrow you, Phoenicium, will visit the brothel shed with a hide of Phoenician purple.]

As we see, Ballio's speech ends with an address to Phoenicium herself, at lines 225–29, describing her as the *deliciae summatum virum* (darling of the top-drawer men). Punning on Phoenicium's name, he then threatens her that unless (*nisi*) she brings him money from the estates of her male friends, "you, Phoenicium, will visit the brothel shed with a hide of Phoenician purple [*poenicio corio*]." Prior to addressing Phoenicium, Ballio likewise speaks to three of his other female brothel slaves in a similarly menacing and abusive tone, associating each with a different group of paying customers: Hedylium with *frumentarii* (grain dealers), Aeschrodora with *lanii* (butchers), Xystilis with oil merchants. He also threatens Aeschrodora with brutal punishment unless (*nisi*) she furnishes him with meat. He tells Xystilis that if there are no bags of oil (*si . . . non*) delivered to him, she can expect intense physical suffering as well.

But in lines 167 and 174 Ballio prefaces these individual addresses with a general description of his clientele as *summos viros* and *viris summis* (top men), thereby identifying all of these men with Phoenicium's *summati viri*. In lines 179–80, he inquires of his female slaves, anaphorically and asyndetically, where the men are to whom they are "darlings, life's treasures, precious pets, sweet kisses, sugarpies, honeybunches" (quibus vos oculi estis, / quibus vitae, quibus deliciae, quibus savia, mammia, mellillae). He hence associates them all with Phoenicium, not only because Plautus has Ballio use the term *deliciae* (darling) for her in line 227 as well, but also because he has had her letter to Calidorus characterize her own pleasure-giving ways in a similar fashion.

By portraying all his female brothel slaves, and all their customers, in language that describes Phoenicium and her elite, presumably educated clientele in particular, Ballio makes a strong impression on Pseudolus. Between Ballio's address to Aeschrodora and that to Xystilis, Calidorus reacts to Ballio's speech by merely declaring, at line 202, that he is "extremely disturbed by this man's words [*sermone*]". But Pseudolus responds to Ballio's *sermo* by voicing his incredulous outrage that young Athenian men like his master do not rise up together to rid the community of this disease (*peste*). Although these young men—unlike Pseudolus himself—are legally free, he characterizes them as enslaved to Ballio by their passions ("ut serviant suos amor cogit").

What is more, Ballio's words help account not only for Pseudolus's changing, increasingly sympathetic attitude toward Calidorus and Phoenicium but also his changing language. Pseudolus speaks of himself here as formerly *stultus* and *indoctus*, stupid and short on learning. While he is literally faulting his earlier failure to understand why young men like his master fall under Ballio's control, it is only after this scene that Pseudolus acquires both the requisite street smarts and speech smarts to defeat Ballio. Indeed, mastering the pimp's talking techniques, along with an impressive battery of tricks, enables Pseudolus to punish Ballio for his cruel enslavement of the workers in his brothel and of Pseudolus's own, freeborn, master.

Through the language that Plautus assigns Ballio here, the playwright also implies that the pimp's words, and style of communication, have heavily influenced those of his brothel slave Phoenicium. As noted at length earlier, her letter, like Ballio's speech, abounds in unusual nouns (both diminutive and invented), verbal padding, and stylistic and sound effects such as asyndeton, anaphora, and rhymed endings. In addition, her letter resembles Ballio's addresses to her and another female brothel slave in its issuance of an *ultimatum* through the employment of a "*nisi*" clause.

Significantly, Ballio issues *ultimata* with the word *nisi* at five earlier points in this same speech: at lines 135, 143, and 144, when threatening all the male slaves, and at lines 178 and 183, when threatening all the females. In line 135 *nisi* prefaces the words "ad hoc exemplum experior" (unless I make trial of you in this whipping way). Ballio employs the verb *experior* again in lines 174 and 176 when he tells the female slaves "I will know and make trial today" (Scibo atque hodie experiar) as to which of them is actually trying to obtain her freedom by enriching him and which merely pretending. After posing three indirect questions to describe what he seeks to discover, he then, in line 176, repeats the words *hodie experiar* (I will make trial today).

Phoenicium, as we have observed, ends her letter in similar language, promising in line 73 to make trial of Calidorus to determine what he does by way of loving as opposed to pretending: "Nunc ego te experiar quid ames, quid simules." Her repeated use of the verb *scio* in line 72 is noteworthy in view of its frequent occurrences in Ballio's speech; indeed, he employs it twice when addressing her in line 226. And her insistence in line 60 that her lover provide the necessary money by *cras* (tomorrow) is noteworthy too: Ballio employs this word in lines 178, 199, 214, and 229, when issuing deadlines first to the female brothel slaves as a group, and then to Aeschrodora, Xystilis, and Phoenicium as individuals.

In the chronology of Plautus's script, Phoenicium's letter of course predates Ballio's speech. But by assigning the pimp a lengthy harangue that reveals his habitual speech patterns, Plautus has Ballio's words illuminate those that his brothel slave uses in convincing her lover to perform to her liking. Since, in the play itself, Pseudolus encounters Phoenicium's letter before Ballio's speech, he is also taking literary lessons from Phoenicium herself, and ultimately Ballio himself, in adopting new talking techniques. These are, as Plautus emphasizes, ways of putting words together that appeal to (even as they enslave) literarily educated young male clients such as his Sappho-evoking master.

The Relation of Plautine Comic Speech to Greco-Roman Social Reality

How, though, is this close textual analysis of Phoenicium's letter and of the resemblances between its language and that of both Pseudolus and Ballio in a fictional Roman comedy of the second century BCE relevant to an investigation of what actually went on in ancient Greek or even in Roman brothels? As Timothy Moore has documented in his discussion of Plautus's *Truculentus*, establishments like Ballio's brothel had counterparts in Plautus's Rome—indeed counterparts that were familiar to his audience.[25] Such evidence by itself suggests that Plautus may be reflecting at least his own Roman reality in choosing to portray, albeit obliquely, Ballio's speech as a model for Phoenicum's letter writing in words that impress her elite and lettered lover and in a style adopted by the lover's clever and resourceful slave.

Studies of earlier Athenian prostitution from an economic perspective allow us to infer that Plautus reflects an earlier Greek reality as well. Edward Cohen, for example, observes that "within their brothels . . . Athenian slaves working as prostitutes are known to have received specialized training, sometimes starting in childhood." He mentions handicraft, catering, medicine, finance, and accounting as possible areas of specialization. He also implies that a similar situation resulted in the training of slave prostitutes in communication skills, although he does not discuss the possibility of "hands-on" training in the form of listening to, and taking writing lessons from, an aggressively entrepreneurial male pimp (2004, 103).[26]

Citing, inter alia, the evidence of Plautus's *Rudens*, James Davidson also calls attention to the existence of schools where anyone could send slaves "to get trained up in musical skills and thus increase their profitability" (2006, 39).[27] In this context, he emphasizes the value of reading and writing as survival skills for the independent female prostitutes whom Anglophone scholars refer to as "courtesans" (2006, 43–44).[28] Such analyses lead to further speculation about enslaved women all over the Mediterranean world who hoped to earn their freedom in brothels. Were they, similarly, "sent away" to acquire such skills, or were these skills that could be acquired "on the job"?

Consequently, it merits notice that Phoenicium's name connects her ethnically, and perhaps geographically, with Carthage, a non-Greek part of the Mediterranean world. In a play staged a mere decade after Rome's victory over the Carthaginians in the Second Punic War, this detail would not have gone unobserved by Plautus's audience. Yet at the same time the name "Phoenicium" derives from a Greek word for her ancestral region. Although Plautus assigns Greek names to most of his dramatis personae, in his comedy all about Carthaginians, the *Poenulus*, two of its Carthaginian characters—Hanno and Giddenis—sport actual Carthaginian names, even as the freeborn Carthaginian girls enslaved by the Greek pimp Lycus have Greek names.[29]

Plautus's portrayal of the Greekly-named Carthaginian Phoenicium, and of her Athenian literary and rhetorical learning environment, may thus offer a humorous critique of both Carthaginian and Greek cultures, one that draws on popular

Roman stereotypes. Phoenicium is, after all, a sex slave from a society associated with verbal and behavioral untrustworthiness who adapts to the elite male culture of a city where words are shown to reign supreme.[30] To be sure, prostitutes plying their trade in Greece also figure in Plautus's comedies that were evidently composed prior to the *Pseudolus*, women who are also represented as having a way with words. At line 923 of the *Miles gloriosus*, for example, the Ephesian *meretrix* Acroteleutium is even praised for speaking charmingly (*lepide*).[31] Yet Plautus does accord special attention to Phoenicium's use of language, and to the resemblances between her writing style and the speaking styles of both Ballio and, eventually, Pseudolus: her writing, her way with words, after all, sets the entire plot in motion.

The *New York Times* columnist Nicholas Kristof has stressed the importance of literacy as a survival skill for female sex workers, reporting that in 2003 he "purchased two teenage girls from the Cambodian brothels that enslaved them and returned them to their families. . . . Building schools doesn't immediately solve the problem of girls currently enslaved inside brothels." Still, he concludes that "literate girls not only are in less danger of being trafficked, but later they have fewer children, care for their children better, and are much better able to earn a decent living" (Kristof 2006). Henry Louis Gates Jr. has underscored the importance of "literacy—the literacy of formal writing" as "a technology and a commodity" with which the right of an African in the eighteenth and nineteenth centuries "to be considered a human being could be traded" (Gates 2001, 111). Did literary and rhetorical skills, however acquired, help Greek and Roman female brothel slaves to survive, gain their freedom, and earn recognition as human beings? Or did they merely add to the profitability of these women for their owners? Plautus would have us believe that these skills were not merely survival tools but also weapons of combating human oppression by portraying them in his *Pseudolus* as ultimately subverting Ballio and thus making life "hard out there for one pimp."[32]

NOTES

Many thanks to Allison Glazebrook and Madeleine Henry, coeditors of this volume; the referees for the University of Wisconsin Press; and Vincent Carretta, Edward Cohen, James Davidson, Jane Donawerth, Robert Gaines, Donald Lateiner, Timothy Moore, and Nicholas Rauh for their valuable suggestions.

1. The date of the *Pseudolus* is attested by the brief headnotes (*didascalia*) found in the Ambrosian palimpsest (*Marco Iunio Marci fili praetore urbano, acta Megalesiis*); see the discussion of Willcock 1987, 1, 30, 95. See also Moore 1998, 196–207, who illuminates the political circumstances in which the play was performed, namely as part of the games celebrating the dedication of a temple to a goddess recently imported from Asia Minor, the Magna Mater. He notes that Plautus may have "found in the desires of the festival's sponsors extra

incentive to make the *Pseudolus* conspicuously special." Certain distinctive features of the play—the lack of a prologue, all-male roster of speaking roles, and striking emphasis on the potential and power of language—do render it both conspicuous and special in the Plautine *corpus*.

2. For the comedy's preoccupation with performance and literary control, see also Moore 1998, 92–125. Of special relevance is Moore's observation that Plautus has "the actors refer repeatedly to their skill at playing the stock characters they portray" and reinforces these allusions by having other characters praise the performance of, among others, Ballio and Pseudolus (1998, 96–97). Other recent studies of reading and writing in this play include Sharrock 1996; Slater 2004; and Jenkins 2005.

3. For an overview of Plautine comedy and its "Saturnalian" affinities, see E. Segal 1987, 1–41; and Richlin 2005, 19–30.

4. As Amy Richlin (2005, 14) emphasizes, scholars over the past half century have been placing an increased emphasis on what is Roman about Plautus and paying less attention to the relationship between Plautus and his Greek originals. Indeed, Richlin's introduction contains a brief background on Roman culture that highlights Roman slavery, prostitution, and the sex-gender system. Nevertheless, the similarities between earlier Greek and Roman cultural practices in the realm of slave prostitution allow scholars such as James Davidson (2006) to utilize Plautine literary representations of commercial sex work as evidence of earlier Greek as well as Roman social realities. Furthermore, Plautus's prominent use of Greek names, phrases, literary allusions and locales—discussed by Richlin (2005, 41–42)—suggests that he is not only recognizing the presence of native Greek speakers in his audience but also taking comic aim at Greek society as it is portrayed in earlier works of literature.

5. For the role of the opening scene as a substitute for an expository prologue, see Slater 1985, 119; and Jenkins 2005, 383. Thomas Jenkins notes that the epistolary reading at the start of the play calls attention to "writing as a medium of communication"; in this way, it highlights persuasive language, both oral and written. Malcolm Willcock (1987, 96) considers whether the lost Greek original inspiring Plautus's play had a prologue. There are, however, no references to this Greek original in the text of the play.

6. See Judith Hallett's interpretation (2006), which takes issue with Emily Hemelrijk's statement that "part of the fun of this letter lies in the contrast between the low status of the girl and the exuberant style of her letter, which bristles with unusual or invented words. By accumulating uncommon words and long-winded phrases Plautus makes fun of the slave-girl's aspiration to use the language of the educated classes" (1999, 198–99).

7. I follow the text of Willcock 1987; all English translations are my own.

8. See Hallett 2006, 40, on the echo of Sappho 31 Lobel-Page, lines 14–16.

9. By associating Phoenicium's handwriting on the wax tablets with her horizontal body, positioned for intercourse, Plautus characterizes, "sexualizes," and trivializes her, much as various ancient writers, particularly those of Greek comedy, did of the Greek Aspasia. See M. Henry 1995, 19, on the "sexual, sexualized, and sexualizing" nature of comic allusions to Aspasia.

10. Niall Slater (1985, 120–21) construes line 74 as "it is tragically written," adding "Pseudolus' comment of course means that the handwriting itself is a tragedy, but I think it may also mean that 'the plot laid out for the play by this letter is a piece of hack writing.' . . . Pseudolus . . . resists this stock New Comedy plot." Yet Plautus also emphasizes Pseudolus's failure to weep, in the way that Calidorus does, at the language and sentiments of the letter, implying that Pseudolus has a negative reaction to them too.

11. For the use of pumice stone to polish books in ancient Rome, see, for example, Catull. 1.2, 22.8; Hor., *Epist.* 1.20.2; and Ov. *Tr.* 1.1.11.

12. As Timothy Moore has suggested (pers. comm.), *genus nostrum* may well signify "slaves" and imply that those in Pseudolus's lowly position do not have the luxury of being sentimental, as does a freeborn man like Calidorus.

13. On the profusion of nouns, many of them new coinages, in this passage, see Hallett 2006, 41; on Latin diminutives generally, see Varro, *De lingua latina* fr. 9–10.

14. On the copious use of asyndeton and alliteration in this passage, see Hallett 2006, 41. Asyndeton is discussed at *Rhetorica ad Herennium* 4.30 and Quint. *Inst.* 9.3.50–54, 4.23; alliteration at *Rhetorica ad Herennium* 4.18.

15. For homoeoptoton, see *Rhetorica ad Herennium* 4.28.

16. For padding, see *Rhetorica ad Herennium* 4.28, which refers to this phenomenon as "*interpretatio* or *synonymia.*" Edward Courtney (1999, 8) speaks of "the accumulation of near synonyms . . . verging on pleonasm" and regards such language as "producing an insistence on clarity."

17. For the date of the *Casina*, see Hallett 1996. Various details in the text allow the inference that Plautus may have written the play, his last, shortly after the death of Scipio Africanus and shortly before he himself died.

18. See the *OLD*, s.v. *deosculor*. This is the only time this word appears in Plautus, and it is not found again until Apuleius, who uses it twice. W. Thomas MacCary and Willcock (1976, 116) observe of the language of this passage that it exhibits "typical Plautine linguistic exuberance."

19. See Thomas 1993 as well as the *OLD* s.v. *passer* (lb) for the erotic associations of *passer* in Catullus and elsewhere.

20. Plautus may, of course, be ridiculing Olympio's love talk. In this play he does not seem to identify with either Olympio or his rival Chalinus; rather, he is represented on stage by the *matrona* and "playwright" Cleostrata. But it warrants emphasis that Chalinus—unlike Pseudolus—does not object to Olympio's mode of self-expression nor to how he fantasizes about Casina expressing herself, but only to Olympio's arrogant assumption that he alone will eventually enjoy Casina's favors.

21. On the most conspicuous stylistic features of this passage from the *Pro Rhodiensibus*, see Courtney 1999, 78–94; the rhymed endings here exemplify homoeoteleuton rather than homoeoptoton, since the present active infinitives rhymed are indeclinable forms.

22. Cf. also 1257–58, which contain an allusion—as do the words of Calidorus in the opening scene—to Sappho 31 Lobel-Page: "Hic omnes voluptates, in hoc / omnes venustates

sunt, / deis proxumum esse arbitror" (Here are all the pleasures, in this are all the joys of love, I think I am extremely close to the gods).

23. The *hapax legomena* assigned to Ballio in this passage include *flagritribae* and *beluatam*. See s.v. *flagritriba* and *beluata* in the *OLD*.

24. Willcock (1987, 41) assigns this line to Pseudolus rather than Calidorus, unlike most editors of the play.

25. See Moore's chapter on the *Truculentus* for the argument, and much evidence, that "Plautus' prostitutes could have appeared . . . relevant to his audience" (1998, 141–42).

26. Cohen cites, inter alia, Konstantinos Kapparis's comment on [Dem.] 59.18 concerning the female brothel keeper Nikarete (1999, 207). As an (anonymous) referee of this essay rightly observed, however, these specialized activities are crafts that might come in handy around the physical space of a brothel and are substantially different from rhetorical skills, which enable those managing and laboring in brothels to communicate with, and satisfy, their customers.

27. Davidson continues, "Investing in the training of slaves, especially of courtesans, male and female, musical or otherwise, was one of the few really dynamic areas of the ancient economy, an area in which a wise investment might produce dramatic returns" (2006, 39). However, he contrasts such slaves with those who were merely sent to a brothel.

28. Davidson comments: "The old-fashioned idea of courtesans as educated may be a fantasy, but it is a fantasy based on the ancient sources, which assume that courtesans can read and write letters, quote lines from Homer and tragedy, and compose elaborate pieces of oratory" (2006, 43).

29. See Richlin 2005, 187–98, for the names assigned to the characters in the *Poenulus* and for the standard Latin words for "Carthaginian."

30. For the Romans' stereotype of the Carthaginians as "untrustworthy, sneaky, slimy"—and the Roman use of *punica fides*, "Phoenician trustworthiness," for "untrustworthiness"—see Richlin 2005, 185.

31. For the date of the *Miles gloriosus*, see Richlin (2005, 10–11), who notes that lines 211–12 may allude to an event involving the playwright Naevius in 205 BCE.

32. These words evoke the lyrics of the 2005 Academy Award–winning song, "It's Hard Out Here for a Pimp" by Djay f/Shug.

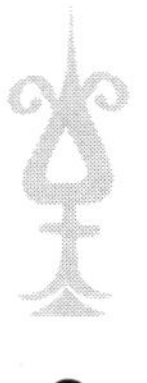

9 Prostitutes, Pimps, and Political Conspiracies during the Late Roman Republic

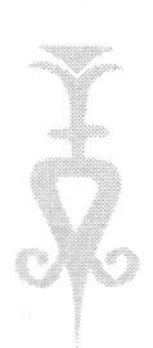

NICHOLAS K. RAUH

A recurring pattern of subversive behavior by courtesans, pimps, and prostitutes, including participation in political conspiracies and underclass violence, is visible in literature of the late Roman Republic (133–27 BCE). Since many of these sex professionals were of eastern Mediterranean origin and reflected trends in the wider Hellenistic world (Herter 1960, 71; Kleberg 1957, 77), the topic falls within the context of this volume. Underclass sex-trade laborers appear repeatedly to have joined in "conspiracies" to undermine the authority of the senatorial aristocracy. According to the textual record, admittedly compiled by members of the elite, female courtesans and prostitutes (*meretrices*, *sagae*) and male pimps (*lenones*) and muggers (*sicarii*) demonstrated the capacity to destabilize the aristocracy's dominant position in society.[1] Two contemporary writers, Sallust and Cicero, appear to have viewed these people as genuine political threats. According to these authors, sex laborers in Rome galvanized urban followings to oppose the aristocracy, gave voice and direction to underclass discontent, and perhaps most seriously influenced the outcome of political events. Our source tradition for this behavior is limited and arises largely from literary forms of dubious authority such as Cicero's political speeches. The entire tradition attesting to the involvement of sex-trade laborers in republican political conspiracies is the product of what specialists in cultural studies identify as "conspiracy theory." Daniel Pipes (1997, 21) defines conspiracy theory as the fear of a nonexistent conspiracy or the perception that a conspiracy exists when proof is lacking. To the degree that our source tradition about renegade pimps and prostitutes arose from a sense of paranoia among members of the senatorial elite, this "anxiety" may appropriately be called *conspiracism*.[2] Conspiracy theory requires that there be a long-standing template for involvement in conspiracy that helps create a delegitimizing myth to denigrate the conspirators. To support my view that Roman conspiracism implicated sex-trade laborers, therefore, the second part of my essay demonstrates that similar accusations were made against sex-trade laborers during the classical Greek era.

Sex-Trade Laborers in Republican Political Conspiracies

An example from the decade of the 70s BCE, when the city of Rome experienced repeated outbursts of underclass violence, illustrates the role of renegade courtesans, pimps, and prostitutes in Roman urban conspiracies. The 70s BCE was marked by the growing menace of Cilician pirates, the slave revolt of Spartacus, repeated mob riots in the capital city of Rome, violence and banditry in the hinterland, native rebellions in Spain, Asia Minor, Illyria, Macedonia, and Thrace, and mutinies by the professional soldiers sworn to safeguard the republic. Evidence suggests that the violent efforts of these disparate elements were sometimes coordinated through hidden lines of communication, occasionally culminating in concerted efforts, that is, conspiracies, to topple the oligarchic regime in Rome. At the center of at least one of these conspiracies stood the Roman courtesan (*meretrix*) Praecia.

During the 70s BCE antagonists of the senatorial regime of the dictator L. Cornelius Sulla openly flaunted their defiance while mobilizing dissent. In 76 BCE L. Magius and L. Fannius, two Roman aristocratic military deserters working for Rome's adversary, Mithridates VI of Pontus, passed through Italy while negotiating an alliance between the king and the renegade Roman general in Spain, Q. Sertorius. Alarmed by reports of their movements, the Roman Senate issued a decree declaring Magius and Fannius public enemies and demanding their arrest. The two men eluded its grasp, however, and journeyed unhindered to Spain, where they negotiated not only with Sertorius but also with Cn. Pompeius Magnus, the Roman general commissioned by the Senate to suppress the Spanish rebellion.[3] Since they conducted their three-month cruise of the Mediterranean in a *myoparo* (a sleek warship popular with pirates) and sojourned in Sertorius's pirate haunt of Dianium, it is likely that Magius and Fannius sailed the Mediterranean sea-lanes under the safe passage of the Cilician pirates.[4] Their sea voyage from Pontus to Spain and back undoubtedly required layovers at a number of Italian ports, which probably explains how the Roman Senate became alerted to their movements. In any event the lines of communication that Magius and Fannius opened between Mithridates, Sertorius, and the pirates culminated in a series of seemingly coordinated assaults on the Roman oligarchy in the following year (75 BCE). The Cilician pirates helpfully shut off the grain supply to Rome.[5] By summer their blockade had provoked bread riots in the Roman forum, where a mob threatened the lives of the consuls, C. Aurelius Cotta and L. Octavius. The intimidated consuls relinquished the Sullan regime's prohibitions against the plebeian tribuneship, and the oligarchy appeared to lose its grip on the city, which was overtaken by fiery tribunes and urban renegades.[6] Mysterious figures, such as P. Cornelius Cethegus, a senator and a notorious political trimmer and social outcast from the previous civil war, suddenly emerged as powerbrokers because of their influence with the mob.[7] In 74 BCE Cethegus compelled newly elected Roman consul L. Licinius Lucullus, a distinguished general and the hand-picked successor to the dictator Sulla, to resort to "bribes and flattery" to secure his military command against Mithridates. Cethegus's humiliation of Lucullus did not end there. If one can believe Plutarch, the object of Lucullus's bribery was not so much Cethegus himself as it was Cethegus's mistress Praecia, a courtesan "whose wit and beauty were celebrated throughout the city":

> For at that time Cethegus through his popularity controlled the city and when he joined Praecia's following and became her lover, political power passed entirely into her hands. No public measure passed unless Cethegus favored it, and Cethegus did nothing except with Praecia's approval. (*Luc.* 6.3)

Despite the brevity of this, our only record of this woman, her emergence as a mob personality during this crisis, seems significant.[8] As Plutarch observes:

> In other respects she was nothing more than a courtesan, but she used her associates and companions to further the political ambitions of her friends, and so added to her other charms the reputation of being a true comrade, and one who could bring things to pass. She thus acquired the greatest possible influence. (*Luc.* 6.4)

Given the meagerness of the surviving record, historians legitimately question its importance, uncertain whether to dismiss it as fiction, exaggeration, or aberration. In any case, the conspiracy failed: Cethegus and Praecia disappeared from view as rapidly as they appeared; Lucullus reduced Mithridates to the status of a refugee; and in the subsequent twelve years Pompey defeated Sertorius, Spartacus, the Cilician pirates, and Mithridates in turn. These successes did little, however, to offset the rising wave of urban uprisings in Rome, suggesting that the underlying social causes of the unrest were deeply rooted.

Roman oligarchic sparring with city mobs continued unabated in the ensuing decades, with conspiracies forged between renegade aristocrats, pimps, prostitutes, and underclass, antisocial elements forming a recurring pattern in urban politics. Organizers of urban protests in Rome, and aristocratic politicians aligned with these organizers, appear to have relied on those who congregated in the shops, bars, taverns, inns, and brothels of the city to mobilize and to galvanize their followings (Rauh, Dillon, and McClain 2008). According to Sallust, for example, pimps, wine dealers, butchers, and knife-brandishing muggers supported the uprising of Sulla's adversary, M. Aemilius Lepidus, the renegade consul of 78 BC (*Hist.* 3.63; cf. 1.77.7 M.). Sallust's moralizing tendencies must be borne in mind when assessing the worth of this information. The same author accused Catiline in 63 BCE of forging an urban conspiracy out of proprietors of shops and taverns, elderly indebted prostitutes (common frequenters of taverns), and wanton male and female aristocrats (*Cat.* 13, 14, 24; cf. Welwei 1981, 66). M. Tullius Cicero, Catiline's principal adversary and another writer with an obvious axe to grind, condemned Catiline's followers as "poisoners, gladiators, robbers, assassins, parricides, forgers, cheaters, gluttons, wastrels, adulterers, prostitutes, corrupters of the youth, and juvenile delinquents" (*Cat.* 2.7; cf. 22). In a rare instance of understatement, Cicero asserts (*Cat.* 4.17) that Catiline recruited his conspirators from the ranks of those generally *qui in tabernis sunt.* As Nicolas K. Rauh, Matthew J. Dillon, and T. Davina McClain (2008, 232) note, this expression appears to refer broadly to anyone "residing in," "deriving profit from," or "earning livings" in Roman shops and taverns. Cicero (*Dom.* 13) describes an ally of Clodius named Sergius as a *concitator tabernariorum.* Of particular concern to Cicero were aristocratic conspirators such as Publicius and Munatius, "whose debts contracted in the *popinae* [tavern brothels] caused no small degree of anxiety to the republic" (*Cat.* 2.4). Preying on the foibles of morally bankrupt aristocrats such as these, Catiline, according to Cicero, organized a debauched coalition in the brothels and taverns of the Roman slums. When Catiline's conspiracy began to unravel, Cicero states (*Cat.* 4.17) that its sole remaining at-large member, P. Cornelius Lentulus, attempted to incite public disturbances by dispatching a pimp (*leno*) throughout the *tabernae.* Simply put, Cicero accused Catiline of having exploited venues of the Roman sex trade as loci for male bonding and political intrigue. Catiline allegedly used the evening banquets and orgies that occurred at these locations to forge a common sense of identity among an otherwise diverse constituency and to generate hostility against the senatorial establishment:

> If in their drinking and gambling parties (Catiline's supporters) were content with feasts and prostitutes, they would be beyond redemption, but tolerable at least to

> the rest of us. But who can tolerate this—that indolent men should plot against the bravest, drunkards against the sober, men asleep against men awake; that men lying at feasts, embracing women of ill repute, languid with wine, crammed with food, crowned with chaplets, reeking of ointments, and worn out with debauchery, belch out in their discourse the murder of all good men and the conflagration of the city? (*Cat.* 2.10)

The importance of these localities, as well as of the sex-trade workers within, to the formation of urban mob conspiracies seems evident, therefore, at least within the context of this literature.

Accusations that underclass conspiracies coalesced in tavern and brothel environments persisted through the end of the republican era. According to Cicero, during the 50s BCE, P. Clodius bolstered his mob following with prostitutes, runaway slaves, gladiators, and muggers (*Mil.* 55).[9] Like Catiline before him, Clodius's mastery of the mob stemmed directly from his ability to recruit "leadership cadres" in the *tabernae*. According to Cicero and Asconius, Clodius's control of Roman workshops and taverns was so complete that in 58 and again in 52 BCE he and his henchmen compelled huge demonstrations in the Roman Forum by summarily closing *tabernae* throughout the city (Cic. *Dom.* 54; cf. 89–90; Ascon. 41, 52 C.).[10] Likewise, according to Cicero, actors, actresses, gamblers, pimps, muggers, and gladiators formed the core of M. Antonius's political support during the 40s. In much the same way that Lucullus suffered humiliation at the hand of Praecia, Cicero, his fellow senators, and all "respectable citizens" were forced to endure the sight of Antony's mistress, a notorious mime and *meretrix* named (Volumnia) Cytheris, conveyed in a litter alongside his wife in the train of his consular legions.[11]

These accusations must be weighed against the fact that our main source, Cicero, regarded nearly every one of these political figures as adversaries. That he relied on slanderous accusations to blacken their reputations in public debate has long been recognized (Kubiak 1989; May 1988; Richlin 1983, 86, 109–10; Tatum 1999, 78, 142). The charge that these and other political enemies were debauched frequenters of taverns and brothels form an unmistakable pattern in his rhetoric.[12] The fact that so much of this information arises from Cicero's oratory appears on the surface to weaken the argument that underclass sex-trade laborers played a significant role in these conspiracies. Modern scholars typically greet the evidence with skepticism, tending either to dismiss it as so much Ciceronian hyperbole or to ignore it altogether.[13] Either recourse fails to acknowledge that Sallust, who was Cicero's contemporary, constructed what was essentially the same *conspiracist* narrative for his depiction of the Catilinarian conspiracy. Even when allowing for the likelihood that Sallust (not to mention later sources) relied considerably on

Cicero's writings for understanding the events, the selective processes employed by modern scholars to construct their knowledge of this affair warrants scrutiny.

Some sort of conspiracy undeniably occurred in 63 BCE. The question remains how many extraneous details surrounding the Catilinarian conspiracy may reasonably be accepted. Whether pimps and elderly prostitutes were fundamental to the formation of this conspiracy falls subject to the same scrutiny as other accusations—for example, that prominent aristocrats were similarly involved, including M. Licinius Crassus, C. Julius Caesar, P. Clodius, M. Antonius, C. Scribonius Curio the Younger, and M. Caelius Rufus.[14] As Pipes observes, "a second challenge to discerning conspiracy theories results from their containing enough truth and reasonableness to make them plausible. An element of veracity gets mixed with a much larger proportion of fantasy" (1997, 31). Robert Robins and Jerrald Post likewise observe, "because paranoia is a distortion of a healthy response to the danger that exists in politics and because threats appear and disappear over time, a perception of enemies may be accurate at one time and inaccurate at another" (1997, 34).

In lieu of proof, we resort to modes of argumentation that are invariably subjective (Pipes 1997, 37). Procedural arguments such as "common sense," "historical judgment," and "scholarly consensus" are typically brought to bear. As cultural studies specialists observe, all three means of interpretation enjoy questionable validity, especially when it comes to delegitimizing popular forms of knowledge such as conspiracy theory. As Clare Birchall observes, commonsensical interpretations are flawed because they imply that a sound interpretation or conversely an unsound interpretation or even, in the case of conspiracy theory, an overinterpretation can be deduced or recognized on the basis of reason (2006, 75). As the example of the list of alleged Catilinarian conspirators demonstrates, good interpretation is often impossible to distinguish from "overinterpretation." Historical judgment, which relies on the presence or absence of contradictory testimony as well as on arguments predicated on a "higher awareness" of the facts surrounding an event, is equally vulnerable owing to its reliance on intrinsically hypothetical constructs. As Birchall notes, "conspiracy theory can suggest that all knowledge is only ever theory; that the relationship between a sign and its referent is necessarily inflected by imaginary processes; and that any transcendental truth claims rely on contingent strategies of legitimization" (2006, 73). Where consensus is concerned, Jean-François Lyotard argues, according to Birchall, that as a means of regulating academic discourse, consensus "merely observes science behaving like any other 'power center whose behaviour is governed by a principle of homeostasis'" (2006, 80). Consensus gains efficiency, in other words, by threatening to eliminate dissident opinions from the realm of discourse. "Individual aspirations need to fall in line with the needs of the system" (Birchall 2006, 80). In short, before rejecting ancient testimony that Roman sex-trade workers were implicated in republican political conspiracies, classical scholars need to reexamine the means by which we go about formulating knowledge in the first place. What is at stake here is not merely the disputed role of renegade courtesans, pimps, and prostitutes in republican urban conspiracies, nor the dubious character of the source tradition, nor even the epistemological standards used to assess this source tradition. Alongside all these issues stands the question how we as classicists are to approach *conspiracist* source traditions and devise knowledge constructs from evidence so heavily rooted in ancient popular culture. As Birchall observes, "the treatment of conspiracy theories by some accepted rational discourses of inquiry highlights a preference at work for only certain knowledges and their strategies of legitimization, prompting the question: what causes the selective acceptance of the acceptable?" (2006, 44).

Sex-Trade Laborers and Ancient Conspiracy Theory

Let us hypothesize that the evidence for the role of Roman sex-trade workers in republican political conspiracies arose from the minds of Cicero and Sallust and that it amounts to little more than deliberate fabrication or at best paranoid delusion on their parts. In this manner the evidence lends itself to analysis according to contemporary models of conspiracy theory, enabling us to gauge whether the character of this testimony was "overinterpretational." As described by Pipes, Robins, and Post, conspiracy theories typically work in two directions—from the bottom up and from the top down.[15] In the case of aristocratic writers such as Cicero and Sallust, the theory would have thus disseminated from the top down. Conspiracy theories of great magnitude usually contain three basic elements: the existence of a powerful evil and a clandestine group that aspires to global hegemony; dupes and agents who extend the group's influence throughout the community so that it is on the verge of succeeding; and a valiant but embattled group that must urgently unite to stave off catastrophe (Pipes 1997, 22). The conspiracy is typically described as already powerful and rapidly growing (Robins and Post 1997, 37). Sometimes the political paranoid's beliefs in conspiracy and hostility originate in reality.[16] Reality aside, the leader's objective remains to induce conflict by generating public hostility against his perceived enemies and to create a bellicose climate that primes his supporters for war. The leader's use of conspiracy theory ultimately nurtures murderous instincts against the accused, depriving them of their humanity and rendering them vulnerable to elimination (Pipes 1997,

177). While hyperbole and personal invective furnished standard tools of argumentation in ancient oratory, the template for conspiracy theory conforms remarkably with the descriptions employed by Cicero and Sallust. In their opinion the Catilinarian conspirators represented a powerful evil and a clandestine group aspiring to dominate Rome; they exploited indebted elements at all levels of society so as to extend their rapidly growing influence; and Cicero clearly perceived himself as the leader of a valiant but embattled group urgently attempting to stave off catastrophe (Favory 1978).

Additional parallels between modern conspiracy theory and the rhetoric of Cicero and Sallust become apparent. Conspiracy theory rarely requires the demonstration of logic or proof; rather conspiracists assume that "things are not what they seem and everything is connected" (Birchall 2006, 34). Conspiracy theories tend to be more rigorously logical and have fewer loose ends than ordinary events in real life. On the assumption that appearances deceive, conspiracists reject conventional information and seek out exotic and little-known variants. Many facts that originally seem correct are inevitably undone by the conspiracist's effort to locate causal relationships where none exist (Pipes 1997, 30).[17] To render their theories "venerable" and less questionable, the conspiracist tends to repeat old explanations and to invoke the authority of predecessors. As Pipes notes, "there is tendency for one conspiracy theory to overlap with another forming a giant web enclosing centuries and continents. Each group is expected to pass on its views and secrets to the next organization" (1997, 29). Not only do conspiracists typically see all conspiracies as linked but they also tend to recirculate the same basic assertions with slight variations and revealing inconsistencies. For example, recent conspiracists attempting to expose the threat of the "Trilateral Commission" invariably invent a direct link to past "conspiracies" such as the Free Masons or the Illuminati, who in turn were attributed descent from the Knights Templar and King Hiram of Jerusalem. Piling on theory on top of conspiracy theory, conspiracists resort to rumor, forgery, an overabundance of learned factoids, and anything else that furnishes their argument an aura of credibility. Much like Cicero and Sallust's denigration of Catiline, the conspiracist attempts to blacken his adversary's reputation beyond repair. Accusations of sexual promiscuity and religious insult form standard conspiracist tactics. As Pipes notes, "conspiracist writings constitute a quite literal form of pornography (though political rather than sexual). . . . Recreational conspiracism titillates sophisticates much as does recreational sex" (1997, 49). To denigrate the conspiracist's adversary as sexually and religiously profligate helps to isolate him from respectable society. This particular facet of conspiracy theory seems highly germane to Cicero's and Sallust's assertions that sex-trade laborers were involved in Roman conspiracies. By identifying Catiline with pimps and prostitutes, Cicero and Sallust may simply have been fabricating salacious details to titillate the imaginations of their audience. Sex-trade laborers in Rome are similarly identifiable with Pipes's dupes and agents who help to extend the conspiracy's influence throughout the community.

In addition to the conspiracist model used to attack adversarial leaders, a similar one is used to indict their followings. Robins and Post explain that conspiracists attempt to dehumanize these followings in the public eye by implicating them in an established delegitimizing myth (1997, 43). Typically the conspiratorial element is portrayed as a clandestine group united by hidden practices and dedicated to the destruction of respectable society. In modern examples the accused groups typically assume the form of an underclass or perpetually marginalized elements of society who have risen beyond their ordinary station in life. "People like to take the newly risen down a peg and a charge of witchcraft could do that" (Robins and Post 1997, 50). Charges of sexual promiscuity and religious deviancy invariably help isolate these elements in societies caught in the grip of imagined conspiracies. The singling out of sex-trade laborers in Rome by Cicero and Sallust conforms remarkably with this facet of conspiracism, since these people were typically non-Roman, of slave origin, alienated, impoverished, and marginalized within Roman society. One other factor that contributes to the mass hysteria directed against a marginalized group is the tendency for outbreaks such as those to occur in disintegrating societies. "In these circumstances, ordinarily self-sufficient and psychologically healthy individuals overwhelmed by a society in chaos swell the ranks of the alienated and psychologically discontented" (Robins and Post 1997, 97). In other words, a society undergoing social and political unrest like the late Roman Republic was particularly vulnerable to conflict induced by conspiracy theories.

As constructed by the narratives of Sallust and Cicero, the role of sex-trade laborers in republican conspiracies conforms well to the model for conspiracism. Underclass, marginalized elements are singled out by our sources and charged with sexual depravity and religious sacrilege alongside leaders such as Catiline, Clodius, and Antonius. And not just sex-trade laborers are singled out: muggers, slaves, foreign ambassadors, and bankrupt veterans and aristocrats are also indicted. One must ask, nonetheless, how writers such as Cicero and Sallust were able to convince the Roman public that sex-trade laborers in the *tabernae* posed a convincing threat to society. Something about their behavior must have given everyday Romans pause for the accusation to have achieved the desired effect of dread and hostility. The character of conspiracy theory, and its tendency to pile theory on top of theory, justifies an investigation of a delegitimizing myth that implicated sex-trade laborers in conspiracies backward through time and space.

In this regard it is interesting to observe that classical and early Hellenistic *hetairai* in Athens reportedly exerted a similarly destabilizing influence on their respective societies. This suggests possibly that Roman sources such as Cicero and Sallust adapted and modeled their descriptions of sex-trade laborers on preexisting stories about Athenian prostitutes. Owing to the existence of pornographic literature that was available to writers in the time of Sallust and Cicero, an assessment of the conspiratorial tendencies of Greek *hetairai* and the concerns they raised for the Athenian public holds potential insight for conspiracism in Rome.[18] The problem of determining whether either of these traditions is reliable, however, remains. Nearly every facet of the behavior of Athenian *hetairai* exists as unsubstantiated rumor, and the women themselves remain so poorly documented that they loom as the ancient equivalent of urban legends (M. Henry 1995, 3–7). It stands to reason, nonetheless, that the greater the similarity between the Athenian and Roman traditions, the greater the likelihood that Sallust and Cicero drew on this earlier testimony to forge their delegitimizing myth.

The Role of Greek *Hetairai* in Athenian Conspiracy Theory

Roman descriptions of the subversive influence of urban sex laborers conform remarkably with those of critics elsewhere in the Mediterranean world, most particularly in the Hellenistic east. According to Greek literature an early (sixth and fifth century BCE) tradition of courtesan-driven *symposia* (drinking parties) in cities such as Athens, Corinth, and Miletus evolved with the conquest of Alexander the Great into a widely dispersed and highly unsettling phenomenon. According to the source tradition, classical and Hellenistic Greek courtesans used their beauty and their talents to extract payment from wealthy males, thus acquiring reputations as rapacious, mercenary, and predatory.[19] The excerpted and abridged record furnished by Athenaeus (13), for example, indicates that prostitutes, particularly highly prized *hetairai*, enjoyed untoward mobility in Athenian society.[20] Admittedly his backward-looking, airbrushed construct of "the great age of the courtesan" displays hyperbole about sex-trade laborers equal to that in the narratives of Cicero and Sallust. The anecdotes he presents for Greek courtesans are collected, arranged, and interpreted in a nostalgic way so as to create a pornographized view of their experience (McClure 2003a; M. Henry 1992). In other words, just as we must take Sallust and Cicero's criticisms with a grain of salt, we must constantly bear in mind the distorted prism through which Athenaeus views Greek prostitution. This having been said, Athenaeus furnishes a detailed list of politicians, philosophers, poets, artists, and actors who communed with Greek courtesans from the sixth to fourth centuries BCE. Apart from the financial drain that these women imposed on their aristocratic lovers, another sinister aspect of their behavior appears to have resulted from the vulnerability of Greek males themselves. According to the literary tradition, members of the Athenian elite repeatedly became emotionally involved with these women. In a few instances Greek courtesans allegedly used the power they held over their lovers to influence if not to usurp political power. Aspasia's alleged influence over Pericles presents only the most celebrated example (M. Henry 1995, 13).[21] The tradition attesting to courtesans assuming political power was even stronger among neighboring monarchies such as Thessaly and Macedonia. The tendency of Aegean and later Hellenistic monarchs to associate with *hetairai* often resulted in the installment of courtesans, such as Thargelia, Philinna, Phryne, Pythionike, Glycera, Lais, and Agathocleia, as royal consorts and queens.[22] This tendency appears to have made leaders of representative governments such as the Athenian democracy and the Roman Republic extremely uneasy. As Aristotle wrote (*Pol.* 1.1269b32), "For what difference is there between a rule of women and a state in which women rule the rulers?" We observe that courtesans were alleged to have frequented all levels of Athenian society, to have drained the financial resources of its leading citizens, and to have posed risks to the well being of Athenian political institutions.

A second source of concern to Athenian elites was posed by elderly, unattractive prostitutes at the bottom of the sex-trade hierarchy. These women were the precursors of the notorious *sagae* of Hellenistic-Roman literature.[23] Many of these, such as Lais and Phryne, had originally enjoyed wealth and notoriety as *hetairai* but were impoverished in old age. Older, "used-up" prostitutes assumed secondary roles as gatekeepers, messengers, caretakers, and suppliers of cosmetics and potions.[24] These elderly prostitutes supplemented diminishing incomes by furnishing the ancient equivalent of a drug trade, servicing fellow prostitutes and others with a wide array of aphrodisiacs, cosmetics, and magical incantations, allegedly handed down from ancient sorceresses of Thessaly.[25] Within the subculture of prostitution these aids and services enjoyed widespread popularity. Just as pimps and innkeepers endured nefarious reputations as thieves, muggers, kidnappers, and murderers, elderly, frail *sagae* were popularly associated with witchcraft, magical potions, and poisonings.[26] Greek and Roman poets indicate that even the most elegant *hetairai* and *meretrices* were never far removed from these crones, relying on them as personal advisors.[27] By positioning themselves beside popular courtesans, *sagae* retained access to the highest levels of elite society and dispensed their goods to the wider community. Anyone who frequented venues of prostitution, therefore, potentially came in contact with women such as these. The fear of this particular aspect of the sex trade was pronounced. According to the literary tradition, L. Lucullus, the general who temporarily aligned with Praecia in 74 BCE, and the poet Lucretius both died from abuse of love potions (*pocula desiderii*.)[28] Horace long persisted in the belief that he had been poisoned by his aging mistress Canidia (*Epod.* 3, 5, 17; *Sat.* 1.8.19–50). Propertius insisted (3.7.24, 4.5.5–20, 4.7.35, 43–44) that the streetwalker Nomas poisoned his courtesan-mistress, Corinna, and that Corinna's friends Petalas and Lalage likewise died mysteriously. Martial derided one particularly loathsome, elderly prostitute as a Thessalian witch (Mart. 2.33, 4.65, 7.67, 70, 9.29, 40, 62, 10.22, 12.22).[29] In short, it is highly likely that Roman sources seized on the literary tradition describing the *sagae* and recirculated it as a form of conspiracy theory. By drawing a connection between a prostitute and Thessalian witches, Martial merely invoked a long-lived, delegitimizing myth about prostitutes in general.

Where evidence for the participation of sex-trade laborers in wider political conspiracies is concerned, the Athenian record is decidedly less substantial than its Roman counterpart. Athenian sources occasionally recognized prostitutes as threats to public safety. For example, several women were allegedly prosecuted for impiety (*asebeia*), murder, and poisoning. Where the capital charge of *asebeia* is concerned, Aspasia, Neaira, Phryne, and possibly Lais were indicted, either because the charge allowed for a broad range of interpretation or because something about the women's behavior was sufficiently alarming to warrant condemnation for sacrilege.[30] Demosthenes allegedly prosecuted two subversive women for poisonings during the late fourth century BCE. One Theoris of Lemnos, described alternately as a priestess (*hiereia*), a prophetess (*mantis*), or a druggist (*miara pharmakida*), was executed along with her entire family allegedly for inciting slaves to plot against their masters.[31] A Ninos, also described as a priestess and a poisoner, was executed for allegedly supplying love potions to young men.[32] While neither of these women are specifically referred to as prostitutes, their activities certainly conform to those of the *sagae*. The late fifth-century *hetaira* Nais was ominously nicknamed Anticyra ("Hellebore," a poisonous flowering plant), allegedly because she had amassed a large quantity of this common poison.[33]

A third source of fear generated by sex-trade laborers in Athenian society may have arisen, therefore, from these women's ability to utilize their popularity to defy public morality. Several Athenian *hetairai* appear to have fostered what Timothy Gilfoyle describes as a "sexual democracy," thereby creating vertical connections across the socioeconomic spectrum that enabled them to forge political associations of a highly improbable sort.[34] The most talented prostitutes successfully enticed wealthy citizens and young aristocrats into an underclass world of sex establishments where they came in contact with social inferiors (Rauh, Dillon, and McClain 2008, 234). As the glue that held this culture together, Athenian *hetairai* appear to have enabled underclass males to impose egalitarian norms on their social superiors (Gilfoyle 1994, 224–50). Although there is little evidence to suggest that Athenian *hetairai* ultimately used this influence to mobilize political conspiracies against the government in the manner described in Rome, they appear nonetheless to have recognized the value of cultivating organized followings in possible imitation of Athenian demagogues. As a result, the Athenian establishment seems to have interpreted these efforts as potential threats to the urban social fabric. This in turn may explain why so many of these women were prosecuted in high-profile trials.

According to Athenaeus, many beautiful prostitutes, including Gnathaina, her granddaughter Gnathainion, Lais, Pythionike, Phryne, Leme, and Pasiphile, imposed egalitarian principles on their lovers, much to the chagrin of those who were elite. Several of these *hetairai* charged the same low price to all their lovers.[35] For Athenaeus to repeat this observation as often as he does suggests that this policy was atypical if not extraordinary.[36] Seemingly insignificant at first glance, the fact that so many women pursued this policy suggests that it was an intentional, if not deliberate, form of mutual imitation. Accordingly, these *hetairai* appear to have engaged in a deliberate effort to render their services affordable to underclass clients and thereby augment the size of their clientele. Some courtesans used these pricing systems specifically to assert their authority over elite lovers. The glamorous Phryne allegedly humiliated the wealthy philosopher Aristippus by charging him an exorbitant fee while allowing the vagabond, Diogenes the Cynic, to visit her for free. She also provoked complaint from the playwright Moerichus by demanding that he pay her a mina while knowingly charging some foreigner a mere two gold pieces.[37] However capricious this behavior may appear, it reinforces the suspicion that Phryne used her sexual attraction to dominate her wealthier clients. Apparently they were powerless to resist. The glamorous and sarcastic Gnathaina went so far as to publish her egalitarian house rules in formal verse, employing language deliberately mimicking that of the peripatetic philosophers. According to Athenaeus (13.579e–585a), Gnathaina "ran her brothel as an open house, offering access to any male able to pay in advance and willing to abide by her published *nomos sussitikos* [banqueting rule]. Its opening line proclaimed, 'This law, equal and the same for all, has been written in 323 verses'" (13.579e–585b; Herter 1960, 102).[38] This fourth-century BCE *hetaira* engaged in sexual liaisons with an array of companions, including the comic playwright Diphilus, the actor Andronicus, an alcoholic gambler named Pausanias, an unnamed Syrian who plied her with small compliments, a parasite (freeloader) named Chaerophon, several rich foreign merchants in the Piraeus, a wrestler, several young boys, including a butcher's apprentice in the marketplace, a soldier, and numerous *mastigias*, a term used generally for whip-scarred slaves and convicts.[39] The fact that several of Athenaeus's anecdotes record witticisms made by Athenian *hetairai* at the expense of such convicts seems particularly significant. The recurring proximity of these criminals to glamorous *hetairai* seems to indicate that some women made a point of adding criminals to the mix of their sexual democracies. Aristocrats desiring to "date" these women, in other words, would have had to pay the same price, wait in the same line, and essentially compete for the attentions of an *hetaira* with the likes of philosophers, actors, parasites, gamblers, athletes, foreign merchants, soldiers, market vendors, youths, slaves, and whip-scarred slaves and convicts.[40] The inevitable result, intended or otherwise, was an effective social leveling in the brothels that was imposed by the *hetairai* themselves. This in turn supports the argument that these women consciously imitated and competed with one another while constructing their popular followings. Returning to the Roman examples for a moment, not only does this pattern of behavior demonstrate how a *meretrix* like Praecia could come to exert some political influence at Rome, but it also helps to explain the sense of alarm that sex-trade laborers incited among the Roman voting public. The lack of evidence for Athenian political conspiracies notwithstanding, the recurring pattern of indictments, prosecutions, and convictions of Athenian courtesans suggests that "respectable society" in Athens feared the popularity of these women every bit as much.

The ultimate danger posed by Athenian *hetairai* emerges from the fact that most of these women were foreigners. They used their popularity to improve their positions in the community, something particularly alarming in a society such as Athens where citizenship was zealously guarded. The *hetaira* Neaira of Corinth crucially illustrates this point (Hamel 2002). As foreigners, typically of slave origin, *hetairai* demonstrated a remarkable degree of upward mobility in Athenian society, on rare occasions transcending that of freeborn Athenian women.[41] This at any rate would appear to be the basis of accusations formulated by Athenian conspiracists. Neaira offers a detailed example of such social infiltration. Like Aspasia, this mid-fourth-century BCE *hetaira* revealed a remarkable talent for ingratiating herself with Athenian male citizens and thereby attaining status in Athenian society disproportionate to her legal standing. Whether the accusations made against her by the Athenian Apollodoros were legitimate is unimportant to the present argument. Since Neaira's record arises from a legal oration employing rhetorical logic that would be admired and emulated by Cicero, her experience offers insight to the kind of fear Athenian "conspiracists" attempted to incite against sex-trade laborers in their audience, in this instance 501 Athenian jurors.[42]

According to the testimony in the speech delivered by Apollodoros sometime in the 340s BCE, Neaira was purchased and raised as a *hetaira* along with six other female children by a slave-madam named Nikarete in Corinth. Neaira and her "sisters" were prostituted as preadolescents and rapidly cultivated friendships with numerous rich foreign customers, especially Athenians.[43] In adolescence Neaira visited Athens on several occasions (during the Great Panatheneia, for example) and associated with men such as the poet Xenocleides, the comic actor Hipparchus, and a wealthy Athenian named Phrynion ([Dem.] 59.24–26). These contacts became important when the opportunity arose for her to purchase her freedom ([Dem.] 59.29). To raise the 20 *minae* purchase price, she summoned to Corinth several of her former lovers including Phrynion, who agreed to purchase her freedom and to relocate her to Athens as his lover. Since Phrynion belonged to a relatively high-ranking family, his decision to live with her opened a potentially significant pathway into Athenian society.[44] Neaira's relationship with Phrynion quickly turned abusive, however, and she fled Athens for Megara, absconding with household goods and servants. Her fortunes declined in Megara, but in 371 BCE she attached herself to yet another Athenian named Stephanus and returned to Athens. According to Apollodoros, Stephanus convinced Neaira to live with him in the city as his wife ([Dem.] 59.35–37). At this point, Neaira's household included her two sons, Proxenus and Ariston, a daughter named Phano (according to Apollodoros a beautiful young courtesan much like her mother [(Dem.) 59.50–52; 59.67–70; 59.73]), two maidservants, and a butler.[45]

According to the prosecution, on arrival in Athens Stephanus and Neaira assumed the guise of a legitimate Athenian married couple (Hamel 2002, 49), even going so far as to pass off her children as Stephanus's legitimate Athenian progeny by a previous marriage.[46] This last ploy led to several potentially embarrassing scandals and ultimately exposed the two of them to the legal trouble that formed the basis of Apollodoros's prosecution. In one instance Stephanus arranged a marriage between Phano and the naïve young Athenian aristocrat Theogenes who had attained the office of *archon basileus* with help from Stephanus himself. As the wife of the *archon basileus* (*basilinna*), Phano performed sacred rites that were exclusively restricted to a select handful of well-born Athenian females.[47] When this sacrilege was exposed, Theogenes had little choice but to divorce his wife and charges were brought against Stephanus and Neaira for *asebeia* ([Dem.] 59.9, 43). The outcome of this litigation is unknown as is the extent to which any of the accusations were shown to be not so much legitimately true as convincing to the Athenian jurors present. Nonetheless the case presented by Apollodoros offers a useful summary of the pattern of sex-trade behavior that provoked anxiety in an Athenian lay audience.

That Apollodoros distorted the record for Neaira is revealed by his decidedly unflattering and inaccurate description of Stephanus, a longtime adversary who had previously prosecuted members of Apollodoros's own family.[48] Konstantinos Kapparis (1998), Debra Hamel (2002) and Allison Glazebrook (2005a) accordingly question other details furnished by Apollodoros, including the charges that Neaira and Stephanus's sons were illegitimate or that Phano worked as a courtesan like her mother. It is not so much the authenticity of these details that concerns us, however, as it is the argument that Apollodoros constructs to sway the minds of the jurors. In much the same manner that Cicero and Sallust would weave lurid depictions of renegade aristocrats and prostitutes colluding to subvert the republic to alarm their audiences, Apollodoros paints a disturbing picture of Neaira's progressive infiltration into Athenian society. He incites his audience with the fear that women like Neaira will use their illicit affairs with Athenian elites to destroy the urban social fabric ([Dem.] 59.89–113). By claiming to be a legitimate Athenian wife and by repeatedly forwarding her illegitimate children as respectable citizens, she made a mockery of past grants of Athenian citizenship so zealously guarded by ballots and legal challenges in the Athenian assembly (89). With equal effrontery Neaira's daughter Phano had conducted sacred rites legally prohibited to those who otherwise obtained legitimately sanctioned grants of citizenship. Even their progeny could not conduct these rites without verifying descent from legitimate Athenian females. Apollodoros insists that the jurors, by failing to convict Neaira of sacrilege, risk rendering the laws that governed grants of citizenship meaningless, polluting the body politic and violating Athens' standing with the gods. Along the same line Apollodoros argues that by acquitting Neaira the jurors would open the floodgates to additional courtesans wishing to pose as Athenian wives, thus imperiling the status of Athenian women themselves. Poor maidens, whose chief attraction lay in their ability as Athenian citizens to procreate legitimate offspring for Athenian males, could thus be replaced by foreign prostitutes free to produce illegitimate children and to obtain for them civic status and the political and religious offices of the state. Drawing on the reputation of courtesans and *sagae* as poisoners, Apollodoros metaphorically depicts these women as poisoners of the state. Neaira comes off as a master schemer determined to undermine the stability of Athenian society.[49] As he argues to the jurors:

> You must cast your vote in the interest of legitimate Athenian women, as well as in the interest of the state, the laws, and the religion. This is the only way that you prevent Athenian women from being held in the same esteem as prostitutes and insure that Athenian women who have been raised by their relatives with the greatest care, grace, and modesty and have been given in marriage according to the laws will not be seen as standing on equal footing with a whore who in numerous obscene ways has bestowed her favors many times a day, catch-as-catch-can, with any and all customers who so desire. (114)

In short, Apollodoros's speech nearly prefigures the political invective employed by Cicero. Apollodoros deliberately exaggerates and distorts the role of Neaira in order to titillate his audience while blackening Stephanus's reputation (Glazebrook 2005a). Conceivably, Apollodoros relies on well-worn delegitimizing myths about Athenian *hetairai* to bias the jury against Neaira and Stephanus.[50] Like Cicero, in other words, Apollodoros employs commonly believed attributes of conspiracy theory to build his case.

From a political standpoint the example of Neaira's behavior hardly compares with that of Praecia. Her ambitions were personal, not political. This suggests that the majority of *hetairai* and *meretrices* in either city were more typically disinterested in political controversies. Given their relationships with local aristocrats, most of these women were possibly more inclined to identify themselves with the prevailing attitude of the hierarchy, an attitude that generally condoned extramarital affairs with prostitutes. Males in both the Roman and Greek hierarchies clearly surrounded themselves with women of this sort and it would appear that only the bravest, most successful, or most popular of these women actually dared to use their celebrity for anything more than personal aggrandizement. What the Roman examples of politically subversive sex-trade laborers may indicate, therefore, is the potential influence these professionals could obtain among the sizable underclass population in Rome. The difference in population size for the two cities—a conservative estimate puts the inhabitants of Rome at 600,000 in the mid-first century BCE and the inhabitants of Athens at 150,000 in the mid-fourth century BCE—possibly explains the differing political ambitions of their respective sex-trade laborers.[51] The breadth of the urban underclass at Rome arguably rendered it more disjointed and uncontrollable to its ruling class. Radical politicians employing sex-trade laborers in their followings were probably better able to plumb the depths of social discontent at Rome and thereby incite public disturbances. In any event, there appear to have been no similar examples of "social revolutions" incited by sex-trade laborers in Athens.

Like Neaira, most Athenian *hetairai* were resident aliens of slave origin whose low status eliminated the possibility of citizenship. As the example of Neaira indicates, the greatest threat conjured up by Athenian conspiracists was the potential for these women to insinuate themselves directly into the urban mainstream, in the process gaining advantage over freeborn citizen females. In the case of a few women such as Thargelia and Aspasia, this ambition was possibly facilitated by the fact that they were originally elite females who were forced to migrate to communities overseas. In addition to their beauty, their talents, and their sexual favors, they brought with them an informed awareness of the potential influence to be wielded by women in their positions. But these sex-trade laborers appear to have focused their attention more on obtaining personal privileges, as demonstrated by the example of Neaira, than they did on instigating popular uprisings per se. In the Athenian mind's eye what the delegitimizing myth about sex-trade laborers indicated was that foreign *hetairai* such as Aspasia and Neaira encountered seemingly endless opportunities for personal advancement. From Lysias to Xenocleides, Hipparchus, Phrynion, Stephanus, Phrastor, Theogenes, and others, Neaira was depicted as an illegitimate social climber and cultural transgressor who used sexual favors to ingratiate herself with Athenian male citizens, insidiously infiltrating respectable Athenian society to obtain rank and standing for her family. What Athenians feared most about women like Neaira, therefore, was the irresistible manner with which they solicited the attention of Athenian men and the success they obtained thereby.

Conclusion

Modern conspiracy theory furnishes a suitable vehicle for analyzing the perceived dangers of sex-trade laborers in ancient Athens and Rome in that it enables us to grasp the extent and character of the fear that sex-trade laborers incited in the general public. The evidence suggests that these fears were long-standing and that ancient conspiracists drew on them to devise delegitimizing myths to defame not only sex-trade laborers themselves but also citizens tainted by association with them. Ancient conspiracy theory directed against sex-trade laborers typically exhibited an "overinterpretation" of the nature of the threat. Conspiracy theory creates what is in essence a forged form of knowledge about the world in question (Birchall 2006, 81). Despite the hyperreal character of this knowledge, conspiracy theory represents a constitutive factor in interpretation prior to the act of any exclusionary gesture. Rather than render a lack of meaning, conspiracy theory helps to expose a condition of the historical reality, namely, that its simulation and iteration in different contexts generates an exaggerated other, an alternative, popular version of the truth. As modern witnesses centuries removed from the societies that constructed delegitimizing myths about Greco-Roman sex-trade laborers, we may legitimately question our ability to reconstruct any accurate knowledge of the threat posed by these professionals, particularly when the content of our available source material is inherently "overinterpretational" in form. Although we can hardly expect to achieve some semblance of reality from this tradition, neither can we afford to disregard the content that it furnishes. As Birchall observes, "conspiracy theory puts on display a possibility of reading, the invisibility of which (achieved through processes of non-recognition or de-legitimization) other knowledge-producing discourses rely upon" (2006, 74). The substance to the threat posed by ancient sex-trade laborers in Rome and Athens remains ultimately "a hidden occluded element" of reality (Birchall 2006, 83). Accordingly, it is fair to question the likelihood that sex-trade laborers played any significant role in urban conspiracies during the late Roman Republic or that *hetairai* exerted a destabilizing influence on the Athenian democracy. As we craft our conclusions, we must recognize their limited value as viable interpretations. As Birchall notes, where conspiracy theory is concerned, "interpretation is never complete because of a profound absence in the text being interpreted and because that same absence conditions any subsequent interpretative text" (2006, 83).

NOTES

I wish to express my gratitude to Allison Glazebrook and Madeleine Henry for encouraging me to address this topic and for steering it through to completion.

1. Many *sagae* (witches) were reputedly former prostitutes (see nn. 25–30 below).

2. For conspiracism, also known as the paranoid style or the hidden-hand mentality, see Pipes 1997, 22; Robins and Post 1997; and Birchall 2006.

3. For the alliance and participants' movements, see Cic. *Verr.* 2.1.87; Ps. Ascon. 244 St.; Plut. *Sert.* 23.3; App. *Mith.* 68; and Cic. *De imp. Cn. Pomp.* 46. For the date of the alliance between summer 76 and spring 75 BCE, see Magie 1950, 1203 n. 1; and Konrad 1994, 149, 177, 197.

4. See Konrad 1994, 149, 177; and Rauh 1997, 263–74.

5. For the grain crisis, see Cic. *Planc.* 54; Sall. *Hist.* 2.45 M.; Cic. *Verr.* 2.3.215; Plut. *Cic.* 6; and Virlouvet 1985, 110.

6. For sources and discussion, see Magie 1950, 1203 n. 1; Rotondi 1922, 365; and Broughton *MRR* 2.96. Sallust's use of the technical expressions *res novae* and *tumultus* (*Hist.* 2.45, 50 M.) suggests that elements opposed to the Sullan establishment posed a serious political threat in 75 BCE (contra Gruen 1974, 6–46). Sallust portrays the consul Cotta pleading with the public for understanding (*Hist.* 2.47.7 M.).

7. Cethegus eluded Sulla's proscriptions to emerge as the leader of a Roman *factio* during the 70s BCE (Cic. *Parad. Stoic.* 5.40; Cic. *Brut.* 178; Cic. *Cluent.* 84–85; Plut. *Luc.* 5–6; Ps. Ascon. 259 St.; Gruen 1974, 39–40). Decried as a traitor in a speech by Sallust (*Hist.* 1.77.20 M.), Cethegus purportedly arranged the extraordinary "pirate command" of M. Antonius Creticus and played some behind-the-scenes role in a jury-tampering scandal.

8. Cicero (*Parad. Stoic.* 5.3.40) corroborates the general lines of Lucullus's bribery without specifically mentioning Praecia. See also *RE* 1.22, 1192.

9. Cicero (*Mil.* 55) compares Clodius's entourage with Milo's; cf. Cic. *Sest.* 2, 39. Cicero's description of Clodius's entourage on the day that he was murdered almost forms a doublet to his description of Catiline's following. For Clodius's gladiators, see Cic. *Sest.* 77–78; Cic. *Att.* 1.16.4, 4.3; Cic. *Mil.* 53; Cic. *Post red. in sen.* 18, 81; Cic. *Dom.* 6, 48, 81; and

Ascon. 31 C. For his thieves, beggars, and runaways, see Cic. *Att.* 4.3.3–5; cf. Hahn 1975; Kühnert 1991; Zeller 1962.

10. Clodius's henchmen closed all the *tabernae* during Milo's trial. Cicero describes one Clodian ally as a *concitator tabernariorum* (*Dom.* 13); cf. Kleberg 1957, 122. Since homeless elements occupied these establishments at the discretion of the *tabernarii*, they could be compelled in this manner to join Clodius's public demonstrations.

11. Cic. *Att.* 10.10.5 (49 BCE); Cic. *Att.* 10.16.8 (49 BCE); Cic. *Phil.* 2.56, 58, 77, 105, 3.35, 5.12; 6.4, 8.26, 10.22, 13.3, 24; *De vir. ill.* 82.2. Volumnia Cytheris the mime was the freed person of Volumnius Eutrapelus, mistress of Antonius, and possibly of the poet Propertius (*Eclog* 10.22, 46). Her love affair with Antonius provoked widespread scandal. At one of Antonius's banquets in 46 BCE Cicero was chagrined to find Cytheris reclining on a neighboring couch (Cic. *Fam.* 9.26.2). However, during the previous year Cicero's wife, Terentia, had approached Cytheris about Cicero's readmittance to Rome (Cic. *Fam.* 14.16.22). For Cytheris's identification as a *meretrix*, see Serv. *Eclog.* 10.1. Apart from Cytheris, Antony's following allegedly included Sergius the mime (Plut. *Ant.* 9), a "convicted gambler," Licinius Dentiliculus (Cic. *Phil.* 2.56; Cass. Dio 45.47.4), a poisoner, Domitius of Apulia (Cic. *Phil.* 11.13), a "bathkeeper," Insteius of Pisaurum (Cic. *Phil.* 13.26; Plut. *Ant.* 65.1), a former "gladiator," Mustela (Cic. *Phil.* 2.8, 106, 5.18, 8.26, 12.14, 13.3; Cic. *Att.* 16.11.3) and a "wagonload of pimps" (Cass. Dio 45.28.1, 47.4; Cic. *Phil.* 2.56–58).

12. Other adversaries attacked similarly included Cn. Calpurnius Piso Caesoninus and P. Gabinius, the consuls of 58 BCE. According to Cicero both of these men practiced debauchery in the brothels; for Caesoninus, see Cic. *Pis.* 13, 18, 22, 42, 53, 67; for Gabinius, see Cic. *Post red. in sen.* 13, 15, 16; cf. Cic. *Pis.* 20, 22; Cic. *Sest.* 18, 20, 22; and Macrob. 2.14.15.

13. Amy Richlin argues that the evidence arises exclusively from "fossilized political invective, kept alive by political motives that have long outlived the protagonists of the stories" (1983, 86; cf. 109). Jeffrey Tatum dismisses the "thuggish" tradition for Clodius's following as Ciceronian invective and nowhere discusses Clodius's alleged association with pimps and prostitutes (1999, 142–48); see further Nippel 1995, 124.

14. Sall. *Cat.* 48 (Crassus), 49 (false witness against Caesar); Plut. *Crass.* 13; Plut. *Cic.* 10, 20; Plut. *Caes.* 7–8. For M. Caelius Rufus, see Cic. *Cael.* 10. Tatum (1999, 209) accepts Rufus's involvement in the conspiracy but not Clodius's. For C. Scribonius Curio and M. Antonius, see Cic. *Phil.* 2.44–46; Val. Max. 9.1.6; Plut. *Caes.* 8.2; and Plut. *Ant.* 2.4; these two offer perhaps the most pertinent examples, since they seem guilty by virtue of their behavior (accusations of debauchery, prostitutes, huge debts) and their associations (Antonius's stepfather P. Cornelius Lentulus Sura was one of the executed conspirators). However, none of the sources specify that they were involved in the conspiracy; see Huzar 1978, 22; and Havas 1990.

15. A "bottom-up" example of popular distrust of political authority is the current belief throughout the Middle East that the attack of 9/11 was engineered by the CIA and the Israeli secret service to legitimize the American invasion of Iraq. A "top-down" example is the belief of the George W. Bush administration that Al Qaeda posed a sufficient domestic threat to warrant eavesdropping on communications of ordinary U.S. citizens.

16. Robins and Post argue further that being a leader in any organization is always somewhat paranoiagenic (1997, 22). Fear of enemies can become a self-fulfilling prophecy.

17. Evidence that appears to contradict a conspiracy theory is typically dismissed as further proof of the same.

18. For pornographic literature in the age of Cicero, see Rauh, Dillon, and McClain 2008, 209–16.

19. For the dangerous reputations of these women, see Xen. *Mem.* 3.11.4; [Dem.] 59.35, 42, 46, 120–25; Plaut. *Asin.* 177; Plaut. *Poen.* 212–13; Plaut. *Truc.* 168; Plaut. *Bacch.* 368–74; Plaut. *Pseud.* 172–229; Ter. *Heaut.* 443; Ov. *Am.* 2.7; Ov. *Ars. am.* 3.661–65; Luc. *Dial. meret.* 10; Alciphr. 4.3, 6, 8, 9; 3, 11.4; Aristaen. 1.4; Phaedr. *Fab.* 4.5.4; and Ath. 13.558c; cf. Herter 1960, 83; J. Davidson 1998, 201–5; Fantham 1975, 72.

20. As Eva Keuls observes, "the striking feature of Athenian mores is not the glorification of pederasty but the extraordinary propensity for prostitution, both heterosexual and homosexual" (1993, 299).

21. Aspasia's controversial biographical tradition requires us to use other examples.

22. Thargelia of Miletus (early fifth century BCE) married fourteen times. When her last husband, Antiochus, the king of Thessaly, died, she assumed his throne and ruled for thirty years (Ath. 13.583c; RE 2.5, 1304; M. Henry 1995, 10). Aspasia allegedly modeled her career on Thargelia (M. Henry 1995, 42). Courtesans were commonplace among Hellenistic kings. Ptolemy Philopator married the *hetaira* Agathocleia, who eventually overturned his rule and was killed by the Alexandrian mob (Ath. 13.577a; Trogus *Prol.* 30; Strabo 17.1.11 [795]; Polyb. 15.33–34; Plut. *Cleom.* 33; cf. 753d). Hieronymus, the tyrant of Syracuse, married the brothel laborer Peitho and made her his queen. Timotheus, the Athenian general, allegedly was the son of a Thracian prostitute, Philetairus the son of a Paphlagonain flute girl named Boa. Aristophon, the orator, had children by a prostitute named Choregis. Demetrius Poliorcetes was passionately in love with the flute girl Lamia by whom he had a daughter (Ath. 13.577). Other couples include Philip II and Philinna (the mother of Philip Arrhidaeus), Demetrius and Mania, Antigonus and Demos, Seleucus the Younger, and both Mysta and Nysa. See Macurdy 1932; and Pomeroy 1984.

23. For the stereotype of the drunken elderly prostitute, see Herter 1960, 102 n. 604.

24. Isae. 6.21; Liv. 39.11.2; Quint. *Decl.* 14.15; Mart. 9.29.9; Plut. *Mor.* 752C; Luc. *Am.* 43; Luc. *Dial. meret.* 1.2, 4.8, 3; Alciphr. 4, 10.4; Herter 1960, 105 n. 671; Bloch 1912, 385.

25. According to Plin. *NH* 28.70, the *sagae* used hegammen, semen, and menstrual blood to induce labor and abortions; the *hetaira* Lais in old age was a midwife and an authority on cosmetics, abortions, and aphrodisiac potions. She invented secret medicines and potions to alter the size of a woman's waist (Ath. 13.587e–f; cf. Plut. *Mor.* 759e–f; 1039a; *Anth. Pal.* 6.1, 6.18–20; Alciphr. fr. 5; Plut. *Truc.* 762). In old age Phryne boasted of a cream that concealed wrinkles, and she employed so many cosmetics that Aristophanes called her cheeks a "drugstore" (Ath. 13.570b–c). For old prostitutes as procuresses, see Plaut. *Cist.* 20–50; and Herter 1960, 90–91 nn. 382–88. For *sagae* and Thessalian witches, see Tib. 1.2.44; for charges of witchcraft, see Nonius Marcellus s.v. *sagae*; Propert. 3.7.24, 4.5.5–20; Hor. *Sat.* 1.8.19–50; Hor. *Epod.* 17.47; Stat. *Theb.* 4.445; and Bloch 1912, 171, 344.

26. Nonius Marcellus s.v. *sagae*; cf. Plin. *NH* 28.70; Tib. 1.2.44; Stat. *Theb.* 4.445; cf. Artemid. *Onir.* 1.78; Plaut. *Truc.* 762; Plaut. *Am.* 1043; Plaut. *Cist.* 20; Apul. *Met.* 1.8; Aug. *Civ. Dei.* 18.18; Juv. 6.610; Procop. *Anek.* 1.11–14; Liv. 39.11.2; Quint. *Decl.* 14, 15; Mart. 9.29.9; Plut. *Mor.* 752c, 759e–f, 1039a; *Anth. Pal.* 6.1, 6.18–20; Moine 1975; Kleberg 1957, 85; Herter 1960, 90 nn. 382–88, 671; Bloch 1912, 344–35; Richlin 1983, 109–10. Given the organic compounds and minerals these women employed, poisonings were a likely consequence.

27. Ovid's Corinna had her Dipsas (*Am.* 1.8), Horace's Canidia her Acanthis and her perfume-dealing Folia (*Epod.* 5.42). Fabulla's cronies included degraded and much abused *fellatrices* (Mar. 8.79).

28. On Lucullus, see Plin. *NH* 25.25; Plut. *Luc.* 43; and *De vir. ill.* 74.8. On Lucretius, see Euseb. *Chron.* 149 Helm; cf. Herter 1960, 105. The evidence does not reveal a direct connection with prostitutes; however, one must ask how men of such high social standing (and/or their servants and lovers) acquired "love potions."

29. For Martial's invective against sexually active older women, see Sullivan 1979, 293; and Richlin 1983, 109. In 9.29 Martial refers to her as a Thessalian witch and as bald, redhead, and blind in one eye (2.33, cf. 4.65). One suspects that Philaenis was a libertine, not a prostitute, although her marriage to a freedman (9.40), someone named Diodorus, suggests that she had registered as a *meretrix*. Cf. Tracy 1977; Bloch 1912, 384.

30. Aspasia was allegedly indicted on *asebeia* and defended by Pericles (Ath. 13. 589e; cf. M. Henry 1995, 15, 135 n. 22). Lysias wrote a speech against Lais (Ath. 13.486e, 492e); Aristogeiton prosecuted Phryne on a capital charge, but she was defended by her lover Hypereides and acquitted (Ath. 13.590d–e). Neaira was indicted for *asebia* ([Dem.] 59.43, q.v. infra). The fifth-century BCE *hetaira* Sinope was so contemptuous of established mores that Demosthenes and others coined a verb, *sinopizō*, after her behavior (Ath. 13.585e; cf. Ath. 13.339a; Hsch. in Suidas s.v.; Dem. 22.56). Archias, the Athenian high priest of the mysteries at Eleusis and a member of the elite Eumolpidai clan, was punished for, among other things, offering a sacrificial victim brought by Sinope (Dem. 50.116; Ath. 13.594a–b). She too was prosecuted, therefore, if only by proxy.

31. The condemnation of this woman resulted from charges of poisoning, sorcery, and corrupting slaves (Dem. 25.79). Demosthenes later accused one of the defendants of fathering children by Theoris as well as of acquiring her skills as a magician, spell charmer, and poisoner. According to Plutarch (*Dem.* 14), Demosthenes also accused Theoris of teaching slaves to cheat their masters; Demosthenes was allowed to propose her sentence and caused her to be put to death. Harpocration s.v. (Dindorf 155) cites the Demosthenic speech; cf. *RE* 2.5, 2237–38.

32. [Dem.] 19.281 with schol. (Dem. 19, sect. 495a); Dion. Hal. *Din.* 11. p. 313, 13R; cf. Keuls 1993, 322.

33. Harpocration s.v. Antikura alleges that Nais was called Anticyra either because she joined drinking bouts of men who were insane with passion or because the physician Nicostratus at his death left to her a large quantity of hellebore; cf. Ath. 13.592c; Joseph. *AJ* 1.60.2. Her name occurs in a list of courtesans furnished by the comic writer Philetairos (fr.

9 *FAC*) as well as in at least three speeches of Lysias (Ath. 13.586f.; *RE* 1.16, 1586–87). In another episode of poisoning furnished by Antiphon (1.10, 14–16, 26), an Athenian woman angry at her husband conspired with a concubine (*pallakē*) to poison both her husband and the concubine's lover. The lover, bored with his mistress, intended to place her in a brothel. Hearing of this the wife gave the concubine what she claimed to be a love potion capable of restoring the respective affections of both men but what was in fact poison. Administered by the concubine as a libation, the poison killed both men. For the pharmaceutical skills of the elderly Lais and Phryne, see Ath. 13.587e–f, 570b–c; Bloch 1912, 348; and Keuls 1993, 322.

34. Gilfoyle's 1994 study furnishes a useful model for the involvement of upper-class elements in underclass leisure culture. He posits that men and women who experience the economic transitions of societies shifting from agropastoral systems to wage-labor-based, urban commercialism inevitably adapt their lives to meet these new challenges and needs. According to Gilfoyle, gender and age-based social dislocations in rapidly emerging wage-labor societies gave rise to a tavern-driven subculture that he describes as nascent "sexual democracy," a phenomenon that could integrate tavern elements from all levels of the social hierarchy (1994, 250).

35. In her rivalry with Phryne, Lais took on a large crowd of lovers, allegedly making no distinction between rich and poor (Ath. 13.589; *RE* 1.12, 513–16). Pythionike "was shared by all who desired her at the same price for all" (Theopompos in Ath. 13.595c). Leme, the mistress of the demagogue Stratocles, was, according to Gorgias, "called *didrachmon* because she visited any who desired her for two drachmas" (Ath. 13.596f.). Pasiphile allegedly ingratiated herself with foreigners (Athen 13.608f; cf. 13.581e, 583c).

36. In other words, glamorous courtesans more typically charged exorbitant prices that placed their services beyond the reach of underclass Athenians. Cf. James Davidson, who draws a distinction between the *mistharnousai* (wage earners) of the brothels (1998, 92) and the *megalomisthoi* (big-fee prostitutes) (1998, 104), who often possessed their own houses. He agrees that women such as Obole and Didrachmon seemed to advertise their prices through their names (118–19).

37. For Phryne's relations with Aristippus and Diogenes, see Ath. 13.558e; for Moerichus, see Ath. 13.583c. Lais became the mistress of Apelles the painter, Demosthenes, Xenocrates, Myron, a Cyrenian noble named Eubates, and a Thessalian named Pausanias (Ath. 13.588–19). For the evidence of three women named Lais, the earliest of whom originated from Hiccara in Sicily and was known to Alcibiades, see *RE* 1.12, 513–16. Phryne, meanwhile, enjoyed the companionship of the Athenian orator Hypereides, an Areopagite named Gryllion, and the sculptors Apelles and Praxiteles (Ath. 13.558e; Keuls 1993, 197). Pythionike became the mistress of Alexander's friend Harpalus, who spent a fortune on her tomb when she died unexpectedly in Cilicia (Ath. 13.595c; *RE* 1.24, 564–66).

38. She either wrote the rule herself or had it put into verse by her lover Diphilus.

39. While living with the poet Andronicus, Gnathenion, the granddaughter of Gnathaina, had sex with a humble coppersmith, referred to by Andronicus as a *mastigias* (Ath. 13.581e). Gnathaina on one occasion made love to a soldier and a *mastigias* simultaneously

(Ath. 13.585a). For repeated reference to relations between courtesans and whip-scarred criminals (*mastigias*), see Ath. 13.580a–b, 581c, 585a, 585c, 585f.

40. They also had to endure the rowdiness and fighting that were commonplace at these establishments (Herter 1960, 103–4).

41. While Aspasia is the most notable example, some would argue that her experience was exceptional or that the tradition about her was otherwise exaggerated or distorted. As an elite female like Thargelia, Aspasia possibly came to Athens determined to assume a place in the social hierarchy (M. Henry 1995, 10).

42. Hamel (2002) follows the argument of Kapparis, both of whom dismiss most of the accusations made against Neaira in this speech. Glazebrook (2005a; 2006) offers detailed analysis of the rhetoric behind this speech and even questions Neaira's status as a *hetaira*. The outcome of the trial is unknown.

43. By posing as a freeborn Corinthian "married with children," Nikarete was able to charge higher fees not only for her own services but for those of the girls. According to the speech, Neaira's older "sister" Metaneira enjoyed relations with Lysias, the celebrated Athenian orator, and was actually invited by him to be initiated into the Eleusinian mysteries in Attica. Nikarete and Neaira reportedly accompanied Mateneira to the initiation ceremony and lodged at the house of Lysias's unmarried friend Philostratus while in Attica ([Dem.] 59.22, 108). Neaira traveled with her lovers elsewhere in the Peloponnesus and to Thessaly, Magnesia, Chios, and Ionia as well.

44. Hamel 2002, 38–39. Phrynion was from the deme of Paeania, the son of Demon and the brother of Demochares. The speaker indicates that Demochares was politically prominent at this time. Once settled in the city, Phrynion and Neaira attended numerous drinking parties, including one hosted by the former Athenian general Chabrias at the Temple of Athena Kolias in Phalerum in 374 BCE. Chabrias hosted the party to celebrate the victory of his four-horse chariot team at Pythian games ([Dem.] 59.33–34; Hamel 2002, 39). He was a leading figure in Athens, elected general at least twelve times. In 376 BCE he won the Battle of Naxos against the Spartans, for which he was awarded a statue in the agora and a grant of *ateleia* by the assembly.

45. According to Hamel, Phano "was not the wanton [Apollodoros] would have us believe" (2002, 79), and the two sons were likely legitimate sons of Stephanus (2002, 48). Kapparis concurs (1999, 269, 270).

46. This is the heart of Apollodoros's prosecution; he accused Neaira of breaking the law by living with an Athenian citizen and posing as his wife. Hamel (2002, 77) rightly observes that nothing more is heard about Phrynion, who had possibly died by the time of the trial or had otherwise come to some resolution with Stephanus.

47. The wife of the archon basileus, called the *basilinna* or queen, played a prominent role in at least one of the state's religious festivals during the three-day festival of the Anthesteria (Hamel 2002, 103). The *basilinna* made secret offerings on the city's behalf and administered an oath to the priestesses who assisted her in the sacred rites. She was also ritually "married" to the god Dionysus; cf. Kapparis 1999; Glazebrook 2005a.

48. For their feud and the indictment of Apollodoros by Stephanus, see Hansen 1976 and Hamel 2002, 117. According to Apollodoros, Stephanus enjoyed a largely unsuccessful career as a sycophant, possessed few prominent political connections, had limited financial means, and worked as an underling of the orator and politician Callistratus of Aphidna ([Dem.] 59.43; cf. Hamel 2002, 65). External evidence indicates, however, that Stephanus was a prominent politician and orator at this time. Scholars generally identify him with Stephanus, son of Antidorides from the deme of Eroadai, an orator who in 347 BCE proposed a motion in the Athenian assembly to renew the alliance with Mitylene. In the same year he appears to have served as a delegate to the Amphyctionic Council that determined the Peace of Philocrates (*IG* 2/3[2] 213, 1. 5 = SIG[3] 205, 5 with [Dem.] 59.121, where his father's name is given; cf. Aeschin. 2.140; Ath. 13.593f.). Despite his long-term relationship with Neaira he played a significant role in Athenian politics until Apollodoros pursued his indictment in the 340s. Hamel (2002, 127) argues that the trial was somehow connected with the Peace of Philocrates as well as with the Athenian embassy sent to Philip in 346 BCE. Stephanus's presumed political allies, Callistratus and Cephisophon, played prominent roles in that affair. Hamel argues that the political machinations of these three probably generated the trumped-up murder charges that Apollodoros endured at about that time.

49. See Glazebrook 2005a; 2006.

50. A remarkably similar fourth-century BCE episode of prostitute as a schemer is furnished by Isaeus 6, *Concerning the Estate of Philoctemon*. In this speech Euctemon, an extremely wealthy and prominent Athenian, fell under the influence of a former slave prostitute named Alce, who was raised in his brothel establishment (*sunoikia*) in the Piraeus (19) and became the lover of Euctemon (21). Much like Neaira and Stephanus, Alce repeatedly urged Euctemon to have her illegitimate sons recognized as his descendents. These attempts were opposed by legitimate family members, resulting in the legal action recorded in the speech (27). In his argument Isaeus raises the same religious and civic scruples in the jury that Apollodoros had in his argument against Phano and Neaira (49).

51. For these figures, see Brunt 1971, 376–88; and Sallares 1991, 102.

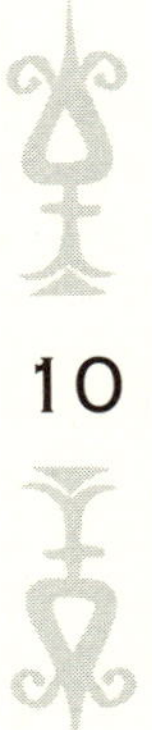

10 The Terminology of Prostitution in the Ancient Greek World

KONSTANTINOS K. KAPPARIS

> She endures cruel and sneering comments—*slut* is often interchangeable with *whore* and *bitch*—as she walks down the hallway. She is publicly humiliated in the classroom and cafeteria. Her body is considered public property: She is fair game for physical harassment. There is little the targeted girl can do to stop the behavior.
>
> Leora Tanenbaum, *Slut!*

Words have power and they can hurt. This conclusion jumps out of the pages of Leora Tanenbaum's study of the sexual reputation of young women in the United States (1999, xvi). The words we use are very telling of what we believe. They reveal our value system, what we consider acceptable and appropriate and what we do not; they reveal our intent and attitudes, whether we speak of someone with respect or contempt; they can express an emotive or dispassionate outlook; they can suggest distant professionalism or personal involvement, specialized research or generic abstraction, precision or vagueness, interest or indifference. Frequently they work on multiple levels—they mean more than one thing, and they are colored by several undertones and background connections. Thus the attempt to reconstruct social attitudes from the terminology used to convey them is often hazardous, complex, and controversial. However, precisely because vocabulary carries some of the complexity of our thinking, it is a subject worthy of exploration and a pathway to a more profound understanding of the conceptual labyrinth that normally accompanies our social structures, values, and interactions. Historians of prostitution in the ancient world have long tried to understand the undertones and connotations of the rich vocabulary in Greek, with emphasis upon the difference between the two main terms *pornē* and *hetaira*, but despite a long debate the results remain inconclusive (for further discussion, see McGinn 2004, 7–9; J. Davidson 2007, 56–71; Henderson 1975, 1–107).

English uses at least twenty words to describe prostitutes. Discomfort with such vocabulary sometimes generates euphemisms, which themselves may eventually become taboo and lead to additional euphemisms (see Henderson 1975, 54–55). This plenitude enables us to describe more accurately the specific type of services that prostitutes offer and to describe how, where, and under what circumstances they practice their trade. Greek fondness for words and accuracy (and the fact that prostitution was legal and practiced for centuries) has generated ten times as many terms as English to describe the rendering of sexual services for a fee. Among these, *pornē/pornos* (literally, "a woman for sale"/"a man for sale") has been the all-inclusive, generic term from the seventh century BCE to the present day, frequently indicating the common prostitute, with no distinctive features, and has generated important compounds and derivatives in many languages (e.g., pornography). A vast number of additional words were used to define specific categories or specializations—for example, *hetaira* (female companion), euphemistically describing a high-class courtesan; *aulētris* (flute player); *psaltria* (singer); *orchēstris* (dancer)—or types and qualities of prostitution—*chamaitupē* (ground beater); *peiōlēs* (cock sucker). Some of these terms have been discussed before (J. Davidson 1997, 73ff.; J. Davidson 2007, 56–71; Kapparis 1999, 408–9; Miner 2003, 19–37; Glazebrook 2005a, 161–87; Fisher 2001, 40ff.), but most remain unexplored.

Here I focus on less common terms for female and male prostitution. I provide without further discussion some common terms or expressions that were indirectly used for prostitutes (e.g., "shameless") or those who behaved like prostitutes (e.g., "filthier than *hetairai*") but that were not really specialized terms. I include any term that has been listed as prostitutional by ancient or Byzantine sources. After offering a brief introduction to lexicographic collections of this invective I explore the origins, meanings, and usages of the words and how they fit into the wider context of social attitudes and stereotypes surrounding this centrally important cultural phenomenon. The present study is intended as only the beginning of a much larger project; it is in a sense a continuation of the discussion Jeffrey Henderson started in the *Maculate Muse*. Henderson has discussed words for genitals and sexual acts but has almost completely excluded the vocabulary of venal sex; moreover his focus is on Attic comedy. This study draws from a much wider pool, including the lexicographers all the way to late Byzantium, and deals primarily with the vocabulary of prostitution.

The Lexicographic Tradition: Ancient and Byzantine Collections of the Invective of Prostitution

Remarkably, there is no Greek word for prostitute before the seventh century BCE. The earliest references to the *pornē*, a word exclusively reserved for a woman whose sexual services one could directly hire, appear in the works of the lyric poets (Archil. fr. 328 West; Alcaeus fr. 117b.26 *PMG*; Hipponax fr. 104 West; Henry, chap. 1 in this volume). In later centuries, as economic prosperity and complex social attitudes encouraged the development of prostitution, more specific vocabulary evolved. From the top end of the market, for which Greek used *hetaira*, to the lowest end of the market, that of the slave brothels of the big cities and harbors, for which words like *chamaitupē* (ground beater) were used, the language found ways to denote and describe prostitution's many faces. By the time of Alexandrian scholarship, the Greek invective of prostitution was so extensive that it merited dedicated study. Aristophanes of Byzantium's *On Insults* (third century BCE) was the first of its kind. With his usual diligence and erudition the great Alexandrian scholar collected terms related to prostitution from previous literature and explained their origin, etymology, and meaning. His collection betrays a literary interest in archaic lyric and Old Comedy and suggests he apparently did not care for colloquialisms currently in use in the streets of Hellenistic Athens or Alexandria. Aristophanes' mission was to try to preserve and explain the literary heritage of classical literature to the new world of Greek speakers that had emerged in the fragments of Alexander's empire. His work does not survive, but extracts are preserved in the work of later scholars and lexicographers, such as Eustathios's *Homeric Commentaries.*

A more thorough and ambitious attempt to categorize the vocabulary of prostitution was undertaken by the second-century Roman scholar and historian Gaius Suetonius Tranquillus (*On Insults and Their Origin*). Suetonius was a man of deep learning, with diverse interests. The same irreverent nature that got him into trouble with the emperor Hadrian is largely responsible for the popularity of his works (e.g., *The Lives of the Caesars*) and has enhanced the value of his lexicographic collection for us. Suetonius did not limit himself to sanctified terminology from high Greek, as had Aristophanes, but included colloquialisms used in the streets, low social circles, and brothels of the contemporary Greco-Roman world. This remarkable example of early lexicography has survived. Suetonius systematically lists his sources, offers largely reasonable semantic and etymological explanations, and sometimes provides a mini-history of a term. Suetonius's collection has been the most influential lexicographic work on the invective of prostitution, all the way to the Palaeologan era (thirteenth to fifteenth centuries), especially in those cases in which compilers were trying to ascertain the origins or etymology of terms.

Julius Pollux (second century CE), a slightly younger contemporary of Suetonius but considerably different in his methods, includes in his *Onomasticon* a rich collection of unusual, rare, obscure, or obsolete vocabulary. Unlike Suetonius, Pollux frequently does not name his sources and does not provide detailed entries or interpretations. He tends to simply list word and phrase clusters, as is typical for ancient and medieval lexicography. Pollux's collection of the prostitutional invective is independent of Aristophanes' and Suetonius's and illustrates how such collections were affected by the interests of the compiler. Ancient and medieval sources provide 101 Greek words for male prostitution; approximately half are given by Pollux and one-quarter by Suetonius. Among the terms given by Pollux, those that imply moral and physical impurity and abuse—for example, *akathartos* (unclean) or *enēsēlgēmenos* (shamed)—outnumber the ones that signify lack of manhood—for example, *gunaikias* (womanliness) (Poll. 6.126)—three to two. In Suetonius, terms that indicate lack of manhood outnumber terms that indicate moral impurity seven to three. These data demonstrate that Suetonius's primary interests are masculinity, gender stereotypes, and the confusion between the two in the circles of male prostitution and that Pollux is concerned with the moral degradation and abuse that the male prostitute willingly suffers when he allows other men to dominate his body.

Pausanias of Attica (second century CE), had obviously read both Aristophanes and Suetonius; the prostitutional vocabulary in his *Collection of Attic Greek Words* is mostly derived from Suetonius but occasionally is enhanced with information from other sources. Pausanias seems to be the primary source for the entries of Suda (ca. 1000 CE), the largest surviving Byzantine reference work, and several other Byzantine lexica. When Hesychius compiled his *Lexicon* in the fifth or sixth century CE, he had at his disposal centuries of classical scholarship and lexicography that had not been available to the scholars of the Hellenistic period or the Second Sophistic. Thus he was in the position to use selectively previous collections of the invective of prostitution and to process their material without feeling the need to adhere very closely to any of them. Photios (ca. 810–ca. 893 CE) likewise is selective and follows sometimes Pausanias, sometimes other sources. Eustathios (twelfth century CE) consulted most of earlier lexicography but is particularly fond of Suetonius, whom he quotes word for word on numerous occasions, frequently adopting his explanations even when these are preposterous. The dictionaries and scholars of the Comnenean (eleventh to twelfth centuries CE) and Palaeologean (thirteenth to fifteenth centuries CE) periods simply reshuffle previously collected materials.

Terminology and Culture: Brothel as Workshop

The oldest attested Greek word for brothel is *ergastērion* (workshop) and appears in the early sixth-century BCE law of Solon, which effectively legalized prostitution by defining the groups of women with whom one could have intercourse without fear of legal consequences. Steven Johnstone argues that *ergastērion* here simply means "workshop" or "warehouse," but undoubtedly Solon was referring to brothels, and this is how the term was understood by Lysias, Plutarch, and Harpocration (Johnstone 2002, 229–56; for an opposing view, see Kapparis 1999, 311–13; Kapparis 2008, 385–87). It is likely that in the sixth century, Greek did not possess a legal term for brothel; Solon used one that clearly implied work of some sort. References to prostitution as "work" are not uncommon or limited to Greek (e.g., [Dem.] 59.22, 26, 30, 32, 36, 37, 39, 50; the English expression "working girl"). The terms *ergatis*, *damiourgos*, and *stegitis* (see under the list of terms for female prostitution) also constitute the brothel as a warehouse or workshop. However, it is remarkable that all terminology referring to prostitution as "work" applies to female prostitution exclusively; there is no equivalent terminology for male prostitutes.

Several scholars in recent years have suggested that the brothels of classical Athens sometimes operated like regular factories, where female prostitutes engaged in tasks like wool work, when they were not busy with clients (see J. Davidson 1997, 86–91, n. 43, for some of the older bibliography; McGinn 2004, 182–238, for custom-built as opposed to generic brothels in the Roman world; Glazebrook, chap. 3 in this volume). This would more easily explain why they were called "workshops," but this interpretation also poses substantial difficulties and still remains to be proven. A more likely explanation probably lies not in the operational practices of the ancient brothels but in the underlying social attitudes. While patriarchal attitudes were such that women working in prostitution might have been accepted as inevitable, albeit disreputable, men performing the same task to satisfy the desires of their male clientele would have been far less tolerated.

Common Place, Public Bodies

A large array of terms referring to male and female prostitutes suggests an understanding of the brothel as a common place and of the bodies in it as public property. Classical authors discuss extensively the division of space between men and women; woman's domain is indoors and men unrelated to the family are excluded from this space. Brothels transgress this traditional division by allowing public access to the private domain and the bodies of the women established in it. The brothel becomes a place that belongs to all in common and, as such, a place where everyone can perform acts that in a regular household would be performed in private. From a legal point of view this perception of the brothel is significant as it allows access to women and sexual acts without fear of consequences. Similar terms are sometimes used for the male prostitute. He is "public," his youth is "cheaper than discarded goods," and the entire population has run over his body.

On the whole, however, the terminology of male prostitution focuses on the sale of the man's body. Unlike the female prostitute, who is easily available and accessible to everyone but does not have control over her body, the male prostitute does have control over his body and his fate and chooses to relinquish this control and make his body, youth, and good looks available to anyone who wants to buy it. In the case of the female prostitute the invective focuses on easy access, but in the case of the male prostitute the focus is on his choice to sell himself; the woman is at the mercy of those who control her body and who can allow or restrict access to her, but the male prostitute is in charge of his fate and thus morally responsible for his choice to forego his right to male privilege and control.

Filth and Physical Degradation

Material evidence from the ancient brothel can only allow us to re-create its atmosphere and conditions of life to a very limited extent. We still must rely on literary sources to approach the experience of the ancient brothel, and these remain remarkably coy. Some sources suggest an environment engulfed in dust and dirt. The common female prostitute has intercourse at the roadside; she is filthy, dusty, a creature of the ground; she has sex in ditches; one can drag her around town. Similar terminology is also used for the male prostitute. He is unclean, disgusting, and dirty, and his testicles are dusty. Although this language might imply moral decadence and degradation to an extent, the images that it creates are too lively, too graphic, to just refer to morals.

Early prostitutional invective in Archilochus or Hipponax does not carry much moralizing undertone but more frequently makes references to unusual sexual practices with humorous, self-deprecating naughtiness. The degradation specifies physical features, for instance, the "filthy hole" of a female prostitute or the white backside of an unmanly male. The poets of Old Comedy were equally inventive with themes of physical degradation, where male prostitutes were concerned: they said they were men who could not have an erection or whose rectums had been so badly abused that they resembled a wide and deep ditch. In later centuries, however, moralizing vocabulary becomes more common.

Moralizing Vocabulary: Sin and Debauchery

Terms that imply moral shame are not widely attested before the Second Sophistic (second to third century CE). Some common and rather generic terms attested before that—"doer of shame"; "filthy"—begin to connote moral decadence in later antiquity, as attitudes toward prostitution gradually become more hostile. Usually this phenomenon is understood as a result of the gradual Christianization of the Roman Empire. A careful study of the vocabulary of prostitution, however, proves that this change in social attitudes preceded the momentum of Christianization and is noticeable already in the collection of Julius Pollux.

Moralizing vocabulary is very limited with regard to female prostitution even in the Christian era, whereas it accounts for a substantial percentage of male prostitutional terminology in later antiquity. The male prostitute is a "doer of shame," "someone who has shamed his body" and his youth; he is "shameless," "deserving of insults and blame," "someone who has tolerated abuse." Society, it seems, had higher expectations of men: women might be forgiven more easily or ignored more readily for giving in to moral inadequacy and allowing abuse of themselves and their bodies in filthy places and in shameful ways, as they were thought to have less developed rational faculties than men. However, for a man to choose to subject himself to this degradation was a sign of unforgivable weakness of character and moral inadequacy.

It is, perhaps, unsurprising that the fiery speeches of the early Christian orators did not pile much castigation on female prostitutes. John Chrysostom in the East and Tertullian in the West, just to mention a couple of prominent names, were more concerned with male decadence and immorality and concentrated most of their efforts on persuading the men to accept monogamy. In the early Christian era, women mattered a lot less because they did not have a strong voice on matters of male monogamy or sexual morality. In the power struggle between the new religion and pagan culture, the immorality of the female prostitute, although taken for granted, did not amount to a crucial factor and only became more emphatically objectionable in later centuries, when Christianity no longer had to fight for its place in the world. However, for a man to allow himself to slip into the position of a woman by hiring out his body and sexual favors was seen as more reprehensible; from the period of the Second Sophistic there are at least thirty different terms to express the moral weakness, shamefulness, and bad reputation of the male prostitute.

Humor

It would be impossible to explore the terminology of prostitution without examining its funny side. As Henderson has demonstrated in an extensive study of the profane in Greek poetry (1975), humor and profanity are closely linked together. Humor is employed sometimes in order to inflict merciless abuse and sometimes to make light of abuse; therefore the precise meaning of the comic vocabulary of prostitution is elusive. Some of the difficulties have been outlined by James Davidson in relation to terms allegedly used for men who had sex with men, including but not limited to male prostitutes (2007, 56–71). The etymology of most is obvious, but pinpointing the precise context in which they were used can be more problematic; the term *lakkoproktos* (ditch ass) is a compound of the word for a deep ditch and the word for anus, but the cultural undertones of this term are much more nuanced. The use of humor in the language of prostitution is a ubiquitous feature of classical Greek culture, although not unique to it, as many contemporary cultures have funny words for prostitute. The poets of Old Comedy in particular concocted a whole array of terms that later lexicographers have collected, such as "man sow," "runner," "ditch ass," "arch whore," "white ass," "whore customs." In addition, there are numerous terms that are not attributed to any particular poet but almost certainly originated in Old Comedy, such as "meat catcher," "man maniac," "rubber," "snatcher."

This creative run seems to end after the classical period. With the exception of some colloquialisms that retain a jocular spontaneity, the vocabulary of prostitution gradually becomes less light hearted and more relentlessly critical and vicious. The shift in attitude from a classical pluralism and a relative sexual openness to a postclassical rigidity and judgmental moralizing is nowhere better attested than in humorless postclassical terminology.

Eunuchs

An unusually high incidence of terms referring to some kind of eunuch appears to suggest a strong presence of eunuchs in the brothels of the ancient world. Castration was not uncommon, especially in the Orient, where eunuchs achieved places of great influence in the courts of Persia and Egypt. In the Byzantine era, some reached high ecclesiastical and political offices. Some of these terms indicate a man whose testicles have been cut or squashed. Some are more generic. Others make a humorous connection to Cybele and her eunuch priests. But how literally we should take the terminology suggesting a strong link between eunuchs and prostitution is difficult to assess. In part, one has to take into account the transgressions of semantic boundaries in medieval Greek, but one also should not assume that the eunuch and the male prostitute were automatically equated, given that in Byzantine culture eunuchs were familiar and well-respected figures; the Byzantines knew the difference. Besides, one common term, *bakēlos* (eunuch), is already in use to indicate a male prostitute in Old Comedy. Undoubtedly eunuch boys worked in brothels, and the eunuch pimp is almost a stereotype in literature, but are we to assume that the brothels of the ancient world were filled with eunuchs? Perhaps the term "eunuchlike" holds the key: it does not refer to a eunuch but to someone who looks like a eunuch, a prostitute with the softness and smoothness of a eunuch, someone who, like a eunuch, has lost his masculine feel. Thus, when male prostitutes are referred to by terms used to refer to eunuchs, it could be that these were not men who had actually been castrated but men whose looks, softness, and conduct resembled that of a eunuch.

Unusual Requests

Sexual acts that took place in brothels were usually left to the imagination of the reader or the audience, with the exception of occasional stereotypical jokes that were more explicit. The terminology of the ancient brothel can shed some light on these secrets. The existence of several words referring to oral sex (e.g., *apomuzouris* for a woman and *peiōlēs* for a man [see under the lists of terms for female and male prostitution]) suggests that it was an expected treat (see also Archil. fr. 42 West; Henry, chap. 1 in this volume). Eupolis's comic subversion of the Homeric adjective *heilipous* (see under the list of terms for female prostitution) suggests a particular sexual position with the woman's legs wrapped around the man. *Kuneira* suggests quick sex with the woman servicing her customer by hand. Clear references to passive intercourse (*kinoumenos*, *peripēgis*) confirm that brothels had men or boys available to be penetrated by the customer. *Tribas* (rubber) clearly refers to lesbian sex and intriguingly suggests that the brothel scene in Lucian's *Dialogues of Courtesans* 6 may not be fantasy. Even more intriguing is the term *kusoniptēs*, which clearly refers to heterosexual sex in which the male prostitute offers oral sex to a female customer, suggesting that women may in fact have paid for the favors of men. "Soiled" or "painted" may even suggest fetishes. *Hippopornos* (horse whore) may simply mean "arch whore," but there could be more to it, if one considers that *kelēs* (racehorse) was the name of a sexual position and *kelētizein* (horseback riding) a term for this act (cf. Ar. *Vesp.* 500–502). Customers probably paid for sexual acts that would be considered unusual and awkward at home. The picture that emerges is not one of a grim place with a rapid turnover of low-class clientele but of a diverse environment shaped by market forces and offering the customer varied choices.

Bending Gender Stereotypes

Audiences were entertained by the humorously inventive vocabulary of the comic poets. High literature, however, tended to more sanctified terms and sometimes, especially in later antiquity, rejoiced in judgmental vocabulary that pointed out the depravity, ruthlessness or immorality of the prostitute. We cannot know for sure the extent to which this very diverse, stereotyping invective reflected practices behind the drawn curtains or inside the cubicles of ancient brothels. However, frequently stereotypes do not function in opposition to daily practice; they simply re-create it in a schematic form. Some terms directly imply cheap sex and some reinforce the cultural stereotype of the sex-loving whore, who is dominated by emotion and lust and thus of weak character. This stereotype is more strongly applied to females. Greek society typically viewed women as having strong sexual desires, but also interpreted a woman's yielding to those desires as a sign that she possessed no rational control.

Eunuchs represent a crossover in gender roles, and this is why their place is perhaps central in this area of ancient life and culture where the traditional gender stereotypes were thrown into chaos, a place where women were not demure, obedient, and obscure figures, as high literature would fancy them to be, but were "notorious around town," "public figures," who "walked the streets," were "easy" and "cheap," and did not hesitate to admit that they enjoyed sex with men. Men, on the other hand, were not the masculine "good and beautiful" figures of the classical ideal. They defied the mandate that their own gender dominate by adopting female behavior and thus becoming half women, half men, effeminate, hairless creatures lacking full manhood, eunuchs, followers of Cybele, or emasculated figures who had adopted feminine toiletry in order to please their clients. Those male prostitutes who adopted these traits deserved to be called the names thrown at men who had lost their testicles. The invective of prostitution is a very accurate reflection of these social and cultural stereotypes and brings them directly and vividly before our eyes. However, the most significant piece of evidence attesting to the importance of prostitution in ancient culture is the sheer number of words that the Greeks invented over the centuries to name and describe it.

Terms for Prostitution

FEMALE PROSTITUTION

akolastos: licentious or lustful (Poll. 6.189).

anaseisiphallos: Suetonius tells us that Hipponax employed this term to slander a specific woman, explaining the etymology: *ana* + *seiō* (to shake back and forth) + *phallos*. All later lexicographic notes (Ael. Dion. e 12; Eust. *Com. Od.* 1.53, 2.275) are based on the note of Suetonius.

anasurtolis or *anasurtopolis*: All sources attribute this term to Hipponax; however, they are divided regarding the form of the name. The correct form appears to be *anasurtopolis*, preserved by Pausanias Atticus (m 27) and Suda (m 1470). The connection with *anasuresthai* is obvious, albeit not straightforward, as that verb has several applicable meanings. It can mean "to reveal by pulling up one's clothing" (cf. Henderson 1973, 21) or "to drag around," which carries connotations of violence against women and the perception of the prostitute as the easy victim of aggression (see Henry, chap. 1 in this volume).

androkapraina: man sow. This seems to be a comic invention (Pher. fr. 186 *PCG*). Several sources quote his verse "man sow and drunkard and sorceress" (but cf. Phrynichus fr. 34 ["sow (*kapraina*) and wandering streetwalker"] and Phot. a 1771; Pollux [7.203] also mentions simple *kapraina*). The etymology suggests a lustful, predatory woman. The verb *kapraō* (or *kapriaō*) was literally used for a sow who had the urge to mate (Arist. *HA* 572b24) and metaphorically to refer women who had wanton, bestial desires for men (Ar. *Plut.* 1024).

apomuzouris: sucker. Aristophanes of Byzantium (fr. 17) interprets this term as "sucking the cock" or "suckling the cock." The etymological connection with *apomuzān* (to suck something dry) can be interpreted both literally in sexual terms and metaphorically in financial terms, indicating a ruthless prostitute who would devastate financially a naïve, infatuated lover.

aselgēs: shameless (Poll. 6.189, 7.202).

bassara/*bassaris*: This term, probably Lydian in origin, was used initially for the dress worn by the Thracian female followers of Dionysus but by extension was used to refer to the Bacchants themselves (*Etym. gen.* s.v.; Ath. 5.198e; Frisk s.v.; Chantraine s.v.). Several lexicographers insist that this word was also used for a prostitute (Suda b 141; *EM* s.v.; Ps. Zonaras s.v.; Sch. Ar. *Nub.* 187); it is used this way in Lycophron (771–72). Suda (b 141) mentions a playful epigram about a prostitute in which the word *bassaris* was used.

borboropē: filthy hole. The obvious etymology—*borboros* (filth) and *opē* (hole)—is correctly identified by Aristophanes of Byzantium (fr. 17 Nauck), who quotes the word in a group of terms for male and female prostitution drawn from comedy (*nothouros, apomuzouris, pandosia* s.v.). Suetonius attributes this term to Hipponax (fr. 135b West). Pausanias Atticus explains it as "unclean." The note of Suda (m 1470) is derived from Pausanias. Eustathios includes Suetonius's comment that Hipponax was slandering a woman for having a filthy birth canal (*paidogonon*). The available evidence suggests that the term was used only by Hipponax.

chalimas: loose. Suetonius connects this term to someone whose body is destroyed by drunkenness and madness, an explanation reiterated by some later sources (Paus. x 1; Eust. *Com. Od.* 4.332). *Etymologicum magnum* (s.v.) and Ps. Zonaras (s.v. *chalimazein*) more accurately explain the term as a reference to a loose woman from *chalasthai* (to be loose, or to decay).

chalkiditis: copper whore. Suetonius says that a prostitute was called *chalkiditis* because of the small value of a copper coin; we can imagine a cheap prostitute in a brothel. All later scholars derive their accounts of the word from Suetonius (Paus. x 5; Suda x 44; Eust. *Com. Il.* 4.835; Eust. *Com. Od.* 2.275).

chamaiteris (also *chamaitairis*): lowly courtesan (Lex. seg. s.v.). The few references in grammarians and lexicographers offer no additional information (Hdn. Gr. 168; Hsch. x 140; Suda x 74; *EM* s.v.). However, the word appears to indicate prostitutes established in brothels, since it suggests intercourse with the clients on the ground (*chamai*) or under humble conditions.

chamaitupē (also *chamaitupis*): ground beater (Ps. Zonaras s.v.) This was a very common term for the lowest class of prostitute from the classical period (e.g., Timocles fr. 24 *PCG*, Theopompos 115 F 225 *FGrH*, Men. *Sam.* 348) down to the late Byzantine period, where we find it in Thomas Magister x 400 (cf. the repeated references to brothels as *chamaitupeia* in the late Byzantine historian Nikephoros Gregoras [1.11, 447, 2.739 al.], a not uncommon usage in modern Greek). The term may have originated in a type of bird of prey that attacks its victim from the ground, not the air, if we believe Aristotle (*HA* 620a31), but undoubtedly it was used for a prostitute because one had sex with a prostitute on the ground (or some cheap mattress on the ground).

damiourgos: public workers. Hesychius (d 192) believed that this term was probably a reference to common prostitutes working their way through the entire city (*dēmos*, Doric *damos*). Cf. *dēmos* below.

deiktērias: showgirl. It is only found in one passage of Polybius (14.11.5). The context suggests that it referred to a common prostitute, although it was euphemistic and serious enough to fit into Polybius's narrative style. The etymology (from *deiknumi*) indicates someone pointed to by the finger (cf. *apodedeigmenon*) and thus notorious in the community as a common prostitute (*koinōn*).

dēmos: public. Suetonius mentions this term among others meaning "prostitute" (supported by a brief note in Hsch. d 841). Obviously the term was used for a public woman who belonged to the entire city (cf. *damiourgos* above).

dromas: runner. Found in drama and historiography to describe a fast-running animal or a female figure exhibiting qualities similar to those of a fast animal. The comic poet Phrynichos subverted the term and used it for a street prostitute (fr. 34 *PCG*).

empelateira: The *Etymologicum magnum* (s.v.), which preserves this term, relates it to *empelazein* (to frequent) and correctly explains it as someone to whom everyone has access.

ergatis: worker. Suetonius attributes this term to Archilochus (fr. 242 West), while Pausanias (m 27) summarizes Suetonius. It is rather curious that we do not encounter this term in other authors considering that the verb *ergazesthai* and the noun *ergasia*, with reference to prostitution, appear repeatedly in an important classical source ([Dem.] 59.22, 26, 30, 32, 36, 37, 39, 50), while *ergastērion* (see under the list of terms for brothel) is a well-attested term for brothel. However, it seems that *ergatis* was used in an abstract or metaphorical sense to indicate the agent or creator of something and retained the positive connotation of a hard-working female (bee: Arist. *GA* 760b14; *HA* 627a12; muse: Callim. fr. 222 Pfeiffer; woman worker: Suda e 2905). Therefore it was not regularly employed as a term for a female prostitute.

erōmenē: Laura K. McClure (2003, 22–25) considers this term to be important in the vocabulary of prostitution, although it means "lover."

eucherēs: easy (Poll. 6.189, 7.202).

gegōnokōmē: notorious around town. This term (cf. *gegōniskein* [to shout loud]) indicates a woman whose name has been spoken aloud all over the town (*kōmē*) and who therefore is notorious and disreputable. Possibly a comic invention, the term is first mentioned by Suetonius, who interprets it as "notorious." Suetonius's alternative interpretation of the etymology as referring to a woman who screams in the streets is adopted by Eustathios (*Com. Il.* 3.405) and may account for the ambiguous explanation of this term offered by Hesychius, namely, that it refers to a "screamer," a woman who cries out loud during sex.

gephuris: bridge woman. Hesychius (g 469), notes that Heracleon, his source, could be mistaken in thinking that the person who stood on a bridge shouting obscenities at pilgrims headed for the Eleusinian mysteries was a prostitute. Others attest that the term meant "foreigner" (Phot. g 96; Suda g 213).

heilipous: This standard Homeric adjective ("with a rolling gait" to describe oxen; e.g., *Il.* 6.424, 9.466; *Od.* 1.92) was parodied by Eupolis (fr. 174 *PCG*), as he listed prostitutes (rolling-gaited women) among the items necessary for a symposium. Suetonius simply mentions the term as a word meaning "prostitute." Pausanias Atticus (g 14, m 27) interprets this adjective as indicative of a sexual position in which the woman wraps her legs around the man, an interpretation repeated by later lexicographers (Hsch. g 1013; Phot. g 234; Eust. *Com. Od.* 1.214).

hierodoulos: hierodule. Normally a word that referred to a temple servant, it was used by Strabo (8.6.20) to describe what he believed to be temple prostitutes in Corinth. This euphemism is still used in modern Greek government documents to refer to professional prostitutes.

hippopornos (alternative feminine form: *hippopornē* [*Vitae Aesopi* 32]): horse whore, giant whore. According to Photios (s.v.) it originated in Old Comedy; Suda (i 575) credits Aristophanes, though the term does not appear in his extant works. It appears in Menander (*Theoph.* 10.19) and sources influenced by him (Ath. 13.565c; Alciphr. 2.31.2, 3.14.1, 4.11.8). Alternative tradition attributes this term to Diogenes the Cynic (Chrysippos fr. 2 von Arnim; Eust. *Com. Od.* 2.60). Probably it was an insult, with the first compound stressing the second.

kapraina: sow. Cf. *androkapraina* above.

kasalbas (alternative forms: *kasalba* [Suda k 446], *kassabas* [*Etym. gud.* k 301; *EM* s.v.], *kassaura* [Hsch. k 2], *kasaura* [Hsch. k 960], *kasauras* [Hsch. k 961], *kassa* [Michael Psellos *Poemata* 6.425; *Etym. gud.* k 302], *katakasa* [*Etym. gud.* k 304; *EM* s.v.], *kassē* [Ps. Zonaras s.v.], *kasoris* [Lycoph. 1385], *kassōris* [Suda k 459], *kasōritis* [Hipponax, according to Eus. *Com. Od.* 2.678; Antiphanes fr. 310 *PCG*]; the related verb is *kasalbazein* [Ar. *Eq.* 355] or *kasoreuein* [Lycoph. 772]): Forms with one sigma are found in classical authors, and forms with double sigma first appear in the Byzantine lexicographers. The profusion of forms suggests that these were common terms in oral discourse. With the notable exception of Lycophron (1385), they only appear in comedy or the lexicographers and thus were likely slang terms denoting low-class prostitutes. Suda specifies that *kasalbas* (or *kasalba*) refers to prostitutes established in brothels (k 446; cf. Sch. Ar. *Eq.* 355a). Suetonius confirms that Antiphanes used *kasōritis* for a common prostitute established in a brothel. Aristophanes used *kasōrion* for a brothel (*Eq.* 1285; see also under the list of terms for brothel). Particularly interesting for our understanding of the socioeconomic background of these terms is the comment of Artemidoros that if one dreams of someone established in a *kasōrion*, this means embarrassment and expense is in his or her future (1.78). The etymology is somewhat unclear; Suetonius's naïve interpretation of *kasalbas* as "someone who first invites the lovers and then pushes them away" in order to take other lovers was adopted by Byzantine lexicographers and scholars (Hsch. k 957; Suda k 447; Sch. Ar. *Eccl.* 1106). Eustathios awkwardly surmises that the word means a woman who calls to her lovers wearing makeup. Suetonius's interpretation of *kasōris* as someone who adorns herself inappropriately is another false etymology adopted by Eustathios (*Com. Il.* 2.678). Perhaps we should relate the word to *kasēs* (Hdn. Gr. 1.63) or *kasas* (Xen. *Cyr.* 8.3.8) or *kassas* (Poll. 7.68 referring to Xenophon), a thick skin or cover used as a saddle. It would make sense if a word meaning "saddle" provided the basis for a series of colloquial terms used to indicate the common, lowbrow prostitute, the one whom everybody "rides," but there is no conclusive evidence to support this suggestion. Chantraine connected it to *kasas* but left unexplained some important questions regarding the precise process of the formation of the word. The rather cryptic note of Frisk (1:797 s.v.) also connects these vulgar words somehow with *kasas* (cf. Latin *scortum*, skin, which means "low prostitute").

katapugōn: Although this term primarily refers to male prostitution (see under the list of terms for male prostitution), some sources attest that *katapugōn* was also used for female prostitution (Suda k 738; Lex. seg. k 270; Choerob. 2.31 Cramer). However, the context of these passages suggests that they may simply be referring to the grammatical gender, not to actual practice. The feminine form attested in inscriptions is *katapugaina* (Milne and Bothmer 1953, 215–24, *anthulē katapugaina*).

katēlusis: descent. Its primary sense is "descent" or "fall," but it was also used metaphorically for a prostitute (Suda k 1051). The connotations suggest a low-class prostitute, and the term is probably a literary invention from later antiquity.

kechramenē: dirty, soiled (Hsch. k 2432).

kreagra: meat catcher. This was a cooking implement that resembled a human hand (Sch. Ar. *Eq.* 722a) and that was used remove meat from a pot (Sch. Ar. *Eq.* 722d). Its metaphorical use is only attested in Suda (e 1800, k 2360), who invokes it to refer to whorish old women. Suda may simply be misinterpreting the passage on which this note is based (Ar. *Eccl.* 1002–4). However, this term does offer itself for use in a prostitutional context and it is tempting to accept the evidence of Suda that it was used for old prostitutes.

kuneira: This term is mentioned by Suetonius, who testifies that it originated in comedy and who cryptically interprets it as "the one pulling the *kuon*, namely, being attracted." Eustathios repeats Suetonius's interpretation (*Com. Od.* 2.147, 148) and tries to make sense out of it by linking it with *choiros* (piglet), a slang word for female genitalia, but misses the fact that *kuōn* was a colloquial term for penis—or at least a part of it, the *frenum praeputii* (Oribasius 50.3.1). Suetonius believed that *kuneira* was an old term from the classical period, because of the employment of the rather archaic *eirō* as the second compound. The use of *kuōn* as a colloquial term for penis in Old Comedy (Pher. fr. 193 *PCG*, also qtd. in Ar. *Lys.* 158 with unambiguous reference to male masturbation) supports the view that this term goes back to the classical period (see *PCG* 7:197–98).

laikastria (alternative form: *lēkastria* [Hdn. Gr. 248.12; Theognostus Gram. 580.2 Cramer; Choerob. 178.16 Cramer]): This colloquial term was quite common both in Old Comedy (Pher. fr. 159 *PCG*; Ar. *Ach.* 529, 537) and in New Comedy (Men. *Per.* 485). The verb *laikazein* is also attested (Ar. *Eq.* 167; Ar. *Thesm.* 57; Cephisodorus fr. 3 *PCG*). The etymology is from *lēkaō*, a rude word for sexual intercourse (Frisk s.v.).

leōphoros: people carrier. Suetonius attributes this term to Anacreon (fr. 60 Gentili). Pausanias Atticus (m 27), Suda (m 1470), and Eustathios (*Com. Il.* 3.918, 937) simply repeat his note. Hesychius (s.v.) defines *leōphoros* as a "public road on which people are carried, which they ride." Undoubtedly a word meaning "wide road" was an insult for a common prostitute who "carried" many each day; this is a particularly ingenious phrase given its connotations of width, easy access, and speed.

lēsitos (alternative forms: *laisitos* [Hsch. l 155], *lasitos* [Hsch. l 373], *lastai* [Hsch. l 373]): The evidence is limited to a few references in the lexicographers (Hdn. Gr. 242.28; Hsch. l 155; Hsch. l 373). Frisk (s.v.) relates it to *lilaiomai* (to desire).

lōgas: The term is found in Hesychius (l 1495). Some scholars connect this term to *legō* (to collect), the idea being that this is a woman who collects men (Frisk s.v.). This interpretation is not entirely convincing.

loupa: she-wolf (Latin, *lupa*). Dionysius Halicarnasseus (1.84.4) first reinterpreted the traditional Roman myth of the she-wolf on the basis of the double meaning of the word *lupa*, which also indicated a low-class prostitute. This meaning is well attested in Roman authors over a long time-span (Plaut. *Epid.* 403; Catull. 99.10; Cic. *Mil.* 55; Mart. 1.34.8; Aug. *De civ. D.* 18.21), and seemingly survived in Romance languages (Adams 1983, 333–35). As Thomas McGinn puts it: "Such terminology emphasizes the rapacious, predatory, and greedy nature of the prostitute as a type, and, at the same time, denies her humanity" (2004, 8).

lupta: *hetaira*, *pornē*: This word appears only in Hesychius (l 1424). There is no further evidence. Frisk (s.v.) relates it to the same root as "to lust."

machlos: wanton (both masculine and feminine). An intriguing term first encountered in the *Iliad* (24.30) and then in Archilochus (fr. 328 West), recurring as late as the historians of the fall of Constantinople (Ducas *Turcobyzantina* 9.4). This widely used term was respectable enough for epic poetry, tragedy (Aesch. *Supp.* 636), and even Christian oratory (John Chrysostom *Commentarii in xii prophetas minores* 1.17, 1.20 al.) and was colloquial enough to be included in every list of low-brow terms for prostitute (Ar. Byz. fr. 15 Nauck; Suet. 1; Poll. 6.188, 7.203; Hsch. o 435, p 1816; Suda b 185, m 306; *Etym. gud.* s.v.). The original meaning of "wanton" seems to have been retained throughout time, and when the word means "prostitute" it refers to lewd and lustful behavior. Frisk gives some credence to the connection with Sanskrit *makha-*, an adjective for a god, meaning "lively, joyous."

mainandros: mad about men. Another witticism similar to *mainas* but more specifically referring to female lust for men (Hdn. *Part.* 76.6; *Com. Arist. Rhet.* 202.12 Rabe).

mainas: maenad. Normally a term used for a maenad, a follower of Dionysus, was particularly suitable as a witticism for a prostitute (Hdn. *Part.* 76.6; cf. Suda s 897) given its connotations of madness and unbridled female sexuality.

maniokēpos: mad garden. Suetonius attributes this term to Anacreon (fr. 164 Gentili) and interprets it as "the woman who is crazy about copulation." He derives it from *mainesthai* (to be mad) and *kēpos* (literally, "garden," which he interprets as referring to the pubic region). Pausanias Atticus (m 27) follows Suetonius closely but paraphrases *kēpos* as "member." Eustathios states that a woman who opens up her garden, so that whoever is willing can pick her fruit, must be mad (*Com. Od.* 1.190). Most interesting is his explicit interpretation of the *kēpos* as the birth canal (*Com. Od.* 2.275 [*paidogonon*]). Although each one of the two compounds of *maniokēpos* is clearly understood, their binding is skillfully ambiguous. Is the first compound attributive to the second (e.g., something like "mad beaver"; I use the word "beaver" as a recognizable English metaphor of similar texture), or does the second compound refer to the first (e.g., something like "mad with regard to her beaver")? Unlikely as the explanation of Eustathios may appear in narrow linguistic terms, culturally it is not far off.

Megarikai Sphinges: Megarian Sphinxes. Several sources attribute this term to the comic poet Callias (fr. 28 *PCG*), implying that he used it for a specific group of prostitutes (e.g., Hsch. m 486). Elsewhere the term is reported as simply meaning "prostitute" (Diogenian *Paroem.* 6.35; Phot. s.v.; Suda m 385) (see Kapparis 1999, 241–42).

misētē: This term attracted attention because of its similarity with the feminine of the adjective *misētos* (hateful), from which it only differs in terms of accent (stress on the penultimate). Grammarians and lexicographers state that *misētē* referred to a loose woman. Aristophanes Byzantios interprets the noun *misētia* as "inclination for sexual encounters." This interpretation was adopted by the grammarian Tryphon (fr. 10 Vels.; cf. Ammon. *Diff. p.* 94 Va = 322 Nickau).

Tryphon seems to be the first who observed the difference in the accent and interpreted *misētē* as "common" (*koinē*) and "easy" (*raidia*). Tryphon also may be the source that, according to Eustathios (*Com. Od.* 1.371), attributed the use of this term to Cratinos (fr. 354 *PCG*) and Sophron (fr. 3.30 *PCG*). The note of Suetonius is based on Tryphon. Pausanias (m 22) also follows Tryphon but adds that *misētē* is derived from *misgesthai* (to have intercourse). A passage from the *Historia arcana* of Procopios concerning Theodora (9.10) seems to support this explanation of the term (see also Sch. Ar. *Plu.* 989 on *misētias*). This interpretation, however, is probably a paretymology, as another passage of Procopios indicates (*Hist. arc.* 9.16), where it is said that thirty servants were not enough to satisfy the insatiable lust of Theodora. There the word *misētia* clearly means "insatiable lust." That the word originally meant "greed" is also confirmed by the note of Photios (s.v.), while Suda (m 607) defines it as "an insatiable appetite for intercourse but in a more general sense greed and stinginess" (cf. m 1113; Sch. Ar. *Av.* 1620; Sch. Ar. *Plu.* 989). The noun *misētia* referring to prostitution is first attested in Pollux (5.115); however, the term *misētē* (and probably the noun *misētia*) came to be associated with the idea of the insatiable whore very early. It may be that Archilochus's subversion of the proverb "a woman with plump, plentiful hips" is responsible for the term (fr. 206 West; cf. Suet.; Herennius Philo m 117). In later centuries the meaning "sexually greedy" became widespread. By the time of Cratinos it appears that this meaning was quite common, when the word was used to refer to insatiable women using dildos (fr. 354 *PCG*).

moicheutria: adulteress (Poll. 6.189, 7.202).

moichidiē: adulteress (*Lexica in opera Gregorii Nazianzeni* m 103).

mulas (also *mullas* [Suda m 1403; Lex. seg. s.v.]): *pornē* (Phot. s.v.). Etymologically it is probably related to *mullainō* (to suck); thus it could be a term for a woman who engages in oral sex (cf. Chantraine s.v. *mulla*).

musachnē: dirty dust. Suetonius attributes the invention of this term to Archilochus (fr. 248 West) and correctly recognizes that it is derived from *musaros* (filthy, dirty) + *achnē* (dust). All later notes by lexicographers and scholiasts are based on Suetonius. Undoubtedly it was used to indicate a low-class prostitute, who had intercourse in dusty, dirty places. It is doubtful that it was used colloquially; most likely it was an Archilochan literary construct.

orchēstris: dancer. The scholiast of Aristophanes defines this term as "dancing *pornai*" (*Ach.* 1093), leaving no room for doubt that ancient female dancers were for the most part specialized prostitutes; the numerous references to dancers in comedy, sympotic literature, and other literary genres confirms this. An interesting passage of the comic poet Metagenes calls them *hetairai* (fr. 4

PCG), possibly beyond their prime, but many other times they are clearly differentiated from the high-class courtesans, flute players, or common prostitutes also invited to the symposium (Ar. *Ach.* 1093–95; Xen. *Symp.* 2.1 al.). Apart from dancing, they were expected to offer sexual favors to the guests, probably for an additional fee, as the passage of Metagenes and other sources suggest.

pacheia: plump. Aristophanes of Byzantium (fr. 18 Nauck) and Suetonius identify Archilochus (fr. 246 West) as the person who gave *pacheia*, which normally means "fat," this meaning by subverting a proverb in order to insult Neoboule (Hsch. e 5658). Suetonius mentions that a prostitute is called this because she is "fed" by many or a lot (*polutrophon*).

pandosia: one who gives herself to everybody. Aristophanes of Byzantium (fr. 17 Nauck) interprets this term as a subversion of Pandora, meaning someone who gives herself to everyone. Suetonius states it was first used by Anacreon (fr. 163 Gentili). Pausanias (m 27) and Suda (m 1470) follow Suetonius, as does Eustathios (*Com. Il.* 3.253, 918, 937, 4.835; *Com. Od.* 2.275), who also adds that a prostitute was called *pandosia* if she was so cheap that everyone could buy her favors.

paragapōmenē: paramour, loved at the side. Attested only by Hesychius (k 2432), this term suggests long-term emotional attachment of the kind that only courtesans or concubines would form with their lovers.

peripolis (alternative form: *peripolos*): patrol. This term appears to be a comic literary invention of Phrynichos (fr. 34 *PCG*) for a streetwalker patrolling the streets.

phorbas: a young, untamed animal (Paus. 5; cf. Ath. 13.573f). Suetonius (2) attests that Sophocles used the word to describe a young woman who goes with many men, because she needs food and maintenance. Pollux (7.203) confirms that it was used for prostitutes. Justin (*Apol.* 27.1) attests that by the second century CE the word had entirely lost its positive meaning and was only used to allude to indecency in boys and girls alike.

pikrainomenē: saddened, disappointed in love. This term is only attested by Hesychius (k 2432). The verb *pikrainō* for a jilted or disappointed lover or for unrequited love is very common in modern Greek.

poluhumnos: much sung. According to Suetonius, this term was used by Anacreon (fr. 165 Gentili) to euphemize a notorious woman.

pordalis/pardalis: leopard (Apion *De glossis homericis* fr. 109; Hdn. Gr. 237; Ael. Dion. p 18; Hsch. p 3009; Phot. p 443; *Etym. gud.* p 452). Although it could have been used as a term for a prostitute, implying the striking appearance and animal qualities of a leopard, the evidence for this is tenuous (Poll. 7.202; Suda p 496) and may well be a misunderstanding of an obscure Aristophanic passage (fr. 494 *PCG*).

procheiros: handy, readily available. The evidence is limited, but the meaning of this term is clear. Suda interprets it, among other things, as *akratēs* (without restraint). Undoubtedly it was used to insult a woman by labeling her easy and lacking in moral restraint, and if it was ever employed colloquially, it would have connoted a cheap whore (Poll. 6.189, 7.202; Suda p 2931).

radia: easy. Like *procheiros* this word was used when the intention was to degrade a woman by suggesting she was a cheap whore (Poll. 6.189, 7.202).

rerupōmenē: dirty, filthy. According to Hesychius (k 2432), this term too was used for a prostitute along with *kechramenē*, *paragapōmenē*, and *pikrainomenē*. The metaphorical use of this verb to indicate moral dirt is well attested among Christian authors (e.g., Did. Caec. *Com. Job* 304; Ephraim Syrus 7.393) but not in pagan Greek, presumably because this concept was not prevalent before the Christian era.

salabakchō: Hesychius (s 88) suggests that the name of Salabaccho, one of the first notorious prostitutes of Attica, came to be used in later times generically for prostitute (Suda k 2692; cf. Ar. *Eq.* 765; Ar. *Thesm.* 805).

satura: Satyra was a proper name used by at least one famous courtesan who lived in the early fifth century. Suetonius and Hesychius (s 255) confirm that this term was used for a common prostitute (*katapherēs*). Its etymological connection with the word satyr would generate connotations of lust and insatiable sexuality.

skammas: Hesychius (s 827) provides the only reference. *Skamma* is a stadium or theater where athletic competitions took place, so this term may refer to a type of prostitution of later antiquity, where strippers entertained the male audience of games and athletic competitions with daring routines (cf. Procopios, *Hist. arc.* 9.11–26; Basil *In ebriosos* 31.448; McGinn 2004, 22–23). The etymological connection with *skaptein* (to dig) inserts an additional level of obscenity.

sobas: This term may have been initially used for a bacchant, but already in Old Comedy it had been converted into a term for a prostitute (Eupolis fr. 373 *PCG*). This sense remained in use through the Byzantine period. The precise context is not clear, but it may have been a reference to a woman with a certain provocative gait, which marked her out as a prostitute in the streets. There is a possible etymological connection with *sobeō* (to bother, to push away).

spodēsilaura: Suetonius first mentions this term, correctly explaining it as a compound of *spodeisthai* (a vulgar verb for sexual intercourse common in Old Comedy) and *laura* (street), indicating a woman who has sex in the streets. Hesychius (s 1538) agrees; Eustathios (*Com. Il.* 3.937, 774; *Com. Od.* 2.275) adds that the term originated in comedy, which sounds probable.

statē: standing. This term (Hesychius s 1974) seems to refer to a prostitute who stood in the street waiting to be picked up.

stegitis: roofer. Although undoubtedly this term referred to prostitutes established in brothels, the precise connotations of it are tantalizingly uncertain, as they have to do with the physical space of the ancient brothel, and our knowledge of this space is limited. A number of sources attest that a brothel was commonly called *stegos* or *tegos* (roof, room on the roof, balcony) and that prostitutes established in it were called *stegitis* or "the women on the roof" (Gregory Nazianzenus *Carmina moralia* 741; cf. Olympiodorus Diaconus *Com. Jer. Ep.* 93.776 ["and the prostitutes on the roof, because he calls the brothel roof"]; see also Poll. 7.202; Hsch. s 1687; Lex. seg. s.v. *tegos*; John Chrysostom *In Matthaeum* 57.370; Suda k 446). The brothel could be called "roof" because of its shabby construction, something like a warehouse or workshop, literally a roof over one's head but not much more. If so, considering that not all brothels were cheap, badly built structures, it would only refer to a particular type of shabby brothel, and thus the term *stegitis* and its variants would have referred to a very low-class prostitute. Alternatively, a brothel could be in a larger building with more than one floor. In this case *tegos* would refer to an upper room or balcony from which the prostitutes solicited passersby, and thus the term *stegitis* would not necessarily have implied the cheapest and lowest of prostitutes. A more definite answer to the whole issue requires further research on the physical space of the ancient brothel.

tribas: rubber. Among the scarce references to female homosexuality, this term provides important information about the practices of lesbian sex in the brothels of the ancient world (e.g., Luc. *Dial. meret.* 5). It was used for women who had sex with other women (Ptol. *Tetr.* 3.15.8; Manetho Astrol. 4.358; Hephaestion Astrol. *Apot.* 152.36, 176.2; Suda o 169; John Kamateros *Introductio in astronomiam* 849) and often for women who paid to have sex with other women (Timaeus *Lex. plat.* e 987a; Hsch. d 1689, e 6489; Phot. e 25; Suda e 3273; Sch. Clem. *Protr.* 337 [where the term is synonymous with lesbian in the modern sense]). The word *tribas* is not found in Attic authors. The scholiast of Lucian (80.5.2 Rabe), undoubtedly a scholar of extraordinary learning, provides the precise etymology from *tribō* (to rub together) and interprets it as a reference to sex between two women. The term was certainly meant to be a vulgar insult, as passages like that of the scholiast of Clement ("the polluted 'rubbers'") confirm.

trioditis: of the crossroads (Latin, *trivia)*. The phrase initially referred to Hecate or Artemis (e.g., Dorotheus Astrol. fr. 3a Pingree; Ath. 7.325d; Damascius *In Phaedonem* 108; John Lydus *De mensibus* 3.10) and was applied to witches.

Philo seems to be the first to use it (*trioditis sobas*) to refer to a prostitute (*De sacrificiis Abelis et Caini* 21; *De fuga et inventione* 153; see also Did. Caec. *Com. Zacch.* 1.45; Constantine Manasses *Compendium chronicum* 5669). The late Byzantine historian John Kinnamos (325 Meineke) uses the term to refer to a princess who might be abused by her future husband and treated as a whore. Apparently it could be used safely in respectable literature, albeit with denigrating intent. One can imagine how an adjective that embodied the idea of dark and secretive feminine powers came to be used to refer to a prostitute, just as several terms initially used to describe worshipers of Dionysus or Cybele ended up being invoked to degrade those followers by equating them and their activities with those of common whores. The adjective *trioditis*, with its connotations of the street, where respectable women did not belong, certainly allows for a secondary meaning suggesting a streetwalker.

MALE PROSTITUTION

achrōmos, *achrōmatos*: colorless, someone who does not blush, shameless (Suda a 4719). The literal meaning must be interpreted from a moral standpoint; blushing from shame signifies virtuous behavior, while the lack of blushing signifies licentiousness (e.g., Philo *Sp. leg.* 3.25).

aischroloichos: licker of shame. An extremely rare term, quoted only by Suetonius, who attributes it to comedy. Eustathios certainly and Photios probably are repeating Suetonius's entry. In fact, Suetonius uses this term to explain *brotoloigos*, a term that initially meant "man killer," and undoubtedly in a comic twist of usages—like that of Aeschylus's *androkmēs loigos* (a man-killing plague) (*Supp.* 678–79)—it was used to indicate a male prostitute. Significant for our understanding of social attitudes toward male prostitution is his superficial justification of *brotoloigos* as a "killer of men"; it is, he says, because such men are responsible for the lack of pregnancies among women.

aischrourgos: worker of shame. This term and the abstract noun *aischrourgia* are both rare and indicate some sort of shameful act, not necessarily sexual (E. *Ba.* 1062; Xen. *Ages.* 9.1; Aeschin. 2.99). From the period of the Second Sophistic, as hostility toward homosexuality increases, the term is frequently encountered more narrowly as a criticism of sexual acts among men (e.g., Philo *De somniis* 2.168; Dio Chrys. *Orationes* 4.102; Galen 12.249 Kühn [*aischrourgon ē kinaidon*]; George Monachos [a Byzantine monk with intensely homophobic views] 324, 650, 653). Whether the term was ever used for a male prostitute, as Pollux seems to suggest (6.126), remains uncertain.

aischunōn to sōma: he who shames his body (Poll. 6.126).

akathartos: unclean (Poll. 6.126).

akolastos: shameless (Poll. 6.126).

anaischuntoteros tōn neōterōn: more shameless than the young (Pollux 6.126). It seems to refer to a man who assumed the passive role in same-sex intercourse after the acceptable age of prime youth.

androgunos: androgynous, literally "man-woman." It is culturally significant that this word has been used for millennia to indicate an intersexual person (e.g., Pl. *Symp.* 189e; Luc. *Dial. D.* 12.1), a eunuch (e.g., Philo *Sp. leg.* 3.40; Dio Chrys. *Orationes* 33.39), an effeminate man (e.g., Philo *De somniis* 1.127; Musonius Rufus 21), the passive male in same-sex intercourse (e.g., Philo *Quis rerum divinarum heres sit* 274), a coward (e.g., Aeschin. 2.127; Men. *Aspis* 242), and sometimes a male prostitute (Diod. Sic. 16.93.4). Particularly interesting is the use of the term in the religious context of the cult of Cybele, where, along with other terms such as *apokopos*, *Attis*, and *bakēlos* (see above and below) or *gallos*, it is employed to indicate a castrated priest (e.g., Philo *Sp. leg.* 3.40; Plut. 338c, 756c; Dio Chrys. *Orationes* 33.39 al.). See also Giammarco 1982, 227–66; Lane 1996, 117–33; and C. Picard 1954, 80–82. The implication is that a man who looked like a woman through the use of feminine toiletry, who acted like a woman by assuming the passive role and allowing another man to penetrate him, or who lacked the conventional manly attributes of body hair, a deep male voice, and the bravery and courage traditionally expected of a man was not fully and truly male (cf. Phot. a 1764: "They called androgynous those who were men by nature but had placed themselves among women and had adopted their lifestyle"). It is difficult to draw clear distinctions among the different meanings of this term, since it seems that the entire semantic field was operant from classical authors such as Hippocrates, Eupolis, and Plato, down to late Byzantine historians (e.g., John Skylitzes *Synopsis historiarum* 14). Curiously, in modern Greek the neuter noun *androguno* is exclusively used for a married heterosexual couple. This usage, first attested in the first century CE (Cyranides 1.2, 3.22), has completely replaced the range of meanings commonly found in classical and medieval Greek. The closest modern Greek comes to the classical/medieval meanings is in the word *androgunaika* (manly woman), indicating a big and/or strong woman, a woman with resonant voice, or sometimes a lesbian. We first encounter the term in the sense of intersexual (e.g., Pl. *Symp.* 189e, 191d; Hip. *Acut.* 28), while Eupolis's comedy *Astrateutoi ē androgunai* suggests that the meaning "womanly" or "cowardly" was also current in the classical period. The term was possibly not used for a male prostitute until the Hellenistic period, when we first encounter it in Diodoros of Sicily (16.93.4) and later in the lexicographers (e.g., Suet. 3; Poll. 6.126). It was primarily used for men who, to use the expression of Photios, "placed themselves among women."

andropornos: man whore (Theopompos 115F 225a; Polybius 8.9.12; Demetrius *Elocut.* 27, 274).

apokopos: cut off. Like other terms for a castrated man, *apokopos* was occasionally used for a male prostitute (e.g., Hephaistion Astr. 16; Basilius Med. *De virginitate* 797.26; Phryn. Gr. fr. 238 Fischer; cf. *androgunos* and *bakēlos* [above and below], *eunouchos*, *gallos*).

aselgēs: shameless (Poll. 6.126).

Attis: See *bakēlos* below.

bakēlos: Like other terms for a castrated man (Phryn. Gr. fr. 238 Fischer; cf. *androgunos* and *apokopos* [above], *eunouchos*, *gallos*), *bakēlos* was used for a male prostitute in Attic Comedy. In the sentence "you are a *bakēlos*" (Alexis fr. 105 *PCG*; Men. fr. 368 *PCG*; Antiphanes fr. 111 *PCG*) the term refers to a man of loose morals. William Arnott, however (1996, 287), is convinced that Alexis meant "male prostitute" on the basis of the translation of Plautus (*Poen.* 1318) as *cinaedus*. Beyond a few references in the lexicographers no other evidence suggests that it was commonly understood as a word referring to a male prostitute. Chantraine believed the word was of oriental origin (s.v.).

bdeluros: scum (Poll. 6.126).

bdelurōteros hetairōn: worse scum than *hetairai* (Poll. 6.126).

brotoloigos: killer of men. See *aischroloichos* above.

brotophthoros: destroyer of men. See *aischroloichos* above.

chalaibasis: a man with a soft, ladylike walk (Suetonius).

chaskax: gaping ass. Mentioned only by Suetonius (and Eustathios [*Com. Od.* 1.78], who copies Suetonius), this also could be a contemporary colloquial term. The meaning derives from *chaskō* (to gape) and rudely jokes about a man who allows a large number of other men to penetrate him. Cf. *lakkoproktos* below.

deisaēs: filthy. Only mentioned by Suetonius, who understands it as "dirty"; cf. *deisa* (filth, dirt [Frisk s.v.]).

dēmokoinos: Primarily used of someone who tortures slaves within the context of judicial proceedings (Antiphon 1.20; Isoc. 17.15). Lycophron seems to have used it for a male prostitute on account of its etymology: *dēmos* (public) + *koinos* (common).

diakeklasmenos: broken. This term refers to gestures considered effeminate (voice: John Chrysostom *In Matthaeum* 58.645; a look: Zeno fr. 246 von Arnim; a song: John Chrysostom *Ad populum Antiochenum* 49.155; words: John *De Davide et Saule*, 54.696; limbs: John Chrysostom *De paenitentia*

49.315; appearance: John Chrysostom *In Matthaeum* 58.645; walking: John Chrysostom *In Matthaeum* 58.645). The origin of the word possibly goes back to castration; if so, it would initially have applied to a eunuch.

dialaos: The comic playwright Cratinos may have intended this to mean "utmost of whores" (Hsch. d 1143; fr. 438 *PCG*). The word can refer to a man who is notorious among people or perhaps a man through whom everyone has gone.

digenēs: Etymologically, a person with both sexes. Aelius Dionysius (a 177) defines it as half man or half woman (cf. Theophylactus *Epist.* 43).

eidomalidēs: Suetonius attests that this term was invented by an unknown lyric poet and that Alcaeus subverted its original meaning to describe someone who used rouge. This suggests that at some brothels, male prostitutes were made up and dressed like female prostitutes.

ekdedēlōkōs eis aischunēn to sōma: someone who revealed his body for shameful purposes (Poll. 6.126).

ekdromas: This term was a comic invention of Eubulus (fr. 10 *PCG*) to indicate a man with a big and attractive backside. According to Suetonius (3), it applied to someone past his early adolescence and thus too old to be someone's beloved.

ekpeporneumenos: whore (Poll. 6.126).

ektethēlusmenos: effeminate (Poll. 6.126).

empeparōnēmenos: bought (Poll. 6.126).

enēsēlgēmenos: shamed (Poll. 6.126).

epipsogos: someone who deserves blame (Poll. 6.126; Ptol. *Tetr.* 3.14.33–35).

epirrhētos: The term appears to be an invention of Archilochus (Orion *Etymologicum* e 55), designating that something that deserved a verbal attack had to be base and shameless. The term was more frequently attested in later antiquity and Byzantium (e.g., Poll. 6.126; Ael. Dion. fr. 104 Hercher; Philostr. *V. Apol.* 1.12, 5.7).

eponeidistos: shameful (Poll. 6.126).

eunouchōdēs: eunuchlike. An alternative form of *eunouchos* (eunuch); a male prostitute (Ael. Dion. a177; Suda a 3822). Cf. *bakēlos* above.

euōnoeros tēn hōran tōn apokērugmenōn ōniōn: cheaper with his body than discarded shopping items (Poll. 6.126).

gunaikias: womanly (Poll. 6.126; Hdn. *Part.* 18). See *androgunos* above.

gunaikōdēs: womanlike (Ptol. *Tetr.* 3.14.33). See *androgunos* above.

gunandros: womanly man. See *androgunos* above.

gunis: womanish. This term, sometimes included in catalogues of terms for prostitutes (e.g., Suet. 3 and Poll. 6.127), in fact indicated an effeminate man.

hēmiandros/hēmigunis: These appear in Synesios (*Epist.* 44.129 Hercher) and Suda (h 392, p 1959). Both terms seem to originate in lyric poetry; *hēmiandros* was seemingly invented by Hipponax to describe an effeminate man, while *hēmigunis* appears to have been used by Simonides (*AG* 6.217) for one of the castrated priests of Cybele. These terms are synonyms that stress the half-male or the half-female part. They were used, like *androgunos*, for an intersexual person, a eunuch, a man with one testicle (Cyril *De adoratione* 68.793), or an effeminate man (Luc. *Dial. D.* 3.1), and possibly for a male prostitute, since it has been included in the list of Suetonius (cf. Eust. *Com. Od.* 1.78).

hermaphroditos: Medical texts identify the term as it is used today (Galen 4.619 Kühn). Byzantine lexica (Suda e 3028; *EM* s.v.; Ps. Zonaras s.v.) suggest that it was used as a term for a male prostitute in later antiquity and in Byzantine Greek.

hētairēkōs: like a *hetaira* (Aeschin. 1.29; Poll. 6.126; Hdn. *Fig.* 91.8 Spengel).

hōran peprakōs: one who sold his youth (Poll. 6.126).

hugros/hugronous: wet (Poll. 6.126)/wet brain (Poll. 6.126). These rare terms may be related to ancient medical perceptions of the female body as wet as opposed to the male body as dry. If so, they mean "womanly" or "thinking like a woman."

hupomalakos: softened (Ptol. *Tetr.* 3.14.33).

itamōteros hetairōn: more reviled than the *hetairai* (Poll. 6.126).

ithris or *ethris*: eunuch (Ael. Dion. a177; Suda a 3822; Michael Psellos *Poemata* 6.417; *EM* s.v.).

kakophēmos: disreputable (Ptol. *Tetr.* 3.14.35).

kallōpistēs: In the classical period this was a derogatory term for a man who took excessive care of his appearance because he was up to no good (Isoc. 1.27; Ar. *Nub.* 1207 ff.; Arist. *Rhet.* 1401b; Alex. Aphr. *in APr.* 342.11). Davidson points out that the term could mean *moichos* or *kinaidos* (cf. Chrysippos fr. 10a von Arnim [*hubristēs ē kinaidos ē moichos*]; J. Davidson 1997, 167–82). From the Hellenistic period forward it refers to male prostitution (Ptol. *Tetr.* 3.14.33; Basil *De legendis gentilium libris* 9.17).

kataischunōn tēn hōran: shaming his youth (Poll. 6.126).

katapugōn: *Pugē* is derived from the Akkadian *puqu*, which means "cleft" or "buttocks" (Azize and Craigie 2002, 54–64). This colloquial term is almost exclusively confined to Attic Comedy, derivative literature (Lucian, Alciphron), and the lexicographers. (For linguistic analysis, see Milne and Bothmer 1953, 215–24). Davidson concludes: "It is used above all to attack men of power, a kind of inverse acclamation, alluding to general bad morals and in particular to sexual degeneracy and untrammeled sexuality" (2007, 70; cf. Dover 1978, 142). The term carries a broad valence: someone who cannot exercise self-control with food (Ar. *Ach.* 77–79), an ill-mannered individual (Ar. *Eq.* 638–39), an antonym of *sōphrōn* (prudent) (Ar. *Nub.* 529), a synonym of *anaischuntos* (Ar. *Nub.*

909). From the classical period on, it described a soft, effeminate man, fond of cosmetics and sex with men (Ar. *Vesp.* 686–67; *Thesm.* 200–201). The first unambiguous reference to its use for a male prostitute is in Lucian (*Tim.* 22).

kateagos: broken. For a fairly short period of time around the first century BCE this participle of a common verb meaning "to break" came to be used as a term for an effeminate man and a male prostitute. The origin of the word possibly goes back to castration, the idea being that it was a kind of breaking, and so would initially have been applied to a eunuch (cf. D.H. *Comp.* 18; Philo *De gigantibus* 4; Musonius Rufus 21.31).

kathubrismenos: insulted (Poll. 6.126).

kinaidos: This very diverse term for any man who did not fit the traditional stereotype of the rugged heterosexual male is first attested in Archilochus (fr. 328 West), beyond doubt indicating a male prostitute. Joseph Azize and Ian Craigie derive the etymology from the Akkadian *qinnatu* (anus) (2002, 54–64, cf. Chantraine s.v.). As Davidson points out, from the fourth century forward it becomes essentially a synonym of *katapugōn* (1997, 167–82). Aeschines uses it as the opposite of *sōphrōn* (2.151). Plato (*Grg.* 494e) speaks about the "terrible, shameful and wretched life" of a *kinaidos*, while Aeschines (1.131) equates *kinaidia* with unmanliness and elsewhere uses it as a term for male prostitution (2.88). Aristotle ([*Phgn.*] 808a) creates an effeminate caricature of the *kinaidos* that is easily recognizable in many cultures. Davidson describes the *kinaidos* as "a 'man-woman' . . . an effeminate sexual seducer of males (mainly)" (2007, 71).

kinoumenos: he who is fucked. A reference to someone passive in same-sex intercourse (Sch. Ar. *Eq.* 878).

klusma: A medical term for an enema (e.g., Hipp. *Mul.* 66; Gal. 1.391 Kühn) and listed among insults for male prostitutes (Poll. 6.126).

kollopodiōktēs: *kollops* chaser. The active partner (cf. *kollops* below), confirmed by several passages (Suet. 3; Suda a 360; Eust. *Com. Od.* 2.267; Sch. Ar. *Nub.* 349a). Beyond that, it is difficult to see how the word could have been used for a male prostitute; it would probably have been used for the lover of prostitutes.

kollops: The passive partner in male/male intercourse, although he is too old to be someone's *eromenos* (Suet. 3). This is a metaphorical analogy to the hard back of the neck of an ox (*kollops*); one who assumed the passive role, although too old, was "hardened."

kubalēs: bent. This term is found only in Suetonius, who convincingly derives it from *kupto* (bend over).

kusoleschēs: Suetonius includes this among terms for male prostitutes but defines it as a foul-mouthed person: *kusos* (slang for female genitalia) + *leschē* (conversation, gossip).

kusoniptēs: This colloquial term is attested by Hesychius (k 4737). The etymology—*kusos* + *niptō* (to wash)—suggests a heterosexual male very fond of women, and thus unlikely to be a male prostitute in a society where male prostitution was practiced for the benefit of men, not women. One must understand that Hesychius is using the word *pornos* in its medieval sense, namely as a term for any kind of unusual sexual behavior.

laikastēs (alternative form: *lēkastēs* [Hsch. l 131]): Unlike the common feminine form *laikastria* (see under the list of terms for female prostitution), the masculine is only attested in Aristophanes (*Ach.* 79), who created the word (Suda l 181).

lakkoprōktos: ditch ass. It is encountered in Eupolis (fr. 385 *PCG*) and in Pollux's list (6.126) as an insult against passive males who had many lovers. Davidson has suggested that the synonym *euruprōktos* (which is never mentioned in a context of prostitution) was primarily used as an insult for politicians and men of power and referred to "talking out of your arse" and only by extension to other modes of anal dilation, whether through buggery or adultery (for adulterers were believed sometimes to be punished by the husbands and fathers they "cuckolded" with a "radish up the arse"). It is possible that *lakkoprōktos* was just as short lived and used in a similar context (2007, 70).

lakkoschēs: This word is only found in Lucian (*Lex.* 12). Like *lakkoprōktos*, it was probably used for a passive male with many lovers.

lasitos: This word is found in Herodian (542.28) and Hesychius (l 373, 155 [*laisitos*]). It is only attested in a few instances in the lexicographers, like the feminine *lēsitos* (see under the list of terms for female prostitution).

lastauroi: men with a hairy ass, and some prostitutes (Hsch. l 384). This term is perplexing because in the entire iconography of male prostitution smoothness and softness are valued features. Unless one assumes a specific reference to some kind of fetish, the term *pornoi* was probably used in its medieval sense, here for a man with pronounced sexuality.

lelugismenos: bent (Poll. 6.126).

leukopugos/melampugos: white ass, black ass. These terms were included in the list of Suetonius, although it is doubtful that they were ever used in a prostitutional context. *Melampugos* appears to have been invented by Archilochus to describe an eagle (Porphyry *Quaest. Hom. Il.* 24.315–16). Attic comedy subverted that sense and used it to refer to a rough, hairy male (Ar. *Lys.* 801–2; Ar.

fr. 61 *PCG*), the one whom sometimes comic poets call *dasuprōktos* (forest ass; cf. Hsch. m 641; Suda m 449) and stereotypically considered as a real man (cf. Ar. *Eccl.* 1–550). By contrast, Alexis (fr. 322 *PCG*) first used *leukopugos* for a soft, effeminate man (Arnott 1996, 804–5).

lōgalioi: Hesychius (l 1494) states that it was both a game and a male prostitute.

lōtax: Included in a list of disreputable crafts (*Constitutiones Apostolorum* 8.32.33), it probably means "flute player." Ps. Zonaras elaborates that *lōtax* means a "male prostitute, or a man who uses perfumes, or someone who spends his fortune on shameless things, like a prostitute and an androgynous man."

machlēs (also *machlōn* [Hsch. m 435]): This word is found in Hesychius (m 431) and is the masculine equivalent of *machlos* (see under the list of terms for female prostitution).

malthakos: soft (Poll. 6.126).

memalagmenos: massaged (Poll. 6.126).

moichos: adulterer. Equated with *pornos* (Hsch. m 1559; *EM* s.v.). Both *moichos* and *pornos* here are used in their medieval meaning, heavily influenced by Christian concepts of monogamy, to indicate any form of inappropriate sexual behavior.

murtōn: This obscure term only mentioned in Lucian (*Lex.* 12) seems related to *murton*, an aromatic plant widely used for perfumes and for medicines; myrtle was also a metaphor for female genitalia because of the shape of its leaves (Plato Com. fr. 188.14 *PCG*).

nothouros: Several lexicographers (Arist. Byz. fr. 17 Nauck; Suet. 3; Hsch. s.v.; Eust. *Com. Il.* 3.253) include this word in the list of terms for male prostitute, although its original meaning is "impotent": *noth-* (dull) + *ouros* (slang for penis).

palimpratos tēn hōran: someone who keeps selling his youth (Poll. 6.126).

palinkapēlos tou kallous: someone who keeps selling his good looks (Poll. 6.126).

pantopraktēs: all-doer (Ptol. *Tetr.* 3.14.33).

paroinos: drunkard (Poll. 6.126).

peiōlēs: someone who desires a penis. *Peos* + *lō* (to desire) (Hdn. Gr. 566.6).

peripēgis: one who has been frequently penetrated. *Peri* + *pēgnumi* (to stick in) (Hsch. p 181).

philoiphas (also *oipholēs*): one who loves intercourse. Aristophanes Byzantios (fr. 15 Nauck) explains these terms as derivatives of *oiphein*/*oiphesthai* (to penetrate/to be penetrated).

poluthrullētos: much spoken (Ptol. *Tetr.* 3.14.33).

proeimenos ta kallista kai peponthōs ta aischista: someone who abandoned the best and suffered the worst (Poll. 6.126).

propetēs: hasty, in the sense of someone lurching forward impatiently. One can easily see why this word would be hijacked (Poll. 6.126) to indicate an eagerly passive partner in male homosexual intercourse.

pros argurion antikatēllagmenos: exchanged (or sold) for money (Poll. 6.126).

pugostolos: someone who adorns his ass. From *pugē* + *stolē* (dress) (Ps. Zonaras s.v.).

schinotrōx or *schinotrōktēs*: mastich chewer. Several sources suggest that this term primarily indicated a soft, effeminate man, fussy with his breath and personal toiletry (Suet. 3; Luc. *Lex.* 12). The etymology is easily recognizable: *schinos* + *trōgō* (to eat or chew). *Schinos* is a tree with aromatic leaves that grows in much of continental Greece. The LSJ gives it as "mastich wood" (= modern Greek *masticha*), which may only be a rough translation. The scholiast of Lucian (46.12 Rabe) says that shameless men were called *schinotrōx* because they did not want to engage in lewd activities unprepared.

spodorchēs: dusty balls. The obvious etymology—*spodos* (dust) + *orchis* (testicle)—suggests that it was colloquial invective for a low-class male prostitute, who had sex in dusty, unclean places or in the streets (cf. *spodēsilaura* under list of terms for female prostitution).

tais hetairais prosomillōmenos: one who mixes with *hetairai* (Poll. 6.126).

tais pornais homotechnos: one who shares the same job with whores (Poll. 6.126).

tēn hēlikian peprakōs: one who sold his prime (Poll. 6.126).

tēn neotēta peprakōs: one who sold his youth (Poll. 6.126).

thēlis tēn pschuchēn: feminine at heart (Poll. 6.126).

thēludrias: A common term for "effeminate" in classical and later Greek (Hdt. 7.153; Ar. *Thesm.* 131; D.H. 7.2.4; Poll. 6.126). The word is a compound of *thēlus* (feminine) and *hudrias* (jar/pot; cf. the underlying cultural construct of female as vessel). For a connection with *keklasmenos/diakeklasmenos*, see *diakeklasmenos* above.

thēlumanēs: mad woman. This term was used to refer to male/male prostitution. The first element of the compound (*thēlus*) is not the object of the second (*mainesthai*) but rather its subject (e.g., "mad and womanish"; cf. Sch. Ar. *Nub.* 355a, 1022b).

thēlumētris: feminine and motherly. Only in Ps. Zonaras (s.v.) and Suda (s.v.).

thrasuteros: more audacious (Poll. 6.126).

PROCURER/PROCURESS

draxōn: grabber. The word seems to have originated in Greek Sicily (Hdn. Gr. 3.1.34 [with the stress on the *ō*]; Hsch. d 2322), possibly for petty thieves who grabbed food from the market place (Hdn. Gr.) or for a pimp (*EM* s.v.; cf. *drattō* [to grab]).

hetairotrophos: whore farmer, he who grows *hetairai*. Although the etymology and meaning are obvious (*hetaira* + *trephō*), it is rare and attested only in later antiquity (Manetho *Astrol.* 4.314; Jul. *Contra Gal.* 208.18; Athan. *Hist. ar.* 20.5; Hsch. p 3044).

krōbulos (also *krobulos, korbulos*): In later antiquity the proverbial expression "the pair of Krobylos" is frequently cited. Although the precise meaning is uncertain, sources agree that it originated from the name of a particularly treacherous real pimp who owned two courtesans. This well-known proverbial expression generated the common noun *krobylos* (pimp).

mastropos (masculine or feminine; also *mastrōpos, mastrua* [Phot. s.v.]): Hofmann, Frisk, and Chantraine relate it to *maiesthai* (to desire or seek) (Hofmann 1950 s.v. *maiomai*; Frisk s.v.; Chantraine s.v.), while medieval lexicographers link it to the term *matruleion* and the root *matr-* (mother); see Eust. *Com. Il.* 1.599; *EM* s.v. *matruleion*; Ps. Zonaras s.v. *matruleion* (the latter two state that the Dorians called the pimps *materes* [mothers]). The medieval interpretation has parallels in many modern languages (including Greek), where terms for a female pimp use some form of the word "mother." *Mastropos* was widely used from the classical period (e.g., Ar. *Thesm.* 558; Xen. *Symp.* 3.10, 4.56; Theopompos 115 F 227 *FGrh*) down to the second millennium (e.g., Michael Psellos *Oratoria minora* 13.27) and into modern times. Like the term *pornē*, we encounter it in a wide range of literary forms from lewd jokes in Old Comedy to serious historiography and even in the writings of the Byzantine monks (e.g., Theo. Stud. *Epist.* 31.45).

matrulis (alternative form: *matrulla* [Eust. *Com. Il.* 1.599]): Most sources connect this form with *mastropos* (see above); here, however, the connection with the stem *mater-* (mother) is clearer. Haprocration (s.v. *matruleion*) suggests that the term applied to an older pimp in a low-class brothel.

maulistēs (feminine: *maulistria* or *maulis*): This word is noted by Photios (s.v. *pugostolos*) and Suda (p 3114). It is possibly of Lydian origin (Frisk s.v.). Alternative spellings—*mablistēs*/*mablistria* (Phot. [s.v. *mastropos*, s.v. *pugostolos*])—are probably the product of Byzantine pronunciation. The oldest attestation is Hesychius (s.v. *proagōgos*); after that it is attested a number of times in Byzantine grammars and lexica (Phot. [s.v. *pugostolos*]; Choerob. 181.24 Cramer; Suda m 271; *Etym. gud.* m 381 al.) without context. For *maulistērion* (brothel coin), see Henry, ch. 1 in this volume.

pornoboskos: shepherd of whores, whore keeper. The term first appears in fifth-century comedy (Myrtilus fr. 5 *PCG*; Ar. *Pax* 849; Plato Com. fr. 174 *PCG*), which may suggest that it was a comic creation that found its way into daily usage. By the middle of the fourth century the orator Apollodoros considered it appropriate for use in a court of law ([Dem.] 59.30, 68; Aeschin. 1.124, 188, 3.214; Hyp. 1.22). From then on, like *mastropos,* it had a wide range of usages and was invoked by comic playwrights as well as by the church fathers (e.g., Joh. Dam. *Sacra parallela* 95.1560). After the ninth century it is almost exclusively limited to lexicographers and scholiasts, suggesting that it gradually fell out of use.

pornotelōnēs: whore-tax collector. The only attested instance is in Philonides (fr. 5 *PCG*), strongly suggesting that this was a joke of the comic poet.

pornotrophos: whore feeder. Like *hetairotrophos,* this rare term is first attested in Philo (*De fuga et inventione* 28) and then sparsely in Christian authors (Euseb. *De mart. palaest.* 5.3; Pall. *Dial. Joh. Chrysost.* 31) and the scholiast of Aristophanes (*Plu.* 149).

proagōgos: procurer/promoter. This euphemism became the primary term for pimp, albeit with a somewhat officious tone, from the pre-Socratic philosophers (e.g., Hippias F 5a Diels-Kranz) and Old Comedy (e.g., Ar. *Nub.* 980; Ar. *Vesp.* 1028) to the church fathers (e.g., Gr. Naz. *In laud. Cypriani* 35.1180.32) and late Byzantine historians (e.g., Nic. Greg. 3.185.16), all the way up to the modern period, where it is the primary term used in government documents. *Proagōgos* is attested almost as often as the other two main terms, *mastropos* and *pornoboskos,* combined.

BROTHEL

chamaitupeion: The form *chamaitupia* mentioned by Hesychius probably does not mean "brothel," but "prostitution," as he admits in a rather confused note (Hsch. x 138). The noun *chamaitupē* (see under list of terms for female prostitution) seems to have come first, and from it a noun for brothel was derived. The first evidence for *chamaitupeion* (Dionysius fr. 422 von Arnim) appears approximately half a century after the first attested instance of *chamaitupē.* The sources suggest that the term was used for a low-class brothel or tavern, an abusive and vile environment, where drunken customers would fight (e.g., Philo *Quis rerum divinarum heres sit* 109; Philo *De somniis* 1.88; Luc. *Nigr.* 22; Jul. *Eis tous apaideutous* 7.21). (For inns and taverns as establishments of prostitution in the Roman world, see McGinn 2004, 15–22.) *Chamaitupeion* is used in modern Greek where it has acquired a more educated tone and can be safely used formally.

ergastērion: This widely used euphemism for brothel literally referred to any kind of workplace, shop, or workshop (Aesop 59.1 [a coppersmith's workshop];

Hdt. 4.14 [a fuller's shop]; Isoc. 18.15 [workshops and stores of the agora]; Dem. 25.52 [barbershop and perfumery]; Dem. 37.9 [knife factory]). It is used in the Solonian law that effectively legalized prostitution by excluding from the force of the adultery laws any woman who practiced some form of prostitution ([Dem.] 59.67; see Kapparis 1999, 311–13; Fisher 2001, 260–62; Rosivach 1995, 2–3; Glazebrook 2005b, 34–53). Aeschines (1.124) explains that any workshop or store that housed a pimp and some prostitutes would be called *ergastērion*, and everyone would understand it as a euphemism for a brothel. In [Dem.] 59.67 Epainetos employs this term for a private residence, where he alleges that prostitution was practiced (see also Artemid. *Onir.* 1.78, 4.9; Ath. 5.220e).

kasaurion (alternative forms: *kasaureion* [Poll. 6.188], *kassaurion* [Hsch. k 2], *kasalbion* [Sch. Ar. *Eq.* 1285]: This term is found in Photios (s.v.) and the scholiast of Aristophanes (*Eq.* 1285). Like the corresponding nouns (*kasalbas*), the lack of a commonly accepted lexicographic form, as well as their frequent occurrence in the lexica but absence from high literature, suggests that these were colloquial terms in frequent use.

kasōrion (alternative form *kasōreion* [Hsch. k 1002]): This word is attested by Herodian (366.11) and Artemidoros (*Onir.* 1.78).

kēlōston: the abortion place. This intriguing term seems to be a creation of Lycophron (1387) based on the assumption that abortion was common in brothels (*FLG* 135; cf. Eust. *Com. Il.* 1.111; Sch. Lycoph. 1385; on abortion in ancient brothels, see Kapparis 2002, 107–13). This meaning of *kēloō*, although uncommon, is confirmed independently by other sources (*LSJ* s.v.).

kinēterion: Davidson believes that Eupolis used this term for brothel and translates it as "fuckery" (40 Eupolis 99.27 *PCG*; J. Davidson 1997, 84 and n. 38). However, this is far from certain; the term as it appears in *PCG* is a reconstruction.

koineion: common place. Herodian first makes this word synonymous with *porneion* (3.2.536). It is also attested in later lexicographers (Hsch. k 3254; Phot. s.v.; Suda k 2552; Ps. Zonaras s.v.; Lex. seg. k 280) without explanation.

matruleion (also *mastruleion* [Phot. s.v.], *mastrulleion* [Ps. Zonaras s.v.]): This word appears in Ps. Zonaras (s.v.). The connection with the stem *mater-* (mother) is clear. Harpocration says that this term applied to a brothel with older women who would allow the guests to get drunk. This note, repeated in several Byzantine lexica, suggests a low-class brothel/inn that provided alcoholic beverages and sex. In use from the fourth century BCE (Dinarchus fr. 48.5 Conomis; Men. *Epit.* 692), the term was widespread then and later.

oikēma: building. Like *ergastērion* this generic euphemism for brothel was current from the classical period forward (Aeschin. 1.74, 123; Lys. fr. 326 Tur.); Hesychius believed that this usage was normal in Attic authors (o 246). It was quite common in later Greek too (Apoll. *Vita Aeschinis* 9; Poll. 7.201, 9.45; Dio. Cass. 60.31.1, 79.13.3; Origen *Homiliae in Ezechielem* 396.26).

porneion: This is the primary term for brothel in use from the classical period (Antiphon 1.14; Ar. *Vesp.* 1283; Aeschin. 1.124) down to the late Byzantine era (Zonaras *Epit.* 2.34.30, 3.117.28) and into modern times. It was colloquial enough to be used in Old Comedy (Ar. *Ran.* 113; Xenarchos fr. 4.4 *PCG*) and sufficiently proper to be used forensically (Aeschin. 1.124) and in serious literature (e.g., Callisthenes 124 F 5 *FGrH*; Jos. *AJ* 19.357; John Chrysostom *Adv. Judaeos* 48.847 al.).

pornoboskeion: A rare term found only in Byzantine scholars (e.g., Sch. Ar. *Vesp.* 1353) but conceivably originating earlier (cf. *pornoboskos* above).

stegos: See *stegitis* under the list of terms for female prostitution.

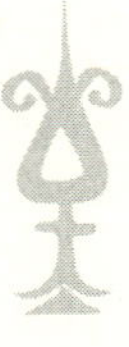

Conclusion

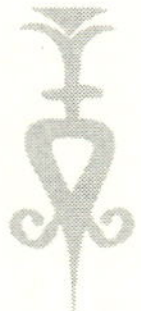

Greek Brothels and More

THOMAS A. J. MCGINN

This book, which traces its origins to a panel organized at the annual meetings of the Archaeological Institute of America, presents a number of new developments welcome not only to students of ancient Greek women, sexuality, and material culture but also to those who investigate these phenomena as they are manifested at other times and places.[1] Its salient issues are: What can we know of the origins of Greek prostitution? How are we to understand the categories of *hetaira* and *pornē*? To what degree did the Greek prostitute endure exploitation or enjoy a certain autonomy? Were Greek prostitutes marginalized and, if so, what does this mean? Underlying these issues is the problem of defining "prostitute" and "prostitution." Other matters of import include brothels. How are they identified and where are they located? Did the Greeks practice a form of moral zoning as has been famously argued for the Romans? Did they have other venues for prostitution such as cribs?

The ancient sources for prostitution, as with other matters related to sexuality, often present a stark and unappealing choice. We can either accept the evidence we have, which we have good reason to suspect is defective, or we can build a hypothesis less directly dependent on these sources, but whose plausibility might be questioned for that very reason.[2] In certain animated short films, a character is presented climbing out on the branch of a tree, then producing a saw to separate the branch from the tree; after the sawing is complete, the tree rather than the branch crashes to the ground. The sensation will not be unfamiliar to many historians of ancient prostitution.

In what follows, I highlight the various approaches taken to the questions I just raised, suggesting how the evidence and methods used by the authors can illuminate our understanding, without my being obliged to register agreement or disagreement on every possible point of interest. After illustrating some of the challenges that confront the student of ancient Greek prostitution by drawing on comparative evidence from Rome, I suggest how this volume can serve as the springboard for future research on this subject.

Madeleine M. Henry's paper, "The Traffic in Women: From Homer to Hipponax, from War to Commerce," views the early history of Greek prostitution as developing out of the practices of rape and sexual exploitation of women by men. The Homeric poems were foundational in this sense as well as others: they "provide a functional or performative definition of masculinity that entails male sex right over women." All mortal females in these works are vulnerable to the possibility of capture, rape, and sexual enslavement. This potential fate is almost taken for granted, embedded in the deep structure of patriarchy seen to operate here. Homer (a term of convenience for the tradition behind the poems) presents us with "a prestate version of the formation of the 'sexual contract,'" in which prostitution, as it is commonly conceived and defined, does not appear but is clearly prefigured.

Women are not just metaphorically objectified in the Homeric poems, for they are literally objects: "Woman is a prize or gift of honor, a *gĕras*." Honor accrues to the male protagonists through their accumulation of women, among other achievements. Homer both celebrates and questions this code of values, evincing an occasional glimmer of sympathy for women. There is not really a contradiction at work here if we compare sexual slavery with slavery conceived more broadly; occasional expressions of sympathy for the fate of individual slaves need not constitute a criticism of slavery itself. So it holds with certain key aspects of the status and role of women we may plausibly identify as belonging to the deep structure of patriarchy. It is fair to say that Homer's critique of heroic values centers on relations between men rather than on relations between men and women, a point thoroughly consistent with Henry's conclusions about the *Iliad*. Similar assumptions are at work in the *Odyssey*. Women are enslaved, dehumanized, and sexually exploited, as a matter of routine. With rare exceptions, "the sexual violence goes unexamined." Henry's focus on lower-status women in the poem departs from much previous scholarship concerned with goddesses and upper-class women.

"Prostitutional scenarios," if not prostitution itself, are attested in the fragmentary works of Archilochus and Hipponax. The evidence is sketchy, but, taken together with Herodotus's tale of Rhodopis and depictions on vases (the interpretation of which is neither easy nor straightforward), it suggests that by the end of the sixth century at the latest the Greeks knew prostitution (see also Hartmann 2002, 142–47). This makes possible, though of course it cannot guarantee, the historicity of Solon's "municipal brothel."[3] One can certainly say that, true or not, the story says something very important about the relationship between Athenian democracy and women's status, and that the news is not good.

Allison Glazebrook makes a distinct contribution to our understanding of the material remains of the brothel in "*Porneion*: Prostitution in Athenian Civic Space." Here we run directly into the thorny problem of brothel identification. The evidence of literature and vases, though tantalizing, is in the end not all that helpful, apart from providing some indications perhaps of temporary, mobile, or even what might be described as domestic brothels. As in other cultures, notably the Roman, there does not appear to have been a brothel building type, making them difficult to identify in the archaeological evidence as well (cf. Aeschines 1.124). The three criteria offered by Andrew Wallace-Hadrill for identifying brothels in ancient Pompeii (1995, 52), briefly, design (masonry beds), erotic art, and relevant graffiti, are not much help even in that context and less so for other Roman cities, such as Rome itself and Ostia.[4] The same appears to hold for ancient Athens on the evidence presented by Glazebrook.

Glazebrook offers the most comprehensive account to date of possible Athenian brothels (cf. J. Davidson 2006, 36). The foremost candidate is the famous Building Z in the Kerameikos, just inside the city wall. While many scholars believe that this was a brothel in its third iteration, the late fourth century Z3, when it offered fairly extensive drinking and dining facilities, in addition to lodgings, it may also have furnished prostitutional services during the building's first two phases dating to the fifth century (Ault 2005, 149–50).[5] Absolute certainty is impossible, but there is a strong possibility that in at least one of its first three phases Building Z was a brothel of the inn- or lodging-house type, one of the three categories identified for Roman brothels: the purpose-built brothel (of which the famous Pompeian Lupanar is the only known example), the tavern-brothel (with rooms upstairs and/or in back, some of which might be used for lodging), and the inn or lodging house (where food and drink also might be available) (McGinn, forthcoming).[6] The categories appear to suit the evidence for possible brothels at Athens, though problems of excavating, preserving, and reporting this evidence may impede assignment of specific examples with precision to one category or the other.

Glazebrook also finds possibilities in the neighboring Building Y, which in its second and third phases (roughly contemporaneous with Z3) evidently offered drinking and dining facilities but no lodgings, perhaps placing it under one of the subtypes of the second category. The availability of venal sex is suggested by an inscription that names a woman who may be a prostitute, Boubalion. She also suggests that a fourth-century structure near the modern Olympic equestrian center might have been a brothel; it appears to have offered lodging, on-site drinking, and a bathing facility. An inscription names a woman, Nannion, who may be a prostitute. A more obscure example, adduced in a note, has been located in the Piraeus. It should be stressed that the evidence for venal sex at all four of these establishments is scant, certainly by the standards of ancient Pompeii.[7]

Another venue for prostitution may have been cribs, that is, single rooms lying off a street or in back of a bar. None have been located at Athens, but Pompeii has as many as thirteen possible examples (McGinn 2004, 291–94). Importantly some literary uses of the word *oikēma* appear to refer to cribs, an idea put forward by James Davidson (1998, 90–91). Glazebrook makes two significant qualifications to his suggestion: she notes that *oikēma* might also refer to a brothel or, better, a booth within a brothel, such as we find, perhaps, in Z3, and she expresses skepticism that cribs were more pleasant for prostitutes than brothels.[8]

One piece of evidence not given for Roman brothels but found in large numbers in Z3 are loom weights (153 examples, according to Knigge 2005, 71). These and three large cisterns that were unearthed suggest the presence of a textile factory. Women textile workers are known from Athenian vases, and debate has long raged over whether the women shown there are prostitutes (e.g., Hartmann 2002, 250–51; McClure 2003a, 162, 221). The finds here support the thesis that they are likely to be prostitutes, in the sense that the evidence for weaving at Z3 supports the identification of weavers as prostitutes and vice versa without being probative, since the two categories did not completely overlap. Presumably, the women in Building Z3 wove textiles when they were not entertaining customers, which is consistent with the premise that the brothel inmates were slaves, ex-slaves, or lived in slavelike conditions, giving their owners a motive to make as productive use of their time as possible (see E. E. Cohen 2006, 104).[9] It is likely that these brothel prostitutes were highly exploited, as Glazebrook cogently argues. If true for Z3, this does not mean that all prostitutes were weavers or all weavers were prostitutes. Less obvious is that loom weights in some contexts might help identify a brothel, a criterion that does not hold for every other culture with prostitution.[10]

Glazebrook significantly observes that some brothels were made to appear more pleasant to *clients*. We know or have good reason to believe from other cultures, such as Rome, that some brothels were evidently tricked out in a manner perhaps designed to appeal to members of the subelite who had the cash to enjoy a faux-elite atmosphere at least on a short-term basis. This might explain some of the upmarket appointments of Building Z3 and strengthen the argument for its identification as a brothel.[11] There is evidence that eating and drinking took place at the site; not only have fine ware and cookware been discovered but also some rooms have been identified as *andrōnes* or banqueting spaces. There are three mosaic floors and two courtyards, the larger of which is equipped with a fountain. The appointments for Building Y appear to be even more upmarket, which does not necessarily mean the clientele was elite.

Glazebrook also develops the thesis that Athens had no moral zoning, that is, no official policy segregating brothels away from or into certain areas of the city. The scarcity of archaeological evidence for brothels makes certainty impossible, but there is simply no evidence to support the existence of an official policy of this kind, despite the efforts of some scholars to turn the Kerameikos, for example, into a "red-light district."[12] Such zoning is incongruent with what we know of pre-Christian attitudes and practice in the configuration of urban space.

In "Bringing the Outside In: The *Andrōn* as Brothel and the Symposium's Civic Sexuality," Sean Corner focuses on what might be described as the ideology of domestic space by way of challenging the argument of Leslie Kurke (here I simplify if not oversimplify) that the fundamental division between the Athenian *hetaira* and *pornē* lay in their respective assignments to the private and public spheres. Corner posits that each is an element of the public realm; the importation of the *hetaira* into the household for symposia held in the male-centered space of the domestic *andrōn* represents an intrusion, as it brings the outside into the house. Social class also inflects his thesis, which identifies the *hetaira* as an upper-class phenomenon and the *pornē* as a lower-class one. At the same time, he argues, these "were not antithetical but parallel figures," the former like the latter a commodity.[13] Corner challenges the views of James Davidson and especially Kurke that the two were so very different. Corner further raises significant problems of categorization in the prospect of a brothel-in-an-*oikos*. If Glazebrook is right about the existence of temporary brothels there might be more to say about this aspect of the problem. Corner's argument supports the case that no moral zoning existed at Athens; if not probative of such, it is certainly suggestive. The evidence for Pompeian "sex clubs," I believe, supports some elements of Corner's thesis (about as much as comparative evidence can).

Clare Kelly Blazeby's "Woman + Wine = Prostitute in Classical Athens?" presents a view of the symposium as aristocratic and exclusive that contrasts with Corner's argument that it is at bottom a public institution that brings the city into the otherwise private house. Part of the contrast is contextual. Kelly Blazeby proposes to explain attitudes toward the tavern and women's role in it, especially as drinkers, and Corner is trying to elucidate usages regarding the symposium and women's role in it, especially as sexual partners. It is possible that the symposium was a more diverse institution than most authors seem to allow. Even so, it cannot have been all things to all Athenians, and scholars will be left to choose between one version and the other, if they do not develop theories of their own.

Kelly Blazeby argues that Athenian women were accustomed to drinking wine but were not necessarily prostitutes for this reason. The assertion is plausible, though difficult to prove with the available evidence. Kelly Blazeby is certain that the representations of women drinking on vases reflect reality, which, if true, does not tell us precisely what the nature of that reality was.[14] Were women drinkers on vases prostitutes, or was it possible to represent respectable women engaged in such an activity? One might attempt to distinguish between depictions of women drinkers with and without clothes, but there are no guarantees even here of a neat resolution of the problem.[15] In my view, Kelly Blazeby's general argument that prostitutes were not the only drinkers among Athenian women is best supported by the evidence of Aristophanes, above all in the passages of the *Thesmophoriazusae* she discusses. Nonetheless the picture they draw is hardly favorable, which suggests that drinking by Athenian women was so strongly disparaged that, as a matter of representation, wine plus woman all too often did equal "nonrespectable" woman.[16]

For Helene A. Coccagna in "Embodying Sympotic Pleasure: A Visual Pun on the Body of an *Aulētris*," the iconography of prostitutes on Attic vases does not admit much doubt. While no single element guarantees such an identification, "it is generally agreed that a combination of factors such as nudity, *auloi*, and a sympotic context makes the identification as a prostitute here secure."[17] Her main subject is a late sixth-century red-figure cup attributed to Oltos depicting a woman copulating with an amphora. Both the woman and the amphora (standing in for its contents) are objects of consumption. Unsurprisingly, the symposium objectifies women but with the twist that the sexual polarities so dear to Foucauldians are reversed, or at least muddled. Coccagna reads the vase not as suggesting that all women are prostitutes but rather as implying that prostitutes represent all women in their unsated and insatiable sexual appetite. Another possibility she raises, albeit very indirectly, is whether the Oltos cup also objectified men. If so, this would be a rather subversive gesture, a critique of the male as the ideal sexual partner for women.[18] Though difficult, the idea is not easily discarded.

Nancy Sorkin Rabinowitz's case study, "Sex for Sale? Interpreting Erotica in the Havana Collection," also tackles the problem of identifying the status of women, including naked women, on Athenian vases. Her approach is marked by caution, as "vase painting is not primarily naturalistic in technique" but rather is ruled by conventions informed by various technical and aesthetic considerations. "As with any art form, there is considerable room for interpretation of what it is that we are seeing," and thus the danger arises of permitting modern concerns and assumptions to determine our understanding of the evidence. What is more, we almost always experience these vases either in a modern publication, such as a catalogue, or in a museum collection, which can further distort their interpretation.

What do we make of a depiction on a pot of a man offering a gift, such as a bag of what is presumably money, to a woman? What does it tell us about the status of the woman? Is she respectable or not, and if not, what kind of nonrespectable woman is she? A lowly brothel prostitute or a romanticized (by the painter or the viewer) *hetaira*, if indeed we can agree on what a *hetaira* was? Perhaps we moderns import more certainty or ambiguity into our own understanding than there might have been in antiquity. For example, do Building Z's loom weights speak for or against a confusion of wives and prostitutes in representations of women and looms on vases?

Rabinowitz's open-ended approach raises more questions than it answers. I share her skepticism over the degree of utility afforded by the Etruscan findspots of many Athenian vases in determining the status of women depicted on them. She concludes with others that the women having sex on one side of a well-known double-sided cup from the Louvre are indeed prostitutes and that they cast a similar light on the respectable-looking woman holding a lyre on the other side. Where such corroborating evidence is absent, however, she wants to leave open the possibility that activities we would regard as innocent in our culture are depicted as such by the Athenian vase painters. Apart from some exceptions that are relatively easy to recognize, are respectable women typically shown as playing the flute on vases?[19] To what extent does the fact of representation mark out an otherwise blameless activity as something transgressive and so signal the status of the woman depicted?[20]

We return to the challenging problem of brothel identification with T. Davina McClain's and Nicholas K. Rauh's "The Brothels at Delos: The Evidence for Prostitution in the Maritime World." The authors explicitly reject the relevance of the three criteria developed by Wallace-Hadrill for Pompeii, because, in their view, they are too closely linked to the highly unusual Purpose-Built Brothel to serve as a "universal template" for brothels elsewhere.[21] They then lay out the historical context that makes the presence of prostitution on Delos likely in the period after the Third Macedonian War. The establishment of a major center for trade in luxury goods and slaves attracted prosperous merchants from Italy as well as the Near East. Most frequented the island exclusively during the summer sailing season. Accordingly, the sale of sex tended to be seasonal, which, the authors argue, militates against the development of brothels on the Wallace-Hadrill template.

McClain and Rauh find alternative criteria for brothel identification in representations of phalli and the clubs of Heracles. They argue that the former might signify more than just an apotropaic device and even that at times they do not serve this purpose at all. Instead the phalli sometimes point the way toward brothels, in their view, just as the clubs also signal their presence. They invoke one of the three criteria, that of design, as I have recast it, arguing that a series of small cubicles lying off a common corridor might indicate a brothel, without insisting, as Wallace-Hadrill does, on the presence of a masonry bed.[22] They posit seven possible brothels in the areas to the north and south of the Sacred Lake, a clustering that, if these were indeed brothels, probably reflects a series of attempts to develop commercial opportunities rather than to effect "moral zoning." Once we depart the confines of the Purpose-Built Brothel at Pompeii, we must learn to be comfortable with possibility rather than certainty in the practice of identifying ancient brothels. A port city like Delos surely had prostitution, and at least some of this must have been organized in the form of brothels. One notes the absurd difficulties of identifying brothels in the port city of Ostia as an analogy to what we encounter on Delos and can reasonably expect to find elsewhere (McGinn 2004, 226–31).

Judith P. Hallett, in "Ballio's Brothel, Phoenicium's Letter, and the Literary Education of Greco-Roman Prostitutes: The Evidence of Plautus's *Pseudolus*," asserts, in the teeth of a trend that has claimed Plautus as evidence for Roman society, that we learn from his plays about Greek or, as she terms it, "Greco-Roman" prostitution.[23] Her examination of the intersection between gender and speech is of interest. Hallett shows how a moral evaluation drives Pseudolus's analysis of Phoenicium's rhetoric as expressed in her letter to Calidorus, a moral evaluation that is strongly influenced by considerations of gender. Hallett invokes the rhetorical practice of Cato the Censor, and its favorable reception by Favorinus and Gellius in the second century CE, to suggest how "a double standard for assessing men's and women's words evinces itself yet again."

In "Prostitutes, Pimps, and Political Conspiracies during the Late Roman Republic" Nicholas K. Rauh argues that allegations of participation by prostitutes and pimps in political conspiracies during this period were used to delegitimize the opposition to the senatorial aristocracy at Rome. He uses the modern analysis of "conspiracy theory" for this purpose. The role of prostitutes and pimps in such enterprises even in the late Roman Republic seems to have been fairly marginal. The marginality of prostitutes is confirmed—doubly confirmed, I would argue—if in a paradoxical manner. Without necessarily subscribing to a Roman version of modern conspiracy theory, we can accept that some members of the upper classes alleged an association with marginal types not only to undercut their opponents but also to define themselves as elite and their values as traditionally Roman.

Konstantinos K. Kapparis introduces us to source material of vital importance for understanding the degree of marginalization endured by ancient Greek prostitutes with his "The Terminology of Prostitution in the Ancient Greek World."[24] His extensive treatment examines the lexicon as it appears from the archaic period down to late antiquity. The extent to which antiprostitution invective amounts to insults against prostitutes is striking: the vast majority of terms are precisely devoted to attacks on prostitutes, especially females. The emphasis of the abusive language directed at male prostitutes falls on ideas of masculinity and gender stereotypes, (and their violation). With women we find some terminology suggesting male qualities but also a number of terms directed at behavior—or rather at a character—deemed depraved, rapacious, and predatory and further associated openly or by implication with animals, effectively dehumanizing the prostitute. It is as if both female and male prostitutes are thought to inflict upon themselves a category mistake, with this difference: the male prostitute is, in general, blamed for a category error of gender, the female prostitute for a category mistake of species. Kapparis himself takes a different view, but I would note that a higher degree of marginalization of female prostitutes is consistent with the more intense level of exploitation he sees imposed upon them. One would like to see Kapparis's valuable collection of terms relevant to the study of ancient Greek prostitution realize its full potential in future by being fleshed out, equipped with a full set of indices (including a source index) and published as a freestanding reference work. Its potential as a resource for future study is very great indeed.

How does *Greek Prostitutes in the Ancient Mediterranean* advance our understanding of ancient Greek prostitution? The origins of Greek prostitution are located in a context of extreme exploitation, one of sexual slavery and rape. As a collection, the essays mute the contrast between *hetaira* and *pornē*, partly owing to their overall emphasis on brothels, which means that the focus falls more exclusively on the latter. In addition, Corner's argument that the distinction between *hetaira* and *pornē* was less important than is sometimes thought, plus the repeated assertions that representations of female drinkers, naked women, and so forth are or *could be* respectable women, helps to fade the *hetaira* from view. Not that the presence of the *hetaira* in such contexts would necessarily spell less marginalization for her.[25] Coccagna's essay suggests that women were objectified in a highly degrading manner. Kapparis's contribution reinforces the general trend, serving as a powerful closing complement to Henry's opening essay. As a result, the degree of exploitation and marginalization endured by ancient Greek prostitutes emerges as pronounced.

Thanks to the work of these authors, we now understand better the paradoxical nature of the Athenian prostitute's marginalization. The absence of a policy of moral zoning meant that prostitution was found throughout the ancient city and was far from invisible. It was not per se illegal, though some legal constraints were placed upon it (see, for example, E. E. Cohen 2000b). Prostitution was legitimized through being taxed by the state, and customers might be obligated at law to pay their fees.[26] Given the existence of the tax, the state perhaps had an interest in seeing the prostitute's fee paid; both the tax and the obligation to pay the fee are consistent with a high degree of exploitation.[27] A classic contrast emerges between the centrality of prostitution as a cash-rich business profitable to those in a position to exploit it, whose ideological importance is suggested, for example, by the story of Solon's brothel (regardless of whether this tale is literally true), and the degradation, marginalization, and sheer exploitation endured by prostitutes themselves.[28]

Some promising results concern brothels: there are as many as four possible examples in the archaeological record for classical Athens, with more possibilities on Hellenistic Delos. The criteria used for identifying these brothels, in important ways different from those put forward for ancient Pompeii, are more thoroughly elaborated here than before. Certainty remains elusive, but it is clear that this is something we are going to have to learn to live with. To be sure, some of those identifications are more certain, even much more certain, than others. While they are not now attested in the material evidence, a more nuanced case emerges for the existence of cribs in ancient Athens. A similar point holds for the argument made here against moral zoning in ancient Athens. Proof of this is lacking and will probably never be forthcoming in any definitive sense. But the burden has shifted to those who would argue that the number and location of brothels, cribs, and other venues for prostitution were determined by the state. Prostitution was a highly visible and widespread enterprise, not far to seek in ancient Athens, at any rate.

Also of interest is the sympotic context in which a good deal of ancient Greek prostitution flourished. This is visible not only in the appointments of some of the brothels discussed by Glazebrook but in the dynamics of the symposia examined by Corner and Kelly Blazeby. It is a theme that runs rife throughout the various and varying treatments of representations of women on vases, not just that by Kelly Blazeby but those by Coccagna and Rabinowitz as well. This association too finds a certain resonance in the Roman evidence, not just in the fact of the tavern-brothel, the most common type found, at least at Pompeii, but also in the atmospherics of the other two types, which seem to have routinely offered clients an opportunity to drink as well. This is not at all surprising in the context of the lodging house or inn, but it is more remarkable in the case of the Purpose-Built Brothel, which sported more than one dining and drinking facility upstairs (McGinn, forthcoming).

More remains to be said, without doubt. This collection highlights a need for greater sustained engagement with the *hetaira*-controversy. What, in particular, are the implications of the *hetaira* for the picture rendered here of the prostitute as socially marginal? What conclusions can we draw about the status of women depicted on Athenian vases? These issues are separate but related; one hopes in any case for the emergence of a scholarly consensus for both problems, however remote this possibility may now seem. What more can be said about part-time, casual, and seasonal prostitution (see E. E. Cohen 2006, 119)? What does the evidence for venal sex tell us about the institution of marriage (see C. Patterson 1994; Hartmann 2002; Glazebrook 2005b, 38)? Surely there is more to say on the subject of the honor/shame syndrome raised by Henry.[29] Finally, what overall conclusions can we draw from the practice of prostitution about the nature of patriarchy in ancient Greece?

One caution might be registered as we look forward to further developments in our understanding of ancient Greek prostitution. There has been for some time a tension in the scholarship between believers and skeptics regarding the value of the evidence, though in recent years the pendulum appears to have swung more decisively in favor of the latter, who verge at times on hyper-skepticism, in my opinion. The uncertainties are great and cannot be ignored. All the same, there is room for hope that we can do a better job in the future of steering a safe course between the Scylla of underestimating and the Charybdis of overestimating the presence of venal sex in the ancient Greek city.

NOTES

1. The panel, under the title "The Hellenic Brothel as Space, Place, and Idea," was organized by the editors of this volume and held in January 2007 in San Diego. I was honored to be the respondent to the papers presented on that occasion.

2. See McGinn 1998a for a discussion of this problem in the context of the evidence for Caligula's brothel on the Palatine.

3. There are at least three possibilities: (a) the brothel is an utter invention; (b) Solon did found it as the tradition suggests; (c) it is a later institution attributed to Solon. The third is worth consideration. See Halperin 1990, 99–102; and Hartmann 2002, 248–49. Vincent Rosivach (1995) and Frank Frost (2002) argue for the first.

4. To the "design criterion" I add a series of small rooms off a common corridor, an idea I borrow from Matteo Della Corte (McGinn 2004, 198–204).

5. Z3 dates from ca. 325/320 to ca. 307 BCE. Ursula Knigge (2005, 49, 78–79), identifies its function as a cloth production facility and inn, staffed in part by prostitutes. There were at least twenty-two rooms. Knigge further identifies Building Z in its first (ca. 430–ca. 420 BCE) and second (ca. 420/410–ca. 400 BCE) phases as an unusually large private residence (Knigge 2005, 6, 27, 28, 47–48).

6. Greek literary evidence supports the existence of one or more of these categories: Euctemon owned one *sunoikia*, evidently a brothel of the lodging-house type, in the Piraeus, and another in the Kerameikos, where wine was sold, a fact lent emphasis by the speaker, so

perhaps it was a tavern-brothel with lodgings (Isae. 6.19–21). Relying on the Latin tags to identify the archaeological remains of venues for the "hospitality industry" can be problematic (Ellis 2004). The same appears to hold for the Greek terminology as well, meaning words such as *sunoikia* and *katagōgion*; see McGinn 2006. Bradley Ault (2005, 144) discusses the difficulty of identifying examples in the material evidence.

7. Even the Pompeian evidence is rarely decisive in identifying a brothel and suggests possibilities rather than certainties (McGinn 2004).

8. A consensus does seem to be forming that male prostitution in classical Athens was largely a crib phenomenon (J. Davidson 1998, 90–91, 332; E. E. Cohen 2006, 119). Glazebrook expresses reservations.

9. The distinction between slave and free in such contexts was likely to have been less clear than one finds in law and literature in general. See Glazebrook 2006, 130. On the slave and/or alien status of the prostitutes in Z3, see J. Davidson 1998, 86–88; and Hartmann 2002, 251.

10. A silver amulet showing Aphrodite as the evening star was found at Building Z3 (Knigge 2005, 210). While this supports the identification as a brothel in this instance, it seems too unusual to qualify as a criterion to be applied in other cases.

11. As Glazebrook notes, citing James Davidson, some brothels tried to emulate a sympotic atmosphere. See also Ault 2005, 149.

12. Some literary evidence argues against the phenomenon of zoning: Aeschines (1.124) (cited by Glazebrook) as well as Xenophon (*Mem.* 2.2.4), who suggests that prostitution was widespread in classical Athens. Further, the implication that Stephanus operated a brothel in his *oikos* seems to rely on the idea that there was no identifiable Athenian "red-light district," in the Kerameikos or anywhere else ([Dem.] 59.41 [cf. 65] with C. Patterson 1994, 209; J. Davidson 1998, 112–13). "Red-light districts" were areas into which brothels and the practice of prostitution were zoned—so that they could be banned elsewhere—in various experiments with regulationism during the late nineteenth and early twentieth century in the United States. In other words, the term reflects the implementation of a practice of moral zoning. Another reason to avoid it, in my view, is that it tends to exaggerate the local profile of brothels. Even where we can be certain they were present, as in the Roman Subura, they were just one element in the urban mix of residential and commercial buildings (McGinn 2004, 21).

13. Support for this thesis is found in some of the literary evidence, above all, Apollodoros's general identification of prostitute with alien and slave ([Dem.] 59.110–15 [cf. Dem. 57.45] with C. Patterson 1994, 205; Glazebrook 2005a, 164, 166–69).

14. For the impasse in the scholarship on the status of women represented on Athenian vases, see J. Davidson 2006, 33. The work of Sian Lewis (2002; 2006) has been very influential here.

15. Not all naked women depicted on Athenian vases were *hetairai* (Lewis 2002, 102). But on naked women drinkers, see Venit 1998, 126–28; and Neils 2000, 204–5, 208–9, 212–13. For women depicted in sympotic contexts as *hetairai*, see also Hartmann 2002, 149–57; and A. Steiner 2007, 176, 206–10, 244, 293–94.

16. See also Xen. *Oec.* 9.11, which appears to allow for moderate consumption of wine by women, and Ath. 11.481c–d, which cites the comic poet Pherecrates lampooning women's—alleged—overfondness for wine.

17. On the low sexual and social status of female flute players, see McClure 2003a, 21–22; Glazebrook 2005b, 45; and J. Davidson 2006, 37–41. Sheramy Bundrick (2005, 92–99) finds some depictions on vases of evidently respectable women playing on *auloi*, but they seem exceptional and are not associated with sympotic contexts and/or nakedness (cf. 111–16). See also Neils 2000, 214–15, 225; and Sutton 2000, 191.

18. For more possible social satire on (archaic) Athenian vases, see Shapiro 2004, 9–10. For transgressive aspects of depictions on vases, see Osborne 1996, 68–69, 72; and A. Steiner 2007, 206–10, 244 (cf. Hartmann 2002, 156).

19. It might be easier to conclude that the depictions of women on vases do not necessarily reflect reality in a straightforward way but can stand in a degree of tension with that reality. The result is not inevitable that prostitution as a social phenomenon is exaggerated. One notes how citizen female prostitutes existed alongside the ideologically motivated pretense that they did not in fact exist: see Cohen 2000, 115, 126; McClure 2003a, 12, 25; Glazebrook 2005a, 163; and Glazebrook 2006, 138; cf. Brock 1994, 344.

20. The conundrum has been well put by Jessica Rabbit when she famously declared, "I'm not bad . . . I'm just drawn that way."

21. One problem with the criterion of "design" is that a series of small rooms (or "cubicles"), with or without masonry beds, might have served as quarters for slaves, not as a venue for prostitution (Ault 2005, 142; McGinn, forthcoming).

22. Other criteria they invoke in the notes include indications of "a consumption of water exceeding the requirements of an ordinary domicile" and location.

23. In fact, a number of scholars, including James Davidson (cited by Hallett), have argued (or assumed) in recent years that Plautus can be used as evidence for Greece: Cohen 2000, 129; Dalby 2002, 114–15; E. E. Cohen 2006, 109; see also the nuanced take of Scafuro 1997, 16–19, on law.

24. For more evidence of how language marginalizes Greek prostitutes, see the recent study of the Attic orators by Glazebrook 2005a and Glazebrook 2006. Cf. Miner 2003, 30.

25. Representations of *hetairai* (if that is the correct term) on vases can be marginalizing: see Neils 2000, 206, 222, 225; and Sutton 2000, 200.

26. See Aeschines 1.119 (tax) and 1.158 (fees) with E. E. Cohen 2000b, 131–32; and E. E. Cohen 2006, 99–100. The latter point is more tenuous than the former, on which see also Pollux (7.202, 9.29).

27. If the state claimed a share, this does not mean that all or even most prostitutes were able to retain the remainder for themselves: see McGinn 2004, 52–53.

28. For a different perspective on the exploitation inflicted on Athenian prostitutes, see E. E. Cohen 2006, 110–14. The evidence presented in this volume suggests that Athenian prostitutes are accurately described precisely as prostitutes and not as "sex workers." For the distinction, and its application to the Roman evidence, see McGinn 2004, 71–77.

29. There is an implicit challenge here to the skepticism recently expressed by William Harris (2005, 26–29) on this subject, that I, for one, would gladly see developed further.

References

Adams, J. N. 1982. *The Latin Sexual Vocabulary*. Baltimore, MD.

———. 1983. "Words for Prostitute in Latin." *Rheinisches Museum* 126:321–58.

Adam-Veleni, P. 1997. "Ballaneio Progenestero tis agoras Thessalonies." *To Archaeologiki ergo sti Makedonia kai Thraki* 11:351–64.

Anhalt, E. K. 1993. *Solon the Singer: Politics and Poetics*. Lanham, MD.

Arnott, W. G. 1996. *Alexis: The Fragments*. Cambridge, UK.

———, ed. and trans. 2000. *Menander*. Vol. 3. Cambridge, MA.

Arthur, M. B. 1983. "The Dream of a World without Women: Poetics and the Circles of Order in the *Theogony* Prooemium." *Arethusa* 16:97–116.

Ault, B. A. 2005. "Housing the Poor and Homeless in Ancient Greece." In *Ancient Greek Houses and Households: Chronological, Regional, and Social Diversity*, ed. B. A. Ault and L. C. Nevett, 140–59. Philadelphia.

Austin, M. 1993. "Alexander and the Macedonian Invasion of Asia: Aspects of the Historiography of War and Empire in Antiquity." In *War and Society in the Greek World*, ed. J. Rich and G. Shipley, 197–223. New York.

Azize, J., and I. Craigie. 2002. "Putative Akkadian Origins for the Greek Words *Kinaidos* and *Puge*." *Antichthon* 36:54–64.

Bakhtin, M. 1984. *Rabelais and His World*. Trans. H. Iswolsky. Bloomington, IN.

Balot, R. K. 2001. *Greed and Injustice in Classical Athens*. Princeton, NJ.

Barber, E. W. 1994. *Women's Work: The First 20,000 Years*. New York.

Barry, K. 1995. *The Prostitution of Sexuality*. New York.

Beard, M. 1991. "Adopting an Approach II." In *Looking at Greek Vases*, ed. T. Rasmussen and N. Spivey, 12–35. Cambridge, UK.

Beard, M., and J. Henderson. 1998. "With this Body I Thee Worship: Sacred Prostitution in Antiquity." In *Gender and the Body in the Ancient Mediterranean*, ed. M. Wyke, 56–79. Oxford.

Beazley, J. D. 1931. "Review of *Corpus Vasorum Antiquorum*, Athens (Greece 1) by K. A. Rhomaios and S. Papaspyridi (1930)." *Journal of Hellenic Studies* 51:121.

———. 1948. *Some Attic Vases in the Cyprus Museum*. London.

Bell, S. 1994. *Reading, Writing, and Rewriting the Prostitute Body*. Bloomington, IN.

Bellen, H., and H. Heinen, eds. 2001. *Fünfzig Jahre Forschungen zur antiken Sklaverei an der Mainzer Akademie 1950–2000: Miszellanea zum Jubiläum*. Forschungen zur antiken Sklaverei 35. Stuttgart.

Benjamin, W. 1972. "A Short History of Photography." *Screen* 13.1:5–26.

Benner, A. R., and F. H. Fobes, eds. and trans. 1949. *The Letters of Alciphron, Aelian and Philostratus*. Cambridge, MA.

Bennett, J. M. 1996. *Ale, Beer and Brewsters in England: Women's Work in a Changing World, 1300–1600*. Oxford.

Bérard, C. 1989. "The Order of Women." In *A City of Images: Iconography and Society in Ancient Greece*, ed. C. Bérard et al., trans. D. Lyons, 89–108. Princeton, NJ.

Bérard, C., et al., eds. 1989. *A City of Images: Iconography and Society in Ancient Greece*. Trans. D. Lyons. Princeton, NJ.

Bérard, C., C. Bron, and A. Pomari, eds. 1987. *Images et société en Grèce ancienne*. Lausanne.

Bergquist, B. 1990. "Sympotic Space: A Functional Aspect of Greek Dining Rooms." In *Sympotica: A Symposium on the Symposion*, ed. O. Murray, 37–65. Oxford.

Bers, V., trans. 2003. *Demosthenes, Speeches 50–59*. Austin, TX.

Bicknell, P. J. 1982. "Axiochus Alkibiadou, Aspasia and Aspasios." *Acta Classica* 51:240–50.

Birchall, C. 2006. *Knowledge Goes Pop: From Conspiracy Theory to Gossip*. New York.

Bloch, I. 1912. *Die Prostitution*. Berlin.

Blundell, S. 1995. *Women in Ancient Greece*. Cambridge, MA.

———. 2009. "After the Revolution: Reinterpreting Women on the Greek Pots in Havana." Paper delivered at the Institute for Classical Studies, London.

Boardman, J. 1994. "Settlement for Trade and Land in North Africa." In *The Archaeology of Greek Colonisation*, ed. G. R. Tsetskhladze and F. DeAngelis, 137–49. Oxford.

Bookidis, N. 1983. "The Priest's House in the Marmaria at Delphi." *Bulletin de correspondance hellénique* 107:149–55.

———. 1990. "Ritual Dining in the Sanctuary of Demeter and Kore at Corinth: Some Questions." In *Sympotica: A Symposium on the Symposion*, ed. O. Murray, 86–94. Oxford.

———. 1995. "Ritual Dining at Corinth." In *Greek Sanctuaries: New Approaches*, ed. N. Marinatos and R. Hägg, 45–61. London.

Bookidis, N., and J. E. Fisher. 1969. "Sanctuary of Demeter and Kore on Acrocorinth: Preliminary Report 3." *Hesperia* 38:297–310.

———. 1972. "Sanctuary of Demeter and Kore on Acrocorinth: Preliminary Report 4." *Hesperia* 41:283–331.

———. 1974. "Sanctuary of Demeter and Kore on Acrocorinth: Preliminary Report 5." *Hesperia* 43:267–307.

Bookidis, N., J. Hansen, L. Snyder, and P. Goldberg. 1999. "Dining in the Sanctuary of Demeter and Kore at Corinth." *Hesperia* 68:1–54.

Bookidis, N., and R. S. Stroud. 1997. *Sanctuary of Demeter and Kore: Topography and Architecture*. Corinth 18, pt. 3. Princeton, NJ.

Bothmer, D., von. 1990. Preface. In *Vasos griegos coleccion Condes de Lagunillas: Museo Nacional Palacio de Bellas Artes la Habana Cuba*, 6–7. Zurich.

Bowden, H. 1993. "Hoplites and Homer: Warfare, Hero Cult, and the Ideology of the Polis." In *War and Society in the Greek World*, ed. J. Rich and G. Shipley, 45–63. New York.

Breitenbach, H. 1908. *De genere quodam titulorum comoediae atticae*. Basel.

Brock, R. 1994. "The Labour of Women in Classical Athens." *Classical Quarterly* 44:336–46.

Broneer, O. 1954. *The South Stoa and Its Roman Successors*. Corinth 1, pt. 4. Princeton, NJ.

Brown, P. 2003. *Man Walks into a Pub: A Sociable History of Beer*. London.

Brown, P. G. McC. 1990. "Plots and Prostitutes in Greek New Comedy." *Papers of the Leeds International Latin Seminar* 6:241–66.

Brown, T. L. 2001. *Sex Slaves: The Trafficking of Women in Asia*. London.

Bruneau, P. 1964. "Apotropaia déliens: La massu d'Héraclès." *Bulletin de correspondance hellénique* 88:159–68.

———. 1968. "Contribution à l'histoire urbaine de Délos à l'époque hellénistique et à l'époque impériale." *Bulletin de correspondance hellénique* 92:658–709.

———. 1970. *Recherches sur les cultes de Délos à l'époque hellénistique et à l'époque impériale*. Paris.

———. 1978. "Deliaca II." *Bulletin de correspondance hellénique* 102:109–71.

———. 1979. "Deliaca III." *Bulletin de correspondance hellénique* 103:83–107.

———. 1995. "Deliaca X, no. 71: L'Agora des italiens était-elle un établissement de sport?" *Bulletin de correspondance hellénique* 119:45–54.

Brunt, P. A. 1971. *Italian Manpower, 225 B.C.–A.D. 14*. London.

Budin, S. L. 2003. *The Origin of Aphrodite*. Bethesda, MD.

———. 2006. "Sacred Prostitution in the First Person." In *Prostitutes and Courtesans in the Ancient World*, ed. C. A Faraone and L. K. McClure, 77–94. Madison, WI.

———. 2008. *The Myth of Sacred Prostitution in Antiquity*. Cambridge, UK.

Buitron-Oliver, D. 1995. *Douris: A Master-Painter of Athenian Red-figure Vases*. Mainz am Rhein, Ger.

Bundrick, S. D. 2005. *Music and Image in Classical Athens*. Cambridge, UK.

Burkert, W. 1979. *Structure and History in Greek Mythology and Ritual*. Berkeley, CA.

———. 1985. *Greek Religion*. Oxford.

———. 1991. "Oriental Symposia." In *Dining in a Classical Context*, ed. W. J. Slater, 7–24. Ann Arbor, MI.

———. 1996. *Creation of the Sacred: Tracks of Biology in Early Religions*. Cambridge, MA.

Burton, J. 1998. "Women's Commensality in the Ancient Greek World." *Greece and Rome* 45.2:143–65.

Cahill, N. 2002. *Household and City Organization at Olynthus*. New Haven, CT.

Cameron, A., and A. Kuhrt, eds. 1993. *Images of Women in Antiquity*. Detroit, MI.

Canby, V. 1978. Review of *Pretty Baby*. *New York Times*, April 5.

Cantarella, E. [1987] 2006. *Pandora's Daughters: The Role and Status of Women in Greek and Roman Antiquity*. Baltimore, MD.

Carey, C., ed. and trans. 1992. *Apollodoros against Neaira: (Demosthenes) 59*. Warminster, UK.

Carpenter, T. H. 1997. *Dionysian Imagery in Fifth-Century Athens*. Oxford.

Casadio, V. 1996. *I 'dubbi' di Archiloco*. Supplement to *Museum Criticum*. Pisa.

Chamonard, J. 1922. *Le quartier du théâtre: Etude sur l'habitation délienne à l'époque hellénistique*. Exploration archéologique de Délos 8. Paris.

Chancer, L. S. 1993. "Prostitution, Feminist Theory, and Ambivalence." *Social Text* 37: 143–71.

Chesler, P. 2005. *The Death of Feminism: What's Next in the Struggle for Women's Freedom.* New York.

Clarke, J. R. 1979. *Roman Black-and-White Figural Mosaics.* New York.

———. 1991. "The Decor of the House of Jupiter and Ganymede at Ostia Antica: Private Residence Turned Gay Hotel?" In *Roman Art in the Private Sphere: New Perspectives on the Architecture and Decor of the Domus, Villas, and Insula*, ed. E. K. Gazda, 89–104. Ann Arbor, MI.

———. 1998. *Looking at Lovemaking: Constructions of Sexuality in Roman Art, 100 BC–AD 250.* Berkeley, CA.

———. 2003. *Roman Sex: 100 BC–AD 250.* New York.

Clay, J. S. 1983. *The Wrath of Athena.* Princeton, NJ.

Cohen, B. 2000. *Not the Classical Ideal: Athens and the Construction of the Other in Greek Art.* Leiden.

Cohen, D. J. 1991. *Law, Sexuality, and Society: The Enforcement of Morals in Classical Athens.* Cambridge, UK.

———. 1996. "Seclusion, Separation, and the Status of Women in Classical Athens." In *Women in Antiquity*, ed. I. McAuslan and P. Walcott, 134–45. Oxford.

Cohen, E. E. 1997. *Athenian Economy and Society: A Banking Perspective.* Princeton, NJ.

———. 2000a. *The Athenian Nation.* Princeton, NJ.

———. 2000b. "'Whoring Under Contract': The Legal Context of Prostitution in Fourth-Century Athens." In *Law and Social Status in Classical Athens*, ed. V. Hunter and J. Edmondson, 113–48. Oxford.

———. [2004] 2006. "Free and Unfree Sexual Work: An Economic Analysis of Athenian Prostitution." In *Prostitutes and Courtesans in the Ancient World*, ed. C. A. Faraone and L. K. McClure, 93–124. Madison, WI.

Cole, S. G. 1984. "Greek Sanctions against Sexual Assault." *Classical Philology* 79.2:97–113.

Cooper, F., and S. Morris. 1990. "Dining in Round Buildings." In *Sympotica: A Symposium on the Symposion*, ed. by O. Murray, 66–85. Oxford.

Corbin, A. 1990. *Women for Hire: Prostitution and Sex in France after 1850.* Cambridge, MA.

Corner, S. 2005. "*Philos* and *Polites*: The Symposion and the Origins of the Polis." PhD diss., Princeton University.

———. Forthcoming. "Transcendent Drinking: The Symposium at Sea Reconsidered." *Classical Quarterly.*

Courtney, E. 1999. *Archaic Latin Prose.* Atlanta, GA.

Couve, L. 1895. "Fouilles de Délos." *Bulletin de Correspondance Hellénique* 19:460–516.

Cox, C. A. 1998. *Household Interests: Property, Marriage Strategies, and Family Dynamics in Ancient Athens.* Princeton, NJ.

Csapo, E. 1997. "Riding the Phallus for Dionysus: Iconology, Ritual, and Gender-Role De/Construction." *Phoenix* 51.3–4:253–95.

Dalby, A. 1993. "Food and Sexuality in Classical Greece." *Food, Culture and History* 1:165–90.

———. 2002. "Levels of Concealment: The Dress of *Hetairai* and *Pornai* in Greek Texts." In *Women's Dress in the Ancient Greek World*, ed. L. Llewellyn-Jones, 111–24. London.

Davidson, G. R. 1952. *The Minor Objects*. Corinth 12. Princeton, NJ.

Davidson, J. 1998. *Courtesans and Fishcakes: The Consuming Passions of Classical Athens*. London.

———. 2001. "Dover, Foucault and Greek Homosexuality: Penetration and the Truth of Sex." *Past and Present* 170:3–51.

———. 2004. "*Liaisons Dangereuses*: Aphrodite and the Hetaera." *Journal of Hellenic Studies* 124:169–73.

———. 2006. "Making a Spectacle of Her(self): The Greek Courtesan and the Art of the Present." In *The Courtesan's Arts: Cross-Cultural Perspectives*, ed. M. Feldman and B. Gordon, 29–51. Oxford.

———. 2007. *The Greeks and Greek Love: A Bold New Exploration of the Ancient World*. New York.

DeFelice, J. 2001. *Roman Hospitality: The Professional Women of Pompeii*. Warren Center, PA.

Degani, E. 1984. *Studi su Ipponatte*. Bari.

Delacoste, F., and P. Alexander, eds. 1987. *Sex Work: Writings by Women in the Sex Industry*. Pittsburgh, PA.

Della Giusta, M., M. L. Di Tommaso, and S. Strøm. 2008. *Sex Markets: A Denied Industry*. New York.

Delorme, J. 1960. *Gymnasion: Étude sur les monuments consacrés à l'éducation en Grèce*. Paris.

Delphy, C. 1984. *Close to Home: A Materialist Analysis of Women's Oppression*. Trans. D. Leonard. London.

Deonna, W. 1938. *Le mobilier délien*. Paris.

De Souza, P. 2000. *Piracy in the Graeco-Roman World*. Cambridge, UK.

Detienne, M. 1977. *The Gardens of Adonis: Spices in Greek Mythology*. Trans. J. Lloyd. Atlantic Highlands, NJ.

Dillon, M. 1999. "Post-Nuptial Sacrifices on Kos (Segre, ED 178) and Ancient Greek Marriage Rites." *Zeitschrift für Papyrologie und Epigraphik* 124:63–80.

Dimakis, P. 1988. "Orateurs et Hetaïres dans l'Athènes Classiques." In *Éros et droit en Grèce classique*, ed. P. Dimakis, 43–54. Paris.

Donlan, W. 1985a. "*Philos Pistos Hetairos*." In *Theognis of Megara: Poetry and the Polis*, ed. T. J. Figueira and G. Nagy, 223–44. Baltimore, MD.

———. 1985b. "The Social Groups of Dark Age Greece." *Classical Philology* 80:293–308.

———. 1989. "The Pre-State Community in Greece." *Symbolae Osloenses* 64:5–29.

Douglas, M., ed. 1987. *Constructive Drinking: Perspectives on Drink from Anthropology*. Cambridge, UK.

Dover, K. J. 1978. *Greek Homosexuality*. London.

Downer, L. 2001. *Women of the Pleasure Quarters: The Secret History of the Geisha*. New York.

DuBois, P. 1988. *Sowing the Body: Psychoanalysis and Ancient Representations of Women*. Chicago.

Duchêne, H. 1992. *La stèle du port: Fouilles du port 1: Recherches sur une nouvelle inscription Thasienne*. Athens.

Duchêne, H., and S. Girerd. [1998] 2001. *Delos: A Database of Archaeological Images* (U.S. version). Trans. N. K. Rauh, R. F. Townsend, and J. C. Bednar. New York.

Dué, C. 2002. *Homeric Variations on a Lament by Briseis*. Lanham, MD.

Dunbabin, K. M. D. 1991. "Triclinium and Stibadium." In *Dining in a Classical Context*, ed. W. J. Slater, 121–48. Ann Arbor, MI.

———. 1998. "*Ut Graeco More Biberetur*: Greeks and Romans on the Dining Couch." In *Meals in a Social Context: Aspects of the Communal Meal in the Hellenistic and Roman World*, ed. I. Nielsen and H. S. Nielsen, 81–101. Denmark.

Dupont, F. 1977. *Le plaisir et la loi*. Paris.

Ellis, S. J. R. 2004. "The Distribution of Bars at Pompeii: Archaeological, Spatial, and Viewshed Analyses." *Journal of Roman Archaeology* 17:371–384.

Empereur, J.-Y. 1982. "Les anses d'amphores timbrées et les amphores: Aspects quantitatifs." *Bulletin de correspondance hellénique* 106:219–33.

———. 1983. "Travaux de l'École française à Délos, 1982: Une cour remplie d'amphores à l'est du Lac sacré." *Bulletin de correspondance hellénique* 107:882–86.

Evans, J. 1991. *War, Women, and Children in Ancient Rome*. New York.

Evelyn-White, H. G. 1920. *Hesiod, the Homeric Hymns and Homerica*. London.

Fagles, R. trans. 1996. *Odyssey*. New York.

Fantham, E. 1975. "Sex, Status, and Survival in Hellenistic Athens: A Study of Women in New Comedy." *Phoenix* 29:44–74.

Fantham, E., H. P. Foley, N. B. Kampen, S. B. Pomeroy, and H. A. Shapiro, eds. 1994. *Women in the Classical World*. Oxford.

Faraone, C. A. 1992. *Talismans and Trojan Horses: Guardian Statues in Ancient Greek Myth and Ritual*. New York.

———. 2005. "Priestess and Courtesan: The Ambivalence of Female Leadership in Aristophanes' *Lysistrata*." In *Prostitutes and Courtesans in the Ancient World*, ed. C. A. Faraone and L. K. McClure, 125–38. Madison: WI.

———. 2006. "The Masculine Arts of the Ancient Greek Courtesan." In *The Courtesan's Arts: Cross-Cultural Perspectives*, ed. M. Feldman and B. Gordon, 209–20. Oxford.

Faraone, C. A., and L. K. McClure, eds. 2006. *Prostitutes and Courtesans in the Ancient World*. Madison, WI.

Farley, M. 2007. *Prostitution and Trafficking in Nevada: Making the Connections*. San Francisco.

Favory, F. 1978. "Classes dangereuses et crise de l'État dans le discours cicéronien d'après les écrits de Cicéron de 57 à 52 av. J.-C." In *Texte, politique, idéologie Cicéron: Pour une analyse du système esclavagiste, le fonctionnement du texte cicéronien, 1978–79*, 109–223. Paris.

Ferrari, G. 1986. "Money-bags?" *American Journal of Archaeology* 90:218.

———. 2002. *Figures of Speech: Men and Maidens in Ancient Greece*. Chicago.

Finley, M. I. 1982. "Was Greek Civilization Based on Slave Labor?" In *Economy and Society in Ancient Greece*, ed. B. Shaw and R. Saller. New York.

Fisher, N. R. E. 1988. "Greek Associations, Symposia, and Clubs." In *Civilization of the Ancient Mediterranean: Greece and Rome*, ed. M. Grant and R. Kitzinger, 2:1167–97. New York.

———. 1992. *Hybris: A Study in the Values of Honour and Shame in Ancient Greece*. Warminster, UK.

———. 1999. "Workshops of Villains: Was There Much Organized Crime in Classical Athens?" In *Organised Crime in Antiquity*, ed. K. Hopwood, 53–96. London.

———. 2001. *Aeschines against Timarchos*. Oxford.

Flaubert, G. [1869] 1964. *Sentimental Education*. Trans. R. Baldick. New York.

Foley, H. P. 1984. "'Reverse Similes' and Sex Roles in the *Odyssey*." In *Women in the Ancient World: The Arethusa Papers*, ed. J. Peradotto and J. P. Sullivan, 59–78. Albany, NY.

Foucault, M. 1990. *The Use of Pleasure*. Vol. 2 of *The History of Sexuality*. Trans. R. Hurley. New York.

Foxhall, L. 1989. "Household, Gender and Property in Classical Athens." *Classical Quarterly* 39:22–44.

Frances, R. 2007. *Selling Sex: A Hidden History of Prostitution*. Sydney.

Fraser, N. 1993. "Beyond the Master-Subject Model." *Social Text* 37:173–85.

Friedrich, E. [1924] 1987. *War against War!* Seattle, WA.

Froehner, W. 1876. *Anatomie des vases antiques*. Paris.

Frontisi-Ducroux, F., and J.-P. Vernant. 1997. *Dans l'oeil du miroir*. Paris.

Frost, F. 2002. "Solon *Pornoboskos* and Aphrodite Pandemos." *Syllecta Classica* 13:34–46.

Fulkerson, L. 2002. "Epic Ways of Killing a Woman: Gender and Transgression in *Odyssey* 22.465–72." *Classical Journal* 97:4:335–50.

Gaca, K. 2007. "The Methods and Magnitude of Female Sexual Subjugation through Ancient Warfare." Paper delivered at the American Philological Association annual meeting, San Diego.

Gager, J. G. 1992. *Curse Tablets and Binding Spells from the Ancient World*. Oxford.

Gallet de Santerre, H. 1959. *La Terrasse des lions, le Létoon, et le Monument de granit à Délos*. Exploration archéologique de Délos 24. Paris.

García Márquez, G. [2004] 2005. *Memories of My Melancholy Whores*. Trans. E. Grossman. New York.

Garland, R. 1987. *The Piraeus*. Ithaca, NY.

———. 1991. "Juvenile Delinquency in the Graeco-Roman World." *History Today* 41:12–19.

Gates, H. L., Jr. 2001. "Literary Theory and the Black Tradition." In *Reception Study: From Literary Theory to Cultural Studies*, ed. J. J. Machor and P. Goldstein, 105–16. New York.

Gerber, D. 1976. "Archilochus, Fr. 42 West." *Quaderni urbinati di cultura classica* 22:7–14.

Gercke, P. 1981. *Funde aus der Antike: Sammlung Paul Dierichs*. Kassel, Ger.

Giammarco, R. 1982. "I Galli di Cibele nel culto di età ellenistica." *Miscellanea greca e romana* 8:227–66.

Gilfoyle, T. J. 1994. *City of Eros: New York City, Prostitution, and the Commercialization of Sex, 1790–1920*. New York.

———. 1999. "Prostitutes in History: From Parables of Pornography to Metaphors of Modernity." *American Historical Review* 104:117–41.

Glazebrook, A. 2001. "The Use and Abuse of *Hetairai*: Female Characterization in Greek Oratory." PhD diss., SUNY, Buffalo.

———. 2005a. "The Making of a Prostitute: Apollodoros's Portrait of Neaira." *Arethusa* 38: 161–87.

———. 2005b. "Prostituting Female Kin." *Dike* 8:34–53.

———. 2005c. "Reading Women: Book Rolls on Attic Vases." *Mouseion* 3.5:1–46.

———. 2006. "The Bad Girls of Athens: The Image and Function of *Hetairai* in Judicial Oratory." In *Prostitutes and Courtesans in the Ancient World*, ed. C. A. Faraone and L. K. McClure, 125–38. Madison, WI.

———. Forthcoming. "Prostitution." In *A Cultural History of Sexuality*, vol. 1, *A Cultural History of Sexuality in the Classical World*, ed. M. Golden and P. Toohey. Oxford.

Goldman, H. 1942. "The Origin of the Greek Herm." *American Journal of Archaeology* 46.1: 58–68.

Gomme, A. W. 1925. "The Position of Women in Athens in the Fifth and Fourth Centuries." *Classical Philology* 20:1–25.

Gomme, A. W., and F. H. Sandbach. 1973. *Menander: A Commentary*. Oxford.

Grace, V. R., and M. Savvatianou-Pétropoulakou. 1970. "Les timbres amphoriques grecs." In *L'îlot de la Maison des comédiens*, Exploration archéologique de Délos 27, ed. P. Bruneau et al., 277–382. Paris.

Graham, A. J. 1998. "The Woman at the Window: Observations on the 'Stele from the Harbour' of Thasos." *Journal of Hellenic Studies* 118:22–40.

Graham, J. W. 1974. "Houses of Classical Athens." *Phoenix* 28:45–54.

Gray, D. R. 2003. "Storyville." Paper delivered at the Archaeological Institute of America Association annual meeting, New Orleans.

Gruen, E. S. 1974. *The Last Generation of the Roman Republic*. Berkeley, CA.

Gulick, C. B., trans. 1959. *The Deipnosophists*, by Athenaeus. Vol. 6. Cambridge, MA.

Hahn, I. 1975. "Der Klassenkampf der Plebs urbana in den letzten Jahrzehnten der römischen Republik." In *Die Rolle der Volksmassen in der Geschichte der vorkapitalistischen Gesellschaftsformationen*, ed. J. Hermann and I. Sellnow, 121–46. Berlin.

Hallett J. P. 1989/1990. "Female Homoeroticism and the Denial of Roman Reality in Latin Literature." *Yale Journal of Criticism* 3.1:209–27.

———. 1996. "The Political Backdrop of Plautus' *Casina*." In *Transitions to Empire: Essays in Greco-Roman History, 360–146 B.C., in Honor of E. Badian*, ed. R. W. Wallace and E. M. Harris, 409–38. Norman, OK.

———. 2006. "Gender, Class and Roman Rhetoric: Assessing the Writing of Plautus' *Phoenicium* (*Pseudolus* 41–73)." *Advances in the History of Rhetoric* 9:32–54.

Halperin, D. M. 1989. "The Democratic Body: Prostitution and Citizenship in Classical Athens." In *One Hundred Years of Homosexuality, and Other Essays on Greek Love*, ed. D. Halperin, 88–112. New York.

Halperin, D., J. J. Winkler, and F. Zeitlin. 1990. *Before Sexuality: The Construction of Erotic Experience in the Ancient Greek World*. Princeton, NJ.

Hamel, D. [2002] 2003. *Trying Neaira: The True Story of a Courtesan's Scandalous Life in Ancient Greece*. New Haven, CT.

Hammer, D. 2004. "Ideology, the Symposium, and Archaic Politics." *American Journal of Philology* 125:479–512.

Hansen, M. H. 1976. "The Theoric Fund and the *Graphe Paranomon* against Apollodorus." *Greek, Roman and Byzantine Studies* 17:235–46.

———. [1991] 1999. *The Athenian Democracy in the Age of Demosthenes*. Norman, OK.

———. 1993. "Introduction: The *Polis* as a Citizen-State." In *The Ancient Greek City-State: Symposium on the Occasion of the 250th Anniversary of the Royal Danish Academy of Sciences and Letters*, ed. M. H. Hansen, 7–29. Copenhagen.

Hanson, A. E. 1990. "The Medical Writer's Woman." In *Before Sexuality: The Construction of Erotic Experience in the Ancient Greek World*, ed. D. Halperin, J. J. Winkler, and F. Zeitlin, 309–38. Princeton, NJ.

Harris, W. V. 2005. "The Mediterranean and Ancient History." In *Rethinking the Mediterranean*, ed. W. V. Harris, 1–42. Oxford.

Harrison, E. B. 1965. *Archaic and Archaistic Sculpture*. The Athenian Agora 11. Princeton, NJ.

Hartmann, E. 2002. *Heirat, Hetärentum und Konkubinat im klassischen Athen*. Frankfurt.

Harvey, D. 1988. "Painted Ladies: Fact, Fiction and Fantasy." *Proceedings of the 3rd Symposium on Ancient Greek and Related Pottery, Copenhagen, August 31–September 4, 1987*, ed. J. Christiansen and T. Melander, 242–54. Copenhagen.

Hatzidakis, P. I. 1994. "'House of the Lake,' South Well in the Atrium." In *Eller Aigaio*, 46–73.

———. 1997. "Kritio notio tou Ierou tou Promachonos: Mia taberna vinaria sti Dilo." In *D'Epistemonike sinanantisi gia tin Ellinistiki Keramiki: Chronologika Problimata, klista sunola, ergasteria. Mytilene, Matros, Praktika*, 115–30. Athens.

———. 2003. *Delos*. Athens.

Havas, L. 1990. "Schemata und Wahrheit in der Darstellung der spätrepublikanischen politischen Ereignisse." *Klio* 72:216–24.

Hedreen, G. M. 2006. "'I Let Go My Force Just Touching Her Hair': Male Sexuality in Athenian Vase-Paintings of Silens and Iambic Poetry." *Convivium assisiense* 25.2:277–326.

Hemelrijk, E. 1999. *"Matrona Docta": Educated Women in the Roman Elite from Cornelia to Julia Domna*. London.

Henderson, J. 1975. *The Maculate Muse: Obscene Language in Attic Comedy*. New Haven, CT.

———, trans. 1987. *Lysistrata*. Oxford.

———, trans. 1996. *Three Plays by Aristophanes: Staging Women*. New York.

Henry, A. 2002. "Hookers and Lookers: Prostitution and Soliciting in Late Archaic Thasos." *Annual of the British School at Athens* 97:217–21.

Henry, M. 1985. *Menander's Courtesans and the Greek Comic Tradition*. Frankfurt.

———. 1986. "*Ethos, Mythos, Praxis*: Women in Greek Comedy." *Helios* 13:141–50.

———. 1992. "The Edible Woman: Athenaeus' Concept of the Pornographic." In *Pornography and Representation in Greece and Rome*, ed. A. Richlin, 250–68. New York.

———. 1995. *Prisoner of History: Aspasia of Miletus and Her Biographical Tradition*. New York.

———. 2000. "Athenaeus the *Ur*-Pornographer." In *Athenaeus and His World: Reading Greek Culture in the Roman Empire*, ed. J. Wilkins and D. Braund, 503–10. Exeter, UK.

Herter, H. 1960. "Die Soziologie der antiken Prostitution im Lichte des heidnischen und christlichen Schrifttums." *Jahrbuch für Antike und Christentum* 3:70–111.

Heubeck, A., S. West, J. B. Hainsworth, eds. 1988. *A Commentary on Homer's Odyssey.* Vol. 1, *Introduction and Books I–VIII.* New York.

Hofmann, J. B. 1950. *Etymologisches Wörterbuch des Griechischen.* Munich.

Hooks, S. 1985. *Sacred Prostitution in Israel and the Ancient Near East.* Cincinnati, OH.

Hordern, J. 2001. "Sumerian Asses and Iambic Poetry." *Zeitschrift für Papyrologie und Epigraphik* 136:39–40.

Housman, A. E. 1931a. *D. Iunii Iuuenalis saturae: Editorum in usum edidit.* London.

———. 1931b. "Praefanda." *Hermes* 66.1:402–12.

Hubbard, T. K. 2003. *Homosexuality in Greece and Rome: A Sourcebook of Basic Documents.* Berkeley, CA.

Human Rights Watch. 1995. *Rape for Profit: The Trafficking of Nepali Girls and Women to India's Brothels.* New York.

Humphreys, S. C. 1980. "Family Tombs and Tomb Cult in Ancient Athens: Tradition or Traditionalism?" *Journal of Hellenic Studies* 100:96–126.

———. 1993. *The Family, Women and Death.* 2nd ed. Ann Arbor, MI.

Hunter, V. 1994. *Policing Athens: Social Control in the Attic Lawsuits, 420–320 B.C.* Princeton, NJ.

Huzar, E. G. 1978. *Mark Antony: A Biography.* Minneapolis, MN.

Immerwahr, H. R. 1990. *Attic Script: A Survey.* Oxford.

International Organization for Migration. 2001. *Trafficking in Women and Prostitution in the Baltic States: Social and Legal Aspects.* Helsinki.

Isager, S., and M. H. Hansen. 1975. *Aspects of Athenian Society in the Fourth Century BC: A Historical Introduction to and Commentary on the "Paragraphe"-Speeches and the Speech against Dionysodorus in the Corpus Demosthenicum (XXXII–XXXVIII and LVI).* Odense, DK.

Jackson, A. H. 1993. "War and Raids for Booty in the World of Odysseus." In *War and Society in the Greek World,* ed. J. Rich and G. Shipley, 64–76. New York.

———. 1995. "An Oracle for Raiders?" *Zeitschrift für Papyrologie und Epigraphik* 108: 95–99.

Jameson, M. H. 1990. "Private Space and the Greek City." In *The Greek City: From Homer to Alexander,* ed. O. Murray and S. Price, 171–95. Oxford.

Jashemski, W. F. 1977. "The Excavation of a Shop-House Garden at Pompeii (I.XX.5)." *American Journal of Archaeology* 81.2:217–27.

———. 1979. *The Gardens of Pompeii: Herculaneum and the Villas Destroyed by Vesuvius.* New Rochelle, NY.

Jenkins, T. E. 2005. "At Play with Writing: Letters and Readers in Plautus." *Transactions of the American Philological Association* 135:359–92.

Jobst, W. 1976/1977. "Das 'öffentliche Freudenhaus' in Ephesos." *JÖAI* 51:61–84.

Johnstone, S. 2002. "Apology for the Manuscript of Demosthenes 59.67." *American Journal of Philology* 123:229–56.

Joshel, S., and S. Murnaghan, eds. 1998. *Women and Slaves in Greco-Roman Culture: Differential Equations.* New York.

Just, R. 1989. *Women in Athenian Law and Life.* New York.

Kakavoyianni, O., and I. Dovinou. 2003. In *Archaiologikeis Ereunes stin Merenta Markopoulou: I. Aphroditis*, 34–35. Athens.

Kampen, N. 1981. *Image and Status: Roman Working Women in Ostia.* Berlin.

Kampen, N., and B. Bergmann, eds. 1996. *Sexuality in Ancient Art: Near East, Egypt, Greece, and Italy.* New York.

Kapparis, K., trans. 1999. *"Against Neaira": [D. 59].* Berlin.

———. 2002. *Abortion in the Ancient World.* London.

Karras, R. M. 1992. "The Latin Vocabulary of Illicit Sex in English Ecclesiastical Court Records." *Journal of Medieval Latin* 2:1–17.

———. 1996. *Common Women: Prostitution and Sexuality in Medieval England.* Oxford.

Katz, J. T., and K. Volk. 2000. "'Mere Bellies?': A New Look at *Theogony* 26–8." *Journal of Hellenic Studies* 120:122–31.

Katz, M. 1992. "Ideology and 'The Status of Women' in Ancient Greece." *History and Theory* 31:70–97.

Kavvadias, G. 2000. "Black-Figure *Lekythos* (Secondary Type)." In *Athens, the City Beneath the City: Antiquities from the Metropolitan Railway Excavations*, ed. L. Parlama and N. Stampolidis, 298. Athens.

Keesling, C. 2006. "Heavenly Bodies: Monuments to Prostitutes in Greek Sanctuaries." In *Prostitutes and Courtesans in the Ancient World*, ed. C. A. Faraone and L. K. McClure, 59–76. Madison, WI.

Kellum, B. 1996. "The Phallus as Signifier: The Forum of Augustus and Rituals of Masculinity." In *Sexuality in Ancient Art: Near East, Egypt, Greece, and Italy*, ed. N. Kampen and B. Bergmann, 170–83. New York.

Kelly, P. 2008. *Lydia's Open Door: Inside Mexico's Most Modern Brothel.* Berkeley, CA.

Kelly Blazeby, C. F. 2000. "Drinking in the Athenian Agora c. 475–323 BC: An Archaeological Perspective." MPhil thesis, University of Glasgow.

———. 2006. "*Kapeleion*: Casual and Commercial Wine Consumption in Classical Greece." PhD diss., University of Leicester.

Keuls, E. 1983a. "Attic Vase-Painting and the Home Textile Industry." In *Ancient Greek Art and Iconography*, ed. W. G. Moon, 209–30. Madison, WI.

———. 1983b. "The Hetaera and the Housewife: The Splitting of the Female Psyche in Greek Art." *Mededelingen van het Nederlands historisch Instituut te Rome* 44–45:23–40.

———. 1985. *Reign of the Phallus: Sexual Politics in Ancient Athens.* New York.

Kilmer, M. F. 1993. *Greek Erotica on Attic Red-Figure Vases.* London.

King, H. 1998. *Hippocrates' Woman: Reading the Female Body in Ancient Greece.* New York.

Kitto, H. D. F. 1951. *The Greeks.* Harmondsworth, UK.

Kleberg, T. 1957. *Hôtels, restaurants et cabarets dans l'antiquité romaine.* Uppsala, SE.

Knigge, U. 1982. "Ho astēr tēs Aphroditēs." *Mitteilungen Des Deutschen Archäologischen Instituts. Athenische Abteilung* 97:158–70.

———. 1991. *The Athenian Kerameikos: History, Monuments, Excavations.* Trans. J. Binder. Athens.

———. 1993. "Die Ausgrabung im Kerameikos 1990/91." *Archäologischer Anzeiger* 1:125–40.

———. 2005. *Der Bau Z.* Kerameikos17, pts. 1–2. Munich.

Knigge, U., B. von Freytag gen. Löringhoff, and Gerhard Kuhn. 1995. "Kerameikos: Tätigkeitsbericht 1992–94." *Archäologischer Anzeiger* 209:627–59.

Koch-Harnack, G. 1983. *Knabenliebe und Tiergeschenke.* Berlin.

Konrad, C. F. 1994. *Plutarch's "Sertorius": A Historical Commentary.* Chapel Hill, NC.

Kreeb, M. 1988. *Untersuchungen zur figürlichen Ausstattung Delischer Privathäuser.* Chicago.

Krenkel, W. A. 1988. "Prostitution." In *Civilization of the Ancient Mediterranean: Greece and Rome,* ed. M. Grant and R. Kitzinger, 1291–97. New York.

Kristof, N. D. 2006. "Fighting Brothels with Books." *New York Times,* December 24.

Kubiak, D. P. 1989. "Piso's Madness (Cic. *In Pis.* 21 and 47)." *American Journal of Philology* 110.2:237–45.

Kühnert, B. 1991. *Die Plebs Urbana der späten römischen Republik.* Berlin.

Kurke, L. 1996. "Pindar and the Prostitutes, or Reading Ancient 'Pornography.'" *Arion* 3–4: 49–75.

———. 1997. "Inventing the *Hetaira.*" *Classical Antiquity* 16.1:106–50.

———. 1999. *Coins, Bodies, Games, and Gold: The Politics of Meaning in Archaic Greece.* Princeton, NJ.

———. 2002. "Gender, Politics, and Subversion in the *Chreiai* of Machon." *Proceedings of the Cambridge Philological Society* 48:20–65.

Lane, E. N. 1996. "The Name of Cybele's Priests the 'Galloi.'" In *Cybele, Attis, and Related Cults: Essays in Memory of M. J. Vermaseren,* ed. E. N. Lane, 117–33. New York.

Lapalus, E. 1939. *L'Agora des Italiens.* Exploration archéologique de Délos 19. Paris.

Lear, A., and E. Cantarella. 2008. *Images of Ancient Greek Pederasty: Boys Were Their Gods.* New York.

Lefkowitz, M. 1981. *The Lives of the Greek Poets.* Baltimore, MD.

Lefkowitz, M., and M. Fant. 1969. *Women's Life in Greece and Rome.* Baltimore, MD.

Lentakis, A. 1986. *I porneia: O erōtas stin arkaia Ellada.* Vol. 3. Athens.

Lerner, G. 1986. *The Creation of Patriarchy.* New York.

Levine, D. B. 1985. "Symposium and the Polis." In *Theognis of Megara: Poetry and the Polis,* ed. T. J. Figueira and G. Nagy, 176–96. Baltimore, MD.

———. 2005. "*EPATON BAMA* ('Her Lovely Footstep'): The Erotics of Feet in Ancient Greece." In *Body Language in the Greek and Roman Worlds,* ed. D. Cairns, 55–72. Swansea, UK.

Levine, M. 1995. "The Gendered Grammar of Ancient Mediterranean Hair." In *Off with Her Head!* ed. W. Doniger and H. Eilberg-Schwartz, 76–130. Berkeley, CA.

Lewis, D. M. 1993. "Keeping Roads Clean in Thasos." *The Classical Review* 43:402–3.

Lewis, S. 2002. *The Athenian Woman: An Iconographic Handbook.* New York.

———. 2006. "Iconography and the Study of Gender." In *Images and Gender: Contributions to the Hermeneutics of Reading Ancient Art,* ed. S. Schroer, 23–39. Fribourg, Switz.

Licht, H. 1932. *Sexual Life in Ancient Greece*. Trans. J. H. Freese. London.

Liddel, P. 2007. *Civic Obligation and Individual Liberty in Ancient Athens*. Oxford.

Lind, H. 1988. "Ein Hetärenhaus am Heiligen Tor? Der Athener Bau Z und die bei Isaios (6, 20f.) erwähnte Synoikia Euktemons." *Museum Helveticum* 45:158–69.

Lissarrague, F. 1990a. *The Aesthetics of the Greek Banquet: Images of Wine and Ritual*. Princeton, NJ.

———. 1990b. "Around the *Krater*: An Aspect of Banquet Imagery." In *Sympotica: A Symposium on the Symposion*, ed. O. Murray, 196–209. Oxford.

———. 1990c. "The Sexual Life of Satyrs." In *Before Sexuality: The Construction of Erotic Experience in the Ancient Greek World*, ed. D. Halperin, J. J. Winkler, and F. Zeitlin, 53–82. Princeton, NJ.

———. 1998. "Intrusions aux gynécée." In *Les mystères du gynécée*, ed. P. Veyne, 156–98. Paris.

Lissarrague, F., and F. Frontisi-Ducroux. 1990. "From Ambiguity to Ambivalence: A Dionysiac Excursion through the 'Anakreontic' Vases." In *Before Sexuality: The Construction of Erotic Experience in the Ancient Greek World*, ed. D. M. Halperin, J. J. Winkler, and F. Zeitlin, 211–56. Princeton, NJ.

Liventhal, V. 1985. "What Goes on among the Women: The Settings of Some Attic Vase Paintings of the Fifth Century B.C." *Analecta Romana Instituti Danici* 14:37–52.

Llewellyn-Jones, L. 2003. *Aphrodite's Tortoise: The Veiled Woman of Ancient Greece*. Swansea, UK.

Loomis, W. T. 1998. *Wages, Welfare Costs, and Inflation in Classical Athens*. Ann Arbor, MI.

Loraux, N. 1987. *Tragic Ways of Killing a Woman*. Cambridge, MA.

Ludwig, P. 2002. *Eros and Polis*. Cambridge, UK.

Luke, J. 1994. "The Krater, *Kratos*, and the *Polis*." *Greece and Rome* 41:23–32.

Lutz, H. F. 1922. *Viticulture and Brewing in the Ancient Orient*. Leipzig.

Lyotard, J.-F. 1994. *The Postmodern Condition: A Report on Knowledge*. Trans. G. Bennington and B. Massumi. Manchester, UK.

MacCary, W. T., and M. M. Willcock, eds. 1976. *Casina*, by Plautus. Cambridge, UK.

MacKinnon, C. A. 1989. *Toward a Feminist Theory of the State*. Cambridge, MA.

Maclay, K. 2003. "UC Berkeley's Portrait of Plato Is Ancient Artifact, Not a Fake, Professor Says." *UC Berkeley News*, April 9, http://www.berkeley.edu/news/media/releases/ 2003/04/09_plato.shtml (accessed July 17, 2009).

Macurdy, G. H. 1932. *Hellenistic Queens: A Study of Woman-Power in Macedonia, Seleucid Syria, and Ptolemaic Egypt*. London.

Magie, D. 1950. *Roman Rule in Asia Minor to the End of the Third Century after Christ*. Princeton, NJ.

Mahfouz, N. 2003. *Rhadopis of Nubia*. Trans. A. Calderbank. Cairo.

Manniche, L. 1987. *Sexual Life in Ancient Egypt*. London.

Manville, P. B. 1990. *The Origins of Citizenship in Ancient Athens*. Princeton, NJ.

Marcadé, J. 1969. *Au Musée de Délos: Étude de la sculpture hellénistique en ronde bosse decouverte dans l'île*. Paris.

Marder, T. 1979. "Context for Claude-Nicolas Ledoux's Oikema." *Arts* 54:174–76.

Marzullo, B. [1995–96] 1997. "Archil. fr. 42 W. (Reversa Neobule?)." *Museum criticum* 30–31:37–66.

Masson, O. 1962. *Les fragments du poète Hipponax: Édition critique et commentée*. Paris.

May, J. M. 1988. *Trials of Character: The Eloquence of Ciceronian Rhetoric*. Chapel Hill, NC.

Mayhew, R. 2004. *The Female in Aristotle's Biology*. Chicago.

McCabe and Mrs. Miller. 1971. Directed by Robert Altman. David Foster Productions.

McClure, L. K. 2003a. *Courtesans at Table: Gender and Greek Literary Culture in Athenaeus*. New York.

———. 2003b. "Subversive Laughter: The Sayings of Courtesans in Book 13 of Athenaeus' *Deipnosophistae*." *American Journal of Philology* 124.2:259–94.

McGinn, T. A. J. 1998a. "Caligula's Brothel on the Palatine." *Échos du monde classique/Classical Views* n.s. 42.17:95–107.

———. 1998b. *Prostitution, Sexuality, and the Law in Ancient Rome*. New York.

———. 2002. "Pompeian Brothels and Social History." In "Pompeian Studies," supplement to *Journal of Roman Archaeology* 47:S7–S46.

———. 2004. *The Economy of Prostitution in the Roman World: A Study of Social History and the Brothel*. Ann Arbor, MI.

———. 2006. "Gastgewerbe (Griechisch-römische Antike und Spätantike)." In *Handwörterbuch der antiken Sklaverei*, ed. H. Heinen. CD-ROM. Stuttgart.

———. Forthcoming. "Sex and the City." In *Cambridge Companion to Ancient Rome*, ed. P. Erdkamp. Cambridge, UK.

McGlew, J. 2002. *Citizens on Stage: Comedy and Political Culture in the Athenian Democracy*. Ann Arbor, MI.

Meiser, K. 1904–5. "Kritische Beiträge zu den Briefen des Rhetors Alkiphron." *Sitzungsberichte der Königlichen Bayerischen Akademie der Wissenschaften, Philos.-philolog. und historische Klasse*. 1:191–244; 2:139–240.

Meskell, L. 2002. *Private Life in New Kingdom Egypt*. Princeton, NJ.

Miller, A. M. 1996. *Greek Lyric: An Anthology in Translation*. Indianapolis, IN.

Milne, M. J., and D. von Bothmer. 1953. "*Katapugōn, Katapugaina*." *Hesperia* 22:215–24.

Miner, J. 2003. "Courtesan, Concubine, Whore: Apollodorus' Deliberate Use of Terms for Prostitutes." *American Journal of Philology* 203:19–37.

Moine, N. 1975. "Augustin et Apulée sur la magie des femmes d'auberge." *Latomus* 34:350–61.

Moore, T. J. 1998. *The Theater of Plautus: Playing to the Audience*. Austin, TX.

Morgan, C. H. 1953. "Investigations at Corinth, 1953: A Tavern of Aphrodite." *Hesperia* 22: 131–40.

Morgan, J. 2005. "Domestic Cult in the Classical Greek House." PhD thesis, Cardiff University.

Morris, I. 1996. "The Strong Principle of Equality and the Archaic Origins of Greek Democracy." In *Demokratia: A Conversation on Democracies, Ancient and Modern*, ed. J. Ober and C. Hedrick, 19–48. Princeton, NJ.

———. 2000. *Archaeology as Cultural History: Words and Things in Iron Age Greece*. Malden, MA.

Mossé, C. 1991. "La place de la *pallaké* dans la famille athénienne." In *Symposium 1990: Papers on Greek and Hellenistic Legal History*, ed. M. Gagarin, 273–80. Cologne.

Müller C., and C. Hasenohr, eds. 2002. *Les italiens dans le monde grec: IIe siècle av. J.-C.-Ier siècle ap. J.-C., circulation, activités, intégration*. Paris.

Murray, O. 1983a. "The Greek *Symposion* in History." In *Tria corda: Scritti in onore di Arnaldo Momigliano*, ed. E. Gabba, 257–62. Como.

———. 1983b. "*Symposion* and Männerbund." In *Consilium Eirene XVI: Proceedings of the 16th International Eirene Conference, Prague, 31.8–4.9, 1982*, ed. P. Oliva and A. Frolíková, 47–52. Prague

———. 1983c. "The *Symposion* as Social Organisation." In *The Greek Renaissance of the Eighth Century B.C.*, ed. R. Hägg, 195–99. Stockholm.

———. 1988. "Death and the Symposion." *Aion Arch. St. Ant.* 10:239–57.

———, ed. 1990. *Sympotica: A Symposium on the Symposion*. Oxford.

———. 1990a. "The Affair of the Mysteries: Democracy and the Drinking Group." In *Sympotica: A Symposium on the Symposion*, ed. O. Murray, 149–61. Oxford.

———. 1990b. "Sweet Feasts of the Grape." *Times Higher Education Supplement*, July 6.

———. 1990c. "Sympotic History." In *Sympotica: A Symposium on the Symposion*, ed. O. Murray, 3–13. Oxford.

———. 1991. "War and the Symposium." In *Dining in a Classical Contex*, ed. W. J. Slater, 83–103. Ann Arbor, MI.

———. 1992. "Les règles du *symposion* ou comment problématiser le plaisir." In *La sociabilité à table: Commensalité et convivialité à travers les ages*, ed. M. Aurell, O. Dumoulin, and F. Thelamon, 65–68. Rouen.

———. 1994. "Nestor's Cup and the Origins of the Greek *Symposion*." *Aion Slavastika* 1: 47–54.

———. 1995a. "Forms of Sociality." In *The Greeks*, ed. J.-P. Vernant, 218–53. Chicago.

———. 1995b. "Histories of Pleasure." In *In vino veritas*, ed. O. Murray and M. Tecuşan, 3–17. Oxford.

Murray, O., and M. Tecuşan, eds. 1995. *In vino veritas*. Oxford.

Nagler, M. 1967. "Towards a Generative View of the Oral Formula." *Harvard Studies in Classical Philology* 98:269–311.

Neer, R. 2002. *Style and Politics in Athenian Vase-Painting: The Craft of Democracy, ca. 530–460 B.C.E.* Cambridge, UK.

Neils, J. 2000. "The Other within the Other: An Intimate Look at Hetairai and Maenads." In *Not the Classical Ideal: Athens and the Construction of the Other in Greek Art*, ed. B. Cohen, 203–26. Leiden.

Nevett, L. 1995. "Gender Relations in the Classical Greek Household." *Annual of the British School at Athens* 90:363–81.

———. 1999. *House and Society in the Ancient Greek World*. Cambridge, UK.

Newman, W. L. 1887. *The "Politics" of Aristotle: With an Introduction, Two Prefatory Essays, and Notes Critical and Explanatory*. Oxford.

Nippel, W. 1995. *Public Order in Ancient Rome*. Cambridge, UK.

Oakley, J. H. 2002. "Some 'Other' Members of the Athenian Household: Maids and Their Mistresses in Fifth-century Athenian Art." In *Not the Classical Ideal: Athens and the Construction of the Other in Greek Art*, ed. B. Cohen, 180–202. Leiden.

Ober, J. 1993. "The *Polis* as a Society: Aristotle, John Rawls and the Athenian Social Contract." In *The Ancient Greek City-State: Symposium on the Occasion of the 250th Anniversary of the Royal Danish Academy of Sciences and Letters*, ed. M. H. Hansen, 129–60. Copenhagen.

Ogden, D. 1996. *Greek Bastardy in the Classical and Hellenistic Periods*. Oxford.

———. 1999. *Polygamy, Prostitutes, and Death: The Hellenistic Dynasties*. London.

Oikonomides, A. N. 1988. "The *Pous* of Aegeus (Eur. *Med.* 679) and the *Pous* of Timesikles (*SEG* xxxiv 43)." *Ancient World* 18:45–47.

Olmos, R. R. 1990. *Vasos griegos: Collección Condes de Lagunillas*. Zurich.

———. 1993. *Catálogo de los vasos griegos del Museo Nacional de Bellas Artes de La Habana*. Madrid.

Omlin, J. A. 1973. *Der Papyrus 55001 und seine satirisch-erotischen Zeichnungen und Inschriften*. Torino.

Onishi, N. 2007. "Japan Court Rules against Sex Slaves and Laborers." *New York Times*, April 27.

Osborne, R. 1996. "Desiring Women on Athenian Pottery." In *Sexuality in Ancient Art*, ed. N. Kampen, 65–80. Cambridge, UK.

———. 1998. *Archaic and Classical Greek Art*. Oxford.

Padgett, J. M., W. A. P. Childs, and D. Tsiafakis. 2003. *The Centaur's Smile: The Human Animal in Early Greek Art*. Princeton, NJ.

Pateman, C. 1988. *The Sexual Contract*. Stanford, CA.

Parke, H. W. 1977. *Festivals of the Athenians*. Ithaca, NY.

Patterson, C. 1985. "Not Worth the Rearing: The Causes of Infant Exposure in Ancient Greece." *Transactions of the American Philological Association* 115:103–23.

———. 1990. "Those Athenian Bastards." *Classical Antiquity* 9:40–73.

———. 1991a. "Marriage and Married Women in Athenian Law." In *Women's History and Ancient History*, ed. S. B. Pomeroy, 48–72. Chapel Hill, NC.

———. 1991b. "Response to Claude Mossé." In *Symposium 1990: Papers on Greek and Hellenistic Legal History*, ed. M. Gagarin, 281–87. Cologne.

———. 1994. "The Case against Neaira and the Public Ideology of the Athenian Family." In *Athenian Identity and Civic Ideology*, ed. A. L. Boegehold and A. C. Scafuro, 199–216. Baltimore, MD.

———. 1998. *The Family in Greek History*. Cambridge, MA.

Patterson, O. 1982. *Slavery and Social Death*. Cambridge, MA.

Pellizer, E. 1990. "Outlines of a Morphology of Sympotic Entertainment." In *Sympotica: A Symposium on the Symposium*, ed. O. Murray, 177–84. Oxford.

Pemberton, E. G. 1989. *The Sanctuary of Demeter and Kore: The Greek Pottery*. Corinth 18, pt. 1. Princeton, NJ.

Peschel, I. 1987. *Die Hetäre bei Symposion und Komos in der attisch-rotfiguren Vasenmalerei des 6. –4. Jahrh. V. Chr.* Frankfurt am Main.

Petersen, L. 1997. "Divided Consciousness and Female Companionship: Reconstructing Female Subjectivity on Greek Vases." *Arethusa* 30:35–74.

Phang, S. 2001. *The Marriage of Roman Soldiers (13 BCE—CE 235): Law and Family in the Imperial Army*. Leiden.

Pheterson, G. 1989. *A Vindication of the Rights of Whores*. Seattle, WA.

Picard, C. 1954. "Le phrygien Hector était-il Galle de Cybèle?" *Revue archéologique* 43: 80–82.

Picard, G. 1969. *The Ancient Civilization of Rome*. Geneva.

Pipes, D. 1997. *Conspiracy: How the Paranoid Style Flourishes and Where It Comes From*. New York.

Pomeroy, S. B. 1975. *Goddesses, Whores, Wives, and Slaves: Women in Classical Antiquity*. New York.

———. 1984. *Women in Hellenistic Egypt: From Alexander to Cleopatra*. New York.

———. 1995. "The Contribution of Women to the Greek Domestic Economy: Rereading Xenophon's *Oeconomicus*." In *Feminisms in the Academy*, ed. D. C. Stanton and A. J. Stewart, 180–95. Ann Arbor, MI.

———. 2002. *Spartan Women*. Oxford.

Poo, M. 1995. *Wine and Wine Offering in the Religion of Ancient Egypt*. London.

Pretty Baby. 1978. Directed by Louis Malle. Paramount Pictures.

Pucci, P. 1987. *Odysseus Polutropos: Intertextual Readings in the "Odyssey" and the "Iliad."* Ithaca, NY.

Raaflaub, K. 1993. "Homer to Solon, the Rise of the Polis: The Written Sources." In *The Ancient Greek City-State: Symposium on the Occasion of the 240th Anniversary of the Royal Danish Academy of Sciences and Letters*, ed. M. H. Hansen, 41–105. Copenhagen.

Rabinowitz, N. S. 1993. *Anxiety Veiled: Euripides and the Traffic in Women*. Ithaca, NY.

———. 2002a. "Excavating Women's Homoeroticism: The Evidence from Vase Painting." In *Among Women: From the Homosocial to the Homoerotic in the Ancient World*, ed. N. S. Rabinowitz and L. Auanger, 106–66. Austin, TX.

———. 2002b. Introduction. In *Among Women: From the Homosocial to the Homoerotic in Antiquity*, ed. N. S. Rabinowitz and L. Auanger, 1–33. Austin, TX.

Rabinowitz, N. S., and S. Blundell. 2008. "Women's Bonds, Women's Pots: Adornment Scenes in Attic Vase Painting." *Phoenix* 62:115–44.

Raubitschek, I. K. 1998. *The Metal Objects (1952–1989)*. Princeton, NJ.

Rauh, N. K. 1992. "Was the Agora of the Italians an *Établissement du Sport*?" *Bulletin de correspondance hellénique* 116:293–333.

———. 1993. *The Sacred Bonds of Commerce: Religion, Economy, and Trade Society at Hellenistic Roman Delos, 166–87 B.C.* Amsterdam.

———. 1997. "Who Were the Cilician Pirates?" In *Res Maritimae: Cyprus and the Eastern Mediterranean from Prehistory to Late Antiquity*, ed. S. Swiny, R. L. Hohlfelder, and H. W. Swiny, 263–83. Atlanta, GA.

———. 2003. *Merchants, Sailors, and Pirates in the Roman World*. Stroud, UK.

Rauh, N. K., M. J. Dillon, and T. D. McClain. 2008. "*Ochlos Nautikos*: Leisure Culture and Underclass Discontent in the Roman Maritime World." In *The Maritime World of*

Ancient Rome: An Exploration of New Research on Subjects Relating to the Maritime Life of Rome and Its Vast Empire, ed. R. L. Hohlfelder, 197–242. Ann Arbor, MI.

Rauh, N. K., and T. D. McClain. 1996. "Signs of a Woman's Influence? The Dedications of the Stertinian *Familia* at Delos." *Aevum, Rassegna di Scienze Storiche-Linguistiche e Filologiche* 70:47–68.

Reade, J. E. 1995. "The Symposion in Ancient Mesopotamia: Archaeological Evidence." In *In vino veritas*, ed. O. Murray and M. Tecuşan, 35–56. Oxford.

Reeder, E. D. 1995. Introduction. In *Pandora: Women in Classical Greece*, ed. E. D. Reeder, 13–19. Princeton, NJ.

Redfield, J. 1983. "The Economic Man." In *Approaches to Homer*, ed. C. Rubino and C. Shelmerdine, 218–47. Austin, TX.

———. [1975] 1994. *Nature and Culture in the Iliad: The Tragedy of Hector*. Chicago.

Reinsberg, C. 1989. *Ehe, Hetärentum und Knabenliebe im antiken Griechenland*. Munich.

Restif de la Bretonne, N. E. 1769. *Le pornographe; ou, Ideés d'un honnête-homme sur un projet de réglement pour les prostituées, propre à prévenir les malheurs qu'occassionne le publicissme des femmes*. Paris.

Rhodes, P. 1981. *A Commentary on the Aristotelian "Athenaion Politeia."* Oxford.

Richlin, A. [1983] 1992. *The Garden of Priapus: Sexuality and Aggression in Roman Humor*. New Haven, CT.

———, trans. 2005. *Rome and the Mysterious Orient: Three Plays by Plautus*. Berkeley, CA.

Richter, G., and M. Milne. 1935. *Shapes and Names of Athenian Vases*. New York.

Robins, R. S., and J. M. Post. 1997. *Political Paranoia: The Psychopolitics of Hatred*. New Haven, CT.

Robinson, D. M. 1930. *Excavations at Olynthus*. Pt. 2, *Architecture and Sculpture: Houses and Other Buildings*. Baltimore, MD.

———. 1941. *Excavations at Olynthus*. Pt. 10, *Metal and Minor Miscellaneous Finds: An Original Contribution to Greek Life*. Baltimore, MD.

Rodenwaldt, G. 1932. "Spinnende Hetären." *Archäologischer Anzeiger* 47:7–21.

Roes, A. 1935. "Chronique des fouilles." *Bulletin de correspondance hellénique* 59:299–300.

Rosen, R. 1988. "Hipponax, Boupalos, and the Conventions of the *Psogos*." *Transactions of the American Philological Association* 118:29–41.

———. 1997. "The Gendered Polis in Eupolis' *Cities*." In *The City as Comedy*, ed. G. Dobrov, 73–89. Chapel Hill.

Rosenzweig, R. 2004. *Worshipping Aphrodite: Art and Cult in Classical Athens*. Ann Arbor.

Rosivach, V. J. 1995. "Solon's Brothels." *Liverpool Classical Monthly* 20.1–2:2–3.

———. 1998. *When a Young Man Falls in Love: The Sexual Exploitation of Women in New Comedy*. New York.

———. 1999. "Enslaving 'Barbaroi' and the Athenian Ideology of Slavery." *Historia: Zeitschrift für Alte Geschichte* 48.2:129–57.

Roth, M. 2006. "Marriage, Divorce, and the Prostitute in Ancient Mesopotamia." In *Prostitutes and Courtesans in the Ancient World*, ed. C. A. Faraone and L. K. McClure, 21–39. Madison, WI.

Rotondi, G. [1922] 1962. *Leges publicae populi romani*. Milan.

Rotroff, S. I., and J. H. Oakley. 1992. *Debris from a Public Dining Place in the Athenian Agora. Hesperia* supplement 25. Princeton, NJ.

Roussel, D. 1976. *Tribu et cité: Études sur les groupes sociaux dans les cités grecques aux époques archaïque et classique*. Paris.

Sallares, R. 1991. *The Ecology of the Ancient Greek World*. Ithaca, NY.

Sams, G. K. 1977. "Beer in the City of Midas." *Archaeology* 30:108–15.

Sandbach, F. H., ed. 1990. *Menandri reliquiae selectae*. Oxford.

Scafuro, A. C. 2006. "Identifying Solonian Laws." In *Solon of Athens: New Historical and Philological Approaches*, ed. J. H. Blok and A. P. M. H. Lardinois, 175–96. Leiden.

Scherrer, P., ed. 2000. *Ephesus: The New Guide*. Trans. Lionel Bier and George M. Luxon. Selçuk, Turkey.

Schmitt Pantel, P. 1985. "Banquet et cité grecque: Quelques questions suscitées par les recherches récentes." *Mélanges de l'École française de Rome: Antiquité* 97:135–58.

———. 1987. "Les pratiques collectives et le politique dans la cité grecque." In *Sociabilité, pouvoirs et société*, ed. F. Thelamon, 279–88. Rouen.

———. 1990. "Sacrificial Meal and *Symposion*: Two Models of Civic Institutions in the Archaic City?" In *Sympotica: A Symposium on the Symposion*, ed. O. Murray, 14–36. Oxford.

———. 1997. *La cité au banquet*. Rome.

Schmitt Pantel, P., and A. Schnapp. 1982. "Image et société en Grèce ancienne: Les représentations de la chasse et du banquet." *Révue archeologique* 1:57–74.

Schumacher, L. 2001. *Sklaverei in der Antike: Alltag und Schicksal der Unfreien*. Munich.

Segal, C. 1971. "Andromache's Anagnorisis: Formulaic Artistry in *Iliad* 22, 437–476." *Harvard Studies in Classical Philology* 75:33–57.

Segal, E. 1987. *Roman Laughter: The Comedy of Plautus*. 2nd ed. Oxford.

Shapiro, H. A. 1992. "Eros in Love: Pederasty and Pornography in Greece." In *Pornography and Representation in Greece and Rome*, ed. A. Richlin, 53–76. New York.

———. 2003. "Fathers and Sons, Men and Boys." In *Coming of Age in Ancient Greece: Images of Childhood from the Classical Past*, ed. J. Neils, 85–112. New Haven, CT.

———. 2004. "Leagros the Satyr." In *Greek Vases: Images, Contexts and Controversies: Proceedings of the Conference sponsored by the Center for the Ancient Mediterranean at Columbia University, 23–24 March 2002*, ed. C. Marconi, 1–12. Boston.

Sharrock, A. R. 1996. "The Art of Deceit: Pseudolus and the Nature of Reading." *Classical Quarterly* 46:152–74.

Shelton, J.-A. 1988. *As the Romans Did: A Sourcebook in Roman Social History*. Oxford.

Sherwin-White, S. 1978. *Ancient Cos: An Historical Study from the Dorian Settlement to the Imperial Period*. Göttingen, Germany.

Shipley, G. 1993. "Introduction: The Limits of War." In *War and Society in the Greek World*, ed. J. Rich and G. Shipley, 1–24. New York.

Siebert, G. 1975. "Travaux de l'École française en 1974: Délos, le quartier de Skardhana." *Bulletin de correspondance hellénique* 99:716–23.

———. 1976. "Travaux de l'École française en 1975: Délos, le quartier de Skardhana." *Bulletin de correspondance hellénique* 100:799–821.

———. 1987. "Travaux de l'École française en 1986: Délos, quartier de Skardhana." *Bulletin de correspondance hellénique* 111:628–44.

———. 1988. "Travaux de l'École française en 1987: Délos, la Maison des sceaux." *Bulletin de correspondance hellénique* 112:755–67.

———. 2001. *L'îlot des bijoux, l'îlot des bronzes, la Maison des sceaux*. Vol. 1, *Topographie et architecture*. Exploration archéologique de Délos 38. Athens.

Singleton, V. L. 1996. "An Enologist's Commentary on Ancient Wines." In *The Origins and Ancient History of Wine*, ed. P. E. McGovern, S. J. Fleming, and S. H. Katz, 67–78. London.

Sissa, G. 1990. *Greek Virginity*. Trans. A. Goldhammer. Cambridge, MA.

Skinner, M. 2005. *Sexuality in Greek and Roman Culture*. Oxford.

Slane, K. W., and M. W. Dickie. 1993. "A Knidian Phallic Vase from Corinth." *Hesperia* 62.4:486–94.

Slater, N. 1985. *Plautus in Performance: The Theatre of the Mind*. Princeton, NJ.

———. 2004. "Staging Literacy in Plautus." In *Oral Performance and Its Contexts*, ed. C. J. Mackie, 163–77. Leiden.

Smith, M. A. 1983. "Social Usages of the Public Drinking House: Changing Aspects of Class and Leisure." *British Journal of Sociology* 34.3:367–85.

Snodgrass, A. 1993. "The Rise of the Polis: The Archaeological Evidence." In *The Ancient Greek City-State: Symposium on the Occasion of the 250th Anniversary of the Royal Danish Academy of Sciences and Letters*, ed. M. H. Hansen, 30–40. Copenhagen.

———. 2000. "The Uses of Writing on Early Greek Painted Pottery." In *Word and Image in Ancient Greece*, ed. N. Rutter and B. Sparkes, 22–34. Edinburgh.

Soh, C. S. 2001. "Prostitutes versus Sex Slaves: The Politics of Representing the 'Comfort Women.'" In *The Legacies of the Comfort Women of World War II*, ed. M. Stetz and B. Oh, 69–87. Armonk, NY.

Sourvinou-Inwood, C. 1995. "Male and Female, Public and Private, Ancient and Modern." In *Pandora: Women in Classical Greece*, ed. E. D. Reeder, 111–18. Baltimore, MD.

Stafford, E. J. 2001. "Hangovers in Ancient Greece." *Omnibus* 41:10–11.

Stansbury-O'Donnell, M. 2006. *Vase Painting, Gender, and Social Identity in Archaic Athens*. Cambridge, UK.

Starr, C. 1978. "An Evening with the Flute Girls." *La parola del passato* 33:401–10.

Stehle, E. 1997. *Performance and Gender in Ancient Greece: Nondramatic Poetry in Its Setting*. Princeton, NJ.

Steiner, A. 2007. *Reading Greek Vases*. Cambridge, UK.

Steiner, D. 2002. "Indecorous Dining, Indecorous Speech: Pindar's First *Olympian* and the Poetics of Consumption." *Arethusa* 35:297–314.

Steinhauer, G. 2003. *I ochurosi kai i pili tis Letioneias*. Piraeus, Greece.

Stetz, M., and B. Oh, eds. 2001. *The Legacies of the Comfort Women of World War II*. Armonk, NY.

Stewart, A. F. [1997] 2002. *Art, Desire and the Body in Ancient Greece*. Cambridge, UK.

Stravrakakis, Y. N. 1998. *Newsbriefs: Thessaloniki Brothel*. New York.

Strong, R. A. 1997. "The Most Shameful Practice: Temple Prostitution in the Ancient Greek World." PhD diss., University of California, Los Angeles.

Stroszeck, J. 2003. "Horos Kerameikou. Zu den Grenzsteinen des Kerameikos in Athen." *Polis: Studi interdisciplinari sul mondo antico* 1:53–84.

Sullivan, J. P. 1979. "Martial's Sexual Attitudes." *Philologus* 123:293–300.

Sutton, R., Jr. 1981. "The Interaction between Men and Women Portrayed on Attic Red-Figure Pottery." PhD diss., University of North Carolina, Chapel Hill.

———. 2000. "The Good, the Base, and the Ugly: The Drunken Orgy in Attic Vase Painting and the Athenian Self." In *Not the Classical Ideal: Athens and the Construction of the Other in Greek Art*, ed. B. Cohen, 180–203. Leiden.

Svenbro, J. 1976. *La parole et le marbre: Aux origins de la poétique grecque*. Lund, Sweden.

Symonds, J. A. [1901] 1971. *A Problem in Greek Ethics*. New York.

Talmadge, E. 2007. "Females Were Coerced into Brothels, Even after WWII's End." *Philadelphia Inquirer*, April 26.

Tandy, D. 1997. *Warriors into Traders: The Power of the Market in Early Greece*. Berkeley, CA.

Tanenbaum, L. 1999. *Slut! Growing up Female with a Bad Reputation*. New York.

Tatum, W. J. 1999. *The Patrician Tribune: Publius Clodius Pulcher*. Chapel Hill, NC.

Thalmann, W. G. 1984. *Conventions of Form and Thought in Early Greek Epic Poetry*. Baltimore, MD.

———. 1998a. "Female Slaves in the *Odyssey*." In *Women and Slaves in Greco-Roman Culture*, ed. S. Murnaghan and S. R. Joshel, 22–34. New York.

———. 1998b. *The Swineherd and the Bow: Representations of Class in the Odyssey*. Ithaca, NY.

Thomas, R. 1993. "Sparrows, Hares and Doves: A Catullan Metaphor and Its Tradition." *Helios* 20:131–42.

Thornton, B. 1997. *Eros: The Myth of Ancient Greek Sexuality*. Boulder, CO.

Timm, A. 2002. "Sex with a Purpose: Prostitution, Venereal Disease, and Militarized Masculinity in the Third Reich." *Journal of the History of Sexuality* 11.1–2:223–55.

Todd, S. 1997. "Status and Gender in Athenian Public Records." In *Symposion 1995: Vorträge zur griechischen und hellenistichen Rechtsgeschichte (Korfu, 1–5 September 1995)*, ed. G. Thür and J. Vélissaropoulos-Karakostas, 113–24. Cologne.

Toivari-Viitala, J. 2001. *Women at Deir el-Medina: A Study of the Status and Roles of the Female Inhabitants in the Workmen's Community during the Ramesside Period*. Leiden.

Tracy, V. A. 1977. "The Leno-Maritus." *Classical Journal* 22:62–64.

Trexler, R. 1995. *Sex and Conquest: Gendered Violence, Political Order, and the European Conquest of the Americas*. Ithaca, NY.

Trümper, M. 1998. *Wohnen in Delos: Eine baugeschichtliche Untersuchung zum Wandel der Wohnkultur in hellenistischer Zeit*. Leidorf, Ger.

Tsakirgis, B. 2005. "Living and Working Around the Athenian Agora: A Preliminary Case Study of Three Houses." In *Ancient Greek Houses and Households: Chronological, Regional, and Social Diversity*, ed. B. A. Ault and L. C. Nevett, 67–82. Philadelphia.

Tsetskhladze, G. 2000–2001. "Black Sea Piracy." *Talanta* 22–23:11–16.

Tyrell, W. B., and L. J. Bennett. 1999. "Pericles' Muting of Women's Voices in Thuc. 2.45.2." *Classical Journal* 95.1:37–51.

Venit, M. S. 1998. "Women in Their Cups." *Classical World* 92.2:117–30.

Ventris, M., and J. Chadwick. 1956. *Documents in Mycenaean Greek: Three Hundred Selected Tablets from Knossos, Pylos and Mycenae with Commentary and Vocabulary*. Cambridge, UK.

Vermaseren, M. J. 1977. *Cybele and Attis: The Myth and the Cult*. Trans. A. M. H. Lemmers. London.

Vernant, J.-P. 1988. "Marriage." In *Myth and Society in Ancient Greece*, trans. J. Lloyd, 55–77. New York.

———. 1989a. "At Man's Table: Hesiod's Foundation Myth of Sacrifice." In *The Cuisine of Sacrifice among the Greeks*, ed. M. Detienne and J.-P. Vernant, trans. P. Wissing, 21–86. Chicago.

———. 1989b. Preface. In *A City of Images: Iconography and Society in Ancient Greece*, ed. C. Bérard et al., trans. D. Lyons, 7–8. Princeton, NJ.

Virlouvet, C. 1985. *Famines et émeutes à Rome, des origins de la République à la mort de Néron*. Rome.

von Reden, S. [1995] 2003. *Exchange in Ancient Greece*. London.

Wachter, R. 2003. *Drinking Inscriptions on Attic Little-Master Cups: A Catalogue*. Berlin.

Walkowitz, J. 1980. *Prostitution and Victorian Society: Women, Class, and the State*. Cambridge, UK.

Wallace, R. W. [1983] 1986. "The Date of Solon's Reforms." *American Journal of Ancient History* 8.1:81–95.

Wallace-Hadrill, A. 1995. "Public Honour and Private Shame: The Urban Texture of Pompeii." In *Urban Society in Roman Italy*, ed. T. J. Cornell and K. Lomas, 39–62. New York.

Walter-Karydi, E. 1996. *To Helleniko spiti: Ho exeugenismos tes katoikias sta hysteroklasika chronia*. Athens.

Waring, M. 1998. *If Women Counted*. San Francisco.

Warren, J. 2008. *Pirates, Prostitutes and Pullers: Explorations in the Ethno- and Social History of Southeast Asia*. Crawley, Australia.

Wasowicz, A. 1989. "Miroir ou quenouille? La représentation des femmes dans la céramique attique." In *Mélanges Pierre Lévêque*, ed. M. Madeleine and E. Gery, 82:413–38. Paris.

Wells, J. 1982. *A Herstory of Prostitution in Western Europe*. Berkeley, CA.

Welwei, K. W. 1981. "Das Sklavenproblem als politische Faktor in der Krise der romischen Republik." In *Vom Elend der Handarbeit: Probleme historischer Untersichtenforschung*, ed. H. Mommsen and W. Schulze, 50–69. Stuttgart, Ger.

West, Martin Litchfield. 1974. *Studies in the Greek Elegy and Iambus*. Berlin.

Whitley, J. 2004. "Archaeology in Greece 2003–2004." *Archaeological Reports for 2003–2004* 50:1–88.

Wiegand, T. 1904. *Priene: Ergebnisse der Ausgrabungen und Untersuchungen in den Jahren 1895–1898*. Berlin.

Wilkins, J. 2000. *The Boastful Chef: The Discourse of Food in Ancient Comedy.* Oxford.

Willcock, M. M., ed. 1987. *Pseudolus*, by Plautus. Bristol.

Williams, C. A. 1999. *Roman Homosexuality: Ideologies of Masculinity in Classical Antiquity.* Oxford.

Williams, C. K. 1986. "Corinth and the Cult of Aphrodite." In *Corinthiaca: Studies in Honor of Darrell A. Amyx*, ed. M. A. Del Chiaro, 12–24. Columbia, MO.

Williams, C. K., and J. E. Fisher. 1972. "Corinth 1971: The Forum Area." *Hesperia* 41:143–84.

———. 1973. "Corinth 1972: The Forum Area." *Hesperia* 42:1–44.

Williams, D. 1985. "Women on Athenian Vases: Problems of Interpretation." In *Images of Women in Antiquity*, ed. A. Cameron and A. Kuhrt, 92–106. Detroit, MI.

Williams, H. 1989. "Excavations at Mytilene, 1988." *Échos du monde classique/Classical Views* 33.8:167–81.

———. 1991. "Excavations at Mytilene, 1990." *Échos du monde classique/Classical Views* 35.10:175–91.

Wilson, T. M. 2005. *Drinking Cultures: Alcohol and Identity.* Oxford.

Winkler, J. J. 1989. *Constraints of Desire: The Anthropology of Sex and Gender in Ancient Greece.* New York.

———. 1990. "Laying Down the Law: The Oversight of Men's Sexual Behavior in Classical Athens." In *Before Sexuality: The Construction of Erotic Experience in the Ancient Greek World*, ed. D. H. Halperin, J. J. Winkler, and F. I. Zeitlin, 171–209. Princeton, NJ.

Winks, R. 1972. *Slavery: A Comparative Perspective.* New York.

Worman, N. 2002. "Odysseus, Ingestive Rhetoric, and Euripides' Cyclops." *Helios* 29.2: 101–25.

———. 2004. "Insult and Oral Excess in the Disputes between Aeschines and Demosthenes." *American Journal of Philology* 125:1–25.

Wright, J. 1975. "The Transformations of Pseudolus." *Transactions of the American Philological Association* 105:403–16.

Younger, J. G. 2005. *Sex in the Ancient World from A to Z.* London.

Zeller, M. 1962. "Die Rolle der unfreien Bevölkerung Roms in den politischen Kämpfen der Bürgerkriege." PhD diss., University of Tübingen.

Contributors

HELENE A. COCCAGNA received her PhD from the Department of Classics at Johns Hopkins University. Her dissertation focused on anatomical manipulations of Attic vases.

SEAN CORNER is an assistant professor in the Department of Classics at McMaster University. His research concerns the political culture and society of archaic and classical Greece. He is currently writing a monograph for Oxford University Press, provisionally titled "The Greek Symposium and the Origins of the Polis."

ALLISON GLAZEBROOK is an associate professor of classics at Brock University. Her research focuses on women, gender, and sexuality in ancient Greece. She has published numerous articles including essays on representations of women in Greek oratory, on female prostitution in classical Athens, and on the iconography of women as readers in Attic vase painting. She is currently at work on a book-length study of Athenian prostitution.

JUDITH P. HALLETT is a professor of classics at the University of Maryland, College Park. She has published widely in the areas of Latin language and literature; women, sexuality, and the family in Greco-Roman society; and the classical tradition in the nineteenth- and twentieth-century Anglophone world. Her books include *Fathers and Daughters in Roman Society: Women and the Elite Family* (1984), *Roman Sexualities*, coedited with Marilyn Skinner (1996), and *British Classics Outside England: The Academy and Beyond*, coedited with Christopher Stray (2008).

MADELEINE M. HENRY is a professor of classical studies and chair of the Classical Studies Program at Iowa State University. Her interests include women's history, literary theory and criticism, Greek comedy, and the teaching of Latin. She has published articles on Greek literary criticism, encyclopedic literature, and teaching Horace and Catullus; longer works include *Menander's Courtesans and the Greek Comic Tradition* (1985) and *Prisoner of History: Aspasia of Miletus and Her Biographical Tradition* (1995). She is also working on "Neaera: Writing a Prostitute's Life."

KONSTANTINOS K. KAPPARIS is an associate professor of classics and director of the Center for Greek Studies at the University of Florida. His main research interests are the Attic orators, Athenian law and society, the history of sexuality and gender studies, and Greek medical literature. His publications include a commentary on the speech *Against Neaira*, a monograph on abortion in the ancient world, and two collaborative volumes on Attic law-court speeches.

CLARE KELLY BLAZEBY is a lecturer in classics at the University of Leeds, England, UK. Her PhD thesis examined the archaeology, anthropology, and social history of "casual" wine drinking in classical Greece, with an emphasis on taverns, or *kapēleia*, and their role as nonsympotic alternative drinking locales for nonelite Greeks and others.

T. DAVINA MCCLAIN received her PhD in classical studies from Indiana University. She currently serves as director of the Scholars' College, the honors college at Northwestern State University in Natchitoches, LA.

THOMAS A. J. MCGINN is a professor of classical studies at Vanderbilt University. He is the author of numerous books and articles on prostitution, marriage, and concubinage in ancient Rome. His most recent book is *Widows and Patriarchy: Ancient and Modern* (2008).

NANCY SORKIN RABINOWITZ is the Margaret Bundy Scott Professor of Comparative Literature at Hamilton College. She is the author of *Anxiety Veiled: Euripides and the Traffic in Women* (1993) and *Greek Tragedy* (2008). She is the coeditor of *Feminist Theory and the Classics* (1993), *Women on the Edge: Four Plays by Euripides* (1999), and *Among Women: From the Homosocial to the Homoerotic in the Ancient World* (2002). Her current research is on women in Greek tragedy as subject and object of the gaze and on rape in tragedy.

NICHOLAS K. RAUH is a professor of classics in the Department of Foreign Languages and Literature at Purdue University. His research focuses primarily on cultural and social history and the material culture of the late Hellenistic-Roman republican world. His books include *The Sacred Bonds of Commerce: Religion, Economy, and Trade Society at Hellenistic Roman Delos, 166–87 B.C.* (1993) and *Merchants, Sailors, and Pirates in the Roman World* (2003).

Index

Notes: Ancient sources are listed in this subject index by author when reference is made to their behavior; the index locorum contains references to their written texts.

Page numbers in *italics* indicate illustrations.

Index Locorum

WISCONSIN STUDIES IN CLASSICS

General Editors

William Aylward, Nicholas D. Cahill, and Patricia A. Rosenmeyer

---

E. A. THOMPSON
Romans and Barbarians: The Decline of the Western Empire

JENNIFER TOLBERT ROBERTS
Accountability in Athenian Government

H. I. MARROU
A History of Education in Antiquity
Histoire de l'Education dans l'Antiquité, translated by George Lamb

ERIKA SIMON
Festivals of Attica: An Archaeological Commentary

G. MICHAEL WOLOCH
Roman Cities: Les villes romaines by Pierre Grimal, translated and edited by G. Michael Woloch, together with "A Descriptive Catalogue of Roman Cities" by G. Michael Woloch

WARREN G. MOON, editor
Ancient Greek Art and Iconography

KATHERINE DOHAN MORROW
Greek Footwear and the Dating of Sculpture

JOHN KEVIN NEWMAN
The Classical Epic Tradition

JEANNY VORYS CANBY, EDITH PORADA, BRUNILDE SISMONDO RIDGWAY, and TAMARA STECH, editors
Ancient Anatolia: Aspects of Change and Cultural Development

ANN NORRIS MICHELINI
Euripides and the Tragic Tradition

WENDY J. RASCHKE, editor
The Archaeology of the Olympics: The Olympics and Other Festivals in Antiquity

PAUL PLASS
Wit and the Writing of History: The Rhetoric of Historiography in Imperial Rome

BARBARA HUGHES FOWLER
The Hellenistic Aesthetic

F. M. CLOVER and R. S. HUMPHREYS, editors
Tradition and Innovation in Late Antiquity

BRUNILDE SISMONDO RIDGWAY
Hellenistic Sculpture I: The Styles of ca. 331–200 B.C.

BARBARA HUGHES FOWLER, editor and translator
Hellenistic Poetry: An Anthology

KATHRYN J. GUTZWILLER
Theocritus' Pastoral Analogies: The Formation of a Genre

VIMALA BEGLEY and RICHARD DANIEL DE PUMA, editors
Rome and India: The Ancient Sea Trade

RUDOLF BLUM
HANS H. WELLISCH, translator
Kallimachos: The Alexandrian Library and the Origins of Bibliography

DAVID CASTRIOTA
Myth, Ethos, and Actuality: Official Art in Fifth Century B.C. Athens

BARBARA HUGHES FOWLER, editor and translator
Archaic Greek Poetry: An Anthology

JOHN H. OAKLEY and REBECCA H. SINOS
The Wedding in Ancient Athens

RICHARD DANIEL DE PUMA and JOCELYN PENNY SMALL, editors
Murlo and the Etruscans: Art and Society in Ancient Etruria

JUDITH LYNN SEBESTA and LARISSA BONFANTE, editors
The World of Roman Costume

JENNIFER LARSON
Greek Heroine Cults

WARREN G. MOON, editor
Polykleitos, the Doryphoros, and Tradition

PAUL PLASS
The Game of Death in Ancient Rome: Arena Sport and Political Suicide

MARGARET S. DROWER
Flinders Petrie: A Life in Archaeology

SUSAN B. MATHESON
Polygnotos and Vase Painting in Classical Athens

JENIFER NEILS, editor
Worshipping Athena: Panathenaia and Parthenon

PAMELA A. WEBB
Hellenistic Architectural Sculpture: Figural Motifs in Western Anatolia and the Aegean Islands

BRUNILDE SISMONDO RIDGWAY
Fourth-Century Styles in Greek Sculpture

LUCY GOODISON and CHRISTINE MORRIS, editors
Ancient Goddesses: The Myths and the Evidence

JO-MARIE CLAASSEN
Displaced Persons: The Literature of Exile from Cicero to Boethius

BRUNILDE SISMONDO RIDGWAY
Hellenistic Sculpture II: The Styles of ca. 200–100 B.C.

PAT GETZ-GENTLE
Personal Styles in Early Cycladic Sculpture

CATULLUS
DAVID MULROY, translator and commentator
The Complete Poetry of Catullus

BRUNILDE SISMONDO RIDGWAY
Hellenistic Sculpture III: The Styles of ca. 100–31 B.C.

ANGELIKI KOSMOPOULOU
The Iconography of Sculptured Statue Bases in the Archaic and Classical Periods

SARA H. LINDHEIM
Mail and Female: Epistolary Narrative and Desire in Ovid's Heroides

GRAHAM ZANKER
Modes of Viewing in Hellenistic Poetry and Art

ALEXANDRA ANN CARPINO
Discs of Splendor: The Relief Mirrors of the Etruscans

TIMOTHY S. JOHNSON
A Symposion of Praise: Horace Returns to Lyric in Odes *IV*

JEAN-RENÉ JANNOT
Religion in Ancient Etruria
Devins, Dieux et Démons: Regards sur la religion de l'Etrurie antique, translated by Jane K. Whitehead

CATHERINE SCHLEGEL
Satire and the Threat of Speech: Horace's Satires, *Book 1*

CHRISTOPHER A. FARAONE and LAURA K. MCCLURE, editors
Prostitutes and Courtesans in the Ancient World

PLAUTUS
JOHN HENDERSON, translator and commentator
Asinaria: The One about the Asses

PATRICE D. RANKINE
Ulysses in Black: Ralph Ellison, Classicism, and African American Literature

PAUL REHAK
JOHN G. YOUNGER, editor
Imperium and Cosmos: Augustus and the Northern Campus Martius

PATRICIA J. JOHNSON
Ovid before Exile: Art and Punishment in the Metamorphoses

VERED LEV KENAAN
Pandora's Senses: The Feminine Character of the Ancient Text

ERIK GUNDERSON
Nox Philologiae: Aulus Gellius and the Fantasy of the Roman Library

SINCLAIR BELL and HELEN NAGY, editors
New Perspectives on Etruria and Early Rome

BARBARA PAVLOCK
The Image of the Poet in Ovid's Metamorphoses

PAUL CARTLEDGE and FIONA ROSE GREENLAND, editors
Responses to Oliver Stone's Alexander: *Film, History, and Cultural Studies*

AMALIA AVRAMIDOU
The Codrus Painter: Iconography and Reception of Athenian Vases in the Age of Pericles

SHANE BUTLER
The Matter of the Page: Essays in Search of Ancient and Medieval Authors

ALLISON GLAZEBROOK and MADELEINE M. HENRY, editors
Greek Prostitutes in the Ancient Mediterranean, 800 BCE–200 CE